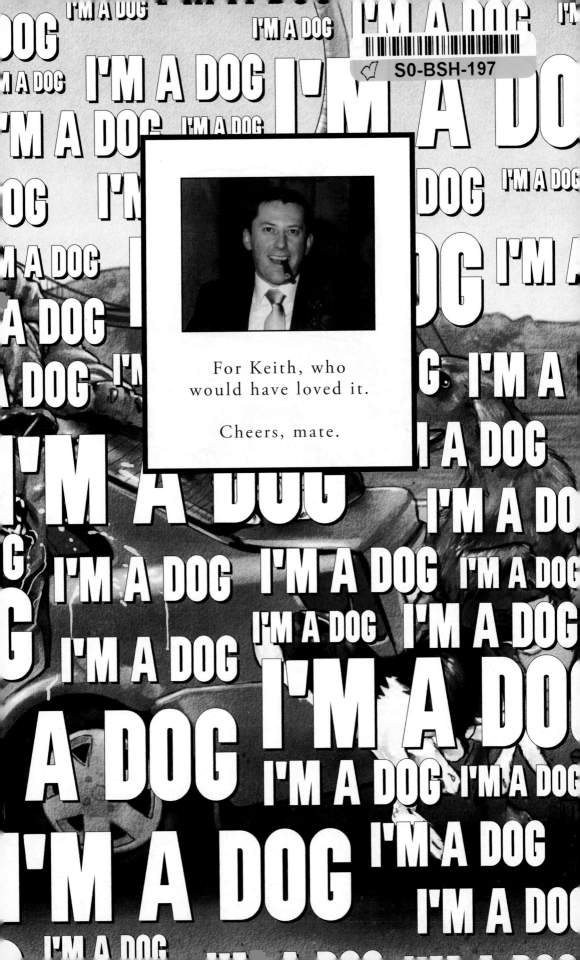

For Keith, who
would have loved it.

Cheers, mate.

S0-BSH-197

FOUR LEGS GOOD TWO LEGS GONE

My reading of American comic books commenced when I was six, in the Bakelite foothills of the later 1950s. This was just before the commencement of the second great costumed-hero pandemic, when the graphic story landscape was a dot-screened jungle of astonishing biodiversity: infant ingénues and amiable foetal spectres, fetish-dressed cowboys and stubbly soldiers, Jane Eyre and Jerry Lewis. There were ginger teenagers with cross-hatched temples making poignant claims to be 'typical' and lithic Kirby aliens with faces like cracked sidewalk whose invasion plans would founder on a last-minute unlikelihood. There were even comic books with animals as their protagonists.

Admittedly, the great majority of this wildlife was from a genus possessing three fingers and an opposable thumb with dapper white opera gloves as an optional extra, but there were still titles wherein a non-human mammal main character could be treated at least semi-naturalistically, at least if one ignored their unusual propensity for solving crimes. Carmine Infantino and Gil Kane were two of the most genuinely gifted stylists of their day, both venerated as creators of a myriad graceful supermen or space-adventurers, and yet it could be argued that their work was never better nor more filled with obvious enjoyment than when they, respectively, delineated Bobo the Detective Chimp and Rex the Wonder Dog. Why this should be so is perhaps not answerable, but it may be that these accomplished artists, like so many other people, found they could invest more real enthusiasm and affection in a living entity if that relationship was not refracted through the ambiguities and shadow-puppetry of even the most simple and vestigial human personality. Perhaps we feel that we know where we stand with individuals who perpetrate this action on more legs than two.

Should we seek further instances of this rewarding use of the so-called 'pathetic fallacy' beyond the still-too-narrow confines of the comic field, in the more venerable and extensive territories of literature we find only a very few examples of such narrative shape-shifting; of such an attempt to conjure the experience of a different species. Disregarding faux-Tibetan Irish handyman T. Lobsang Rampa's spirited pretence at being his own telepathic cat, there doesn't seem to be a lot of seriously depicted literary livestock. Aesop's morally-demonstrative menagerie is obviously intended as anthropomorphic fable, as are Kipling's Just-So jungle denizens; Disney diversions from an age before three-fingered opera gloves. Swift's pained and condescending equine Houyhnhnms are corralled alongside Orwell's barnyard Bolsheviks and Aristophanes' avian allegories in the politico-satiric petting zoo, and when it comes to explorations of a speculated animal intelligence for its own sake rather than as yet another mirror in which we can both admire and criticise ourselves, we're left with still fewer examples. A brief vogue for feline sleuths aside, there are the beast-mythologies of Richard Adams and his imitators and then, towering with spine arched and incisors bared atop the genre's food-chain, there's Jack London's *White Fang*. Otherwise, the pastures of prose would seem relatively bare of fauna, unless it's a tale of us and our activities tricked out in bestial disguise.

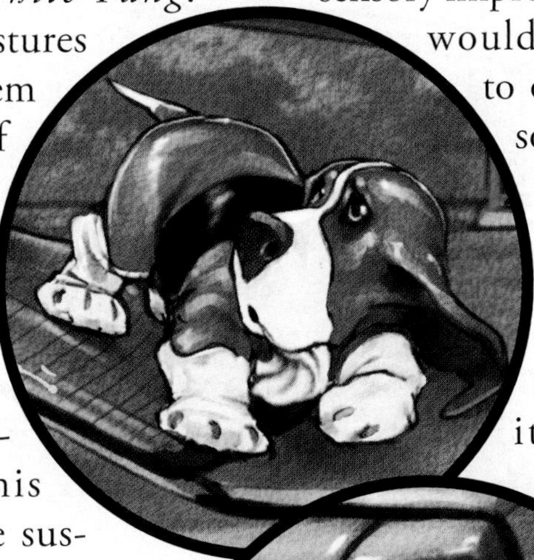

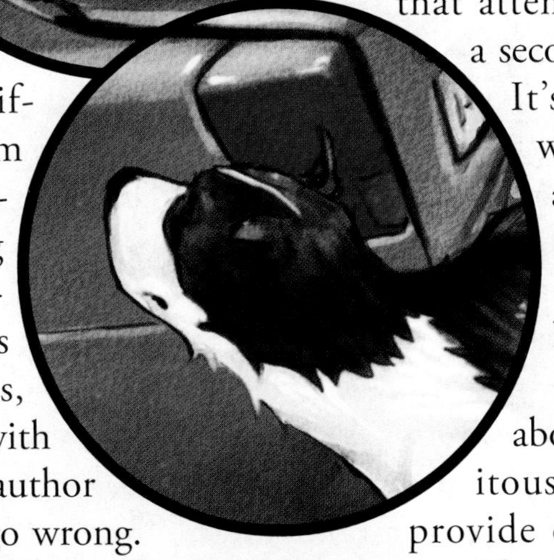

The most probable cause for this depopulation, one suspects, is the enormous difficulty of the enterprise from an intimidated writer's viewpoint, along with a sobering awareness of the undertaking's many hazards. Just as in the thespian professions, when it comes to working with children or animals, for an author there's such a lot that can go wrong. Most evidently, there's the risk of cloying sentiment bringing a diabetic sweetness to the work, especially considering the likelihood that anyone attempting such an enterprise is either an admirer or, potentially, an owner of the animal in question. Even were we to presume a high degree of self-control in our imagined wordsmith there are other, far more serious obstacles, foremost among these being Ludwig Wittgenstein's astute and perhaps insurmountable conclusion that if lions could talk, presumably in our own language, we would nonetheless still be incapable of understanding them. This is to say that the mind of a different species, predicated on a different range of sensory impressions and prerogatives, would be completely alien to our own... although to some extent this would appear to be the case even with other members of the human race, and yet the vast majority of authors, it would seem, make that attempt without a second thought. It's only less-well-tailored animals, apparently, that writers balk at.

All of the above is a circuitous attempt to provide context and the means to properly appreciate the scale and rarity, in any medium, of Garth Ennis and Michael DiPascale's epic cold-nosed tour de force, *Rover Red Charlie*, almost certainly the most affecting and unheralded sequential fiction anyone will read this year. Without apparent effort it surmounts all of the hurdles catalogued above, rounding its woolly plot-threads up and herding them into the pen, an undeniable best-in-show. Relentlessly absorbing from its opening frames, commencing where most homo sapiens-centric tales are of necessity concluded with the absolute extinction of humanity, this extraordinary narrative accomplishes so much without once deviating from the straightforward and muscular tradition of comic strip storytelling which Garth Ennis has both rooted his approach in and extended in its capabilities, that it makes any comprehensive listing of its many virtues highly problematic.

We could start, as the account does, with apocalypse. Innumerable writers, with Garth Ennis and the current author both included, have used World's End as a means of studying the human situation in extremis, hopefully allowing insights into our broader condition. Clearly, with mankind and any of its representatives conspicuously absent for the greater part of its relating, this cannot be what *Rover Red Charlie* is attempting. More ambitiously, we are allowed to witness Armageddon through the eyes, ears and olfactory senses of a species which cannot conceivably aspire to comprehend the great extinction spectacle that it is looking at, the solitary species on the planet other than our own that we could say with some degree of certainty would miss us. For a while.

The book's heart, though, lies in its skilled portrayal and its strenuous imagining of the non-human heroes, villains, and supporting cast. From chickens to Chihuahuas, from hiss-pots to a worryingly alluring incarnation of Lassie, characterisation is impeccable, with nothing in its treatment of animal intellectual or emotional abilities that is anything other than immediately credible. Part of this credibility would seem to be derived from the deft manner in which Ennis handles relative capacity for language-skills among his post-apocalyptic bestiary. The cats have more words than the dogs and everything has more words than the hens. Though some degree of humanising is clearly required for purposes of intelligibility, as in Wittgenstein's robust disclaimer, it should not be thought that Ennis is displaying favouritism or an unrealistic view of canine conversation in his attribution of the most human-like dialogue and responses to his dogs. Recent developments in neuroscience capable of mapping which brain-regions 'light up' in response to verbal stimuli has demonstrated that with both humans and dogs the same cerebral areas are activated in response to the same human words. As to whether basset-hounds can possibly distinguish or in some way even reproduce the intonations of South London, more research is obviously required, although it must be said *Rover Red Charlie* makes a thoroughly convincing case for this daring hypothesis.

Although the sense of characters lived and experienced viscerally as expertly concocted blends of pain, affection and absurdity is customary in Garth Ennis's writing, the enormous contribution made by the perfectly-pitched depictions of both the environment and quadrupedal leads by Michael DiPascale can't be overstated. His facility for lending comprehensible emotive force to animal facial expressions, emphasising and exaggerating without ever venturing into the surely-tempting but disastrous reaches of cartoon, is masterful. It should also be pointed out that even in the halcyon days of Kane and Infantino's animal extravaganzas, no artist was ever called upon to navigate almost a hundred pages without so much as a glimpse of comforting human anatomy or, for the most part, human artefacts. In DiPascale as in his illustrious co-creator we see reassuring old-school craftsmanship writ large, perhaps a sign that almost-extinct values along with endangered genres are slowly returning to their formerly diverse comic book habitats following the decline of a top predator, much as in the ultimate shaggy dog-story that you're fortunate enough to be about to start.

Even amongst its author's lengthy and impressive roster of prior achievements, this book marks a thrilling new departure, and pairs him with about the best imaginable artist for the task. I guarantee that there are passages within *Rover Red Charlie* that will haunt you, irrespective of your status as bird-fancier or ailurophile. For everything I've said about this being an attempt to address animals on their own terms without covertly referencing human issues, it cannot be denied that we cast a long shadow over the events described herein, if only by our yawning absence.

I enjoyed this book immensely, and I can think of no more appropriate means of wrapping up this introduction than recourse to an appropriate quotation from the legendary French songwriter Jacques Brel, one that encapsulates the story here from brush to muzzle:

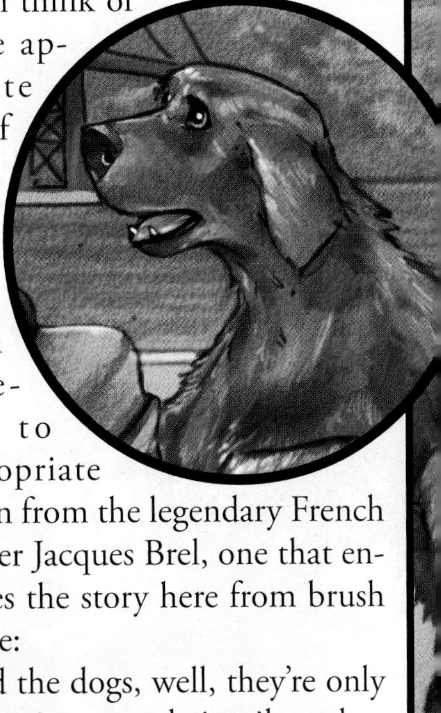

"And the dogs, well, they're only dogs. They just wag their tails as they watch it end."

Greet this astounding book with the Pavlovian reaction it deserves. For my part, I would hope I've drooled enough already to convince you. If not, leave that to the thumping tale itself.

Alan Moore

Northampton—22nd June, 2014

The Ball no Question makes of Ayes and Noes,
But Right or Left as strikes the Player goes;
And He that toss'd Thee down into the Field,
HE knows about it all– He knows– HE knows!

—*Rubaiyat of Omar Khayyam* (tr. Edward Fitzgerald)

•

"You needn't worry about them," said his companion.
"They'll be all right– and thousands like them. If you'll
come along, I'll show you what I mean."
He reached the top of the bank in a single, powerful leap.
Hazel followed; and together they slipped away, running
easily down through the wood, where the first primroses
were beginning to bloom.

—*Watership Down*, Richard Adams

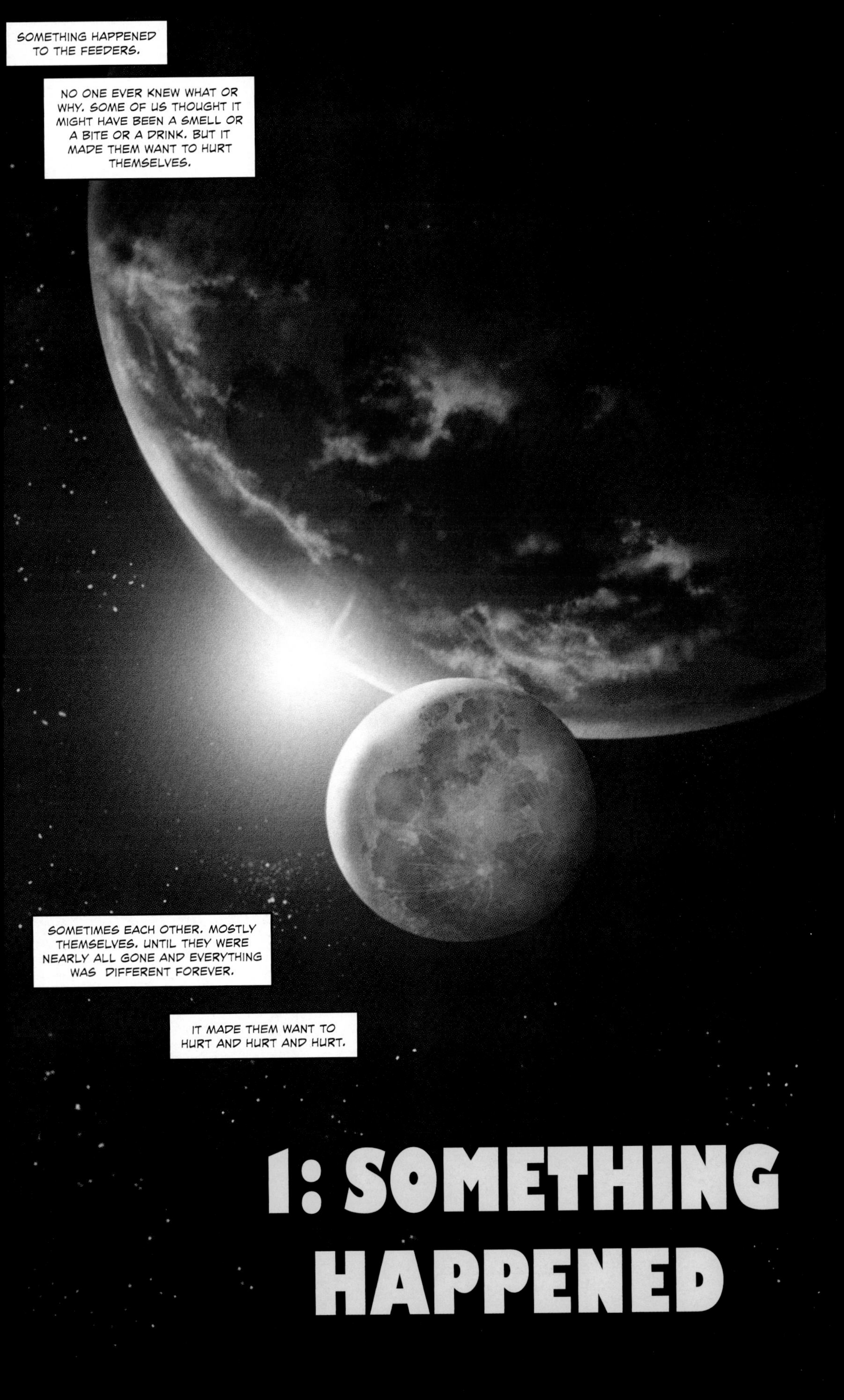
SOMETHING HAPPENED TO THE FEEDERS.
NO ONE EVER KNEW WHAT OR WHY. SOME OF US THOUGHT IT MIGHT HAVE BEEN A SMELL OR A BITE OR A DRINK. BUT IT MADE THEM WANT TO HURT THEMSELVES.
SOMETIMES EACH OTHER. MOSTLY THEMSELVES. UNTIL THEY WERE NEARLY ALL GONE AND EVERYTHING WAS DIFFERENT FOREVER.
IT MADE THEM WANT TO HURT AND HURT AND HURT.
1: SOMETHING HAPPENED

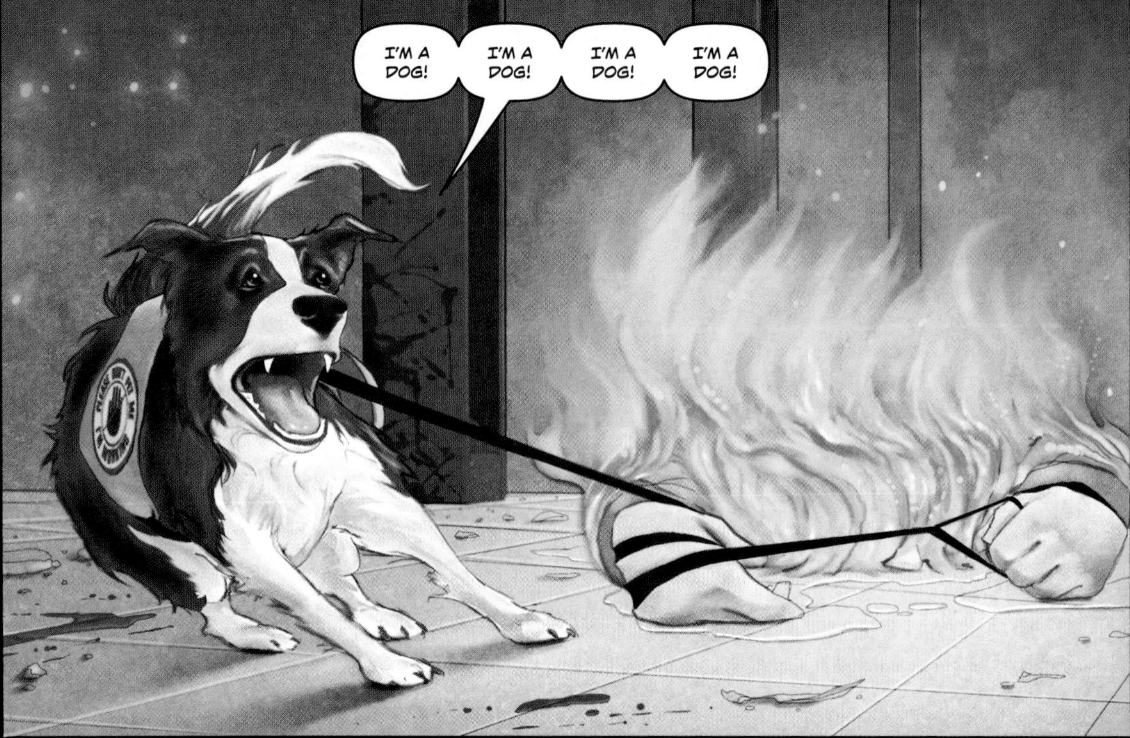
I'M A DOG!
I'M A DOG!
I'M A DOG!
I'M A DOG!

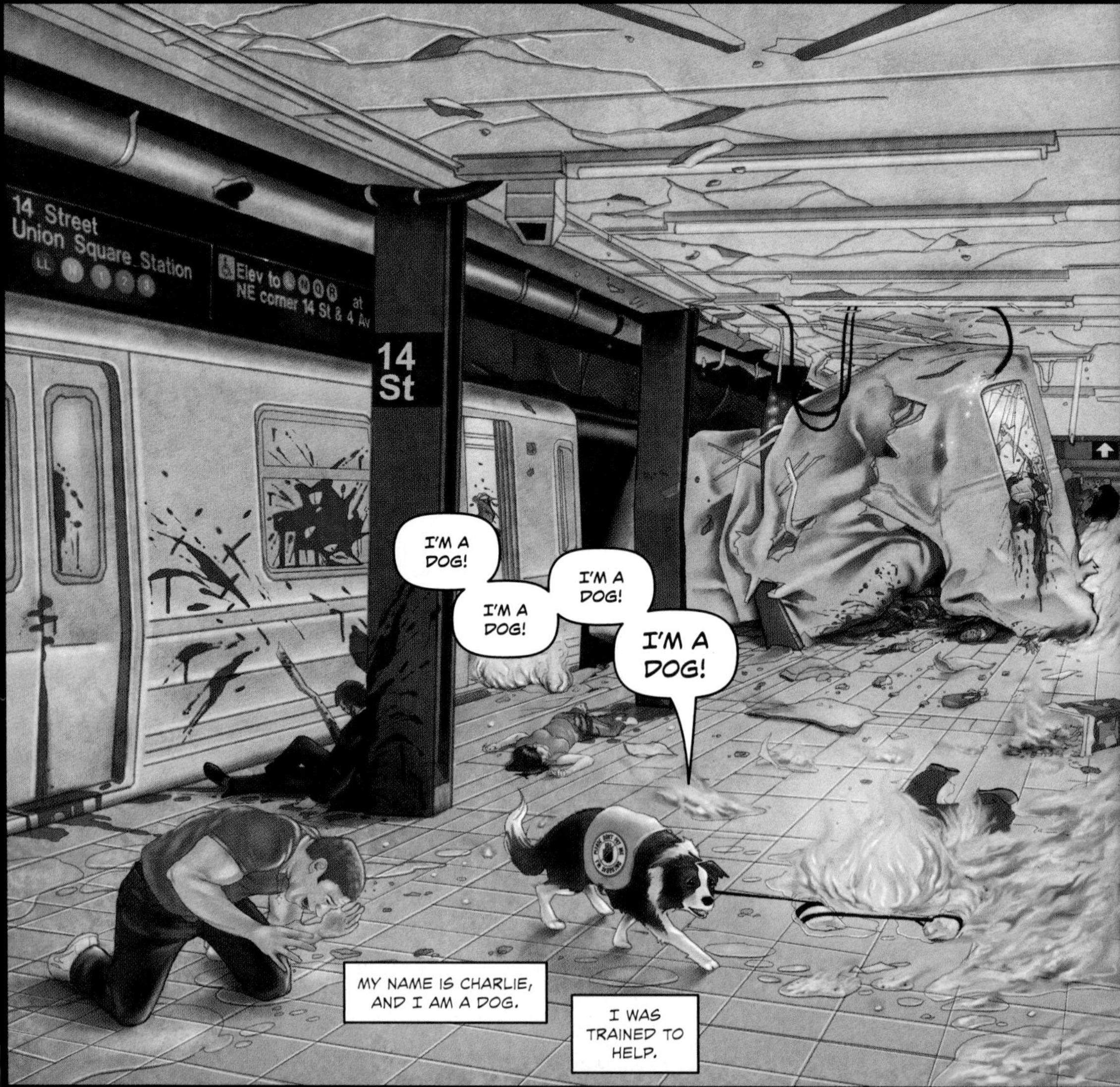
14 Street
Union Square Station
Elev to
NE corner 14 St & 4 Av
14 St
I'M A DOG!
I'M A DOG!
I'M A DOG!
I'M A DOG!
MY NAME IS CHARLIE, AND I AM A DOG.
I WAS TRAINED TO HELP.

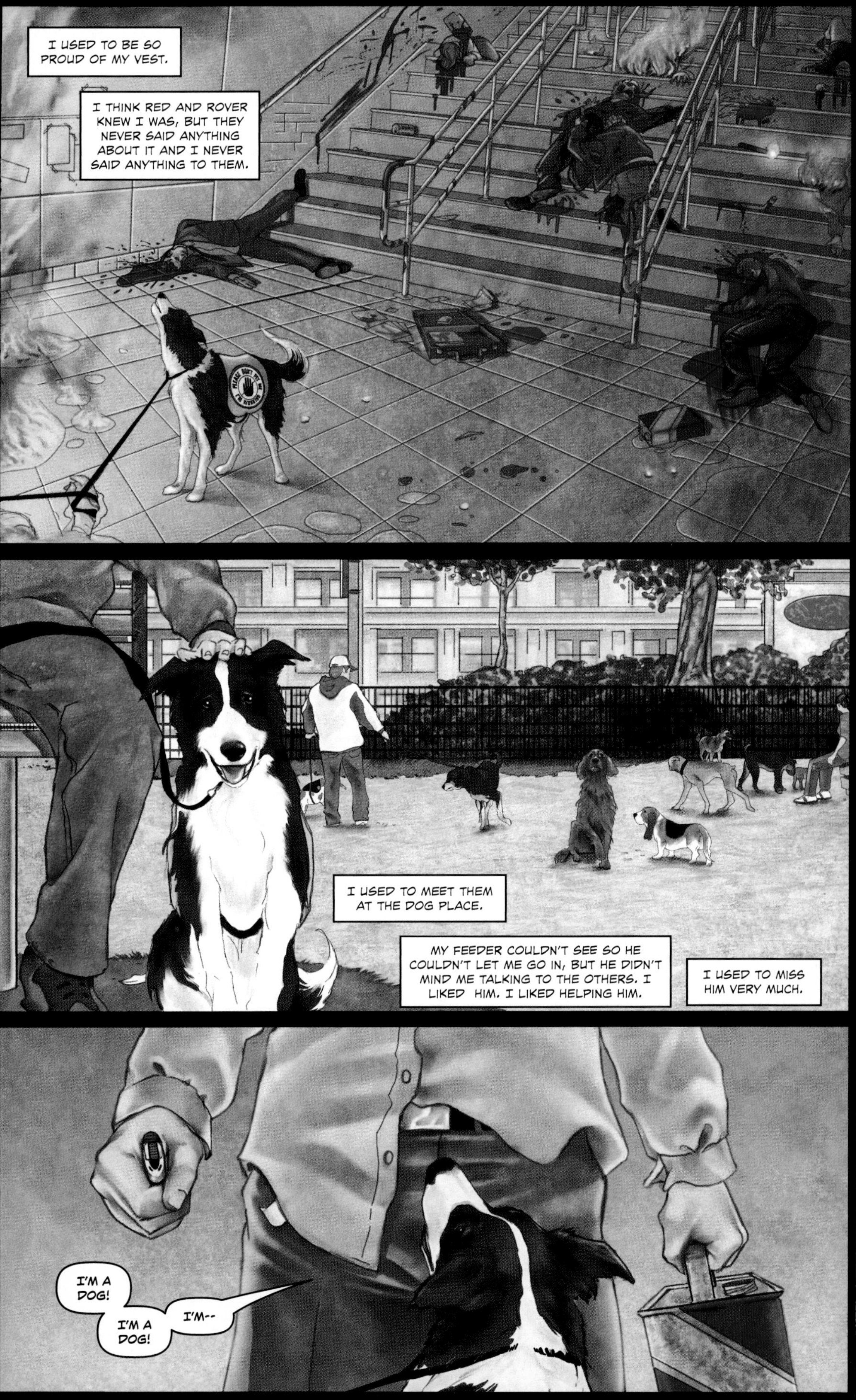

I USED TO BE SO PROUD OF MY VEST.
I THINK RED AND ROVER KNEW I WAS, BUT THEY NEVER SAID ANYTHING ABOUT IT AND I NEVER SAID ANYTHING TO THEM.
I USED TO MEET THEM AT THE DOG PLACE.
MY FEEDER COULDN'T SEE SO HE COULDN'T LET ME GO IN, BUT HE DIDN'T MIND ME TALKING TO THE OTHERS. I LIKED HIM. I LIKED HELPING HIM.
I USED TO MISS HIM VERY MUCH.
I'M A DOG!
I'M A DOG!
I'M--

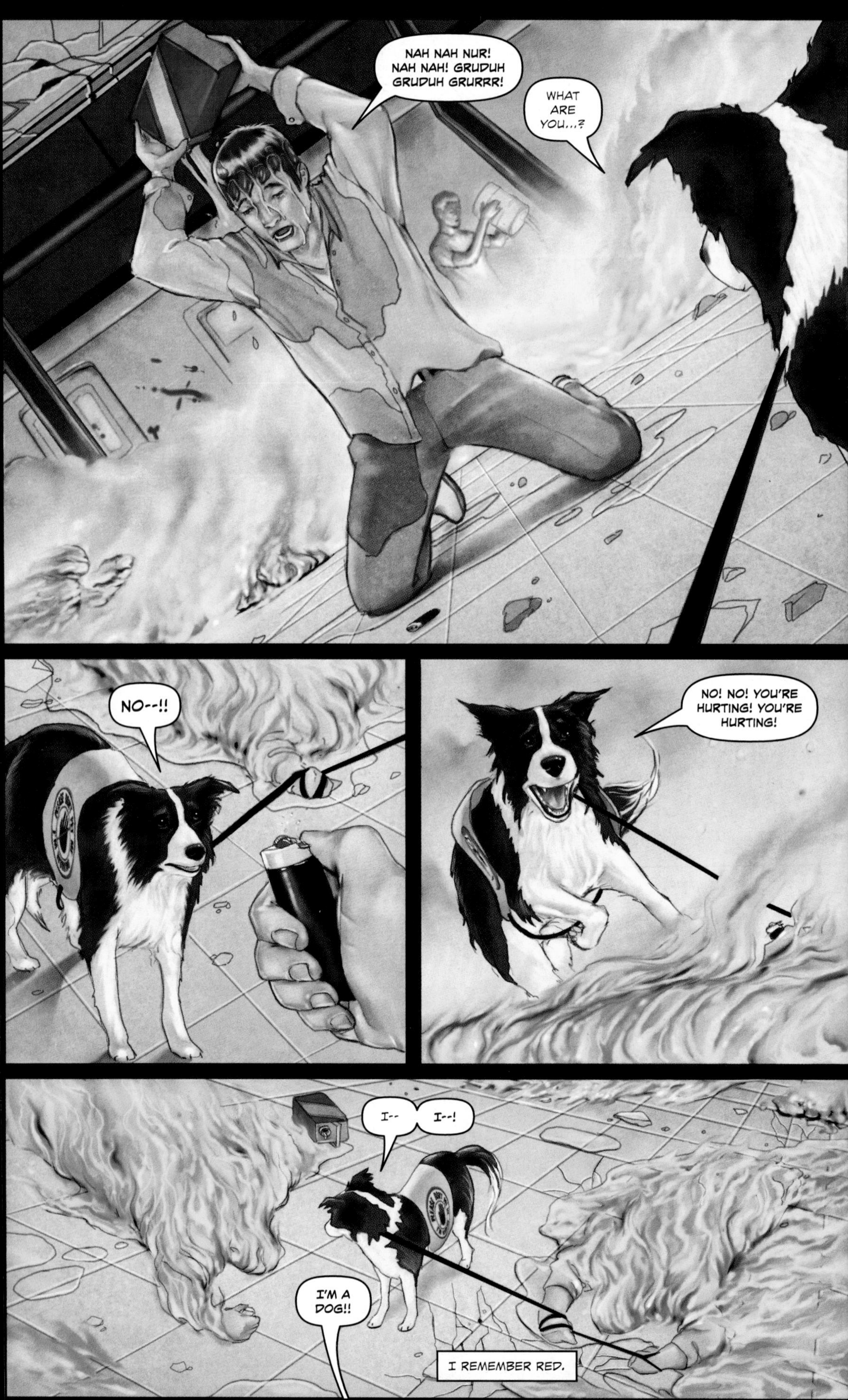
NAH NAH NUR! NAH NAH! GRUDUH GRUDUH GRURRR!
WHAT ARE YOU...?
NO--!!
NO! NO! YOU'RE HURTING! YOU'RE HURTING!
I--
I--!
I'M A DOG!!
I REMEMBER RED.

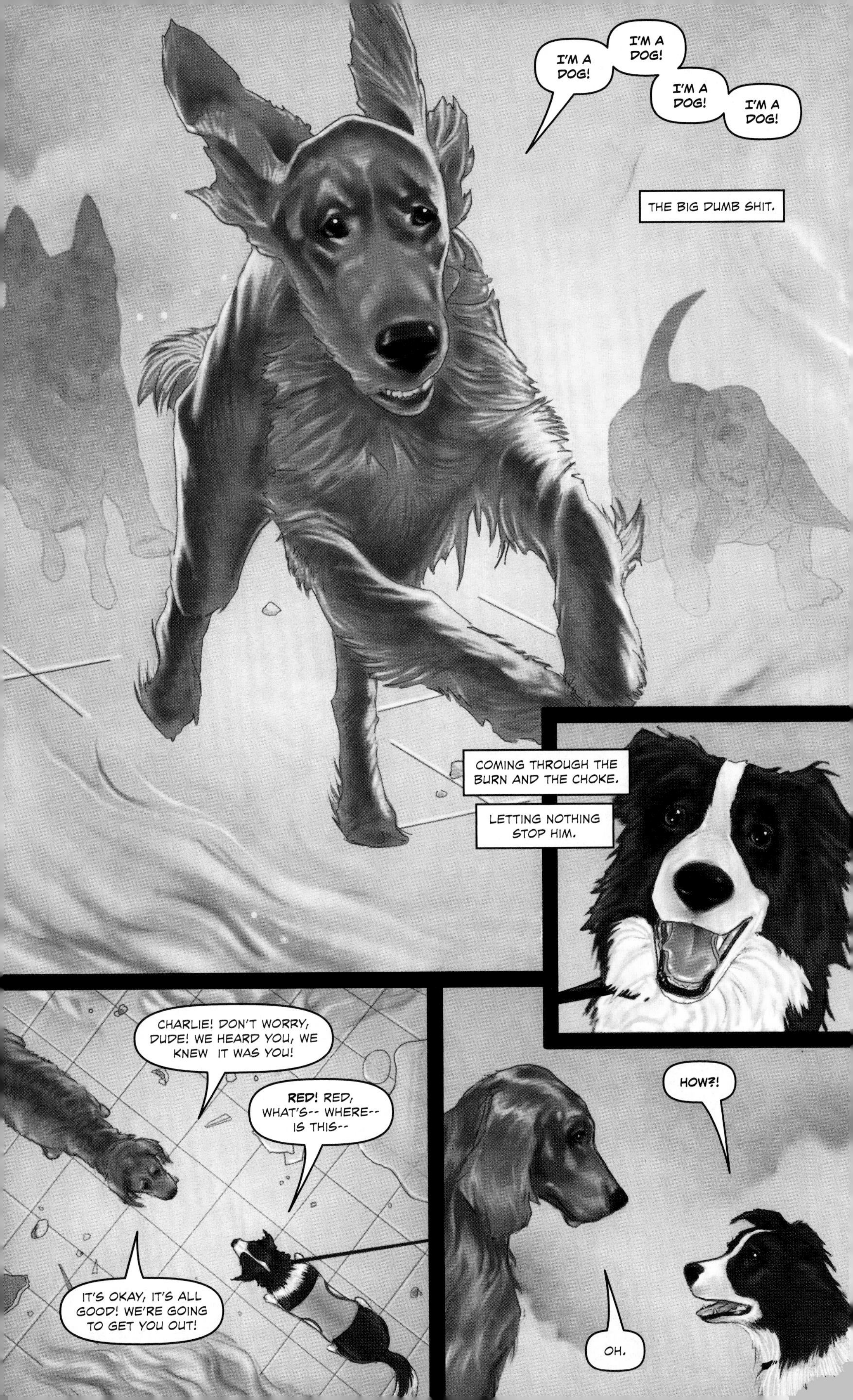
I'M A DOG!
I'M A DOG!
I'M A DOG!
I'M A DOG!
THE BIG DUMB SHIT.
COMING THROUGH THE BURN AND THE CHOKE.
LETTING NOTHING STOP HIM.
CHARLIE! DON'T WORRY, DUDE! WE HEARD YOU, WE KNEW IT WAS YOU!
RED! RED, WHAT'S-- WHERE-- IS THIS--
IT'S OKAY, IT'S ALL GOOD! WE'RE GOING TO GET YOU OUT!
HOW?!
OH.

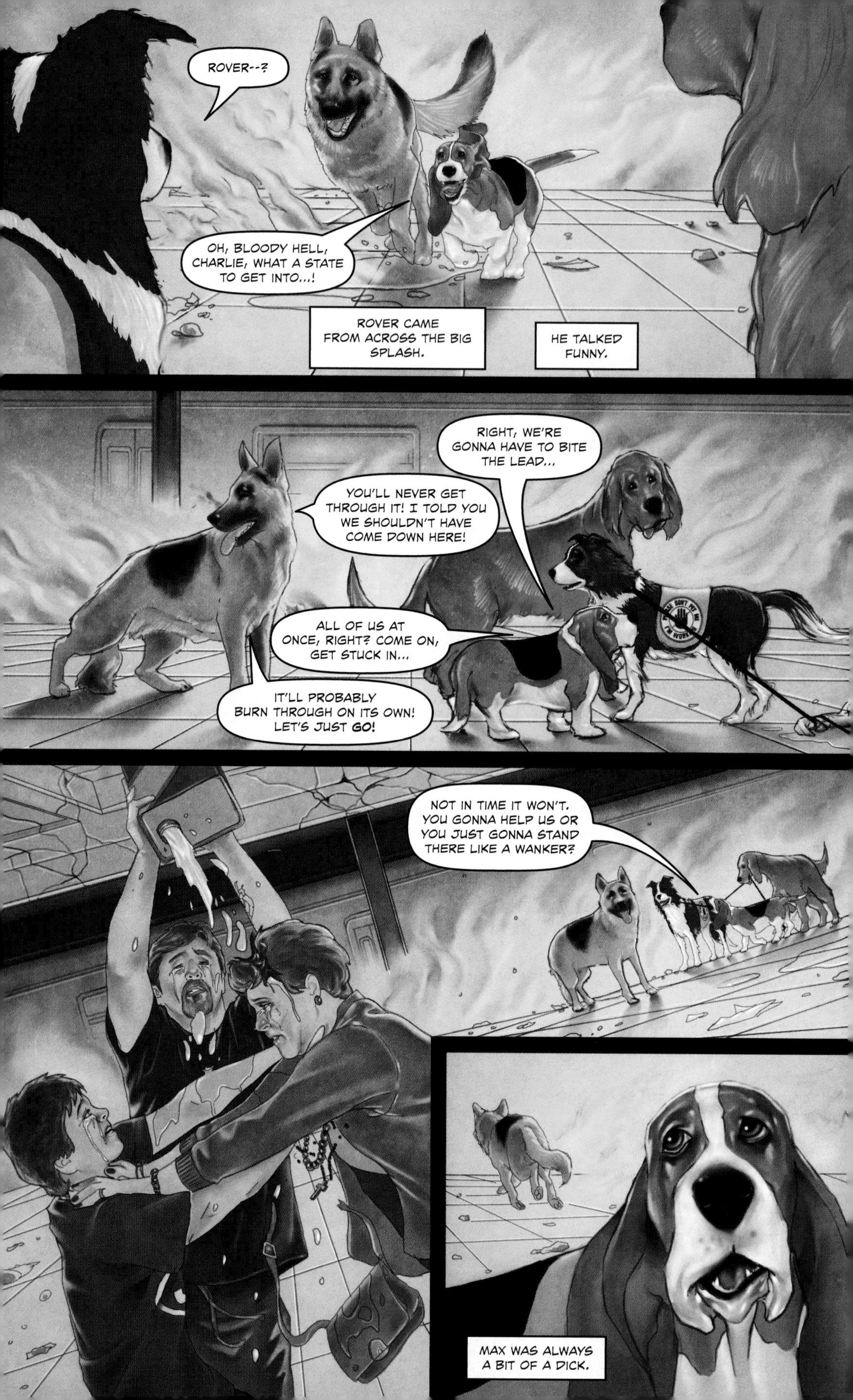
ROVER--?
OH, BLOODY HELL, CHARLIE, WHAT A STATE TO GET INTO...!
ROVER CAME FROM ACROSS THE BIG SPLASH.
HE TALKED FUNNY.
RIGHT, WE'RE GONNA HAVE TO BITE THE LEAD...
YOU'LL NEVER GET THROUGH IT! I TOLD YOU WE SHOULDN'T HAVE COME DOWN HERE!
ALL OF US AT ONCE, RIGHT? COME ON, GET STUCK IN...
IT'LL PROBABLY BURN THROUGH ON ITS OWN! LET'S JUST GO!
NOT IN TIME IT WON'T. YOU GONNA HELP US OR YOU JUST GONNA STAND THERE LIKE A WANKER?
MAX WAS ALWAYS A BIT OF A DICK.

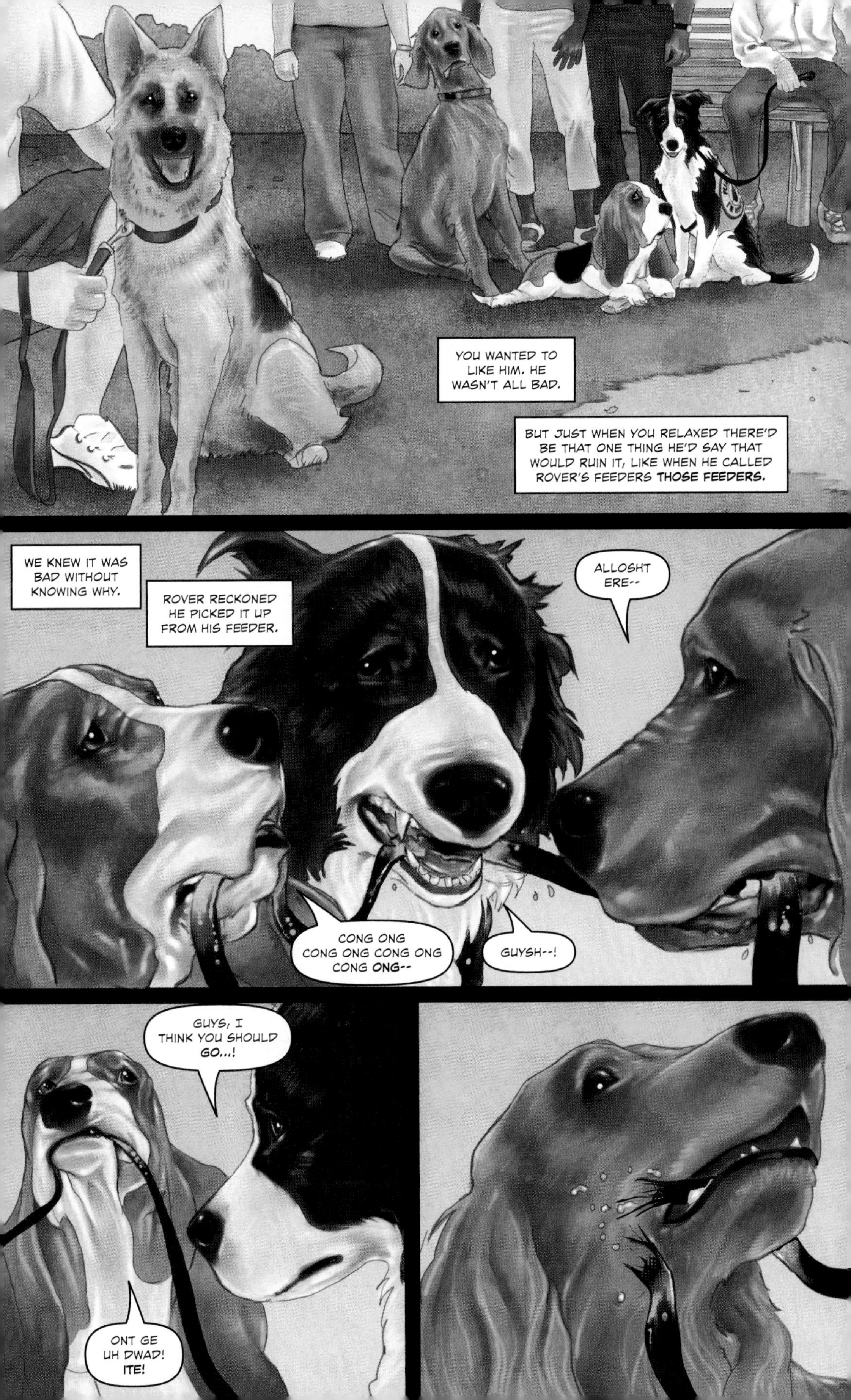
YOU WANTED TO LIKE HIM. HE WASN'T ALL BAD.
BUT JUST WHEN YOU RELAXED THERE'D BE THAT ONE THING HE'D SAY THAT WOULD RUIN IT, LIKE WHEN HE CALLED ROVER'S FEEDERS **THOSE FEEDERS.**
WE KNEW IT WAS BAD WITHOUT KNOWING WHY.
ROVER RECKONED HE PICKED IT UP FROM HIS FEEDER.
ALLOSHT ERE--
CONG ONG CONG ONG CONG ONG CONG **ONG--**
GUYSH--!
GUYS, I THINK YOU SHOULD **GO...!**
ONT GE UH DWAD! **ITE!**

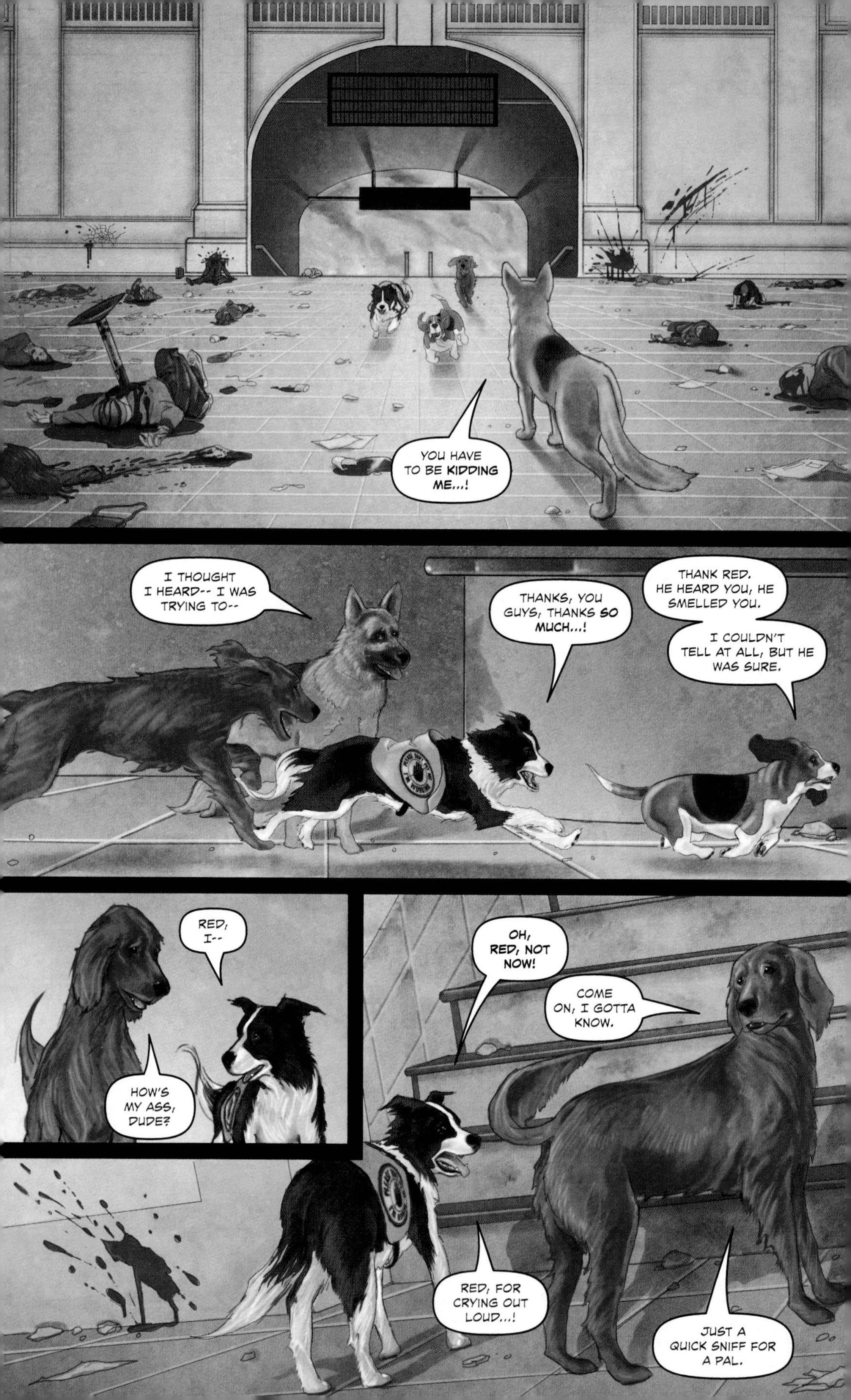
YOU HAVE TO BE KIDDING ME...!
I THOUGHT I HEARD-- I WAS TRYING TO--
THANKS, YOU GUYS, THANKS SO MUCH...!
THANK RED. HE HEARD YOU, HE SMELLED YOU.
I COULDN'T TELL AT ALL, BUT HE WAS SURE.
RED, I--
HOW'S MY ASS, DUDE?
OH, RED, NOT NOW!
COME ON, I GOTTA KNOW.
RED, FOR CRYING OUT LOUD...!
JUST A QUICK SNIFF FOR A PAL.

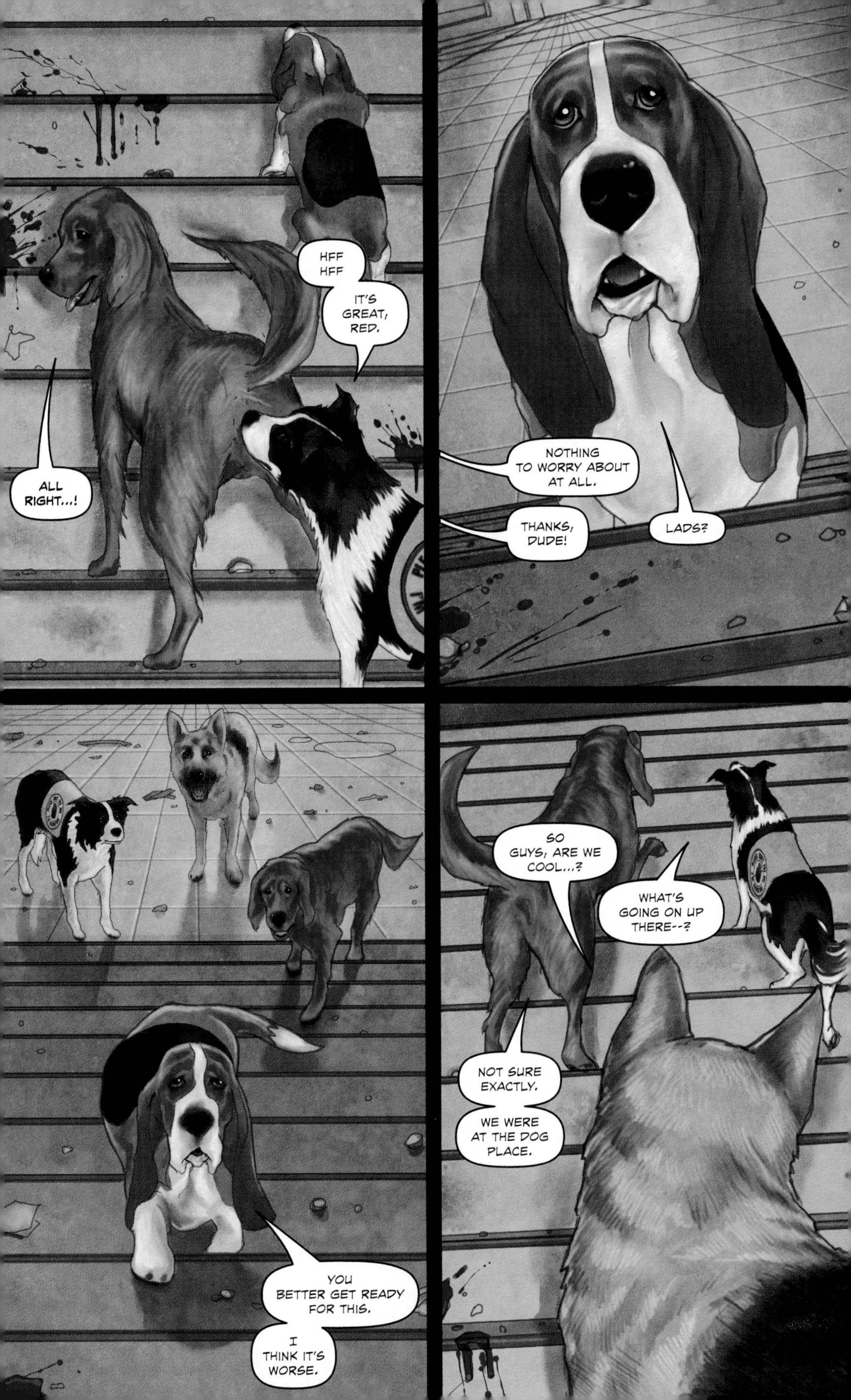
HFF HFF
IT'S GREAT, RED.
ALL RIGHT...!
NOTHING TO WORRY ABOUT AT ALL.
THANKS, DUDE!
LADS?
YOU BETTER GET READY FOR THIS.
I THINK IT'S WORSE.
SO GUYS, ARE WE COOL...?
WHAT'S GOING ON UP THERE--?
NOT SURE EXACTLY.
WE WERE AT THE DOG PLACE.

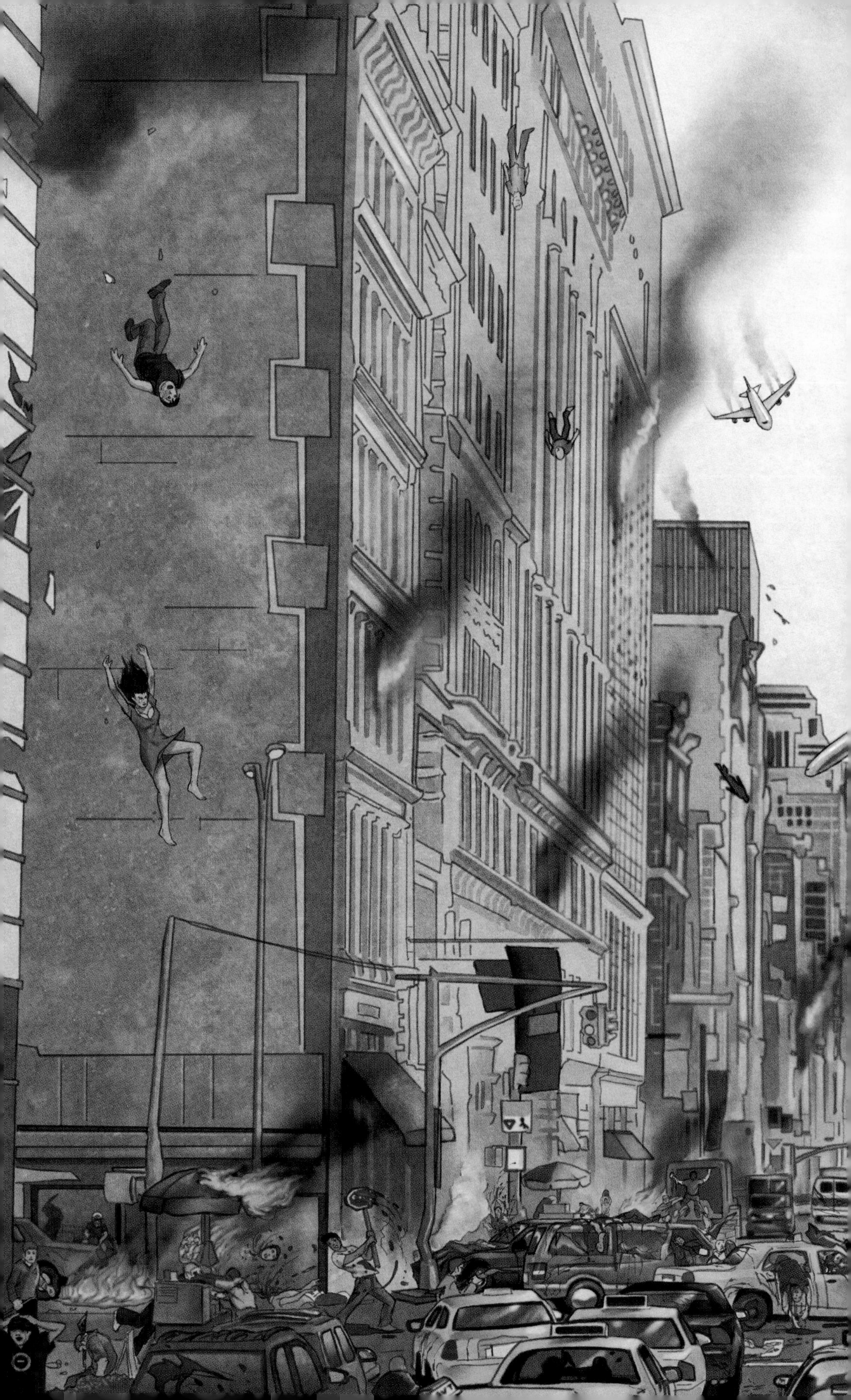

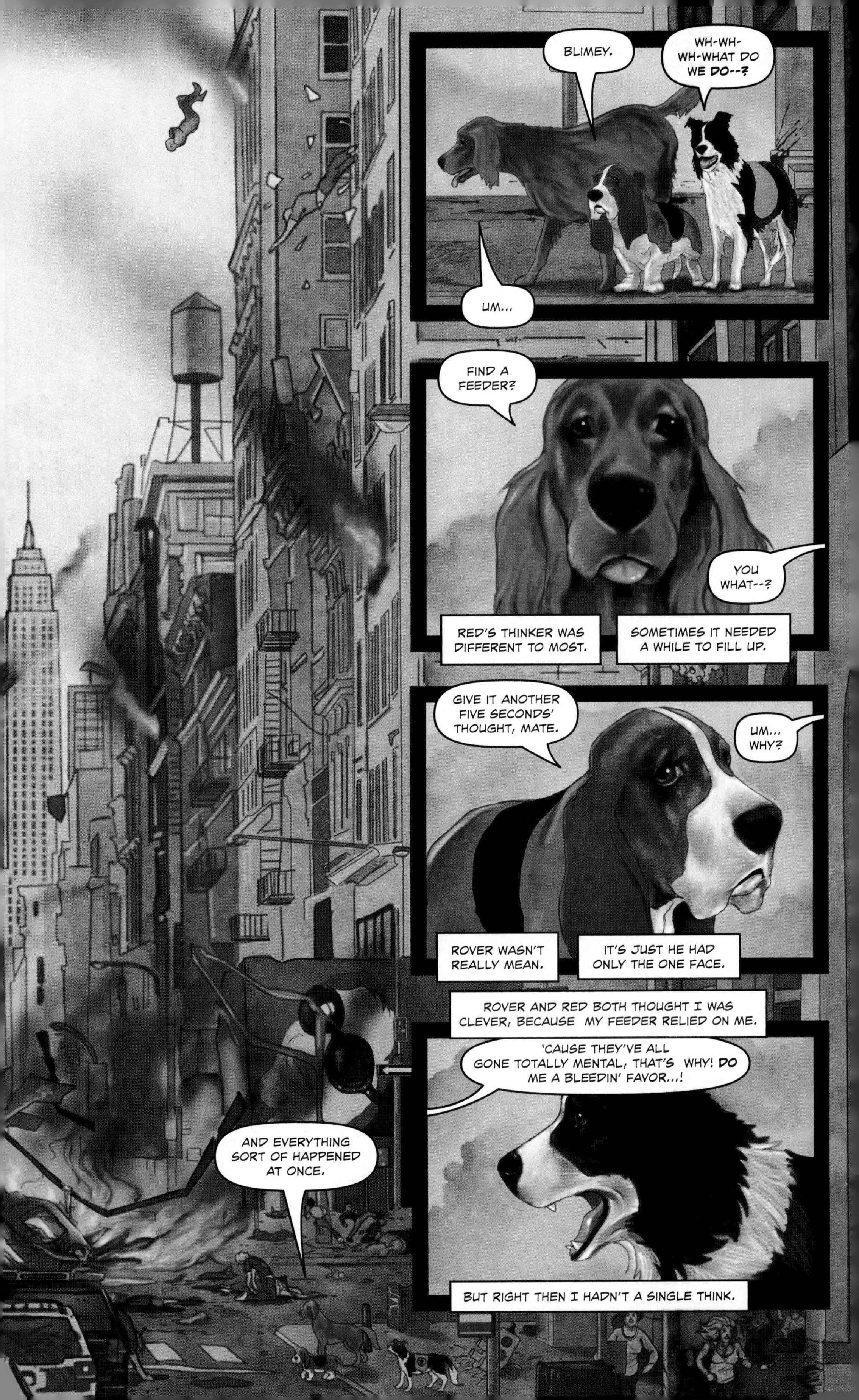
BLIMEY.
WH-WH-WH-WHAT DO WE DO--?
UM...
FIND A FEEDER?
YOU WHAT--?
RED'S THINKER WAS DIFFERENT TO MOST.
SOMETIMES IT NEEDED A WHILE TO FILL UP.
GIVE IT ANOTHER FIVE SECONDS' THOUGHT, MATE.
UM... WHY?
ROVER WASN'T REALLY MEAN.
IT'S JUST HE HAD ONLY THE ONE FACE.
ROVER AND RED BOTH THOUGHT I WAS CLEVER, BECAUSE MY FEEDER RELIED ON ME.
'CAUSE THEY'VE ALL GONE TOTALLY MENTAL, THAT'S WHY! DO ME A BLEEDIN' FAVOR...!
BUT RIGHT THEN I HADN'T A SINGLE THINK.
AND EVERYTHING SORT OF HAPPENED AT ONCE.

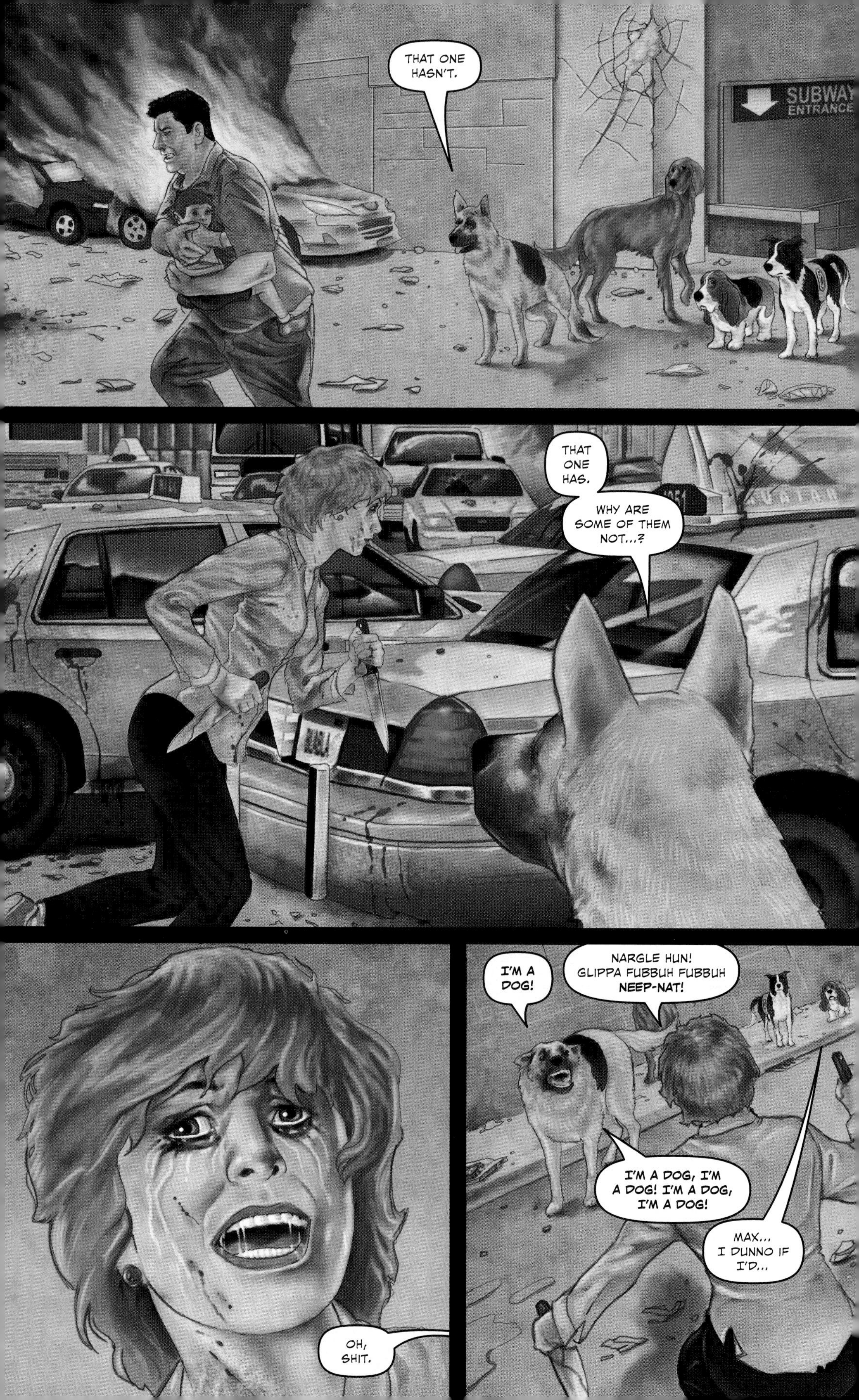
THAT ONE HASN'T.
SUBWAY ENTRANCE
THAT ONE HAS.
WHY ARE SOME OF THEM NOT...?
OH, SHIT.
I'M A DOG!
NARGLE HUN! GLIPPA FUBBUH FUBBUH **NEEP-NAT!**
I'M A DOG, I'M A DOG! I'M A DOG, I'M A DOG!
MAX... I DUNNO IF I'D...

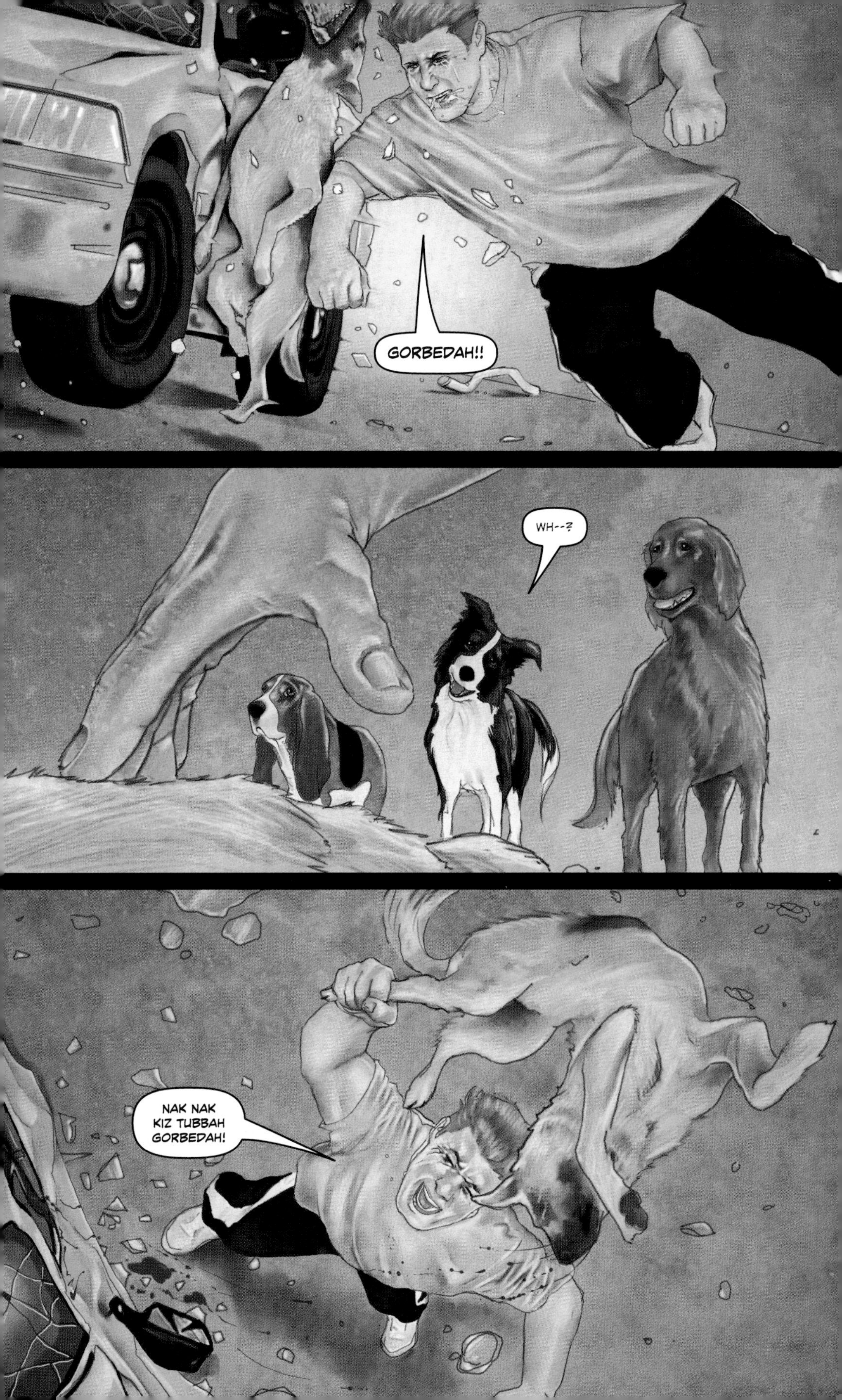
GORBEDAH!!
WH--?
NAK NAK KIZ TUBBAH GORBEDAH!

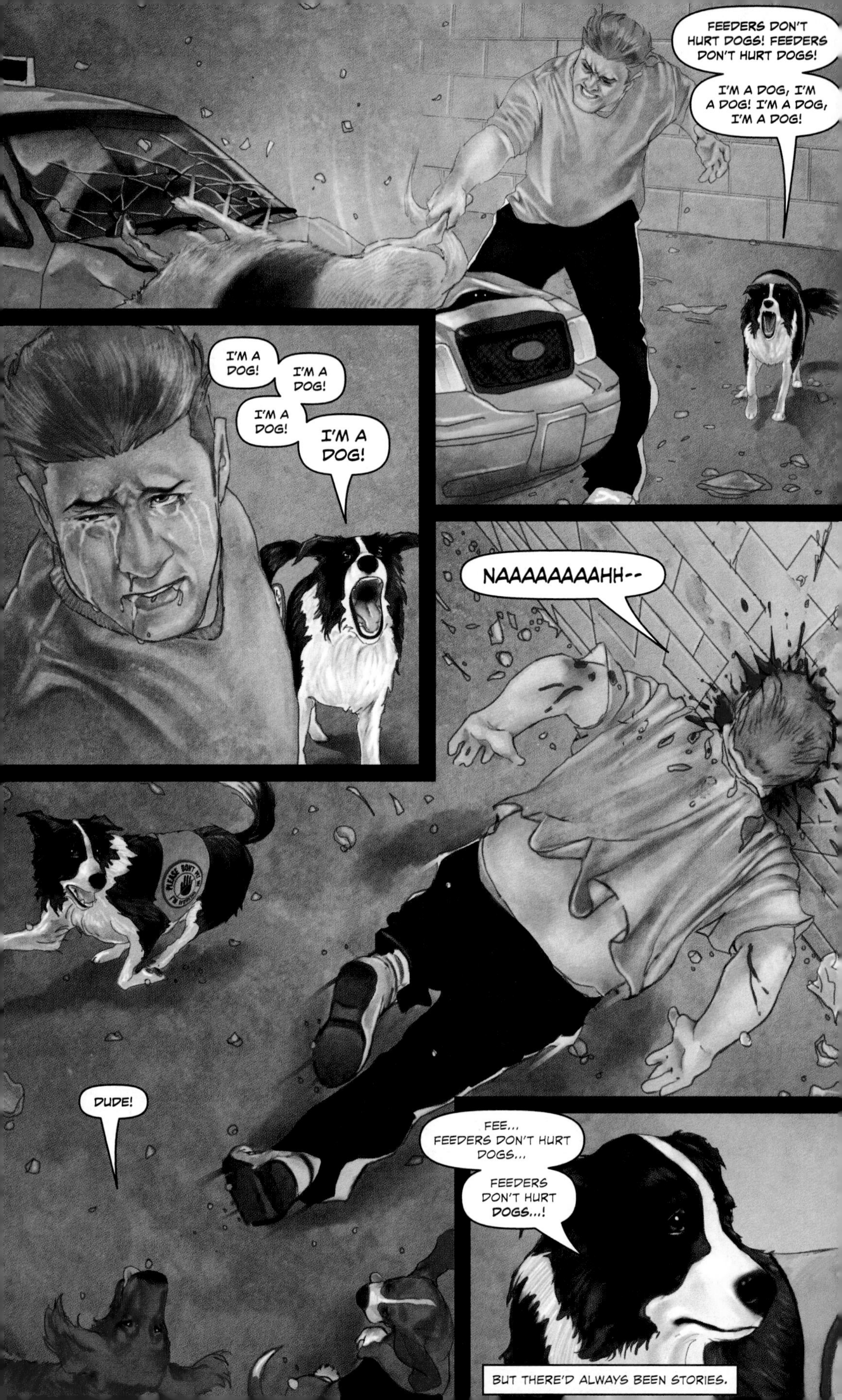
FEEDERS DON'T HURT DOGS! FEEDERS DON'T HURT DOGS!
I'M A DOG, I'M A DOG! I'M A DOG, I'M A DOG!
I'M A DOG!
I'M A DOG!
I'M A DOG!
I'M A DOG!
NAAAAAAAAHH--
DUDE!
FEE... FEEDERS DON'T HURT DOGS...
FEEDERS DON'T HURT DOGS...!
BUT THERE'D ALWAYS BEEN STORIES.

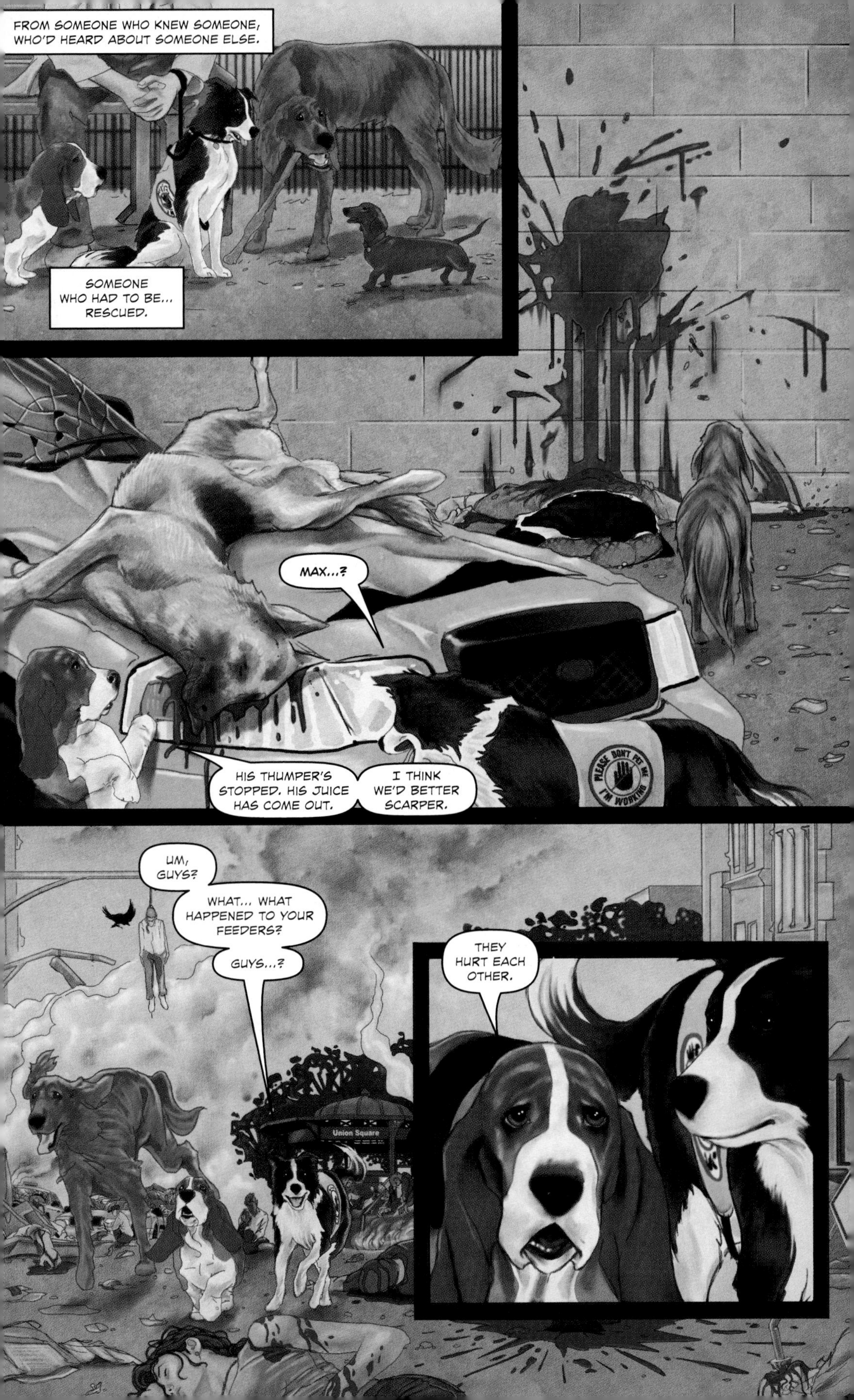
FROM SOMEONE WHO KNEW SOMEONE, WHO'D HEARD ABOUT SOMEONE ELSE.
SOMEONE WHO HAD TO BE... RESCUED.
MAX...?
HIS THUMPER'S STOPPED. HIS JUICE HAS COME OUT.
I THINK WE'D BETTER SCARPER.
PLEASE DON'T PET ME I'M WORKING
UM, GUYS?
WHAT... WHAT HAPPENED TO YOUR FEEDERS?
GUYS...?
Union Square
THEY HURT EACH OTHER.

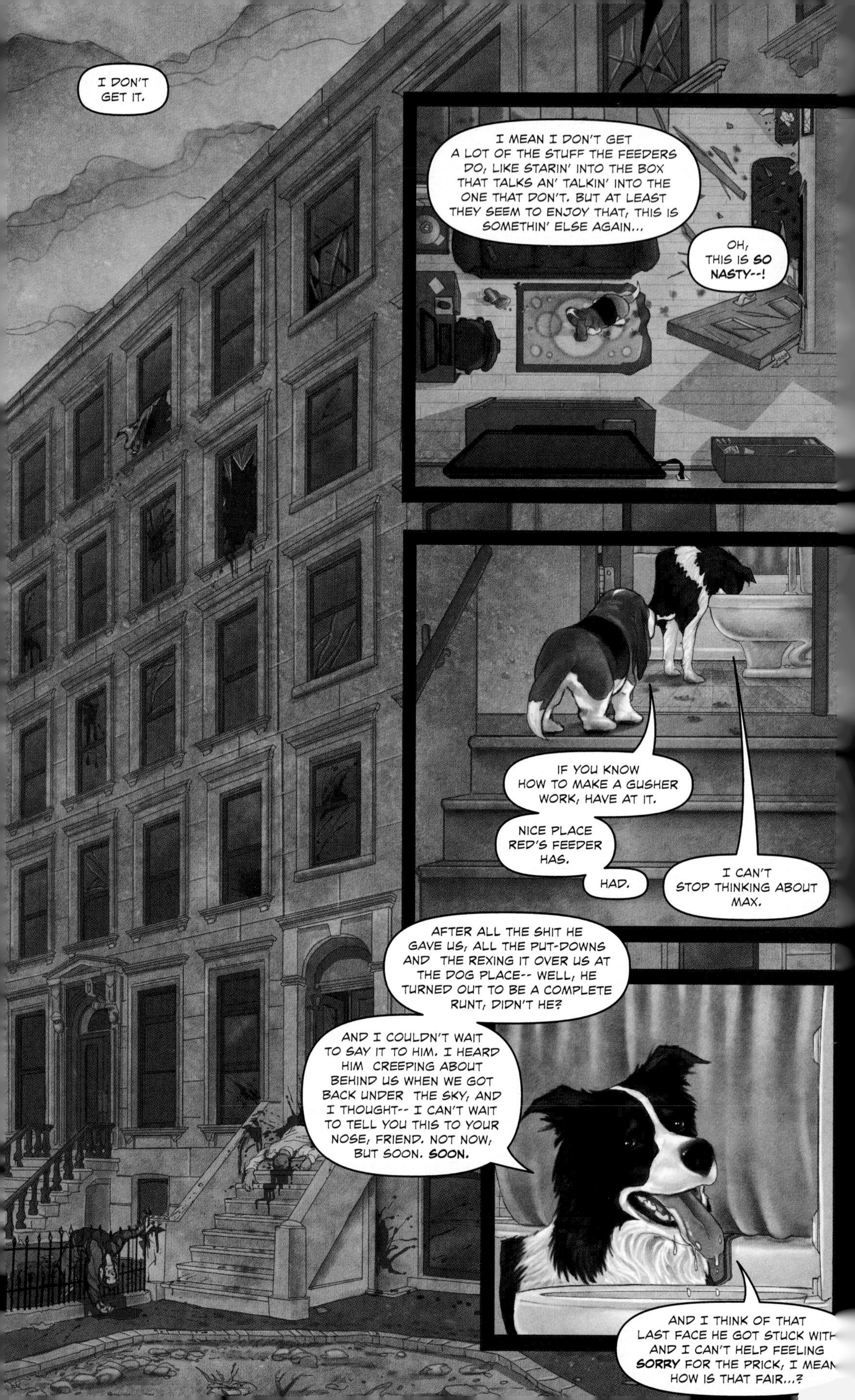
I DON'T GET IT.
I MEAN I DON'T GET A LOT OF THE STUFF THE FEEDERS DO, LIKE STARIN' INTO THE BOX THAT TALKS AN' TALKIN' INTO THE ONE THAT DON'T. BUT AT LEAST THEY SEEM TO ENJOY THAT, THIS IS SOMETHIN' ELSE AGAIN...
OH, THIS IS **SO NASTY--!**
IF YOU KNOW HOW TO MAKE A GUSHER WORK, HAVE AT IT.
NICE PLACE RED'S FEEDER HAS.
HAD.
I CAN'T STOP THINKING ABOUT MAX.
AFTER ALL THE SHIT HE GAVE US, ALL THE PUT-DOWNS AND THE REXING IT OVER US AT THE DOG PLACE-- WELL, HE TURNED OUT TO BE A COMPLETE RUNT, DIDN'T HE?
AND I COULDN'T WAIT TO SAY IT TO HIM. I HEARD HIM CREEPING ABOUT BEHIND US WHEN WE GOT BACK UNDER THE SKY, AND I THOUGHT-- I CAN'T WAIT TO TELL YOU THIS TO YOUR NOSE, FRIEND. NOT NOW, BUT SOON. **SOON.**
AND I THINK OF THAT LAST FACE HE GOT STUCK WITH AND I CAN'T HELP FEELING **SORRY** FOR THE PRICK, I MEAN HOW IS THAT FAIR...?

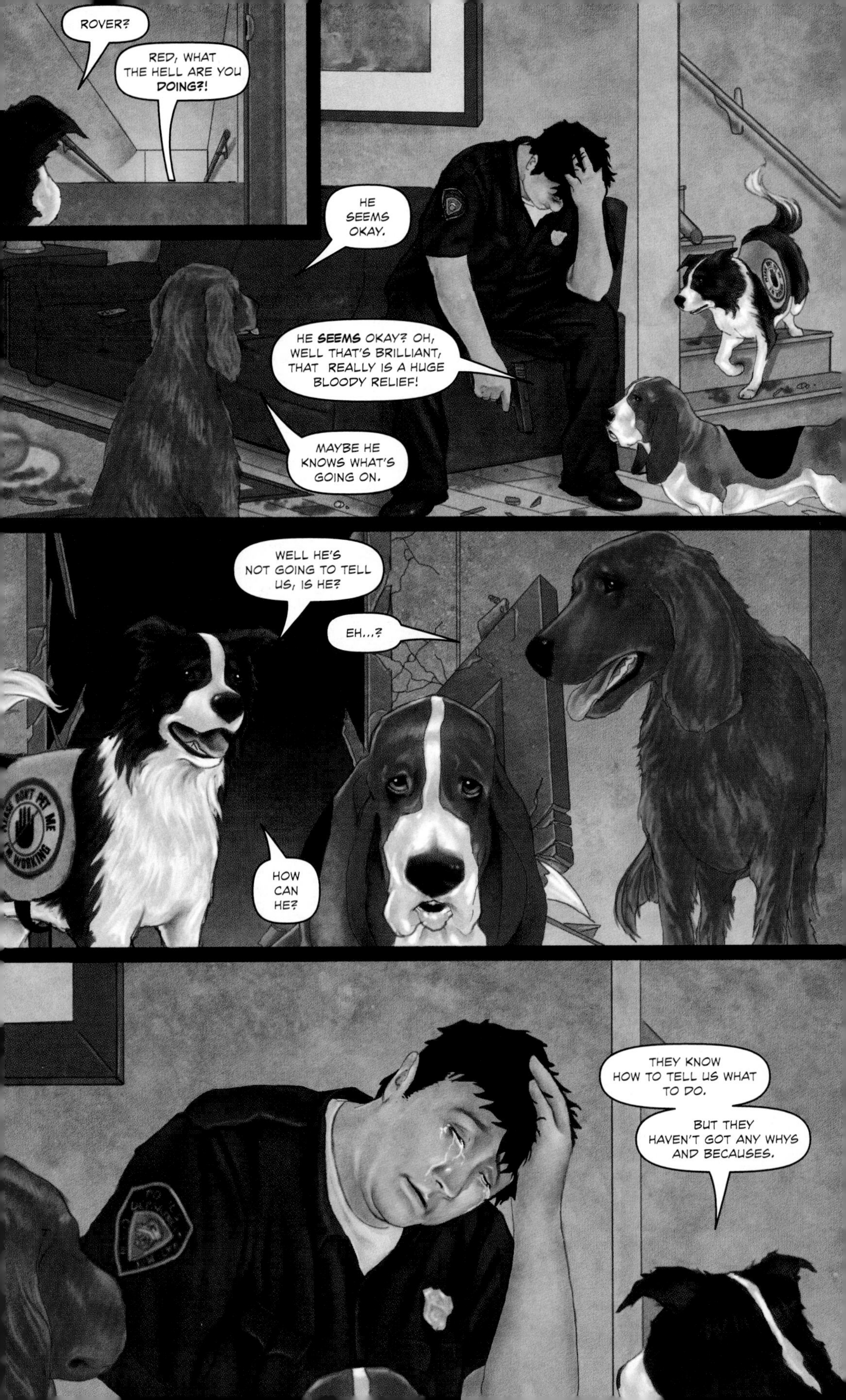
ROVER?
RED, WHAT THE HELL ARE YOU **DOING?!**
HE SEEMS OKAY.
HE **SEEMS** OKAY? OH, WELL THAT'S BRILLIANT, THAT REALLY IS A HUGE BLOODY RELIEF!
MAYBE HE KNOWS WHAT'S GOING ON.
WELL HE'S NOT GOING TO TELL US, IS HE?
EH...?
HOW CAN HE?
THEY KNOW HOW TO TELL US WHAT TO DO.
BUT THEY HAVEN'T GOT ANY WHYS AND BECAUSES.

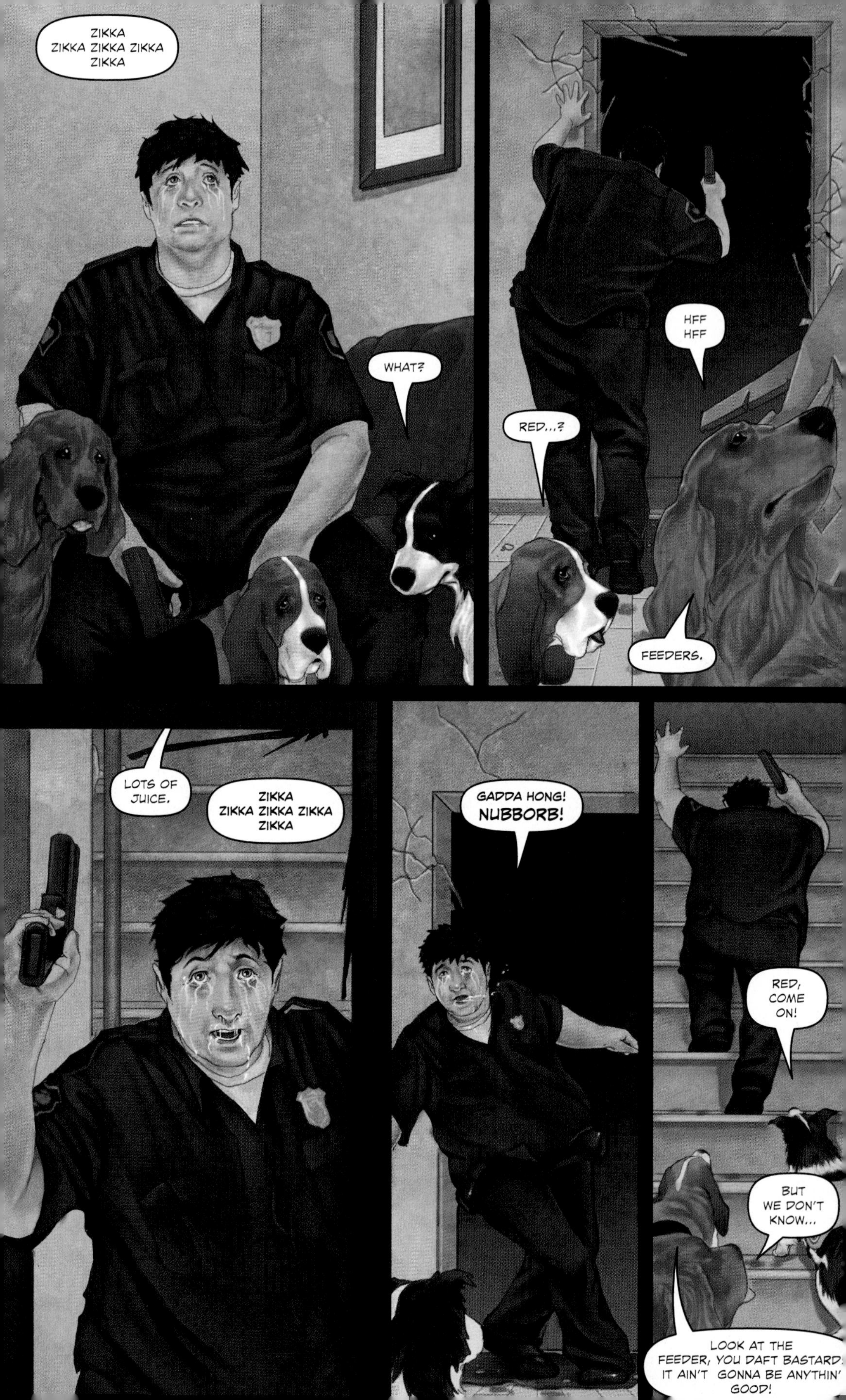
ZIKKA
ZIKKA ZIKKA ZIKKA
ZIKKA
WHAT?
RED...?
HFF
HFF
FEEDERS.
LOTS OF JUICE.
ZIKKA
ZIKKA ZIKKA ZIKKA
ZIKKA
GADDA HONG! NUBBORB!
RED, COME ON!
BUT WE DON'T KNOW...
LOOK AT THE FEEDER, YOU DAFT BASTARD! IT AIN'T GONNA BE ANYTHIN' GOOD!

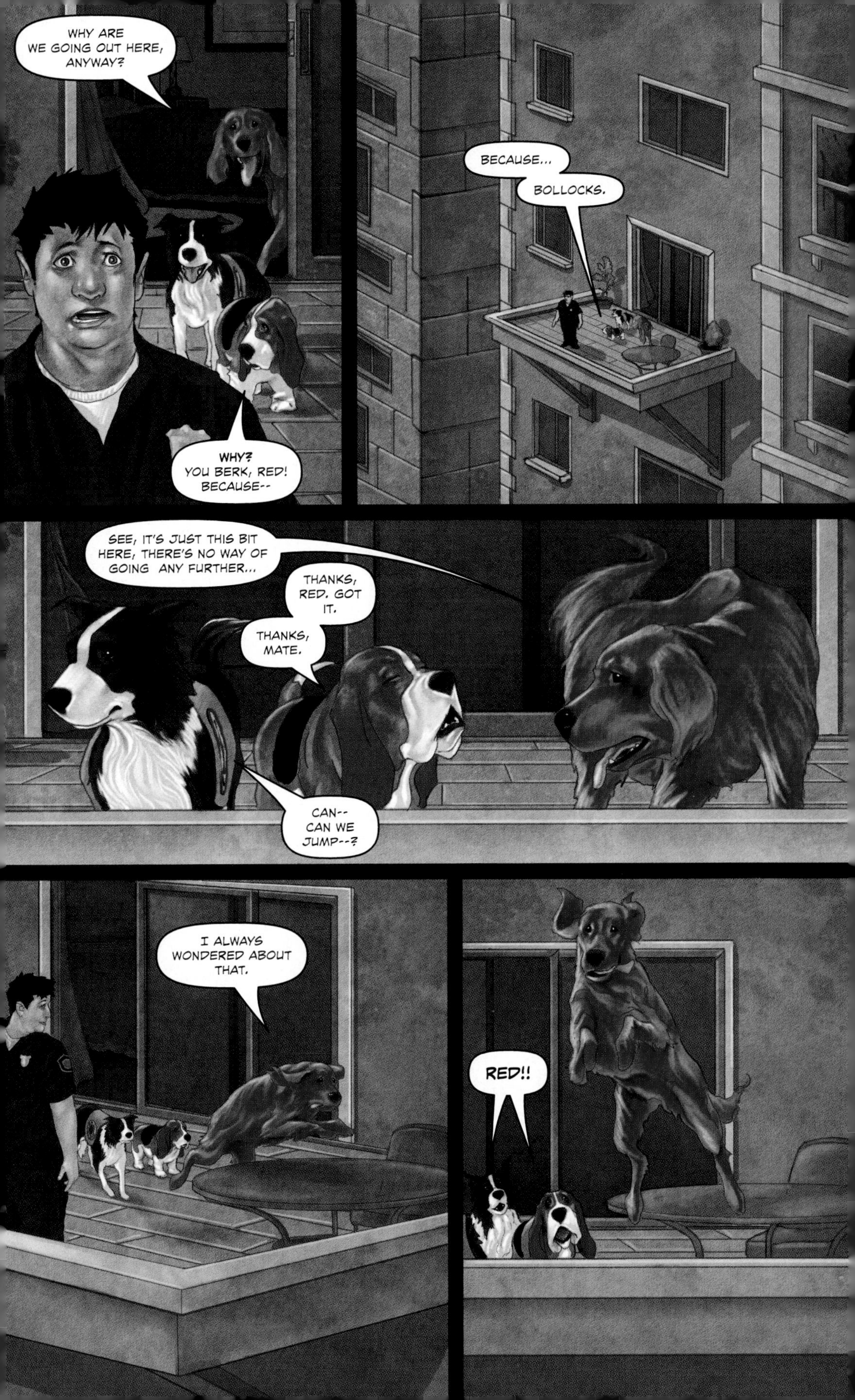

WHY ARE WE GOING OUT HERE, ANYWAY?
WHY? YOU BERK, RED! BECAUSE--
BECAUSE...
BOLLOCKS.
SEE, IT'S JUST THIS BIT HERE, THERE'S NO WAY OF GOING ANY FURTHER...
THANKS, RED. GOT IT.
THANKS, MATE.
CAN-- CAN WE JUMP--?
I ALWAYS WONDERED ABOUT THAT.
RED!!

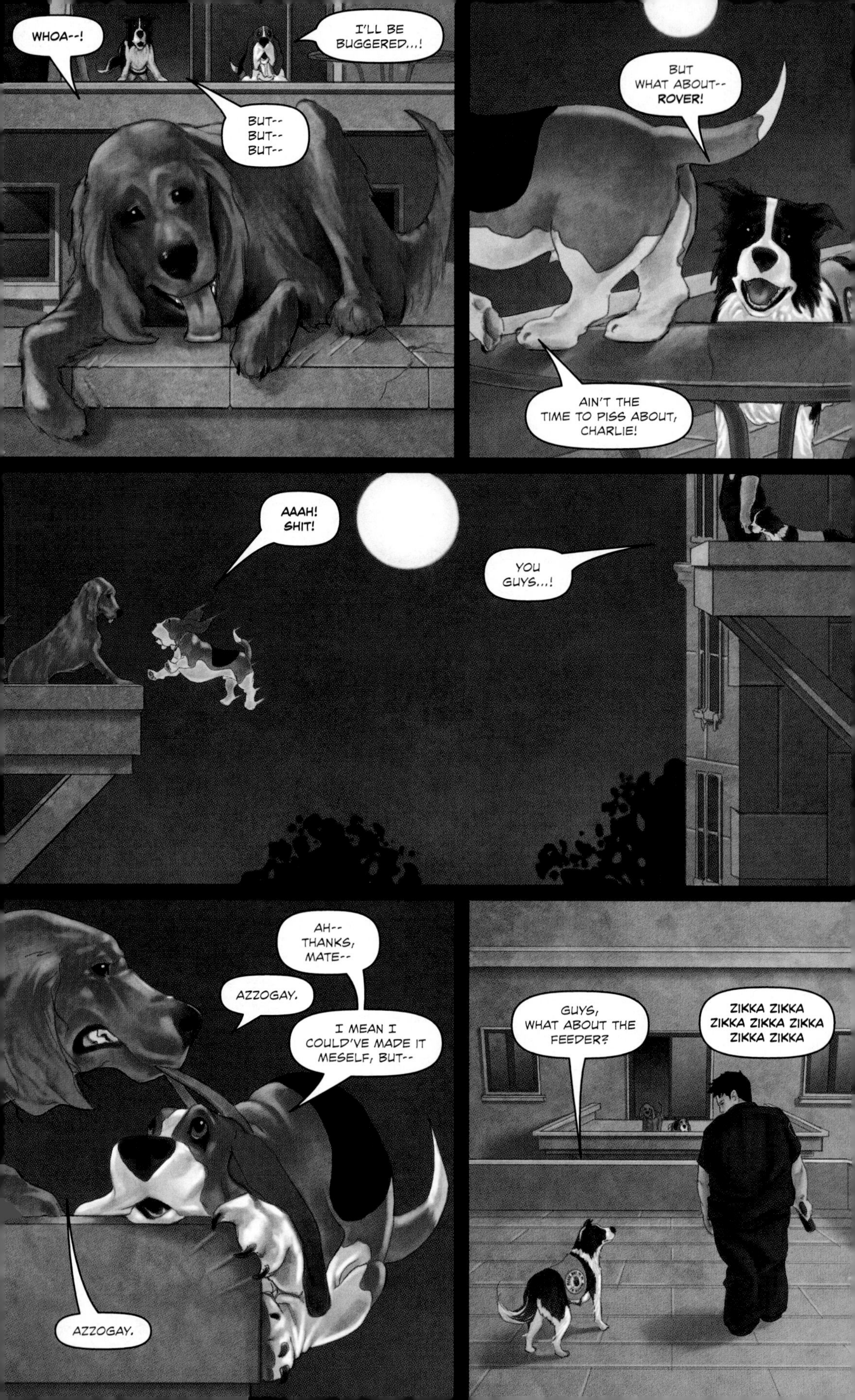
WHOA--!
I'LL BE BUGGERED...!
BUT-- BUT-- BUT--
BUT WHAT ABOUT-- **ROVER!**
AIN'T THE TIME TO PISS ABOUT, CHARLIE!
AAAH! SHIT!
YOU GUYS...!
AH-- THANKS, MATE--
AZZOGAY.
I MEAN I COULD'VE MADE IT MESELF, BUT--
AZZOGAY.
GUYS, WHAT ABOUT THE FEEDER?
ZIKKA ZIKKA ZIKKA ZIKKA ZIKKA ZIKKA ZIKKA

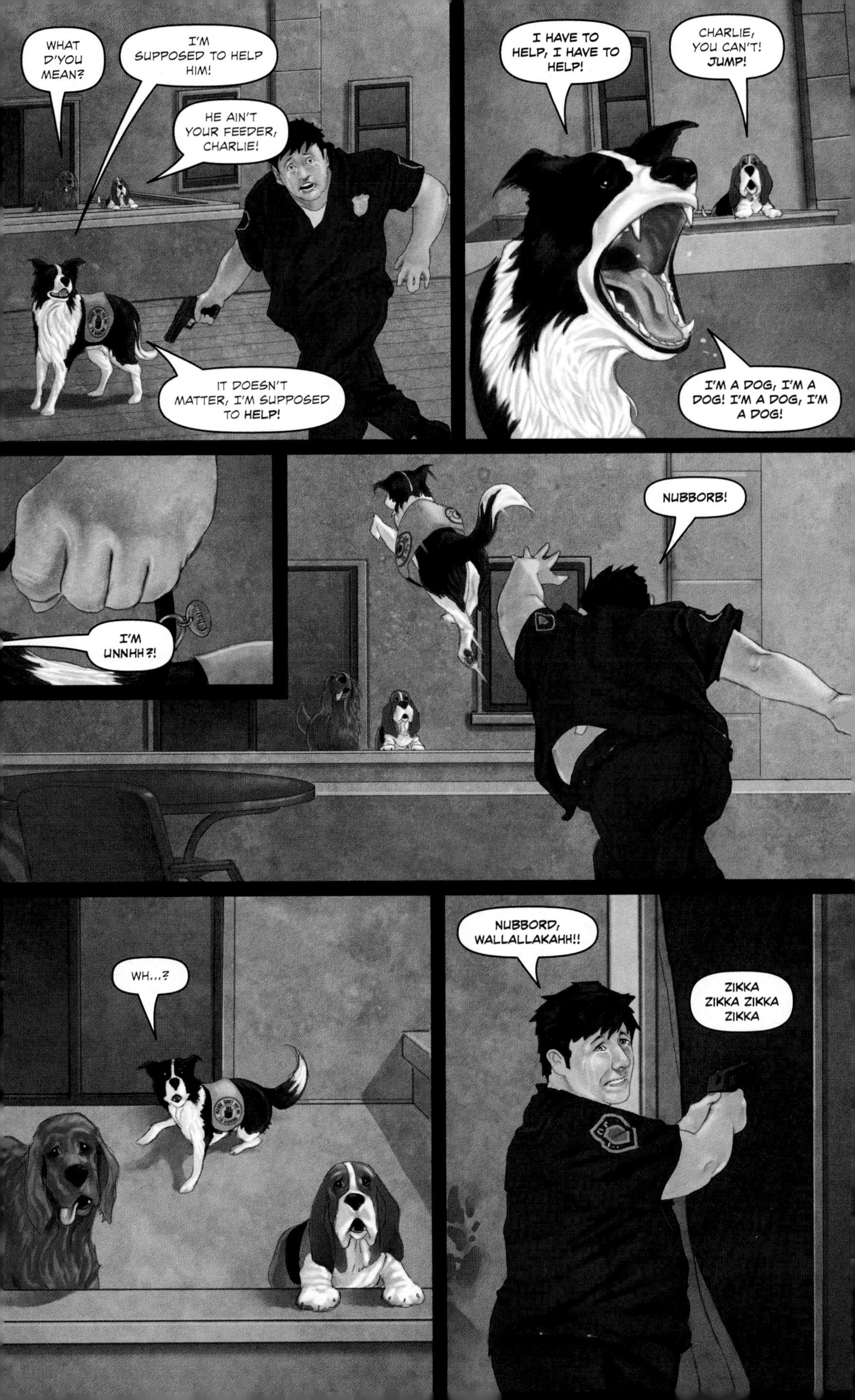

WHAT D'YOU MEAN?
I'M SUPPOSED TO HELP HIM!
HE AIN'T YOUR FEEDER, CHARLIE!
IT DOESN'T MATTER, I'M SUPPOSED TO HELP!
I HAVE TO HELP, I HAVE TO HELP!
CHARLIE, YOU CAN'T! JUMP!
I'M A DOG, I'M A DOG! I'M A DOG, I'M A DOG!
I'M UNNHH?!
NUBBORB!
WH...?
NUBBORD, WALLALLAKAHH!!
ZIKKA ZIKKA ZIKKA ZIKKA

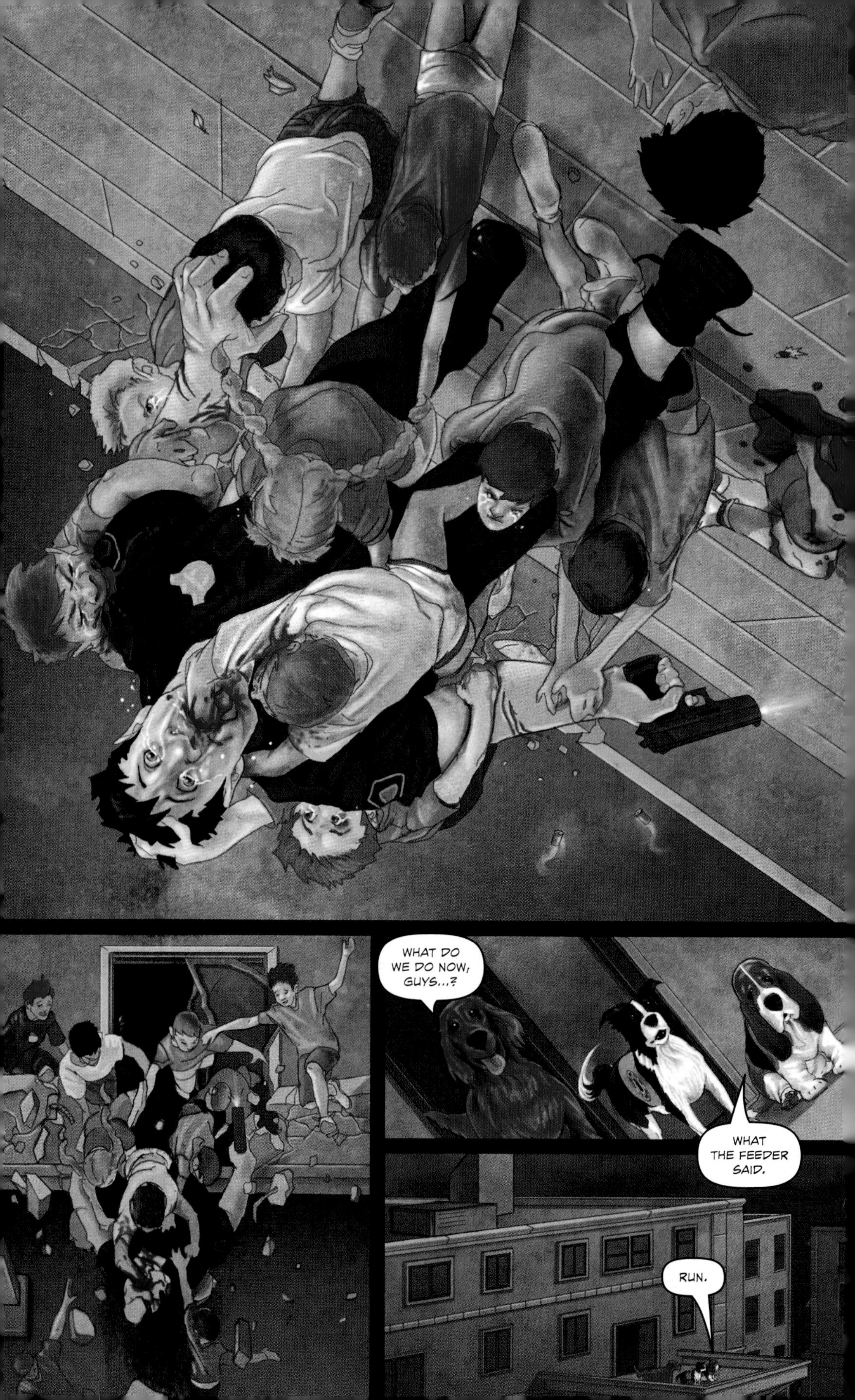
WHAT DO WE DO NOW, GUYS...?
WHAT THE FEEDER SAID.
RUN.

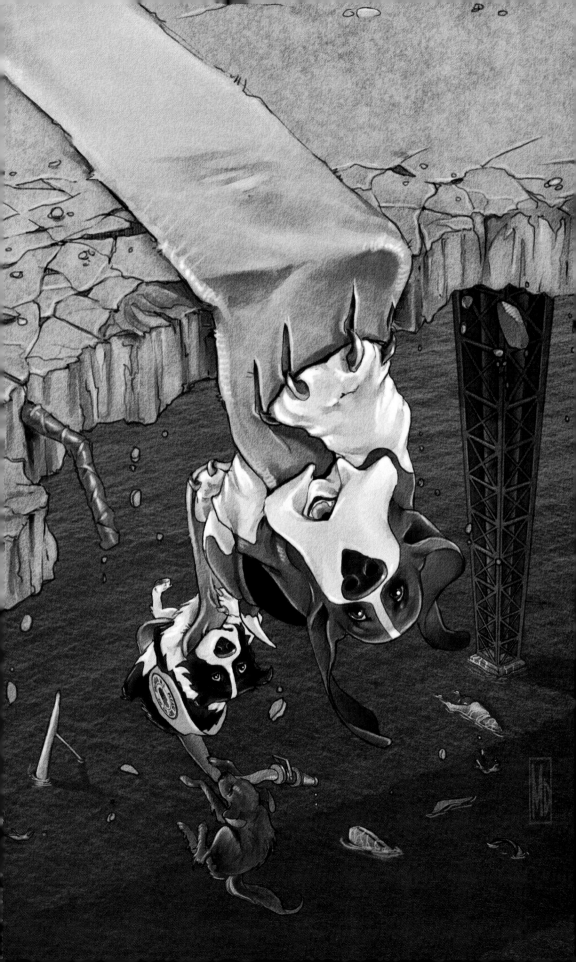

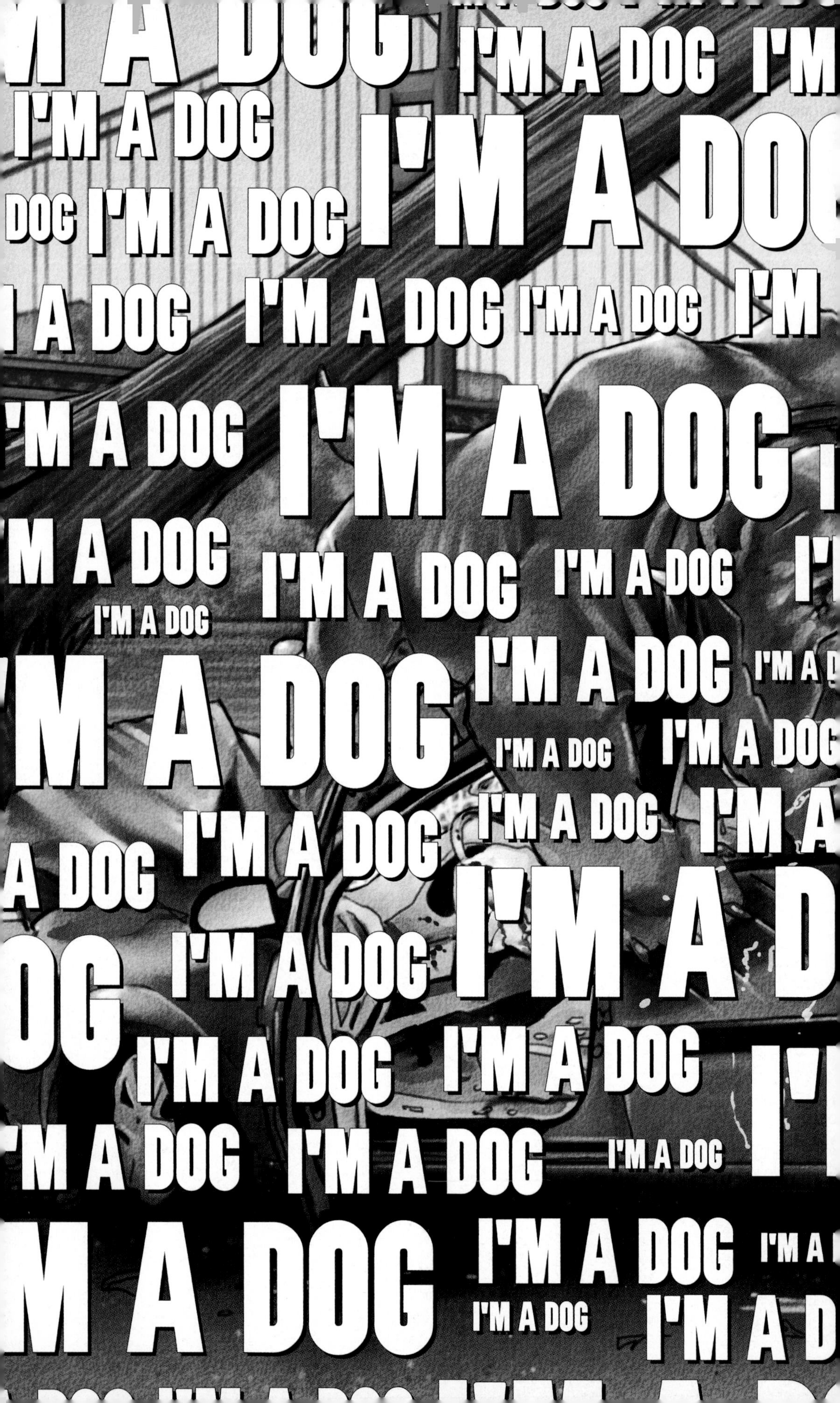

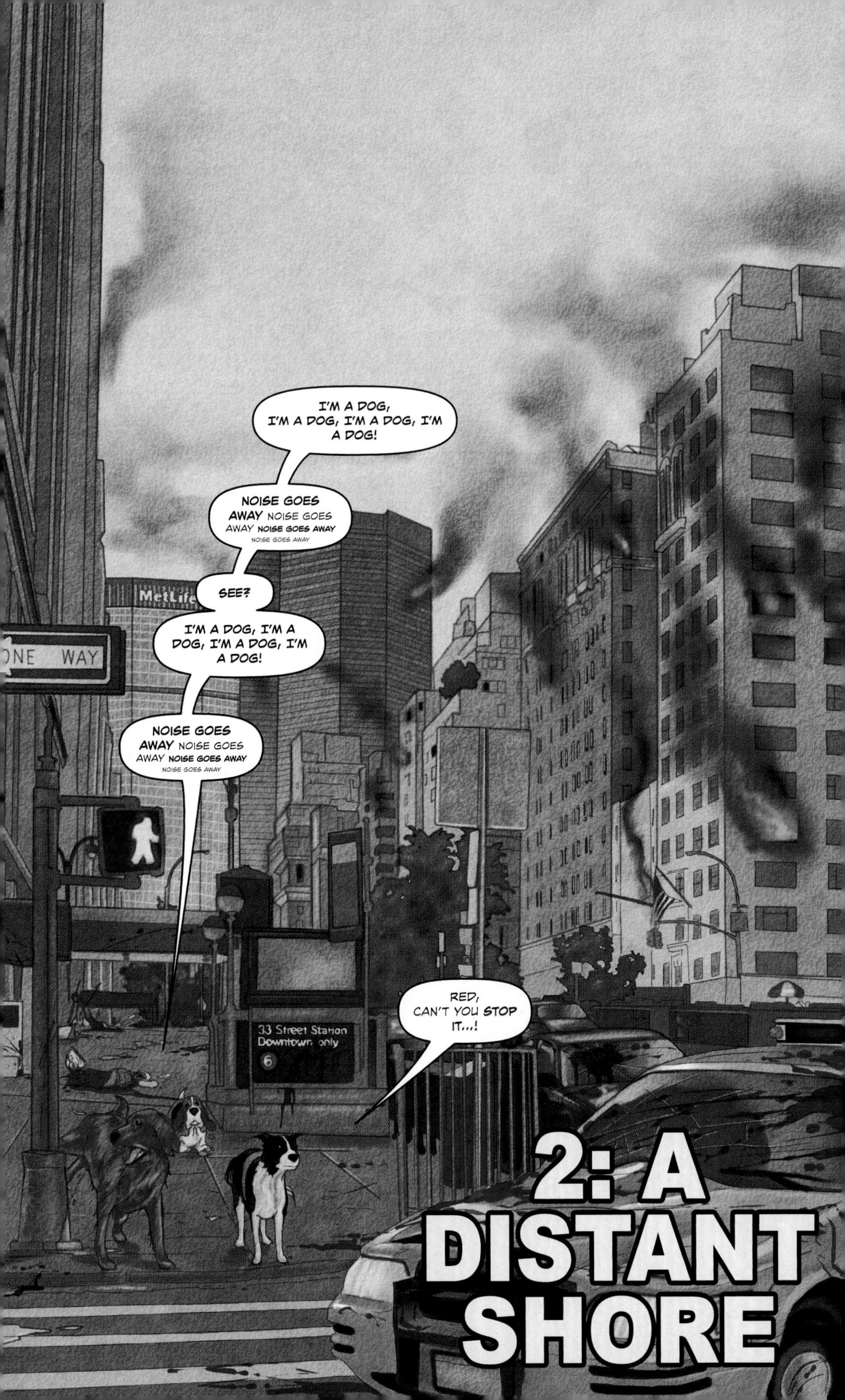
I'M A DOG, I'M A DOG, I'M A DOG, I'M A DOG!
NOISE GOES AWAY NOISE GOES AWAY NOISE GOES AWAY NOISE GOES AWAY
SEE?
I'M A DOG, I'M A DOG, I'M A DOG, I'M A DOG!
NOISE GOES AWAY NOISE GOES AWAY NOISE GOES AWAY NOISE GOES AWAY
MetLife
ONE WAY
33 Street Station Downtown only
6
RED, CAN'T YOU STOP IT...!
2: A DISTANT SHORE

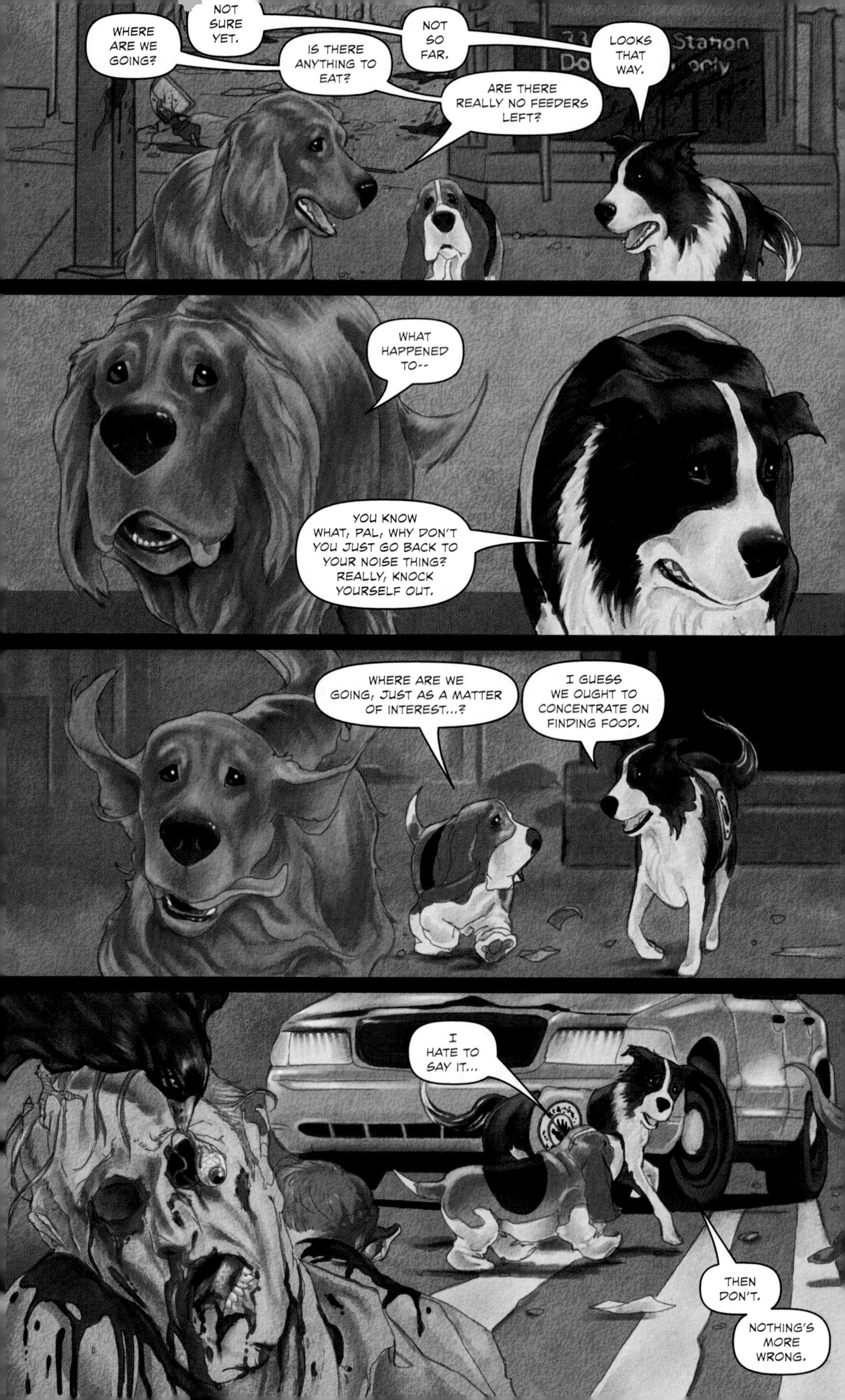
WHERE ARE WE GOING?
NOT SURE YET.
IS THERE ANYTHING TO EAT?
NOT SO FAR.
ARE THERE REALLY NO FEEDERS LEFT?
LOOKS THAT WAY.
WHAT HAPPENED TO--
YOU KNOW WHAT, PAL, WHY DON'T YOU JUST GO BACK TO YOUR NOISE THING? REALLY; KNOCK YOURSELF OUT.
WHERE ARE WE GOING, JUST AS A MATTER OF INTEREST...?
I GUESS WE OUGHT TO CONCENTRATE ON FINDING FOOD.
I HATE TO SAY IT...
THEN DON'T.
NOTHING'S MORE WRONG.

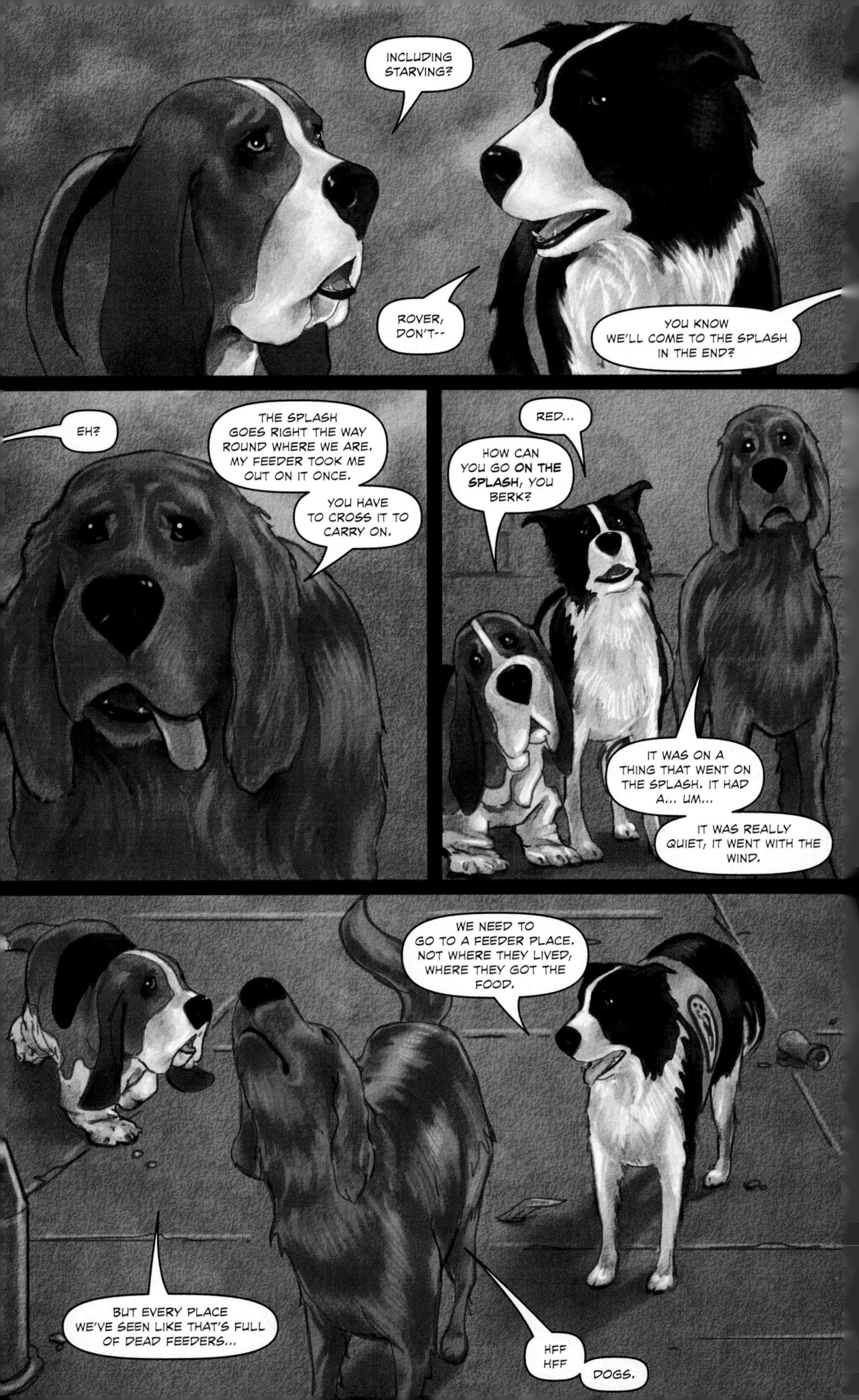
INCLUDING STARVING?
ROVER, DON'T--
YOU KNOW WE'LL COME TO THE SPLASH IN THE END?
EH?
THE SPLASH GOES RIGHT THE WAY ROUND WHERE WE ARE. MY FEEDER TOOK ME OUT ON IT ONCE.
YOU HAVE TO CROSS IT TO CARRY ON.
RED...
HOW CAN YOU GO **ON THE SPLASH**, YOU BERK?
IT WAS ON A THING THAT WENT ON THE SPLASH. IT HAD A... UM...
IT WAS REALLY QUIET, IT WENT WITH THE WIND.
WE NEED TO GO TO A FEEDER PLACE. NOT WHERE THEY LIVED, WHERE THEY GOT THE FOOD.
BUT EVERY PLACE WE'VE SEEN LIKE THAT'S FULL OF DEAD FEEDERS...
HFF HFF
DOGS.

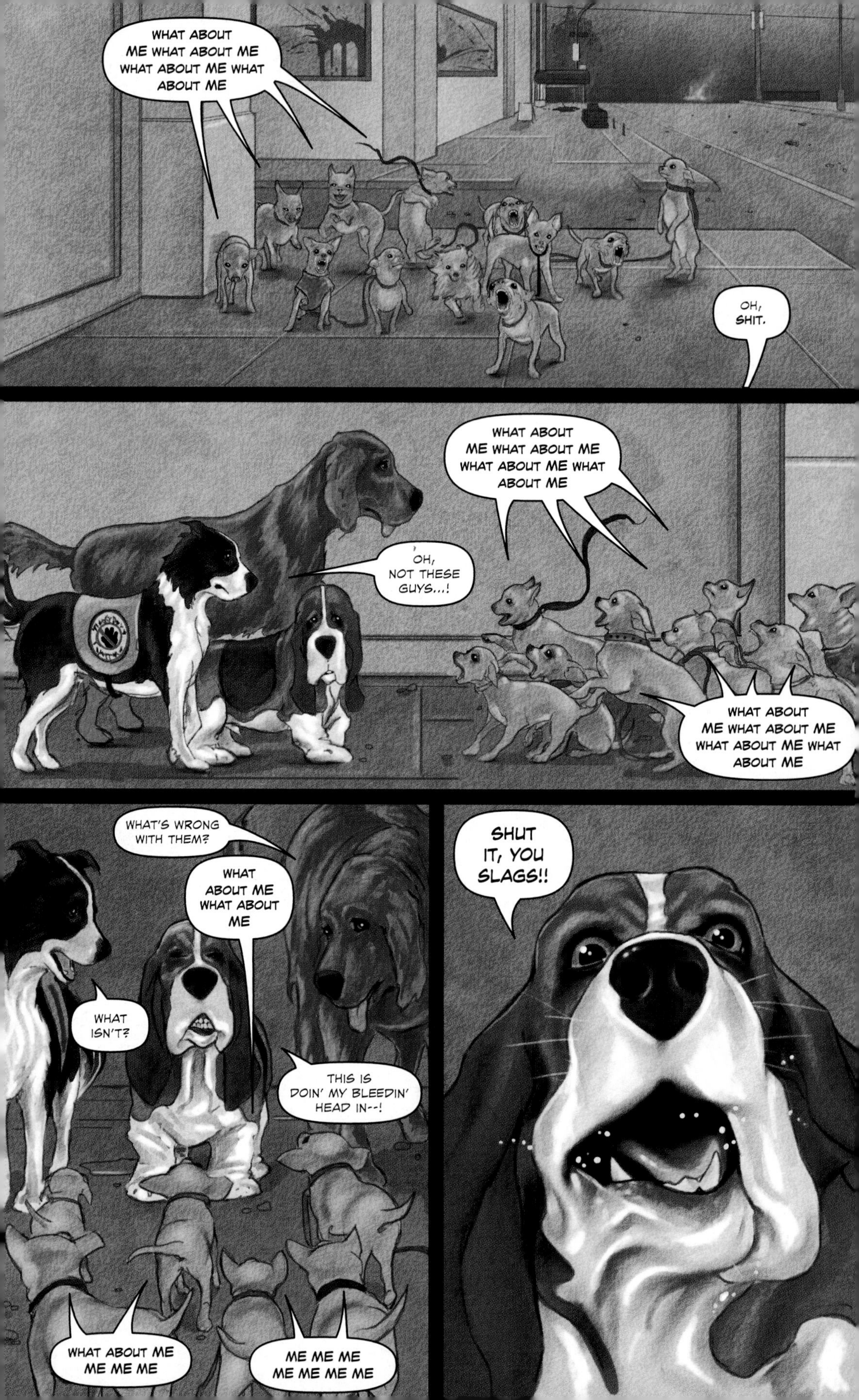
WHAT ABOUT ME WHAT ABOUT ME WHAT ABOUT ME WHAT ABOUT ME
OH, SHIT.
OH, NOT THESE GUYS...!
WHAT ABOUT ME WHAT ABOUT ME WHAT ABOUT ME WHAT ABOUT ME
WHAT ABOUT ME WHAT ABOUT ME WHAT ABOUT ME WHAT ABOUT ME
WHAT'S WRONG WITH THEM?
WHAT ABOUT ME WHAT ABOUT ME
WHAT ISN'T?
THIS IS DOIN' MY BLEEDIN' HEAD IN--!
WHAT ABOUT ME ME ME ME
ME ME ME ME ME ME ME
SHUT IT, YOU SLAGS!!

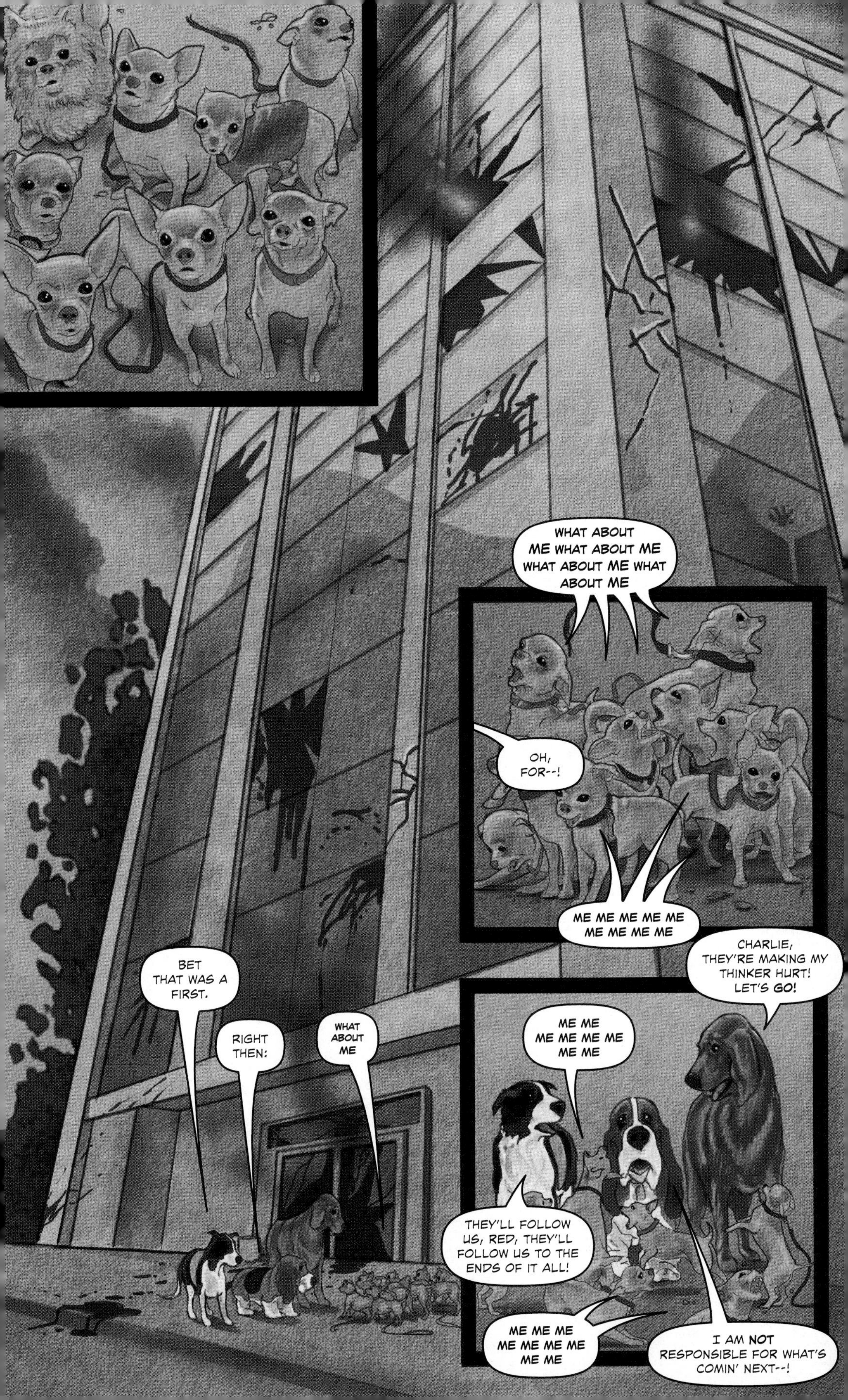
WHAT ABOUT ME WHAT ABOUT ME WHAT ABOUT ME WHAT ABOUT ME
OH, FOR--!
ME ME ME ME ME ME ME ME ME
BET THAT WAS A FIRST.
RIGHT THEN:
WHAT ABOUT ME
CHARLIE, THEY'RE MAKING MY THINKER HURT! LET'S GO!
ME ME ME ME ME ME ME ME
THEY'LL FOLLOW US, RED, THEY'LL FOLLOW US TO THE ENDS OF IT ALL!
ME ME ME ME ME ME ME ME ME
I AM NOT RESPONSIBLE FOR WHAT'S COMIN' NEXT--!

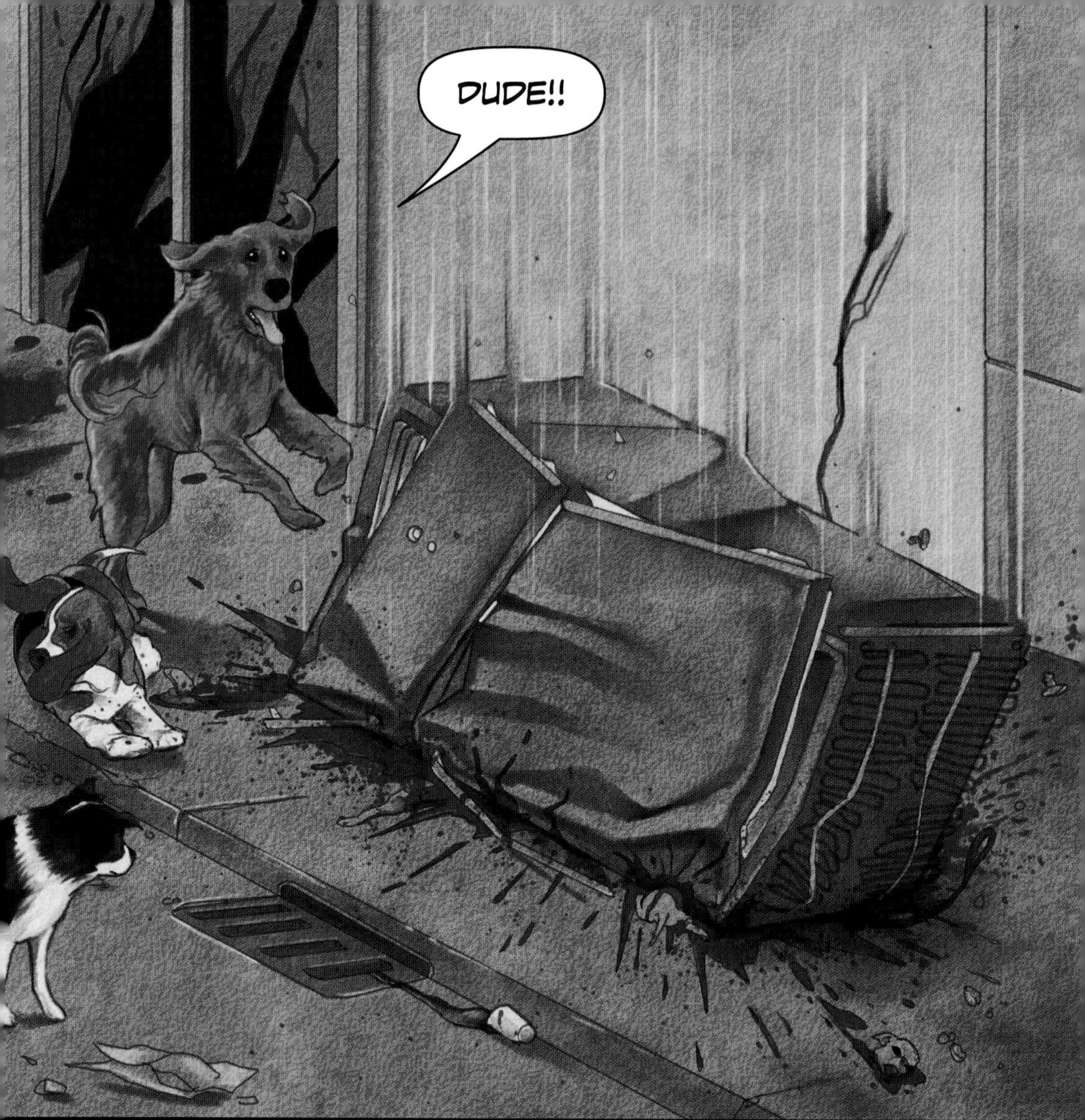
DUDE!!

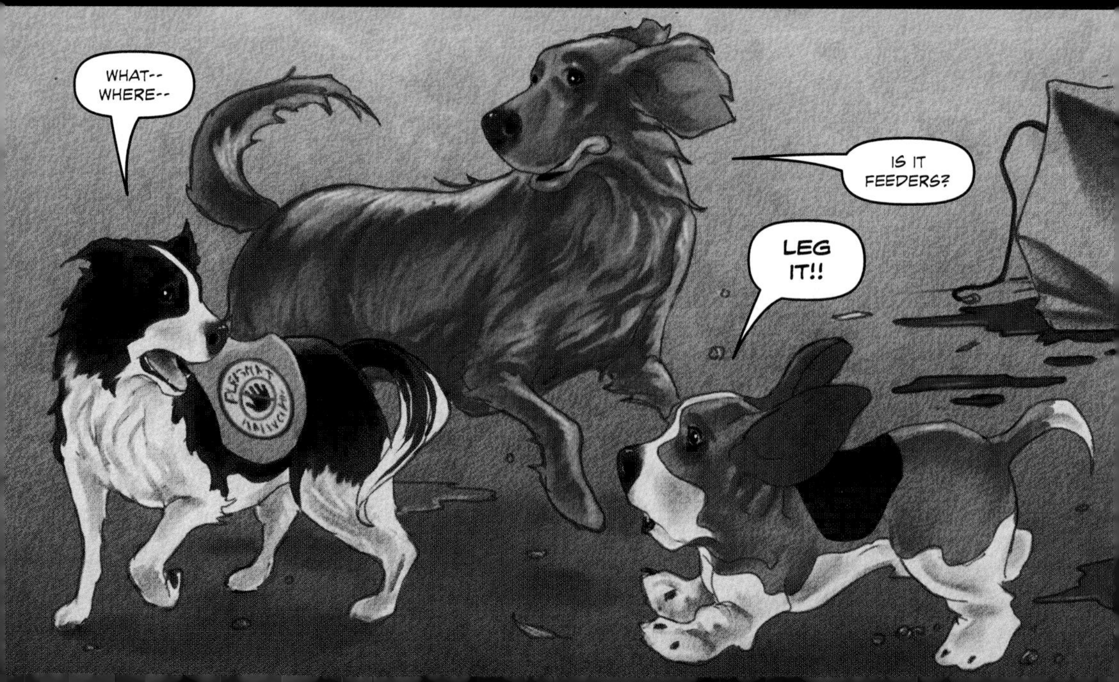
WHAT--
WHERE--
IS IT
FEEDERS?
LEG
IT!!

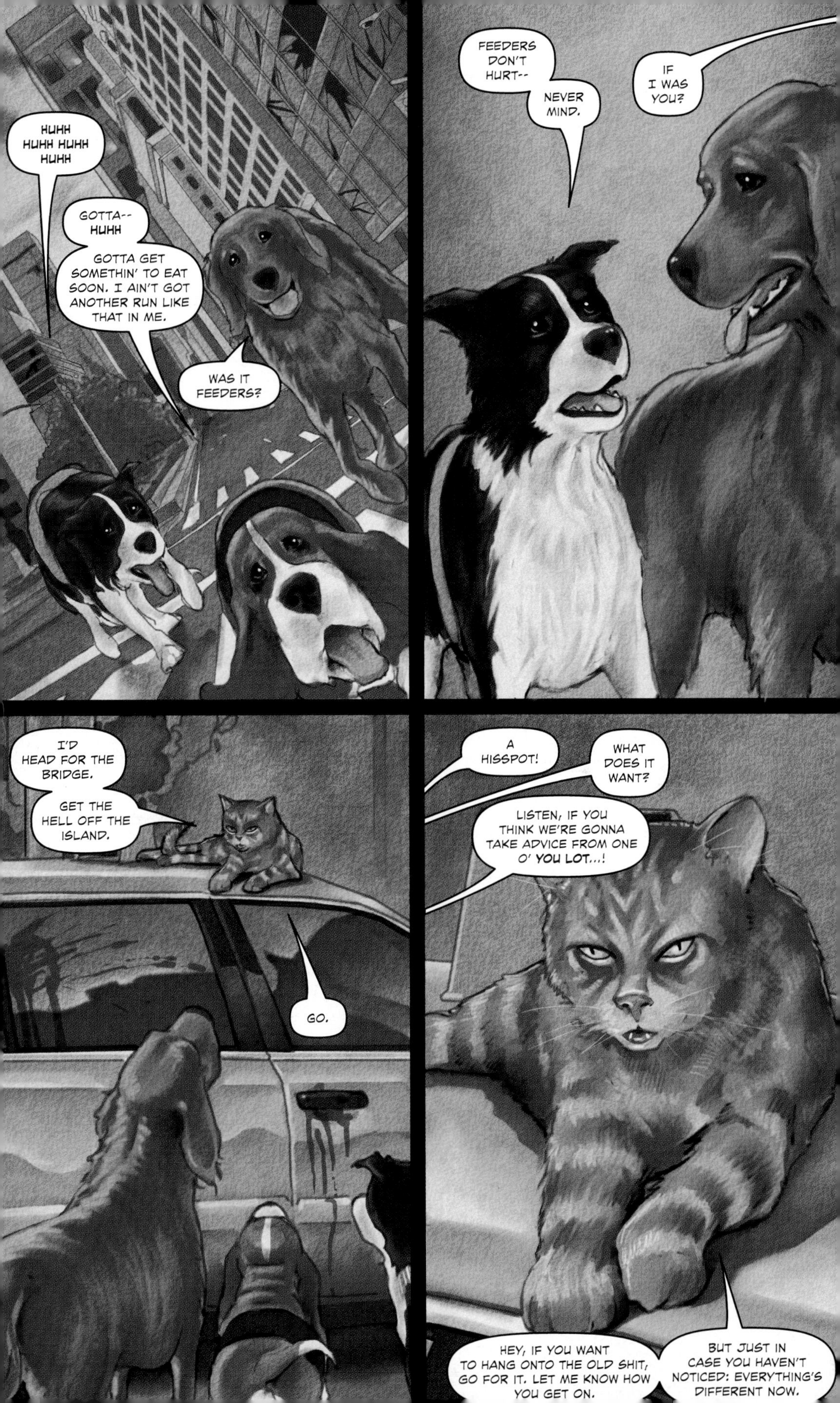
HUHH HUHH HUHH HUHH
GOTTA-- HUHH
GOTTA GET SOMETHIN' TO EAT SOON. I AIN'T GOT ANOTHER RUN LIKE THAT IN ME.
WAS IT FEEDERS?
FEEDERS DON'T HURT--
NEVER MIND.
IF I WAS YOU?
I'D HEAD FOR THE BRIDGE.
GET THE HELL OFF THE ISLAND.
GO.
A HISSPOT!
WHAT DOES IT WANT?
LISTEN, IF YOU THINK WE'RE GONNA TAKE ADVICE FROM ONE O' YOU LOT...!
HEY, IF YOU WANT TO HANG ONTO THE OLD SHIT, GO FOR IT. LET ME KNOW HOW YOU GET ON.
BUT JUST IN CASE YOU HAVEN'T NOTICED: EVERYTHING'S DIFFERENT NOW.

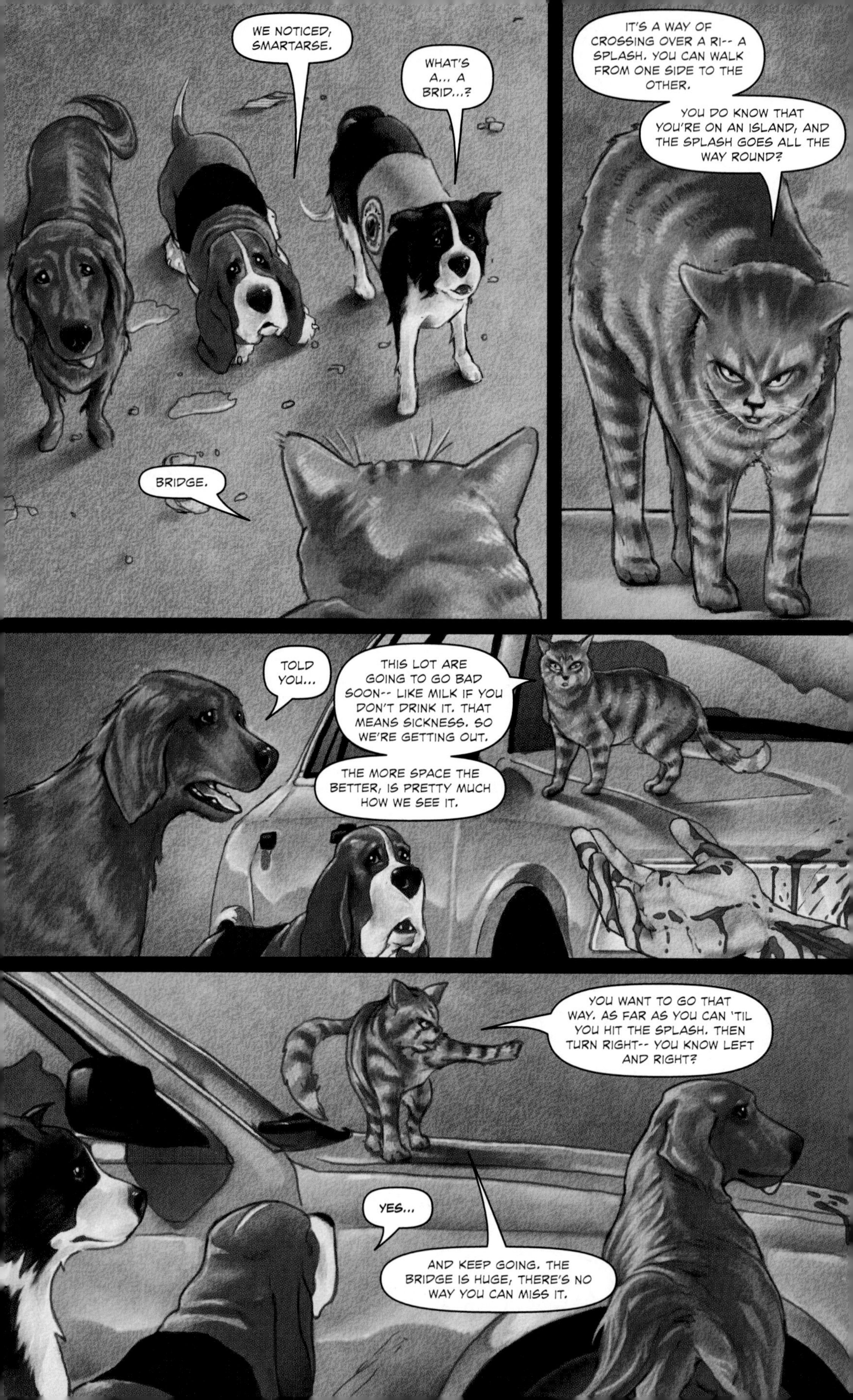
WE NOTICED, SMARTARSE.
WHAT'S A... A BRID...?
BRIDGE.
IT'S A WAY OF CROSSING OVER A RI-- A SPLASH. YOU CAN WALK FROM ONE SIDE TO THE OTHER.
YOU DO KNOW THAT YOU'RE ON AN ISLAND, AND THE SPLASH GOES ALL THE WAY ROUND?
TOLD YOU...
THIS LOT ARE GOING TO GO BAD SOON-- LIKE MILK IF YOU DON'T DRINK IT. THAT MEANS SICKNESS. SO WE'RE GETTING OUT.
THE MORE SPACE THE BETTER, IS PRETTY MUCH HOW WE SEE IT.
YOU WANT TO GO THAT WAY. AS FAR AS YOU CAN 'TIL YOU HIT THE SPLASH. THEN TURN RIGHT-- YOU KNOW LEFT AND RIGHT?
YES...
AND KEEP GOING. THE BRIDGE IS HUGE, THERE'S NO WAY YOU CAN MISS IT.

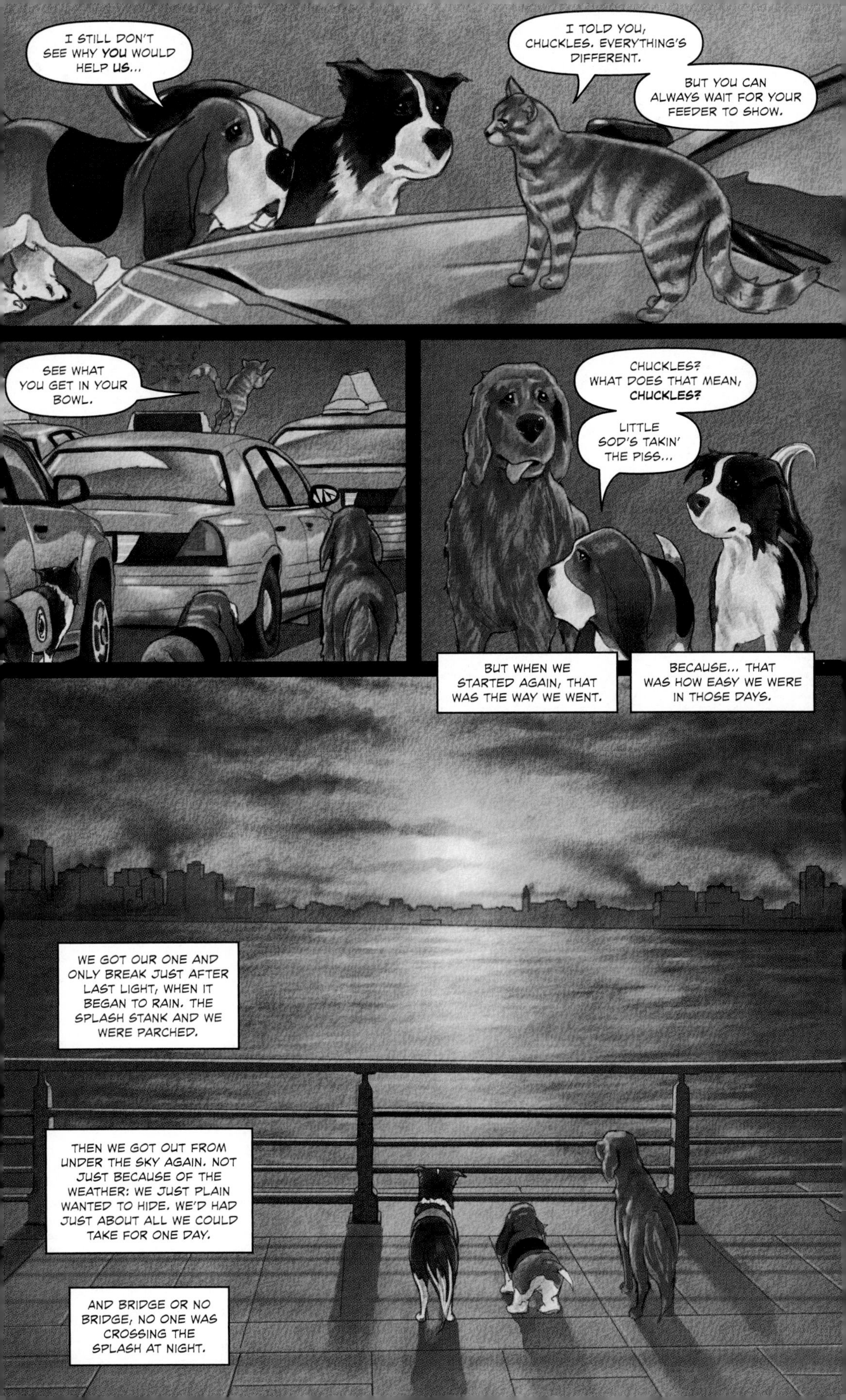
I STILL DON'T SEE WHY **YOU** WOULD HELP **US**...
I TOLD YOU, CHUCKLES. EVERYTHING'S DIFFERENT.
BUT YOU CAN ALWAYS WAIT FOR YOUR FEEDER TO SHOW.
SEE WHAT YOU GET IN YOUR BOWL.
CHUCKLES? WHAT DOES THAT MEAN, **CHUCKLES?**
LITTLE SOD'S TAKIN' THE PISS...
BUT WHEN WE STARTED AGAIN, THAT WAS THE WAY WE WENT.
BECAUSE... THAT WAS HOW EASY WE WERE IN THOSE DAYS.
WE GOT OUR ONE AND ONLY BREAK JUST AFTER LAST LIGHT, WHEN IT BEGAN TO RAIN. THE SPLASH STANK AND WE WERE PARCHED.
THEN WE GOT OUT FROM UNDER THE SKY AGAIN. NOT JUST BECAUSE OF THE WEATHER: WE JUST PLAIN WANTED TO HIDE. WE'D HAD JUST ABOUT ALL WE COULD TAKE FOR ONE DAY.
AND BRIDGE OR NO BRIDGE, NO ONE WAS CROSSING THE SPLASH AT NIGHT.

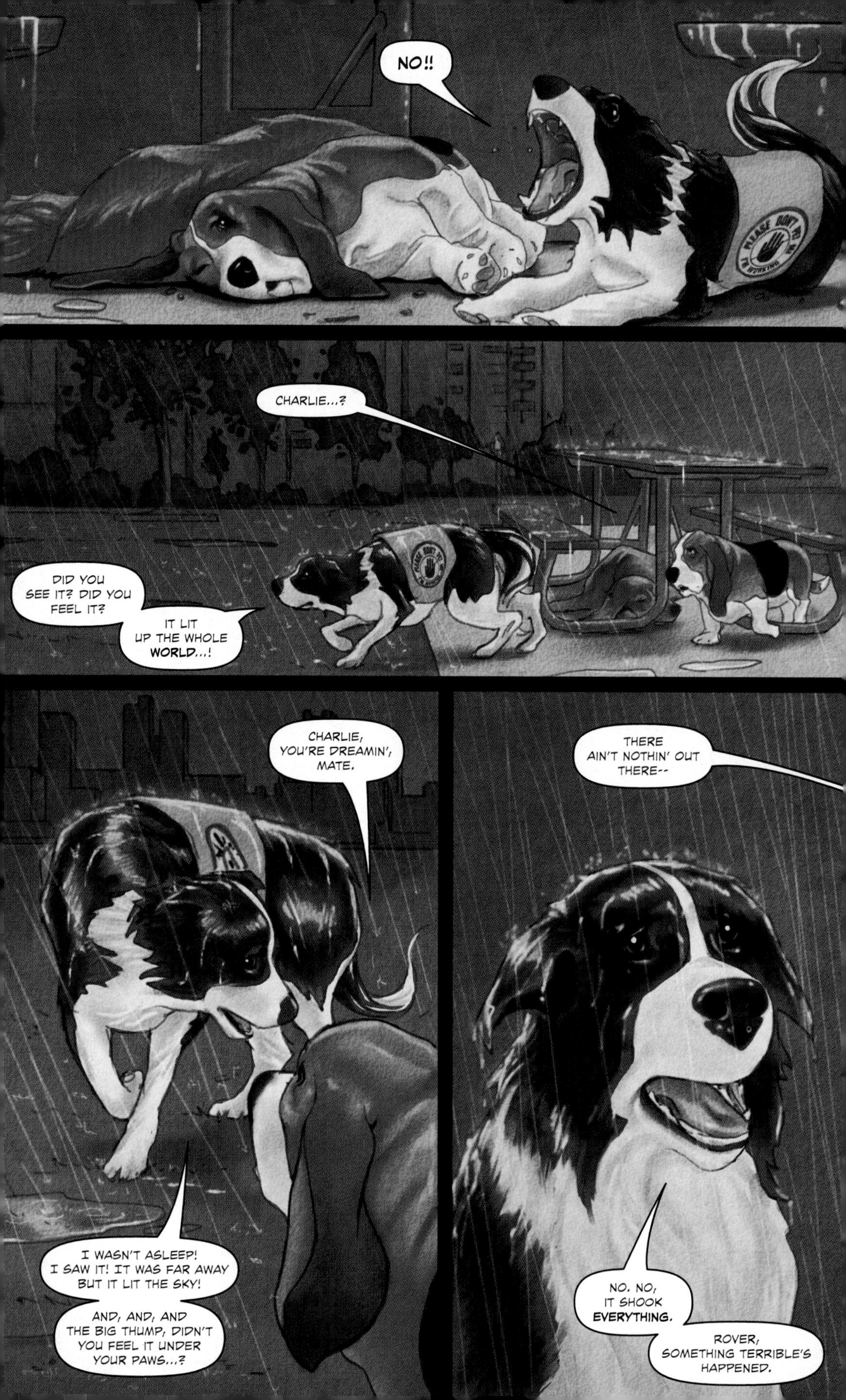
NO!!
CHARLIE...?
DID YOU SEE IT? DID YOU FEEL IT?
IT LIT UP THE WHOLE **WORLD**...!
CHARLIE, YOU'RE DREAMIN', MATE.
I WASN'T ASLEEP! I SAW IT! IT WAS FAR AWAY BUT IT LIT THE SKY!
AND, AND, AND THE BIG THUMP, DIDN'T YOU FEEL IT UNDER YOUR PAWS...?
THERE AIN'T NOTHIN' OUT THERE--
NO. NO, IT SHOOK **EVERYTHING.**
ROVER, SOMETHING TERRIBLE'S HAPPENED.

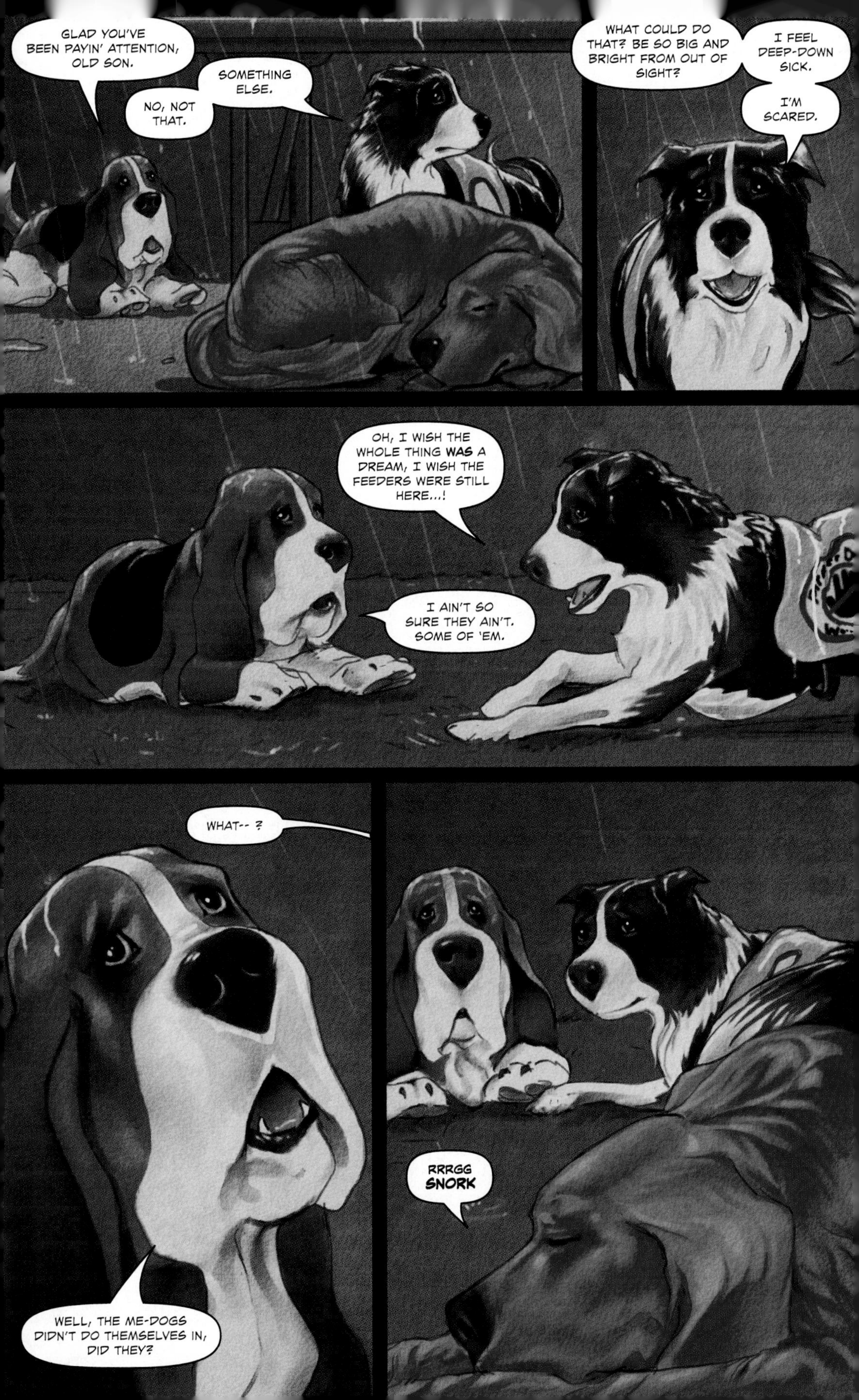
GLAD YOU'VE BEEN PAYIN' ATTENTION, OLD SON.
NO, NOT THAT.
SOMETHING ELSE.
WHAT COULD DO THAT? BE SO BIG AND BRIGHT FROM OUT OF SIGHT?
I FEEL DEEP-DOWN SICK.
I'M SCARED.
OH, I WISH THE WHOLE THING **WAS** A DREAM, I WISH THE FEEDERS WERE STILL HERE...!
I AIN'T SO SURE THEY AIN'T. SOME OF 'EM.
WHAT-- ?
WELL, THE ME-DOGS DIDN'T DO THEMSELVES IN, DID THEY?
RRRGG **SNORK**

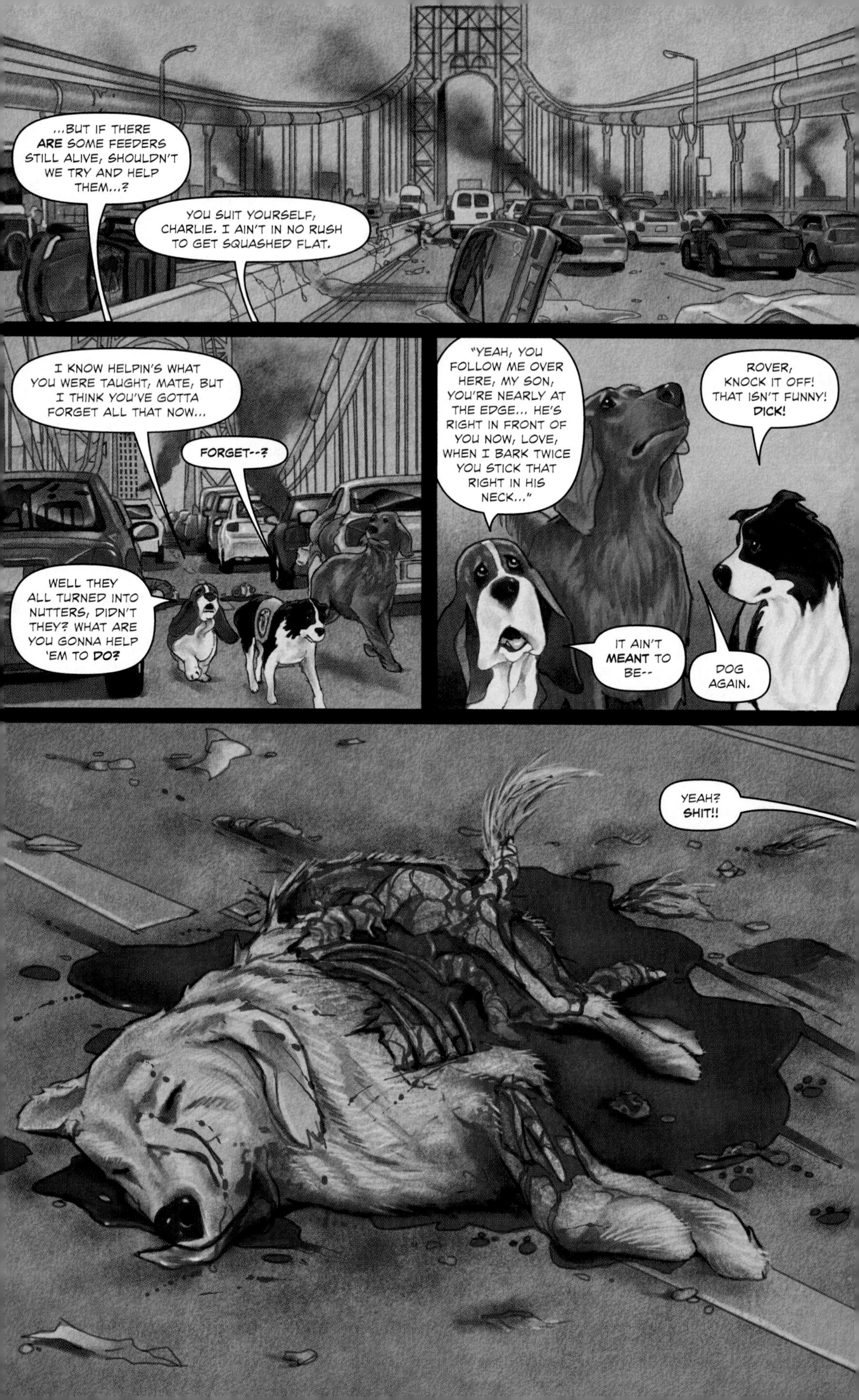
...BUT IF THERE ARE SOME FEEDERS STILL ALIVE, SHOULDN'T WE TRY AND HELP THEM...?
YOU SUIT YOURSELF, CHARLIE. I AIN'T IN NO RUSH TO GET SQUASHED FLAT.
I KNOW HELPIN'S WHAT YOU WERE TAUGHT, MATE, BUT I THINK YOU'VE GOTTA FORGET ALL THAT NOW...
FORGET--?
WELL THEY ALL TURNED INTO NUTTERS, DIDN'T THEY? WHAT ARE YOU GONNA HELP 'EM TO DO?
"YEAH, YOU FOLLOW ME OVER HERE, MY SON, YOU'RE NEARLY AT THE EDGE... HE'S RIGHT IN FRONT OF YOU NOW, LOVE, WHEN I BARK TWICE YOU STICK THAT RIGHT IN HIS NECK..."
ROVER, KNOCK IT OFF! THAT ISN'T FUNNY! DICK!
IT AIN'T MEANT TO BE--
DOG AGAIN.
YEAH? SHIT!!

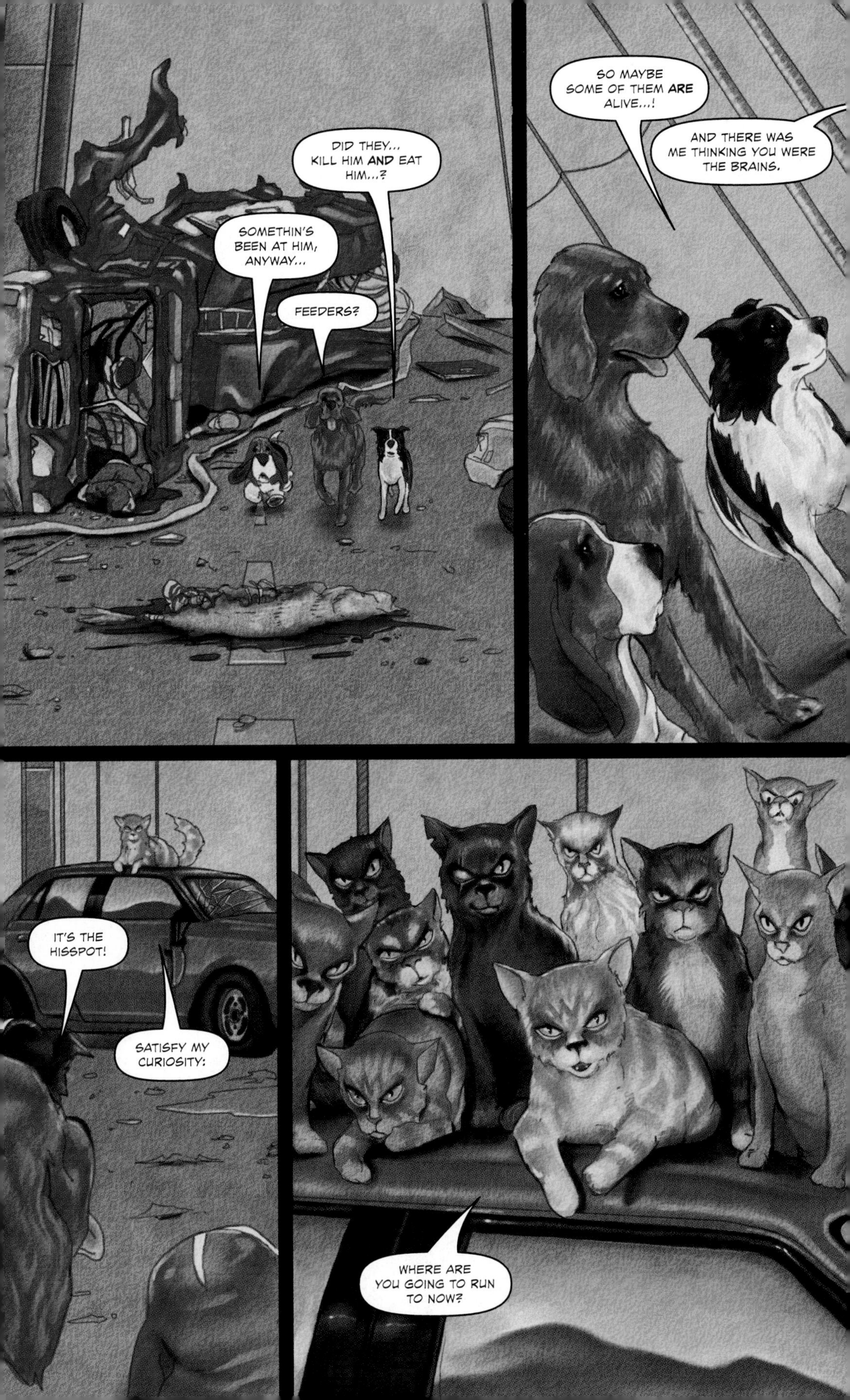
DID THEY... KILL HIM AND EAT HIM...?
SOMETHIN'S BEEN AT HIM, ANYWAY...
FEEDERS?
SO MAYBE SOME OF THEM ARE ALIVE...!
AND THERE WAS ME THINKING YOU WERE THE BRAINS.
IT'S THE HISSPOT!
SATISFY MY CURIOSITY:
WHERE ARE YOU GOING TO RUN TO NOW?

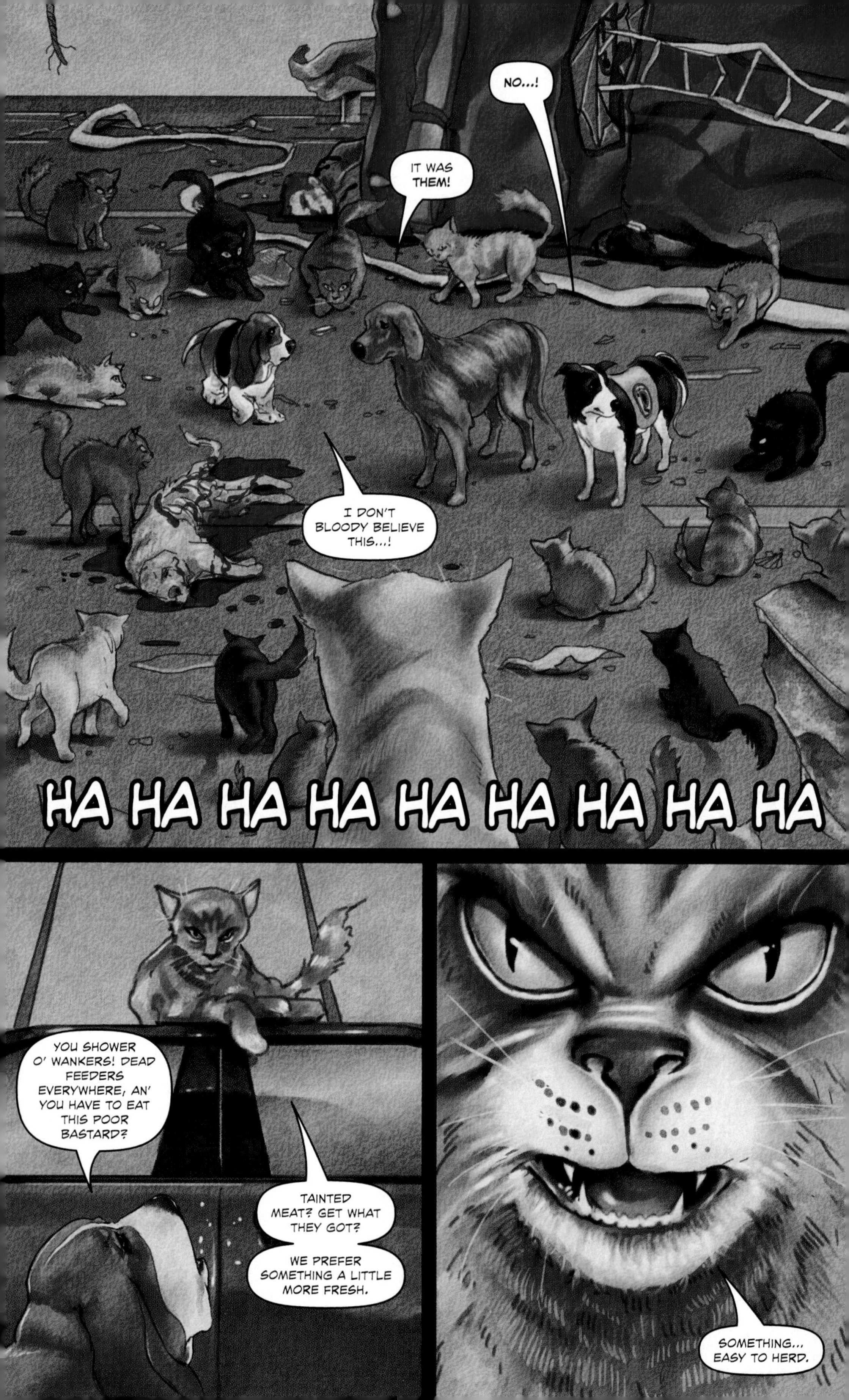
NO...!
IT WAS THEM!
I DON'T BLOODY BELIEVE THIS...!
HA HA HA HA HA HA HA HA HA
YOU SHOWER O' WANKERS! DEAD FEEDERS EVERYWHERE, AN' YOU HAVE TO EAT THIS POOR BASTARD?
TAINTED MEAT? GET WHAT THEY GOT?
WE PREFER SOMETHING A LITTLE MORE FRESH.
SOMETHING... EASY TO HERD.

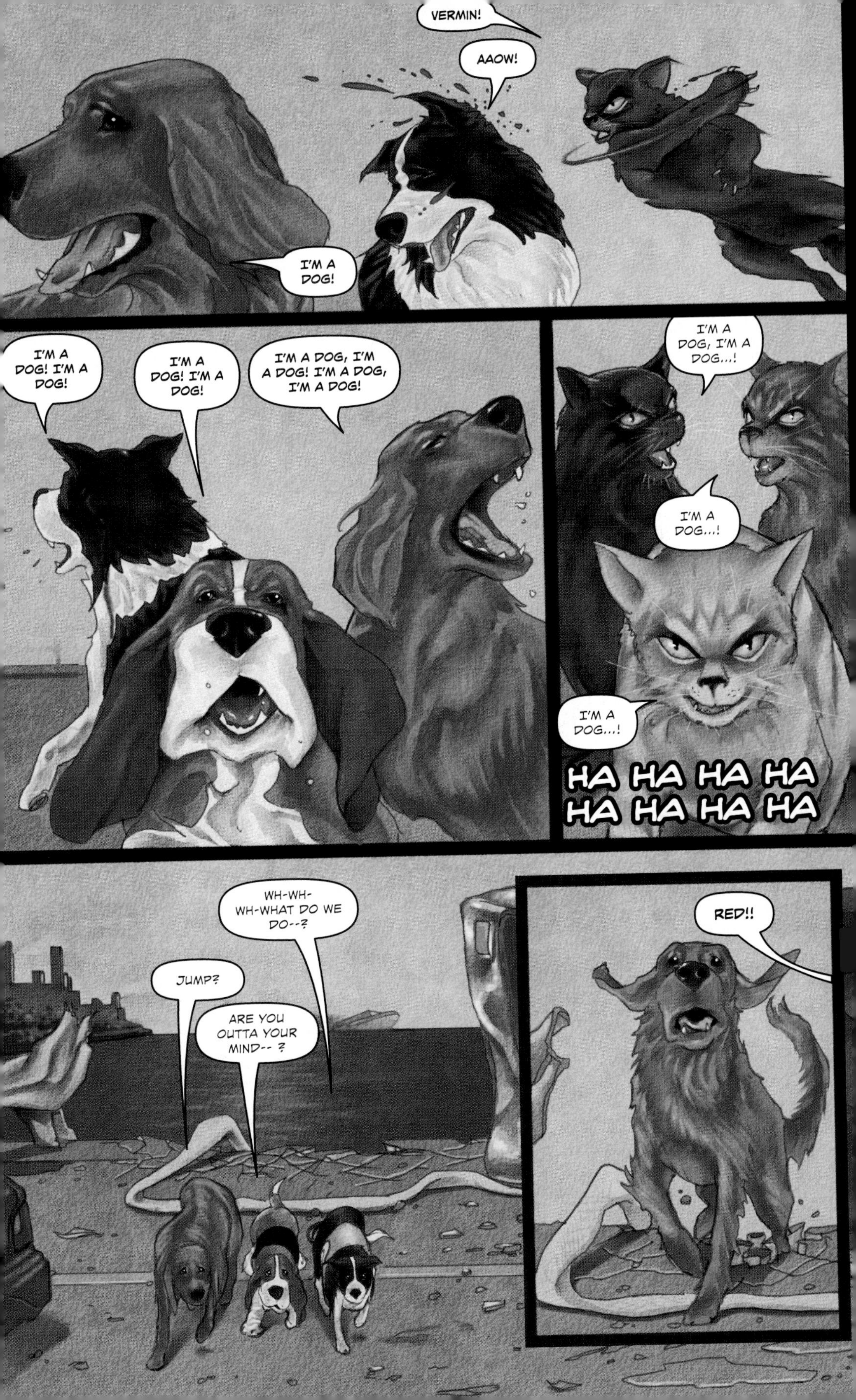

VERMIN!
AAOW!
I'M A DOG!
I'M A DOG! I'M A DOG!
I'M A DOG! I'M A DOG!
I'M A DOG, I'M A DOG! I'M A DOG, I'M A DOG!
I'M A DOG, I'M A DOG...!
I'M A DOG...!
I'M A DOG...!
HA HA HA HA HA HA HA HA
WH-WH-WH-WHAT DO WE DO--?
JUMP?
ARE YOU OUTTA YOUR MIND-- ?
RED!!

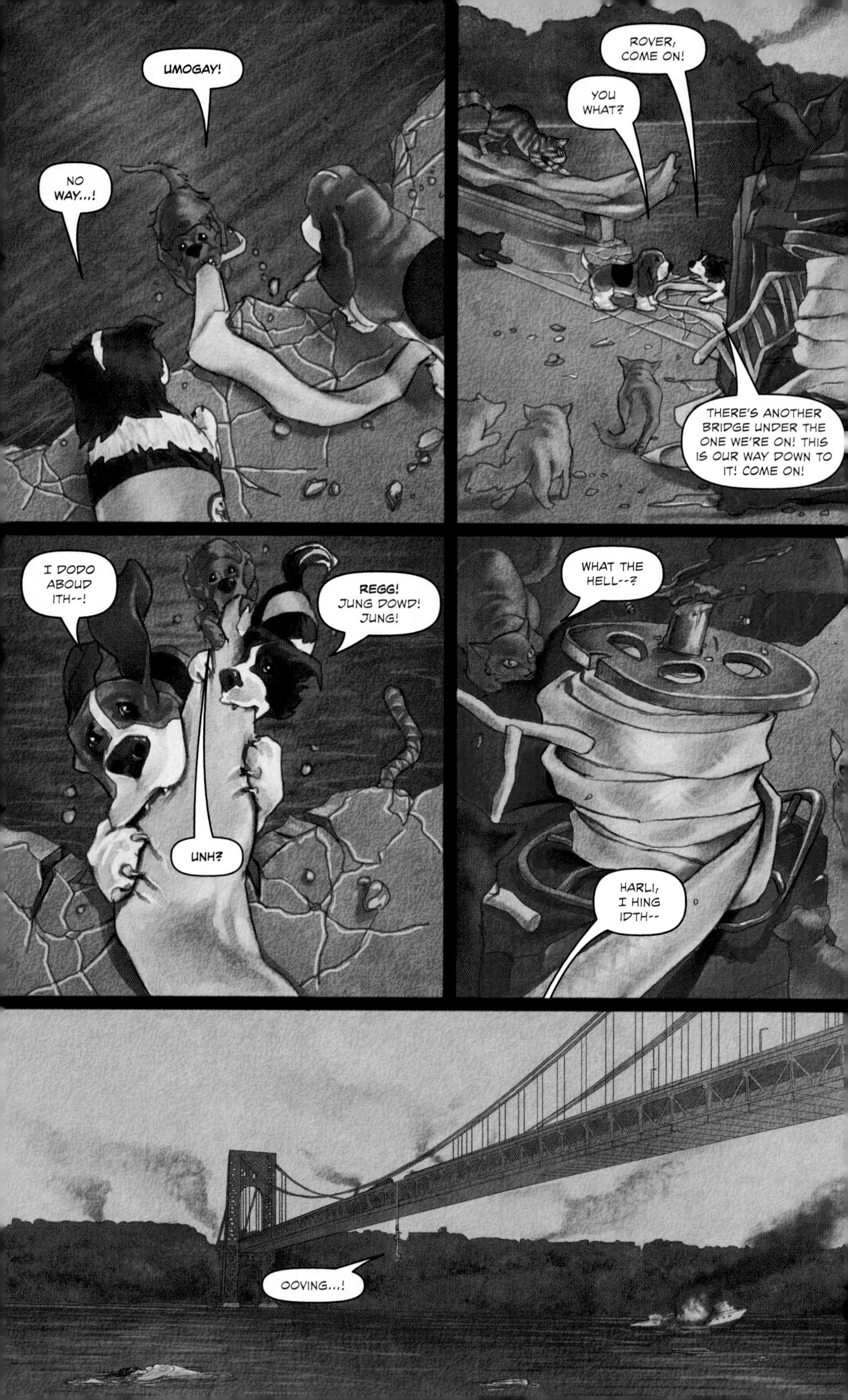
UMOGAY!
NO WAY...!
ROVER, COME ON!
YOU WHAT?
THERE'S ANOTHER BRIDGE UNDER THE ONE WE'RE ON! THIS IS OUR WAY DOWN TO IT! COME ON!
I DODO ABOUD ITH--!
REGG! JUNG DOWD! JUNG!
UNH?
WHAT THE HELL--?
HARLI, I HING IDTH--
OOVING...!

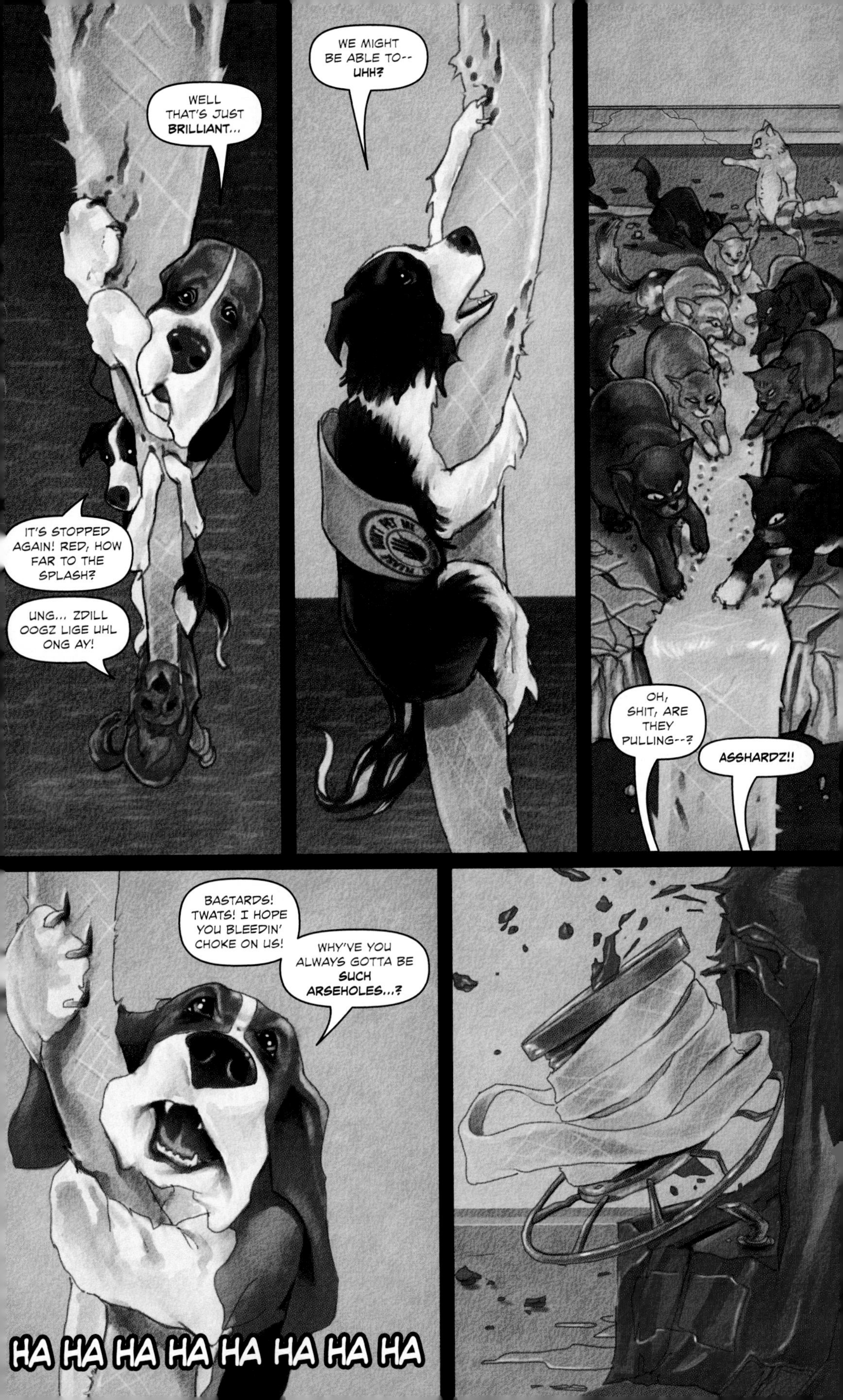
WELL THAT'S JUST BRILLIANT...
IT'S STOPPED AGAIN! RED, HOW FAR TO THE SPLASH?
UNG... ZDILL OOGZ LIGE UHL ONG AY!
WE MIGHT BE ABLE TO-- UHH?
OH, SHIT, ARE THEY PULLING--?
ASSHARDZ!!
BASTARDS! TWATS! I HOPE YOU BLEEDIN' CHOKE ON US!
WHY'VE YOU ALWAYS GOTTA BE SUCH ARSEHOLES...?
HA HA HA HA HA HA HA HA

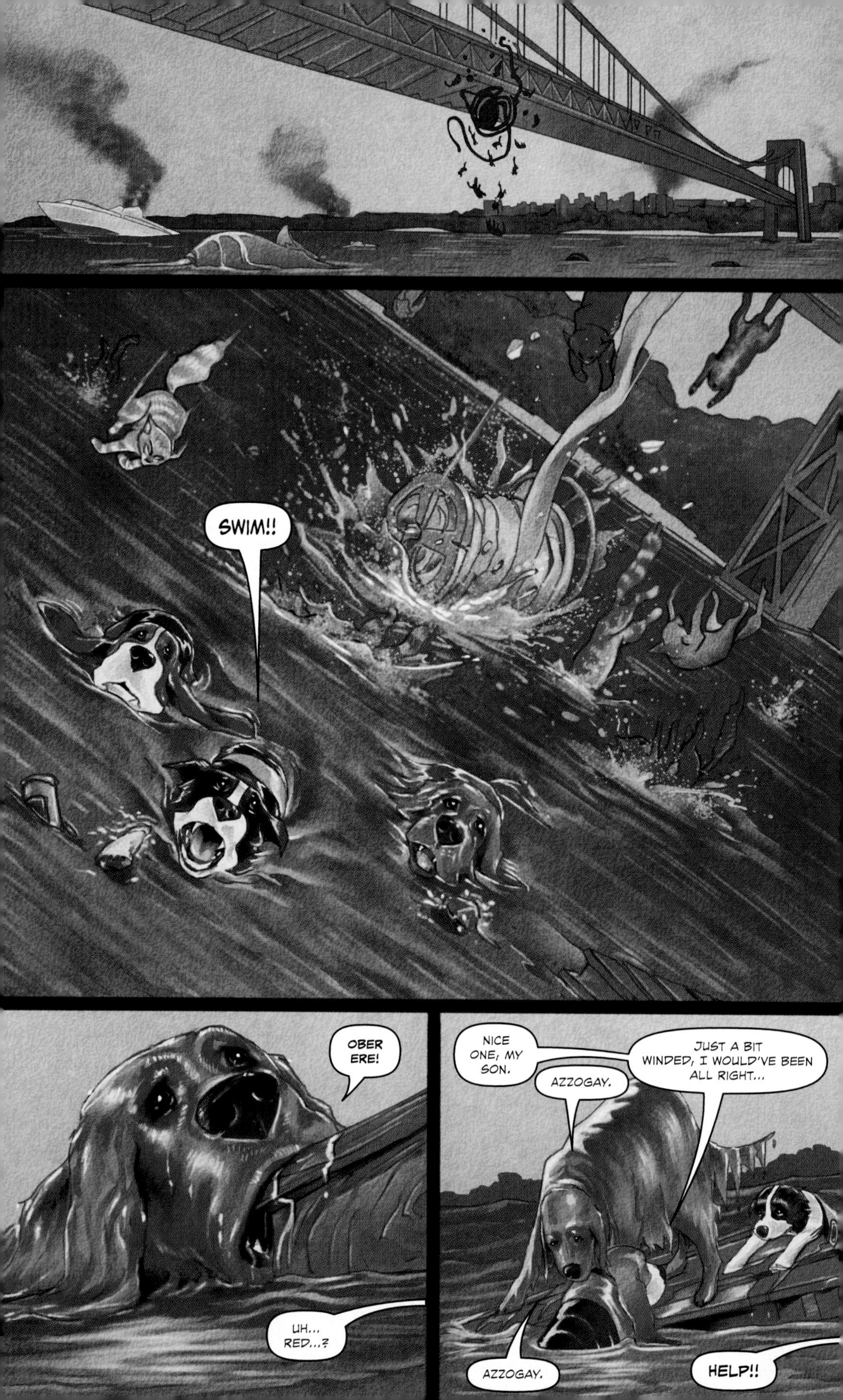
SWIM!!
OBER
ERE!
UH...
RED...?
NICE
ONE, MY
SON.
AZZOGAY.
JUST A BIT
WINDED, I WOULD'VE BEEN
ALL RIGHT...
AZZOGAY.
HELP!!

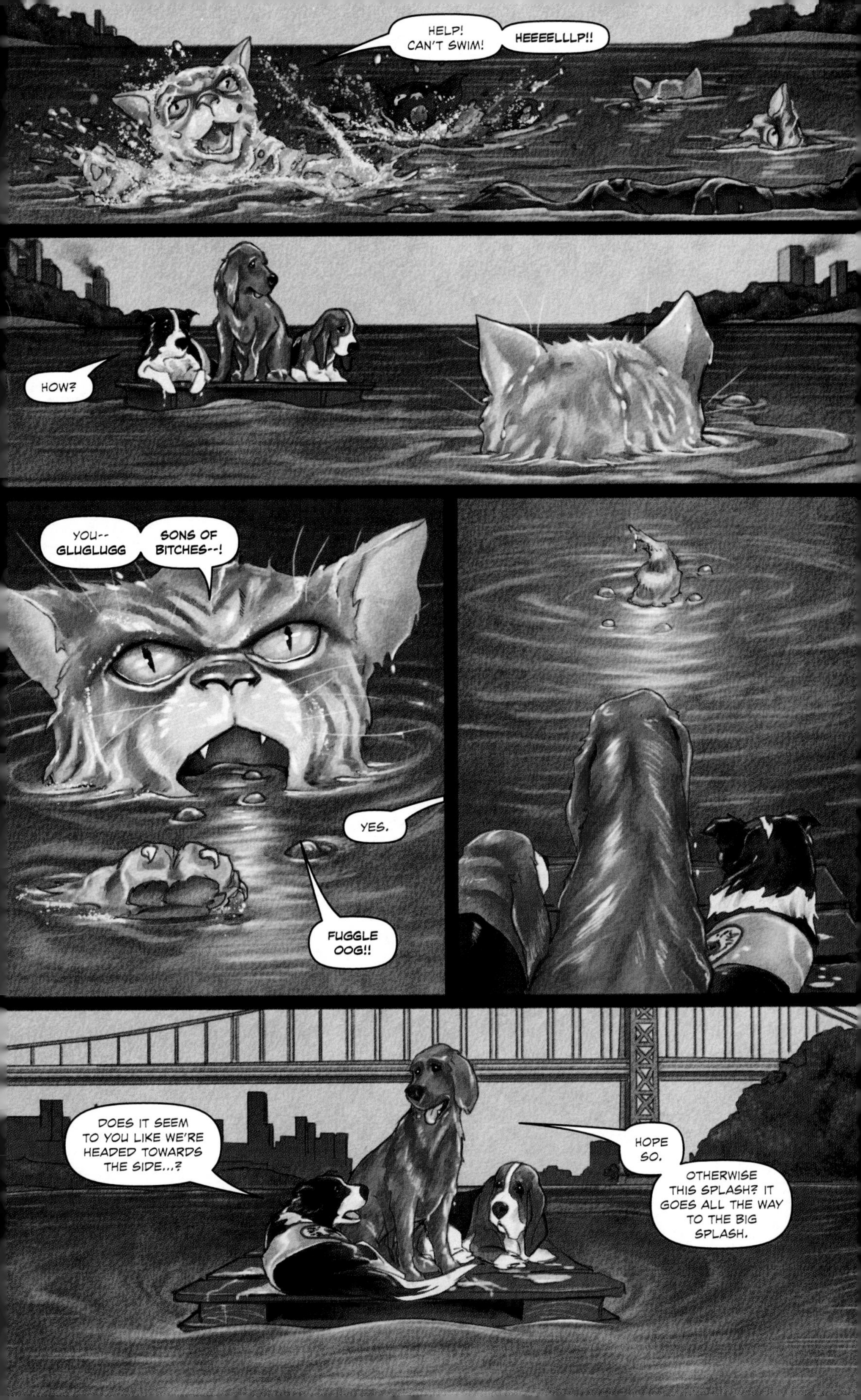
HELP!
CAN'T SWIM!
HEEEELLLP!!
HOW?
YOU--
GLUGLUGG
SONS OF
BITCHES--!
YES.
FUGGLE
OOG!!
DOES IT SEEM
TO YOU LIKE WE'RE
HEADED TOWARDS
THE SIDE...?
HOPE
SO.
OTHERWISE
THIS SPLASH? IT
GOES ALL THE WAY
TO THE BIG
SPLASH.

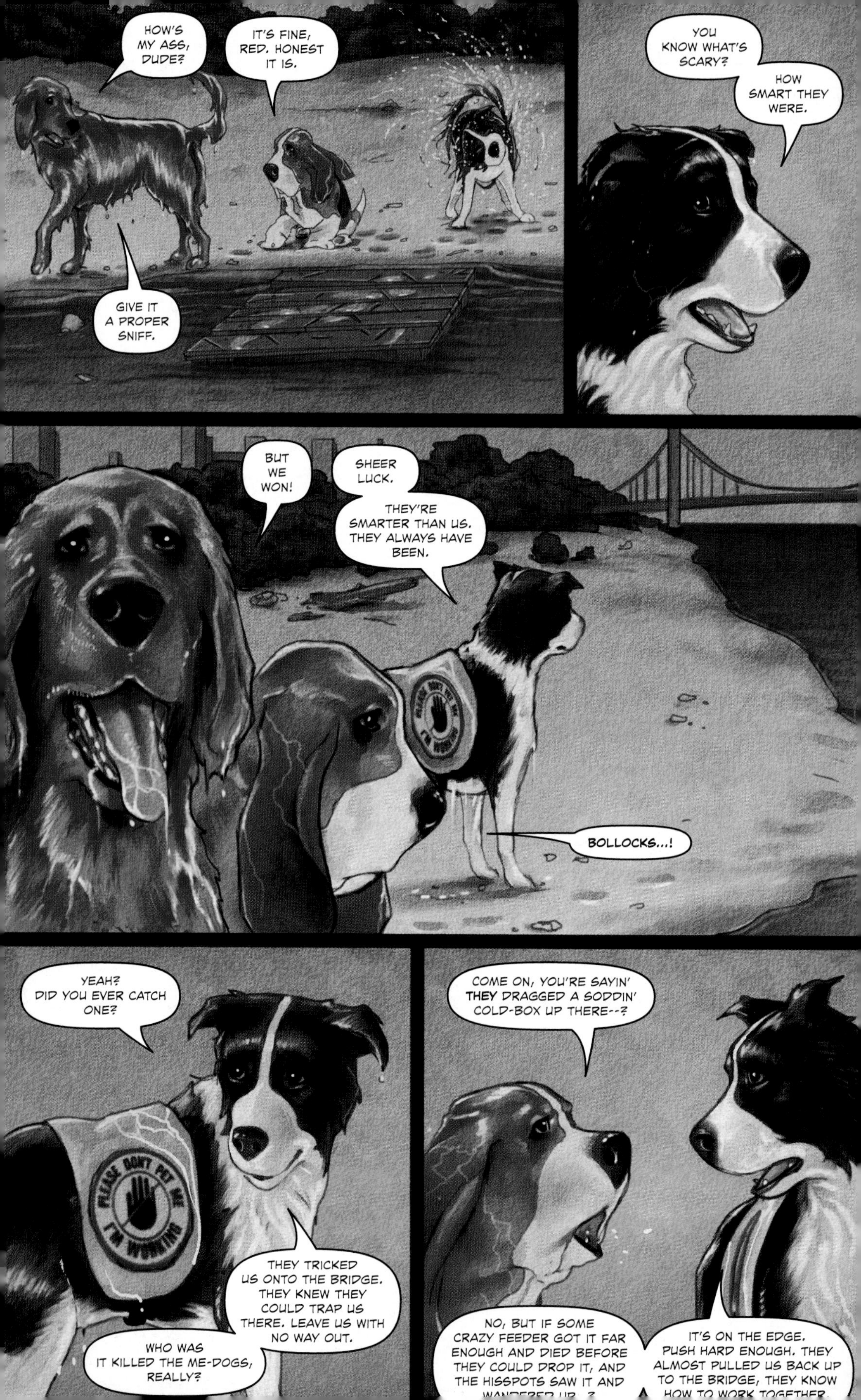
HOW'S MY ASS, DUDE?
IT'S FINE, RED. HONEST IT IS.
GIVE IT A PROPER SNIFF.
YOU KNOW WHAT'S SCARY?
HOW SMART THEY WERE.
BUT WE WON!
SHEER LUCK.
THEY'RE SMARTER THAN US. THEY ALWAYS HAVE BEEN.
BOLLOCKS...!
YEAH? DID YOU EVER CATCH ONE?
PLEASE DON'T PET ME
I'M WORKING
THEY TRICKED US ONTO THE BRIDGE. THEY KNEW THEY COULD TRAP US THERE. LEAVE US WITH NO WAY OUT.
WHO WAS IT KILLED THE ME-DOGS, REALLY?
COME ON, YOU'RE SAYIN' **THEY** DRAGGED A SODDIN' COLD-BOX UP THERE--?
NO, BUT IF SOME CRAZY FEEDER GOT IT FAR ENOUGH AND DIED BEFORE THEY COULD DROP IT, AND THE HISSPOTS SAW IT AND
IT'S ON THE EDGE. PUSH HARD ENOUGH. THEY ALMOST PULLED US BACK UP TO THE BRIDGE, THEY KNOW

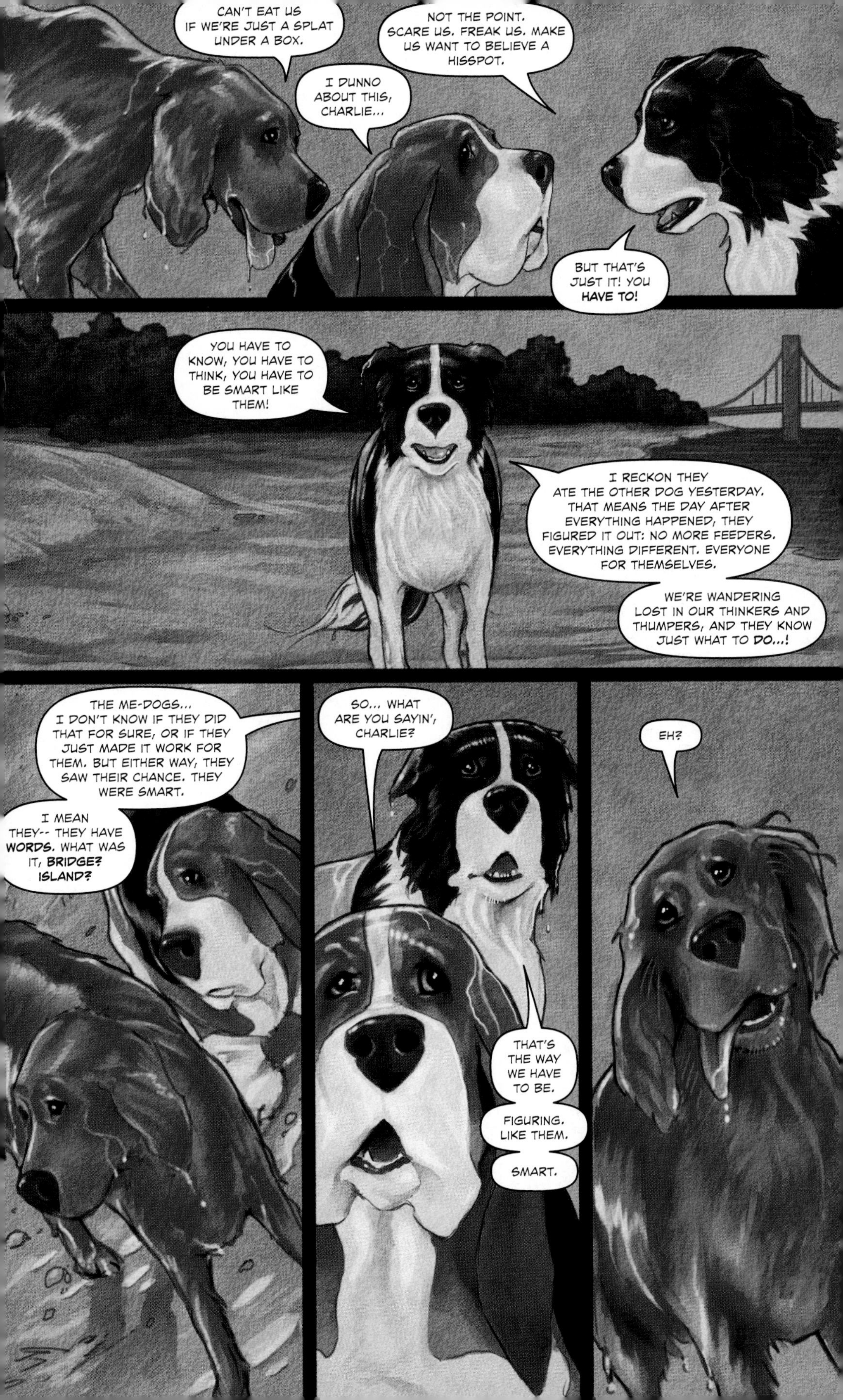
CAN'T EAT US IF WE'RE JUST A SPLAT UNDER A BOX.
I DUNNO ABOUT THIS, CHARLIE...
NOT THE POINT. SCARE US. FREAK US. MAKE US WANT TO BELIEVE A HISSPOT.
BUT THAT'S JUST IT! YOU **HAVE TO!**
YOU HAVE TO KNOW, YOU HAVE TO THINK, YOU HAVE TO BE SMART LIKE THEM!
I RECKON THEY ATE THE OTHER DOG YESTERDAY. THAT MEANS THE DAY AFTER EVERYTHING HAPPENED, THEY FIGURED IT OUT: NO MORE FEEDERS. EVERYTHING DIFFERENT. EVERYONE FOR THEMSELVES.
WE'RE WANDERING LOST IN OUR THINKERS AND THUMPERS, AND THEY KNOW JUST WHAT TO **DO...!**
THE ME-DOGS... I DON'T KNOW IF THEY DID THAT FOR SURE, OR IF THEY JUST MADE IT WORK FOR THEM. BUT EITHER WAY, THEY SAW THEIR CHANCE. THEY WERE SMART.
I MEAN THEY-- THEY HAVE **WORDS.** WHAT WAS IT, **BRIDGE? ISLAND?**
SO... WHAT ARE YOU SAYIN', CHARLIE?
THAT'S THE WAY WE HAVE TO BE.
FIGURING. LIKE THEM.
SMART.
EH?

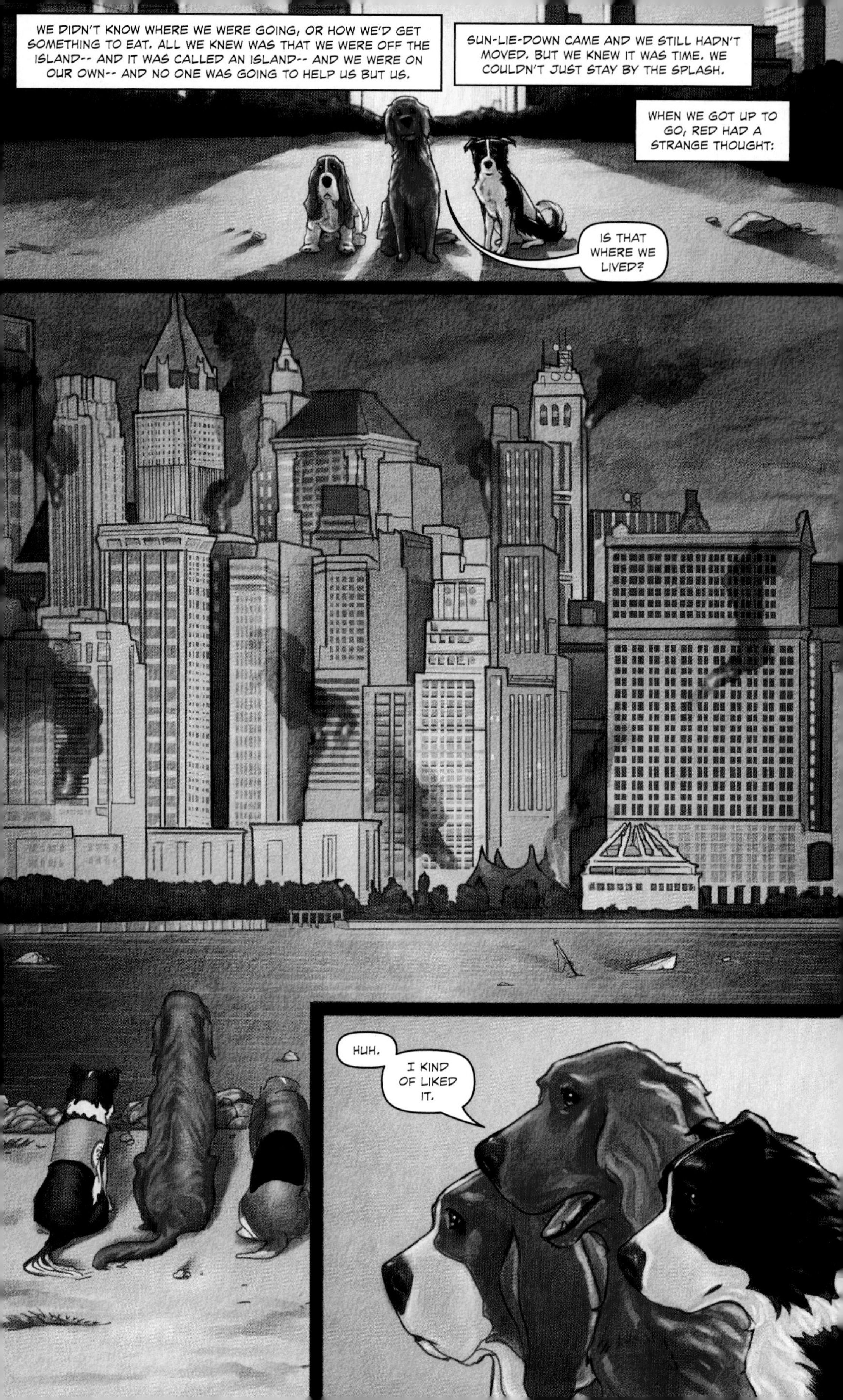
WE DIDN'T KNOW WHERE WE WERE GOING, OR HOW WE'D GET SOMETHING TO EAT. ALL WE KNEW WAS THAT WE WERE OFF THE ISLAND-- AND IT WAS CALLED AN ISLAND-- AND WE WERE ON OUR OWN-- AND NO ONE WAS GOING TO HELP US BUT US.
SUN-LIE-DOWN CAME AND WE STILL HADN'T MOVED. BUT WE KNEW IT WAS TIME. WE COULDN'T JUST STAY BY THE SPLASH.
WHEN WE GOT UP TO GO, RED HAD A STRANGE THOUGHT:
IS THAT WHERE WE LIVED?
IS THAT WHERE WE LIVED?
HUH.
I KIND OF LIKED IT.

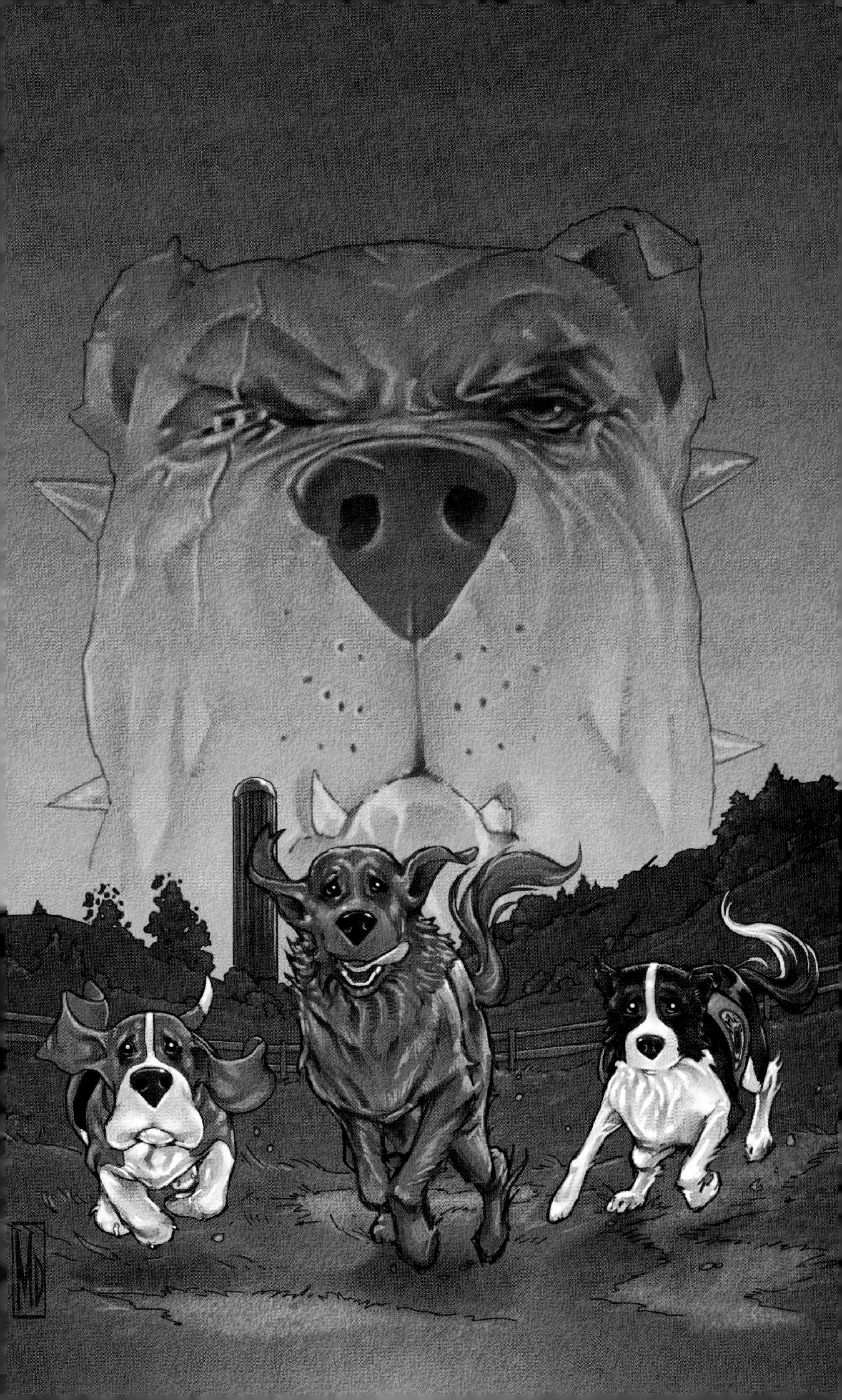

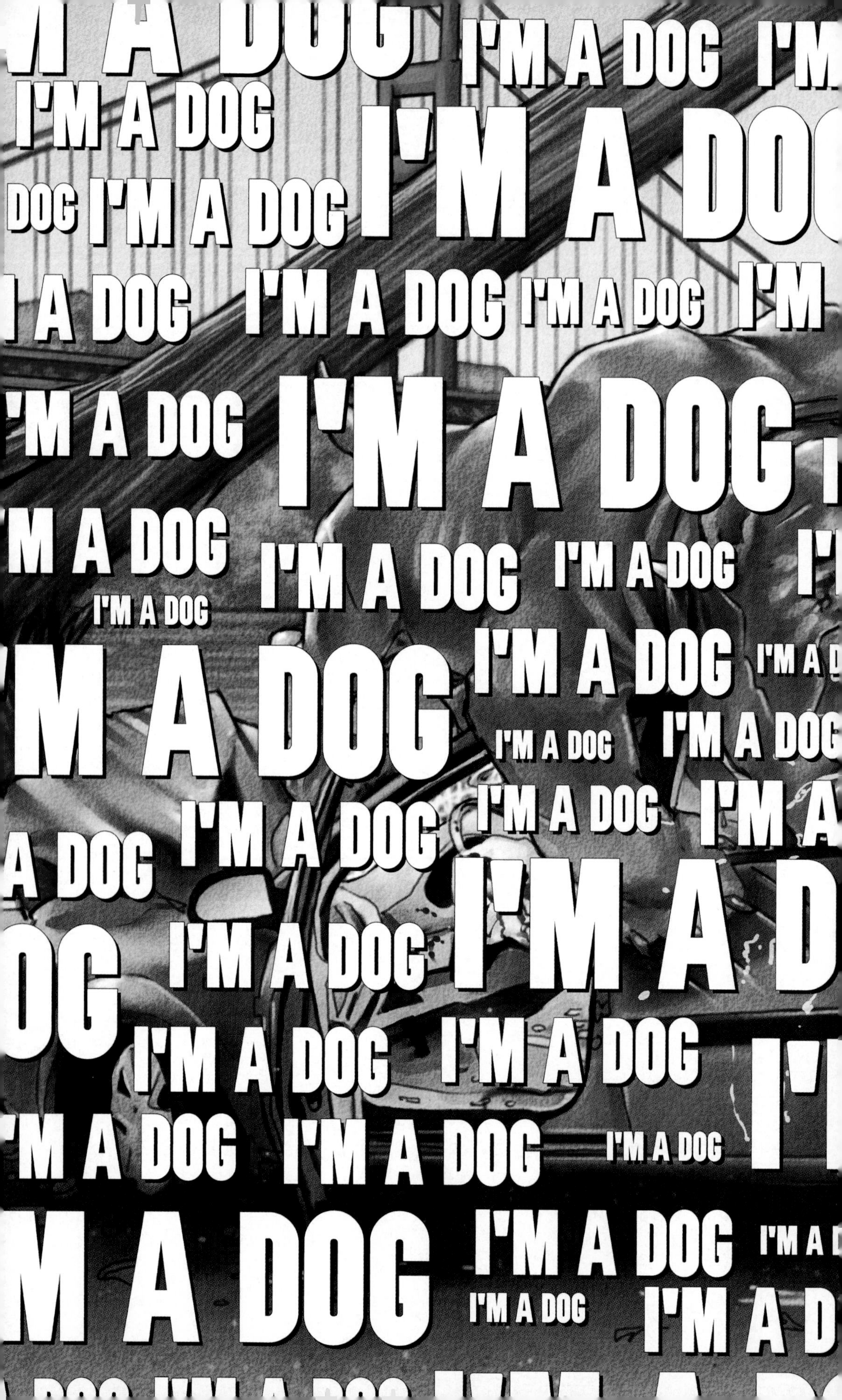

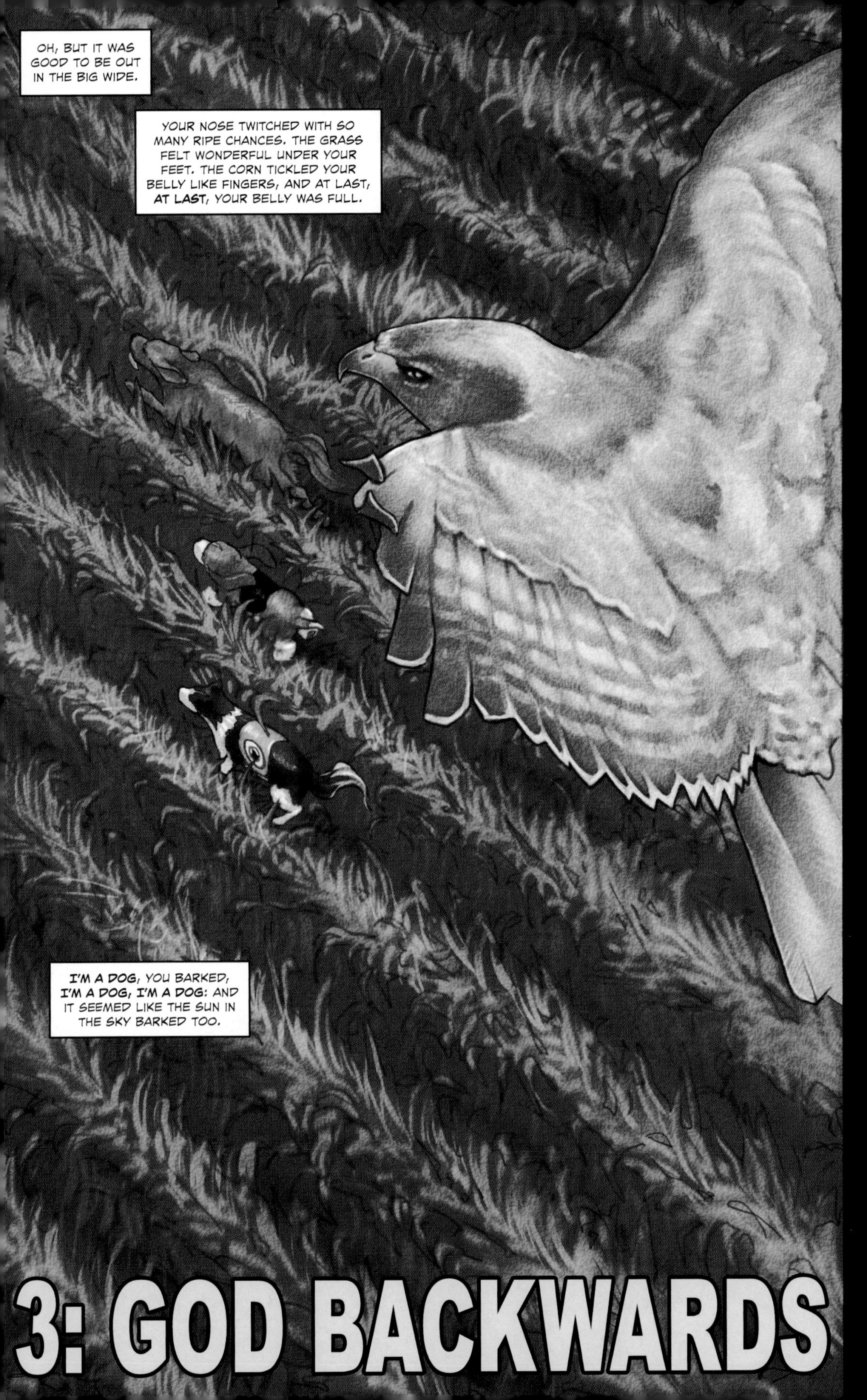
OH, BUT IT WAS GOOD TO BE OUT IN THE BIG WIDE.
YOUR NOSE TWITCHED WITH SO MANY RIPE CHANCES. THE GRASS FELT WONDERFUL UNDER YOUR FEET. THE CORN TICKLED YOUR BELLY LIKE FINGERS, AND AT LAST, **AT LAST**, YOUR BELLY WAS FULL.
I'M A DOG, YOU BARKED, ***I'M A DOG, I'M A DOG***: AND IT SEEMED LIKE THE SUN IN THE SKY BARKED TOO.
3: GOD BACKWARDS

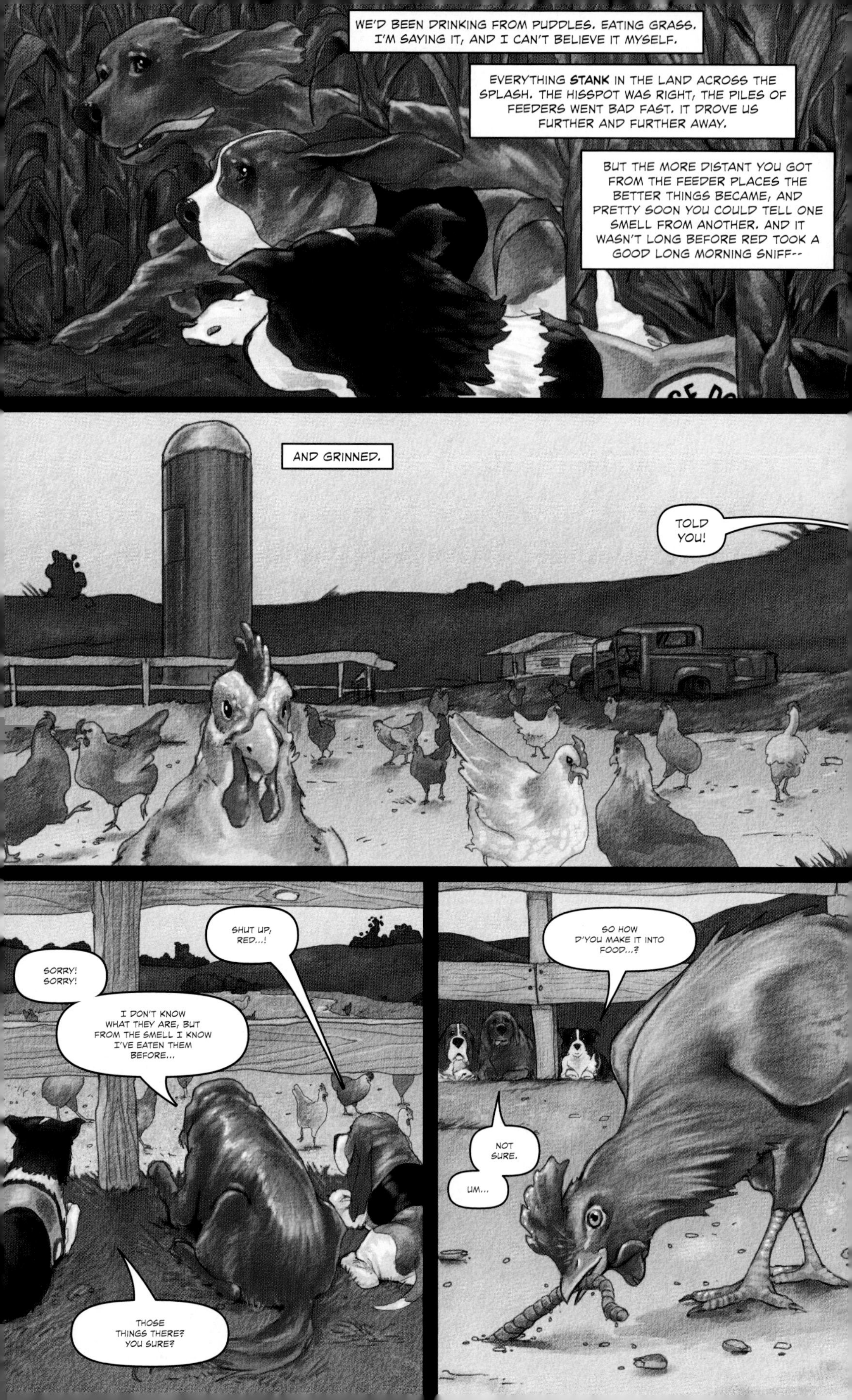
WE'D BEEN DRINKING FROM PUDDLES. EATING GRASS. I'M SAYING IT, AND I CAN'T BELIEVE IT MYSELF.
EVERYTHING **STANK** IN THE LAND ACROSS THE SPLASH. THE HISSPOT WAS RIGHT, THE PILES OF FEEDERS WENT BAD FAST. IT DROVE US FURTHER AND FURTHER AWAY.
BUT THE MORE DISTANT YOU GOT FROM THE FEEDER PLACES THE BETTER THINGS BECAME, AND PRETTY SOON YOU COULD TELL ONE SMELL FROM ANOTHER. AND IT WASN'T LONG BEFORE RED TOOK A GOOD LONG MORNING SNIFF--
AND GRINNED.
TOLD YOU!
SORRY! SORRY!
SHUT UP, RED...!
I DON'T KNOW WHAT THEY ARE, BUT FROM THE SMELL I KNOW I'VE EATEN THEM BEFORE...
THOSE THINGS THERE? YOU SURE?
SO HOW D'YOU MAKE IT INTO FOOD...?
NOT SURE.
UM...

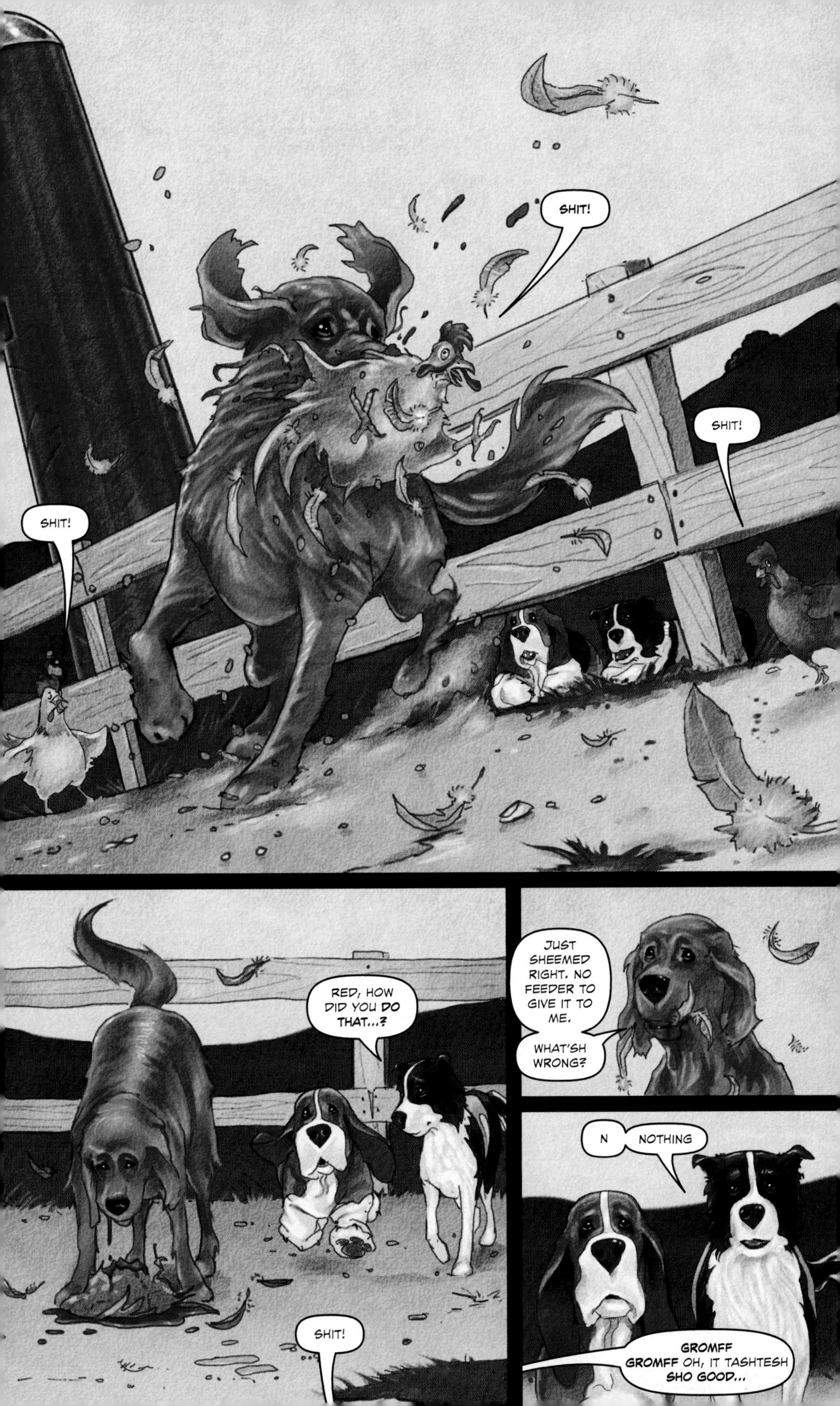
SHIT!
SHIT!
SHIT!
RED, HOW DID YOU DO THAT...?
SHIT!
JUST SHEEMED RIGHT. NO FEEDER TO GIVE IT TO ME.
WHAT'SH WRONG?
N
NOTHING
GROMFF GROMFF OH, IT TASHTESH SHO GOOD...

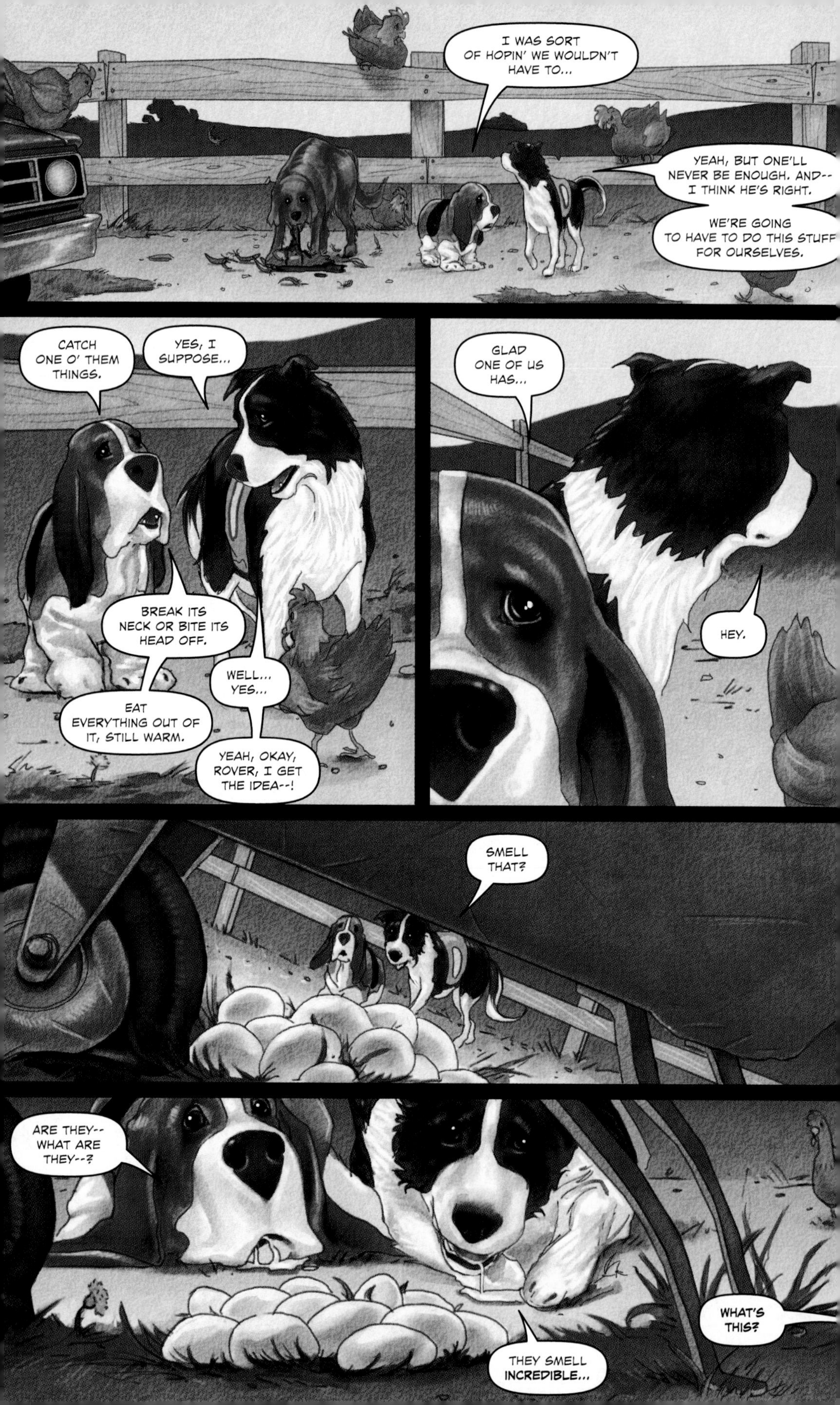

I WAS SORT OF HOPIN' WE WOULDN'T HAVE TO...
YEAH, BUT ONE'LL NEVER BE ENOUGH. AND-- I THINK HE'S RIGHT.
WE'RE GOING TO HAVE TO DO THIS STUFF FOR OURSELVES.
CATCH ONE O' THEM THINGS.
YES, I SUPPOSE...
BREAK ITS NECK OR BITE ITS HEAD OFF.
WELL... YES...
EAT EVERYTHING OUT OF IT, STILL WARM.
YEAH, OKAY, ROVER, I GET THE IDEA--!
GLAD ONE OF US HAS...
HEY.
SMELL THAT?
ARE THEY-- WHAT ARE THEY--?
THEY SMELL INCREDIBLE...
WHAT'S THIS?

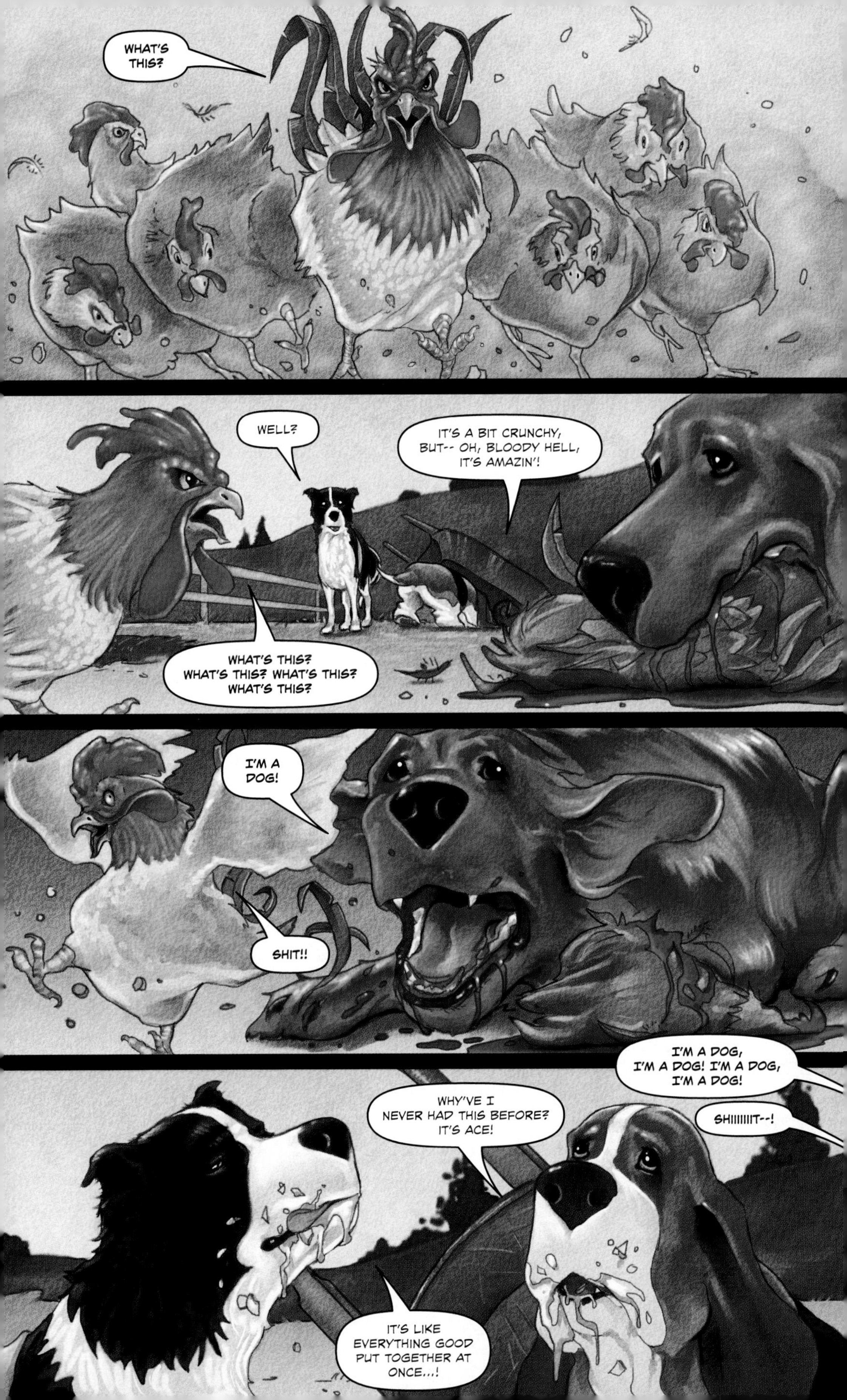
WHAT'S THIS?
WELL?
IT'S A BIT CRUNCHY, BUT-- OH, BLOODY HELL, IT'S AMAZIN'!
WHAT'S THIS? WHAT'S THIS? WHAT'S THIS? WHAT'S THIS?
I'M A DOG!
SHIT!!
I'M A DOG, I'M A DOG! I'M A DOG, I'M A DOG!
SHIIIIIIIT--!
WHY'VE I NEVER HAD THIS BEFORE? IT'S ACE!
IT'S LIKE EVERYTHING GOOD PUT TOGETHER AT ONCE...!

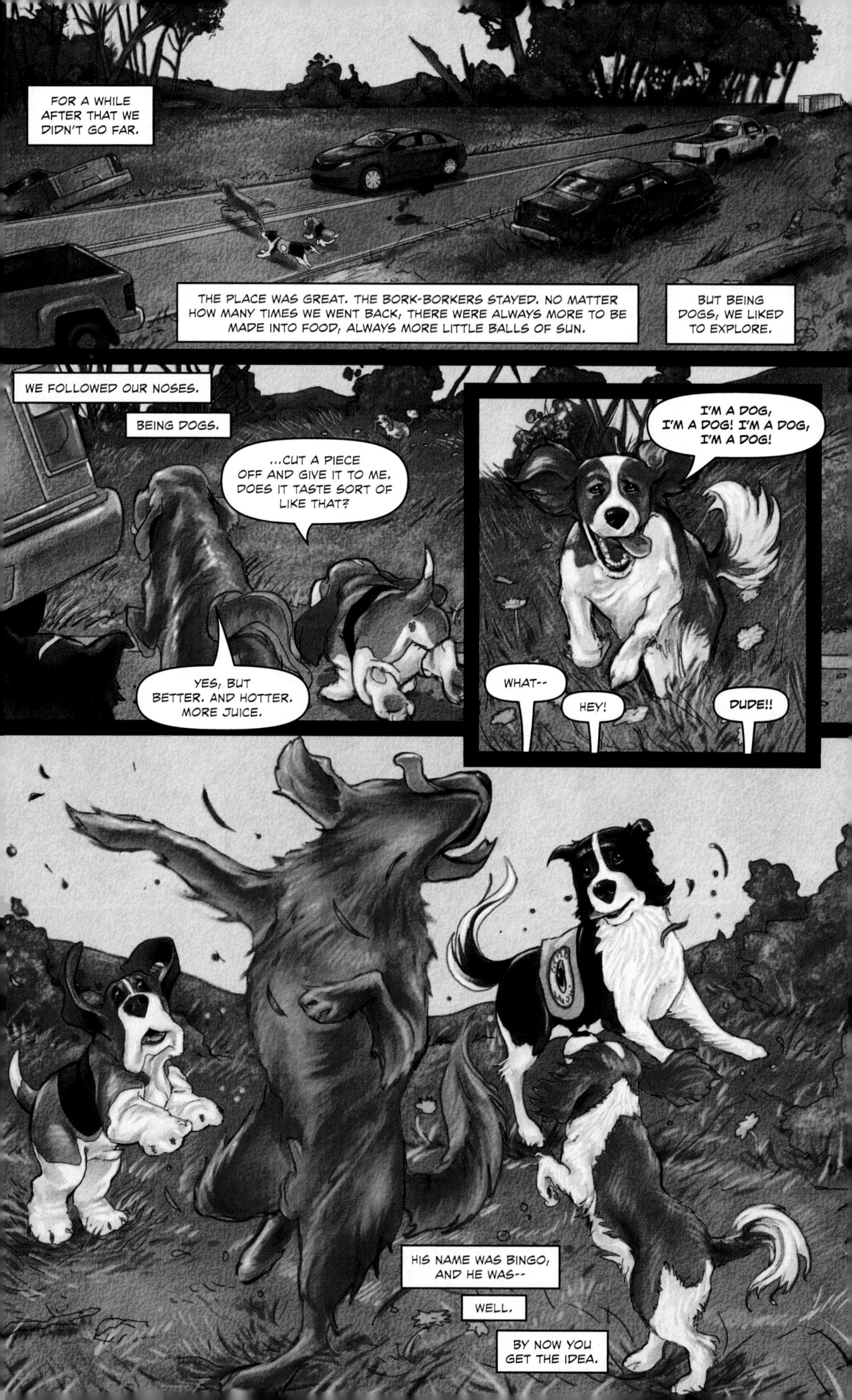
FOR A WHILE AFTER THAT WE DIDN'T GO FAR.
THE PLACE WAS GREAT. THE BORK-BORKERS STAYED. NO MATTER HOW MANY TIMES WE WENT BACK, THERE WERE ALWAYS MORE TO BE MADE INTO FOOD, ALWAYS MORE LITTLE BALLS OF SUN.
BUT BEING DOGS, WE LIKED TO EXPLORE.
WE FOLLOWED OUR NOSES.
BEING DOGS.
...CUT A PIECE OFF AND GIVE IT TO ME. DOES IT TASTE SORT OF LIKE THAT?
YES, BUT BETTER. AND HOTTER. MORE JUICE.
I'M A DOG, I'M A DOG! I'M A DOG, I'M A DOG!
WHAT--
HEY!
DUDE!!
HIS NAME WAS BINGO, AND HE WAS--
WELL.
BY NOW YOU GET THE IDEA.

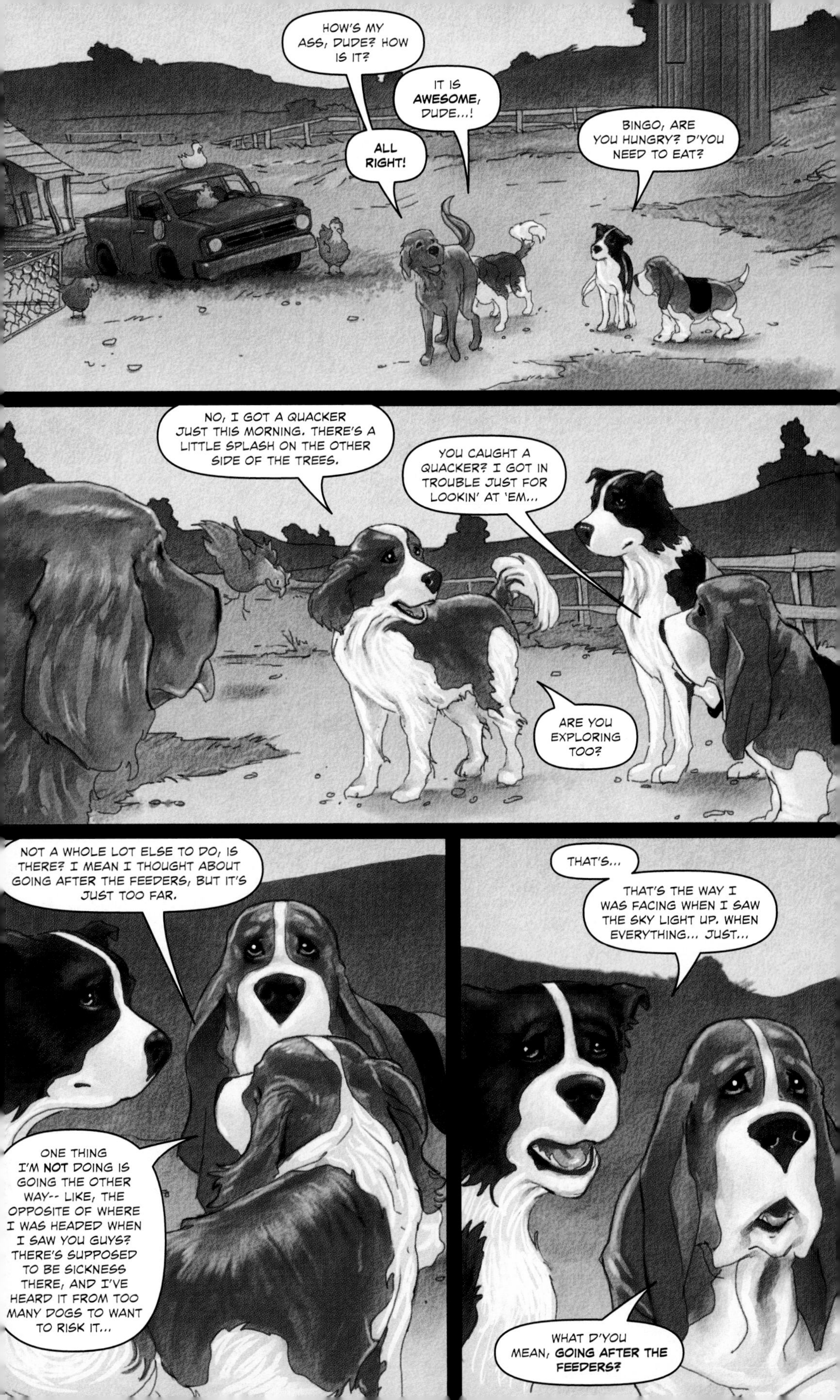

HOW'S MY ASS, DUDE? HOW IS IT?
IT IS **AWESOME**, DUDE...!
ALL RIGHT!
BINGO, ARE YOU HUNGRY? D'YOU NEED TO EAT?
NO, I GOT A QUACKER JUST THIS MORNING. THERE'S A LITTLE SPLASH ON THE OTHER SIDE OF THE TREES.
YOU CAUGHT A QUACKER? I GOT IN TROUBLE JUST FOR LOOKIN' AT 'EM...
ARE YOU EXPLORING TOO?
NOT A WHOLE LOT ELSE TO DO, IS THERE? I MEAN I THOUGHT ABOUT GOING AFTER THE FEEDERS, BUT IT'S JUST TOO FAR.
ONE THING I'M **NOT** DOING IS GOING THE OTHER WAY-- LIKE, THE OPPOSITE OF WHERE I WAS HEADED WHEN I SAW YOU GUYS? THERE'S SUPPOSED TO BE SICKNESS THERE, AND I'VE HEARD IT FROM TOO MANY DOGS TO WANT TO RISK IT...
THAT'S...
THAT'S THE WAY I WAS FACING WHEN I SAW THE SKY LIGHT UP. WHEN EVERYTHING... JUST...
WHAT D'YOU MEAN, **GOING AFTER THE FEEDERS?**

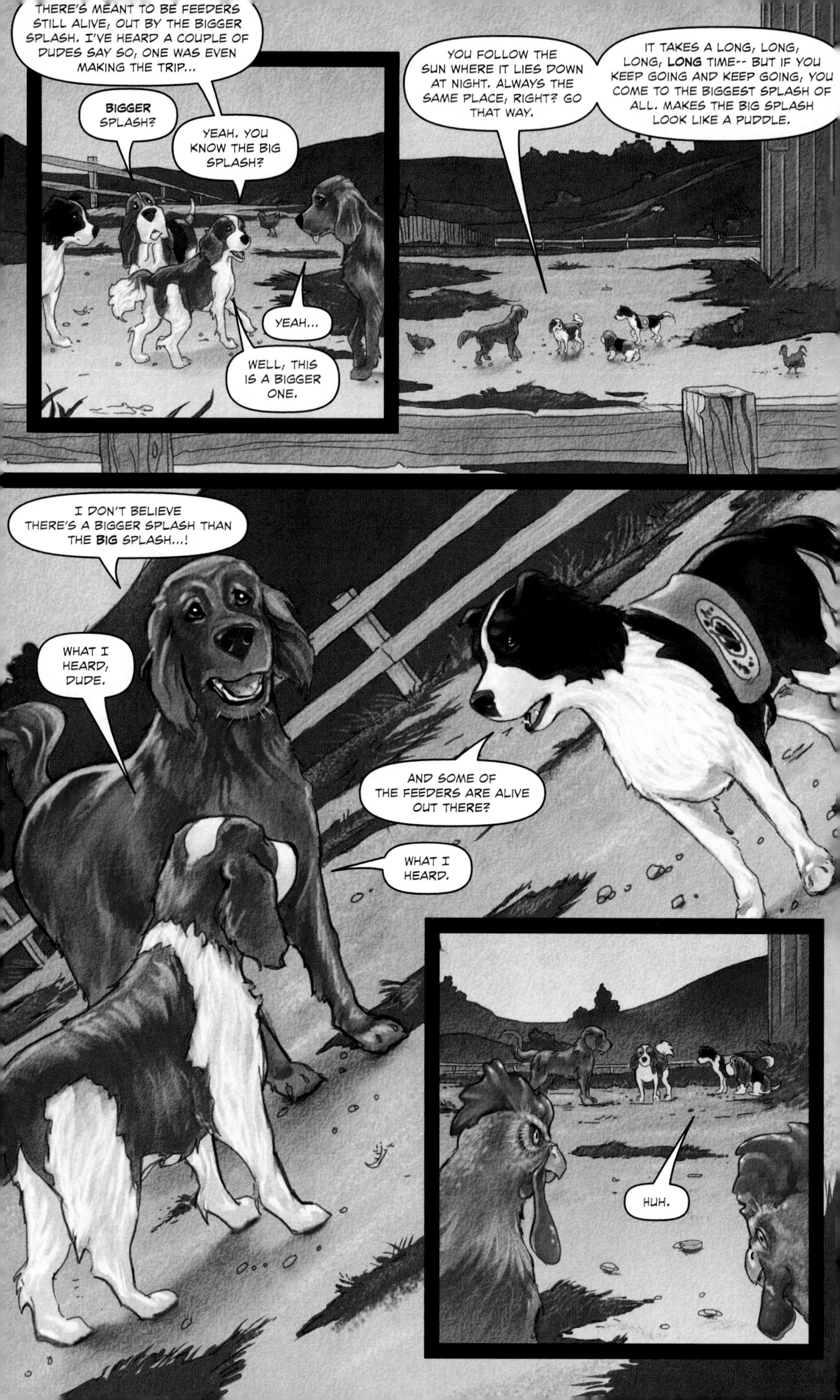

THERE'S MEANT TO BE FEEDERS STILL ALIVE, OUT BY THE BIGGER SPLASH. I'VE HEARD A COUPLE OF DUDES SAY SO, ONE WAS EVEN MAKING THE TRIP...
BIGGER SPLASH?
YEAH. YOU KNOW THE BIG SPLASH?
YEAH...
WELL, THIS IS A BIGGER ONE.
YOU FOLLOW THE SUN WHERE IT LIES DOWN AT NIGHT. ALWAYS THE SAME PLACE, RIGHT? GO THAT WAY.
IT TAKES A LONG, LONG, LONG, LONG TIME-- BUT IF YOU KEEP GOING AND KEEP GOING, YOU COME TO THE BIGGEST SPLASH OF ALL. MAKES THE BIG SPLASH LOOK LIKE A PUDDLE.
I DON'T BELIEVE THERE'S A BIGGER SPLASH THAN THE BIG SPLASH...!
WHAT I HEARD, DUDE.
AND SOME OF THE FEEDERS ARE ALIVE OUT THERE?
WHAT I HEARD.
HUH.

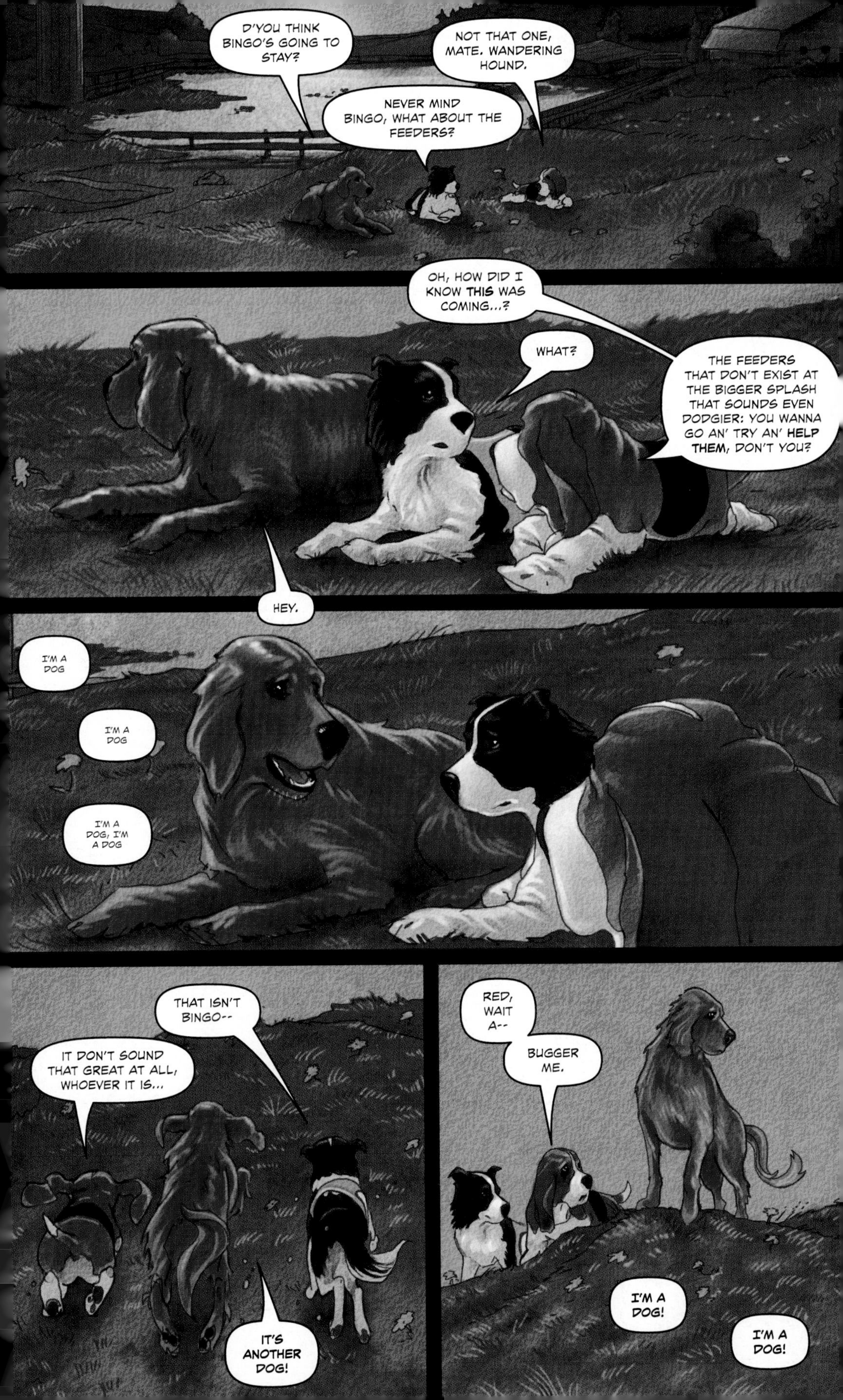
D'YOU THINK BINGO'S GOING TO STAY?
NOT THAT ONE, MATE. WANDERING HOUND.
NEVER MIND BINGO, WHAT ABOUT THE FEEDERS?
OH, HOW DID I KNOW THIS WAS COMING...?
WHAT?
THE FEEDERS THAT DON'T EXIST AT THE BIGGER SPLASH THAT SOUNDS EVEN DODGIER: YOU WANNA GO AN' TRY AN' HELP THEM, DON'T YOU?
HEY.
I'M A DOG
I'M A DOG
I'M A DOG, I'M A DOG
THAT ISN'T BINGO--
IT DON'T SOUND THAT GREAT AT ALL, WHOEVER IT IS...
IT'S ANOTHER DOG!
RED, WAIT A--
BUGGER ME.
I'M A DOG!
I'M A DOG!

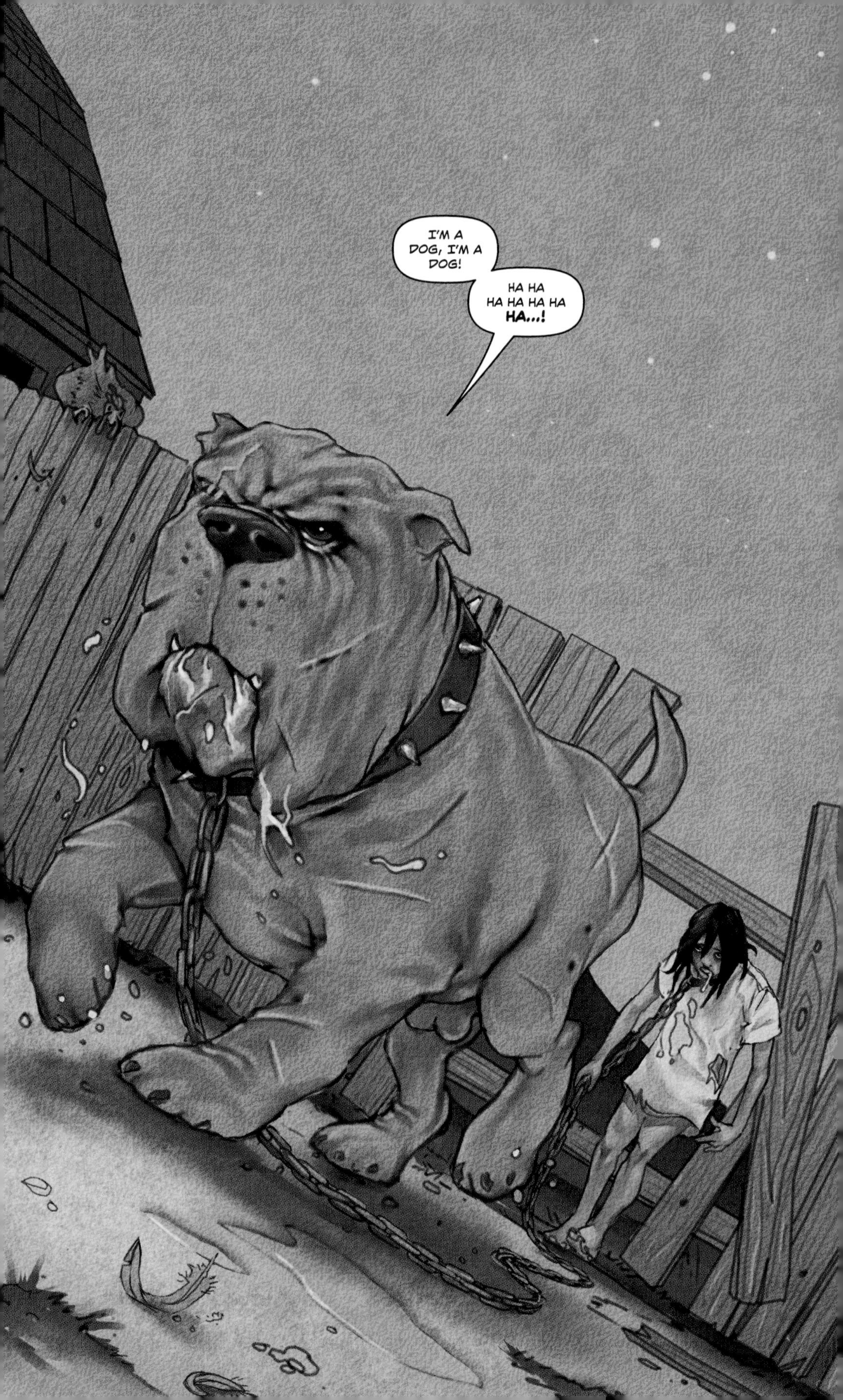
I'M A DOG, I'M A DOG!
HA HA HA HA HA HA **HA...!**

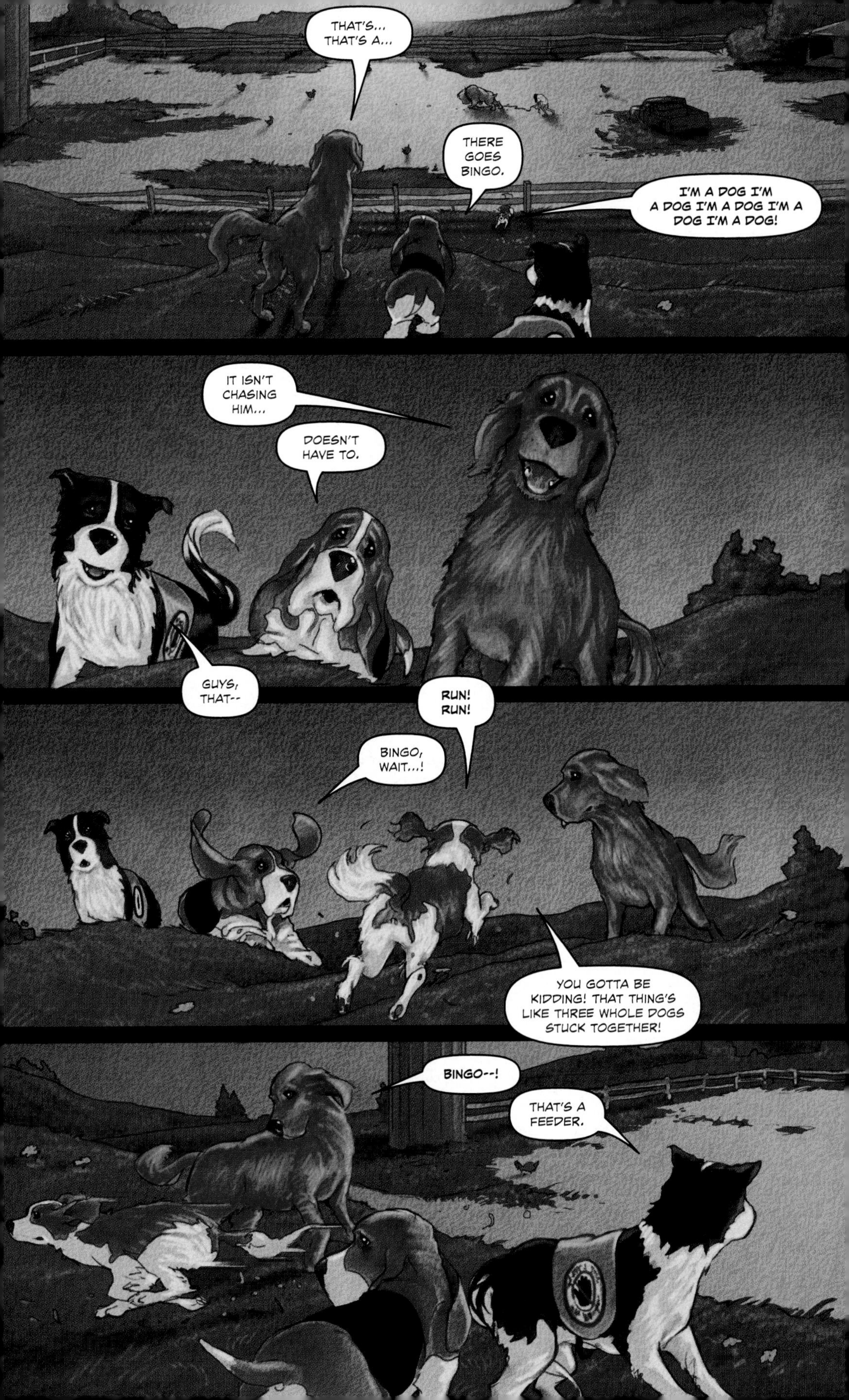
THAT'S... THAT'S A...
THERE GOES BINGO.
I'M A DOG I'M A DOG I'M A DOG I'M A DOG I'M A DOG!
IT ISN'T CHASING HIM...
DOESN'T HAVE TO.
GUYS, THAT--
RUN! RUN!
BINGO, WAIT...!
YOU GOTTA BE KIDDING! THAT THING'S LIKE THREE WHOLE DOGS STUCK TOGETHER!
BINGO--!
THAT'S A FEEDER.

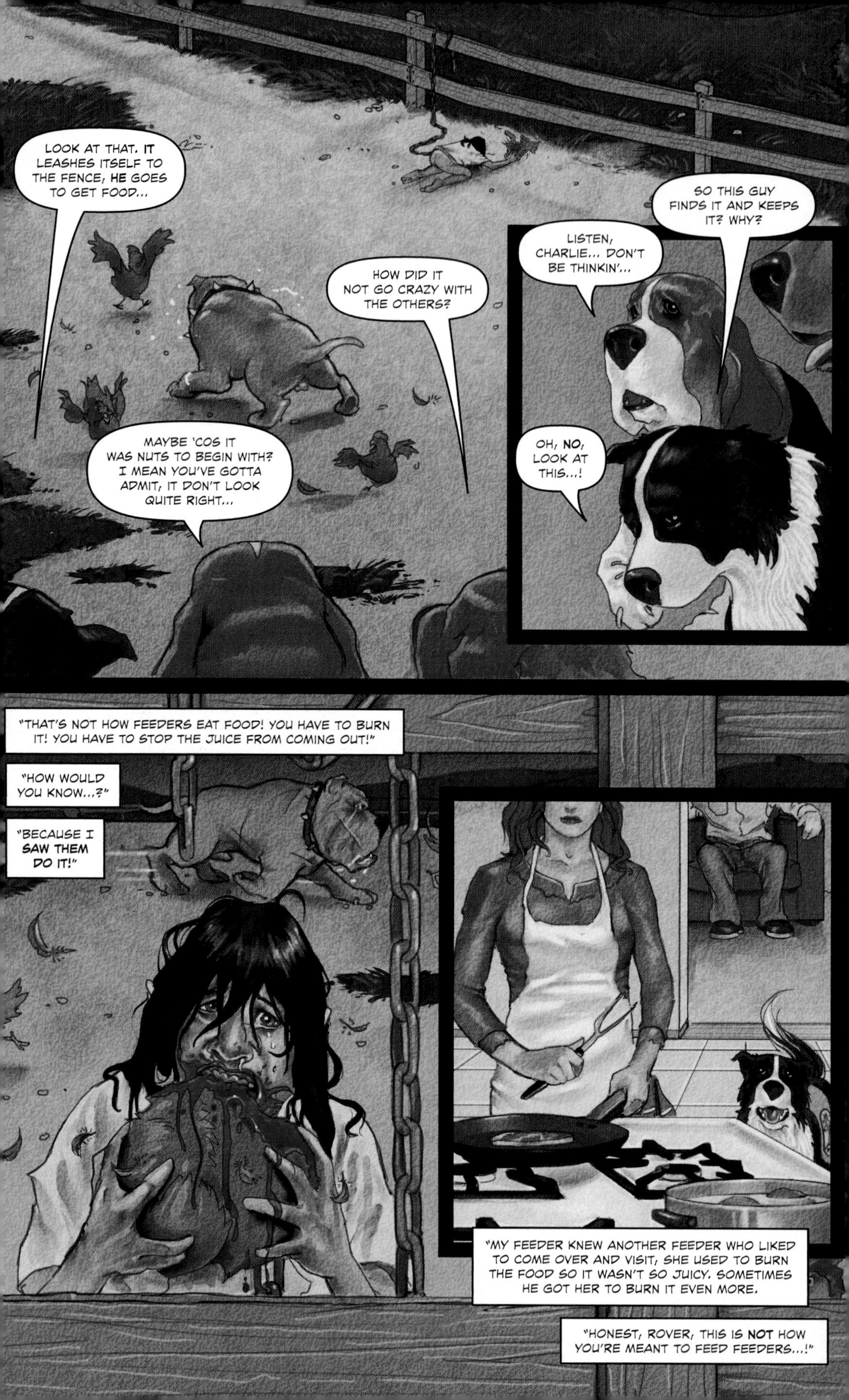
LOOK AT THAT. IT LEASHES ITSELF TO THE FENCE, HE GOES TO GET FOOD...
HOW DID IT NOT GO CRAZY WITH THE OTHERS?
MAYBE 'COS IT WAS NUTS TO BEGIN WITH? I MEAN YOU'VE GOTTA ADMIT, IT DON'T LOOK QUITE RIGHT...
SO THIS GUY FINDS IT AND KEEPS IT? WHY?
LISTEN, CHARLIE... DON'T BE THINKIN'...
OH, NO, LOOK AT THIS...!
"THAT'S NOT HOW FEEDERS EAT FOOD! YOU HAVE TO BURN IT! YOU HAVE TO STOP THE JUICE FROM COMING OUT!"
"HOW WOULD YOU KNOW...?"
"BECAUSE I SAW THEM DO IT!"
"MY FEEDER KNEW ANOTHER FEEDER WHO LIKED TO COME OVER AND VISIT, SHE USED TO BURN THE FOOD SO IT WASN'T SO JUICY. SOMETIMES HE GOT HER TO BURN IT EVEN MORE.
"HONEST, ROVER, THIS IS NOT HOW YOU'RE MEANT TO FEED FEEDERS...!"

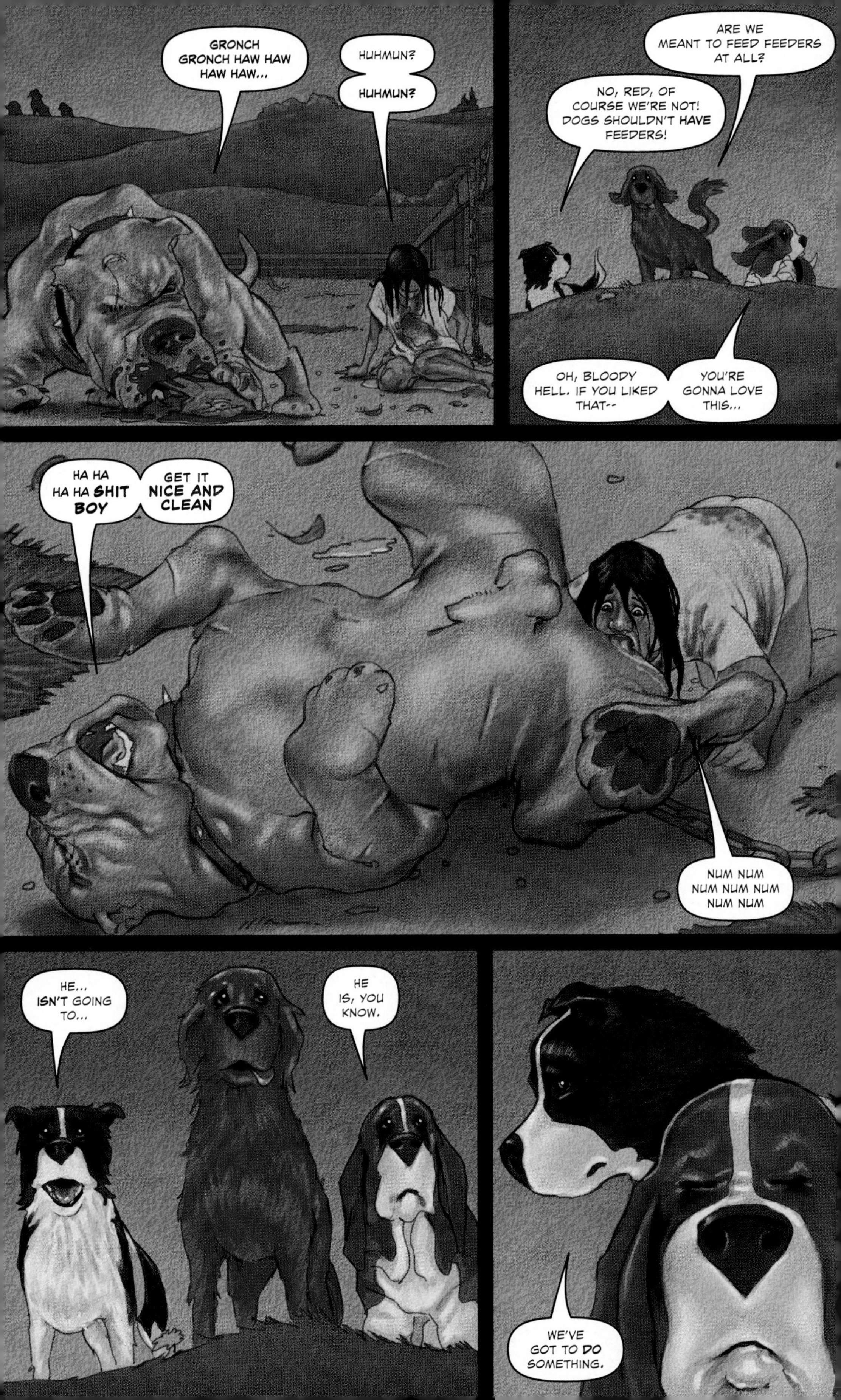
GRONCH GRONCH HAW HAW HAW HAW...
HUHMUN?
HUHMUN?
ARE WE MEANT TO FEED FEEDERS AT ALL?
NO, RED, OF COURSE WE'RE NOT! DOGS SHOULDN'T HAVE FEEDERS!
OH, BLOODY HELL. IF YOU LIKED THAT--
YOU'RE GONNA LOVE THIS...
HA HA HA HA SHIT BOY
GET IT NICE AND CLEAN
NUM NUM NUM NUM NUM NUM NUM
HE... ISN'T GOING TO...
HE IS, YOU KNOW.
WE'VE GOT TO DO SOMETHING.

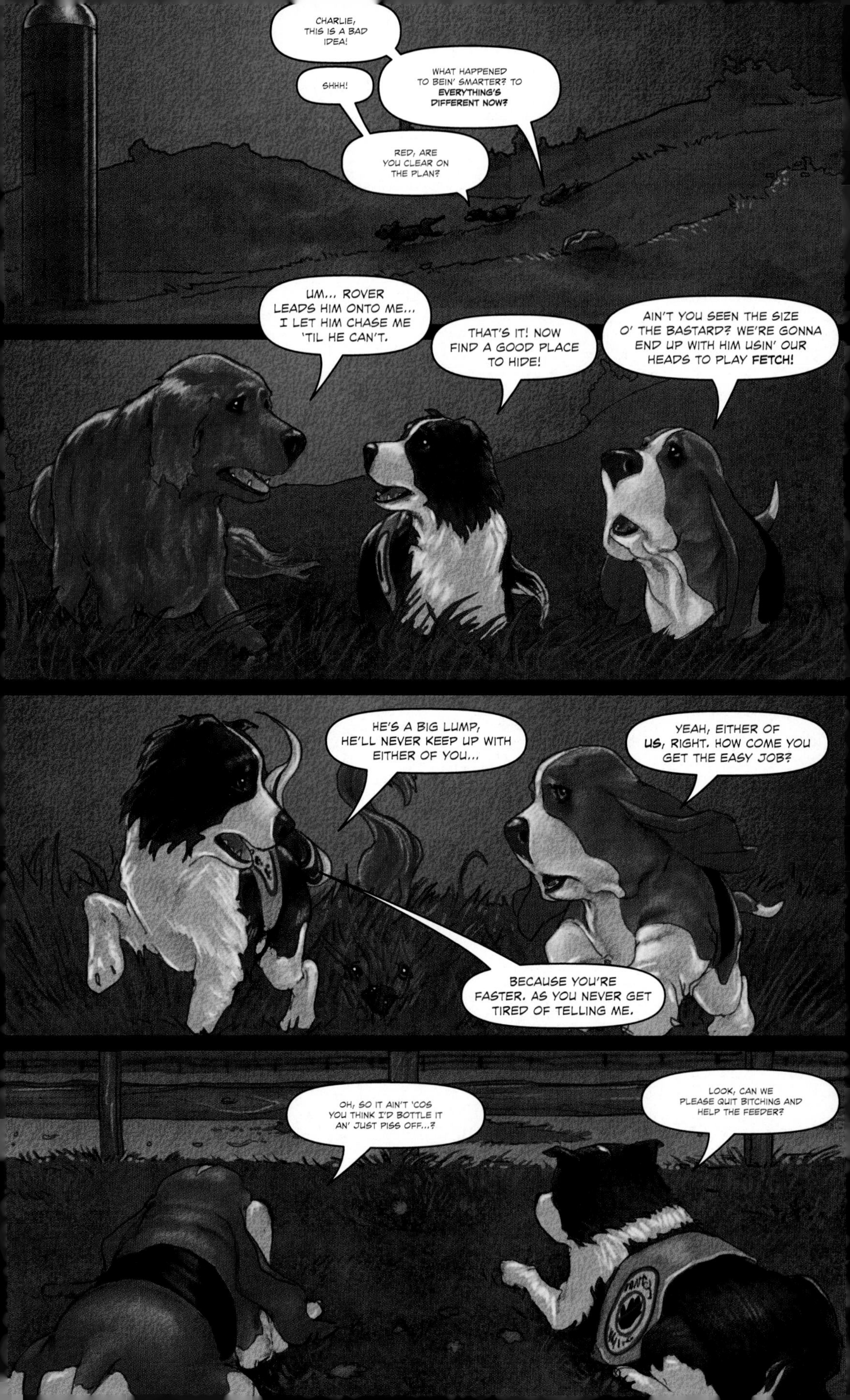
CHARLIE, THIS IS A BAD IDEA!
WHAT HAPPENED TO BEIN' SMARTER? TO EVERYTHING'S DIFFERENT NOW?
SHHH!
RED, ARE YOU CLEAR ON THE PLAN?
UM... ROVER LEADS HIM ONTO ME... I LET HIM CHASE ME 'TIL HE CAN'T.
THAT'S IT! NOW FIND A GOOD PLACE TO HIDE!
AIN'T YOU SEEN THE SIZE O' THE BASTARD? WE'RE GONNA END UP WITH HIM USIN' OUR HEADS TO PLAY FETCH!
HE'S A BIG LUMP, HE'LL NEVER KEEP UP WITH EITHER OF YOU...
YEAH, EITHER OF US, RIGHT. HOW COME YOU GET THE EASY JOB?
BECAUSE YOU'RE FASTER. AS YOU NEVER GET TIRED OF TELLING ME.
OH, SO IT AIN'T 'COS YOU THINK I'D BOTTLE IT AN' JUST PISS OFF...?
LOOK, CAN WE PLEASE QUIT BITCHING AND HELP THE FEEDER?

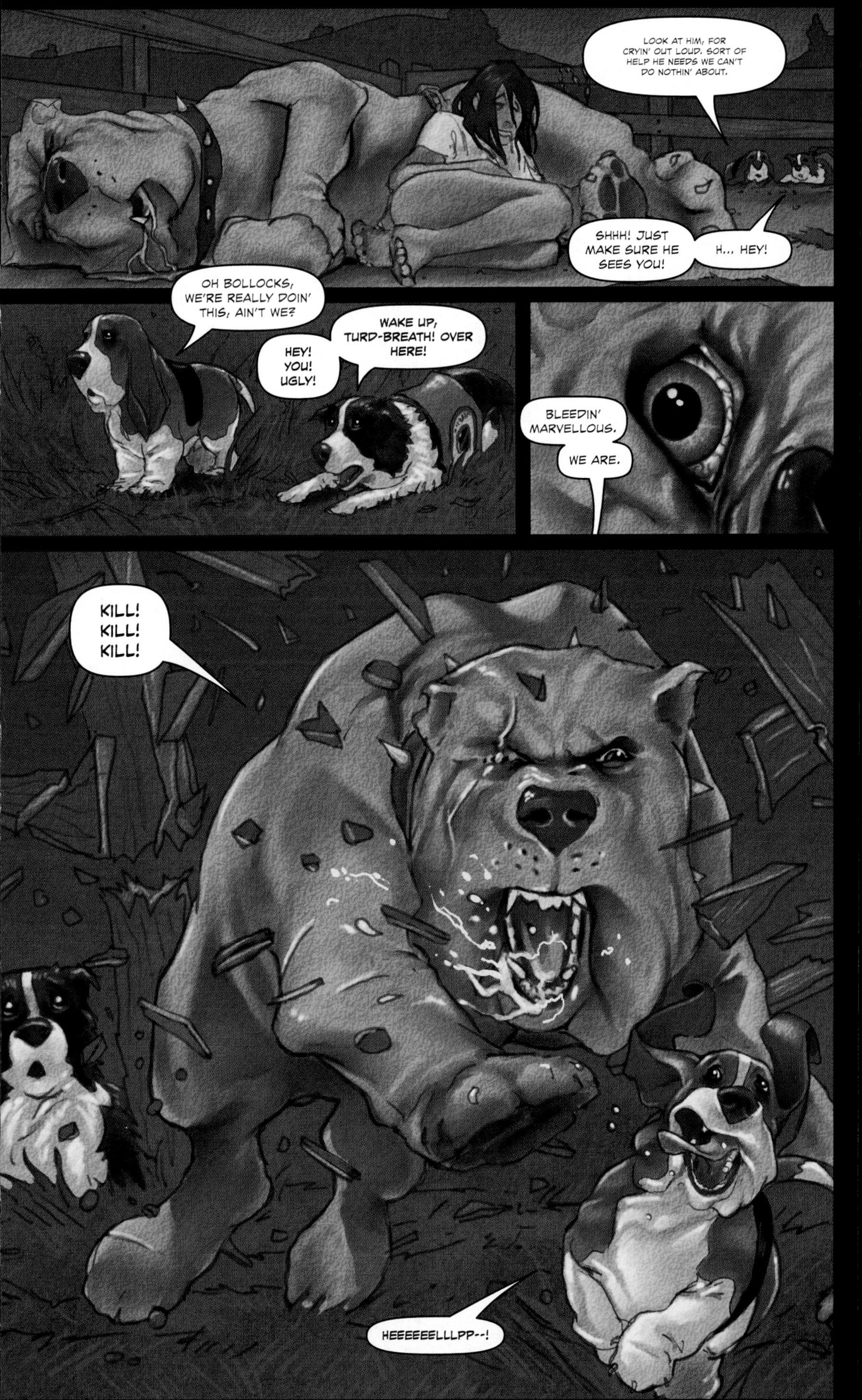
LOOK AT HIM, FOR CRYIN' OUT LOUD. SORT OF HELP HE NEEDS WE CAN'T DO NOTHIN' ABOUT.
SHHH! JUST MAKE SURE HE SEES YOU!
H... HEY!
OH BOLLOCKS, WE'RE REALLY DOIN' THIS, AIN'T WE?
HEY! YOU! UGLY!
WAKE UP, TURD-BREATH! OVER HERE!
BLEEDIN' MARVELLOUS.
WE ARE.
KILL! KILL! KILL!
HEEEEEELLLPP--!

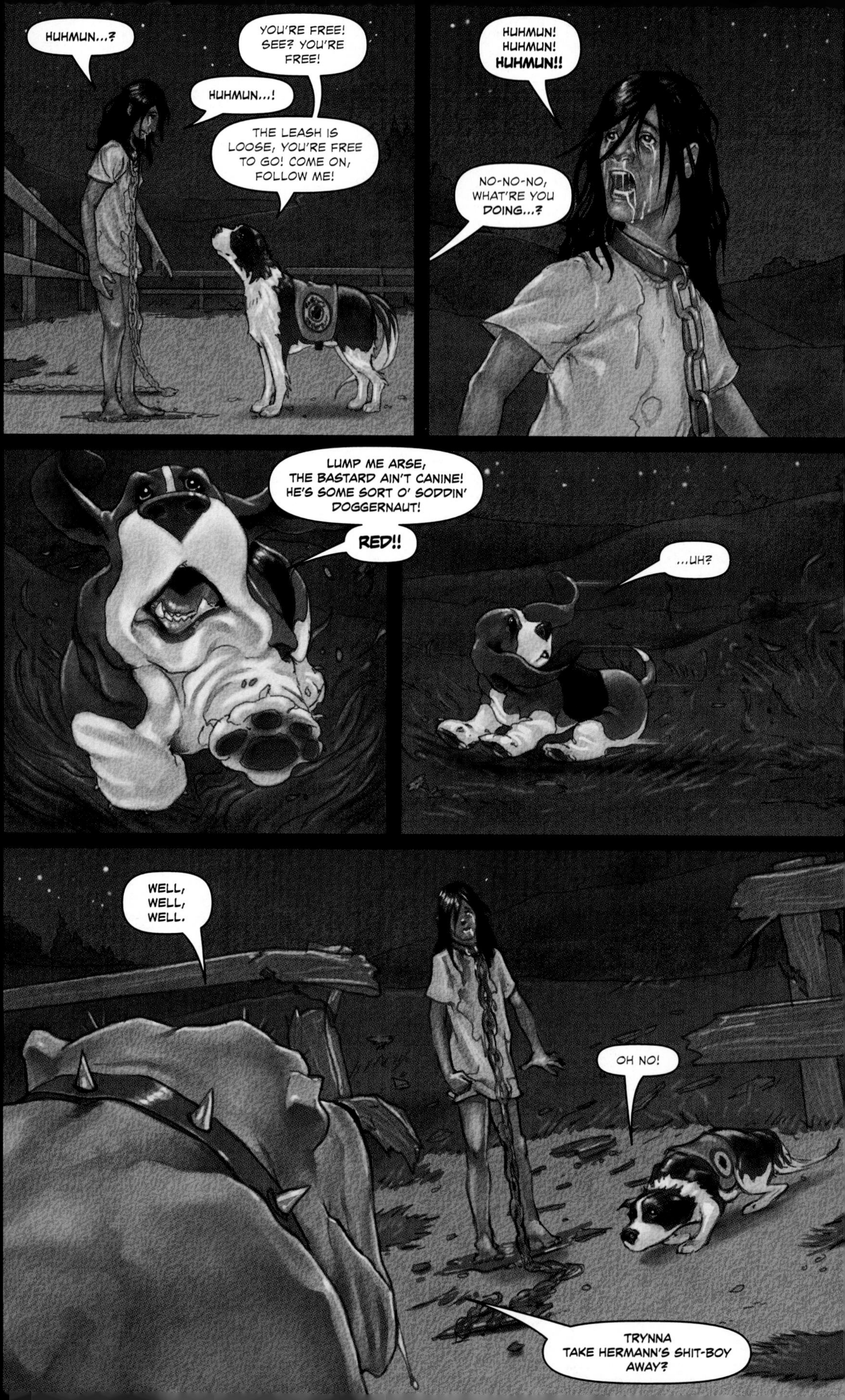
HUHMUN...?
YOU'RE FREE! SEE? YOU'RE FREE!
HUHMUN...!
THE LEASH IS LOOSE, YOU'RE FREE TO GO! COME ON, FOLLOW ME!
HUHMUN! HUHMUN! HUHMUN!!
NO-NO-NO, WHAT'RE YOU DOING...?
LUMP ME ARSE, THE BASTARD AIN'T CANINE! HE'S SOME SORT O' SODDIN' DOGGERNAUT!
RED!!
...UH?
WELL, WELL, WELL.
OH NO!
TRYNNA TAKE HERMANN'S SHIT-BOY AWAY?

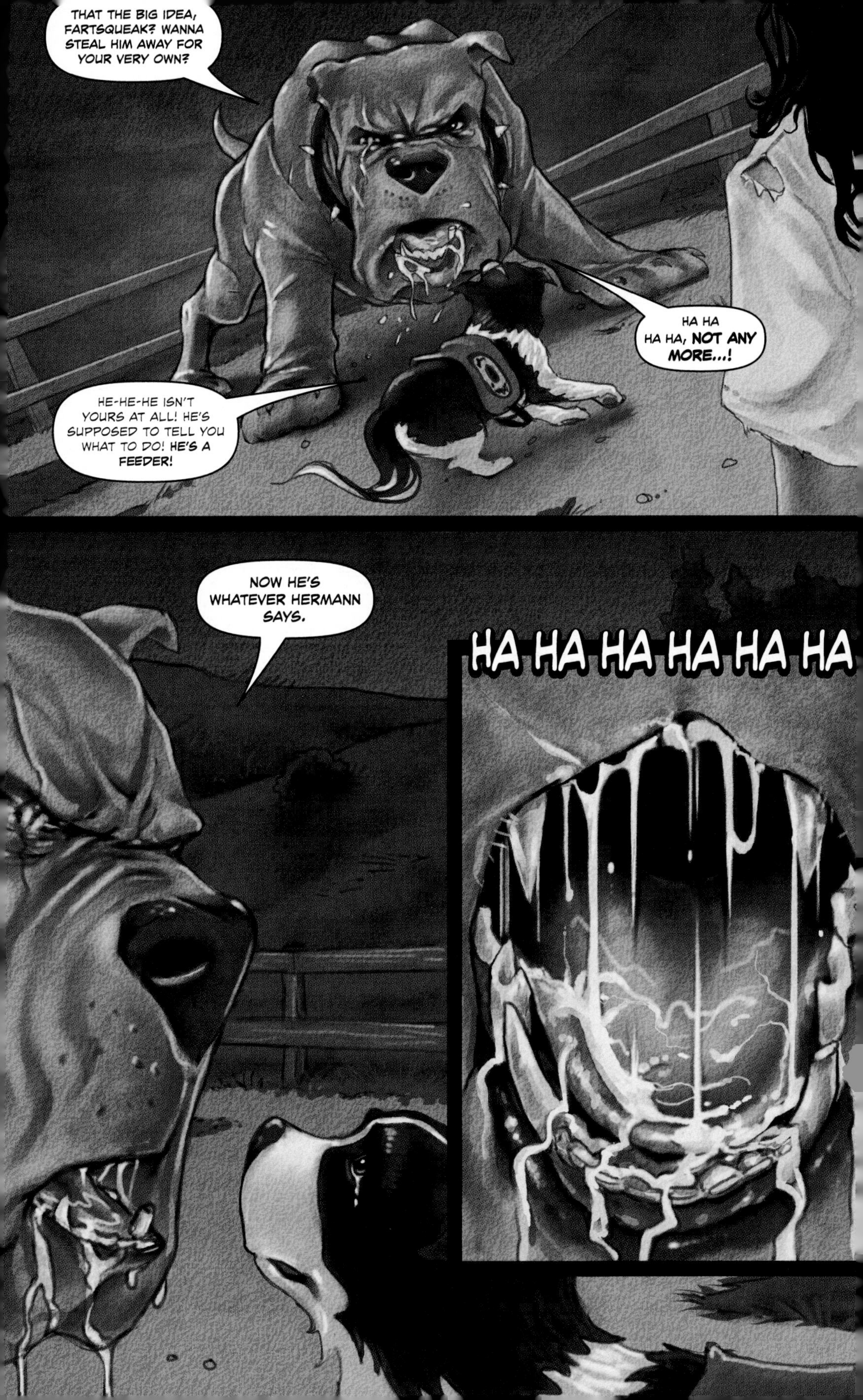
THAT THE BIG IDEA, FARTSQUEAK? WANNA STEAL HIM AWAY FOR YOUR VERY OWN?
HE-HE-HE ISN'T YOURS AT ALL! HE'S SUPPOSED TO TELL YOU WHAT TO DO! HE'S A FEEDER!
HA HA HA HA, NOT ANY MORE...!
NOW HE'S WHATEVER HERMANN SAYS.
HA HA HA HA HA HA

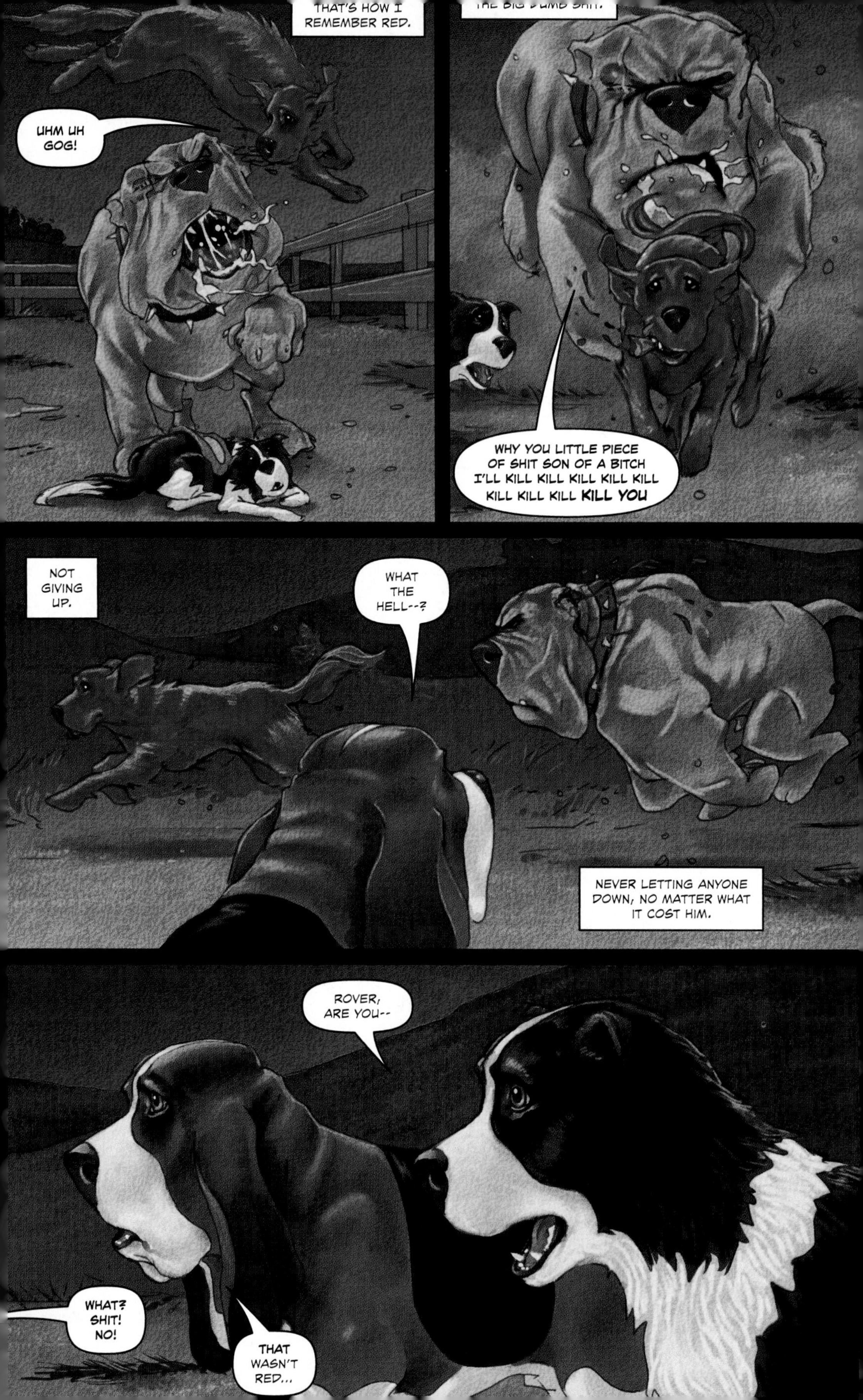
THAT'S HOW I REMEMBER RED.
UHM UH GOG!
WHY YOU LITTLE PIECE OF SHIT SON OF A BITCH I'LL KILL KILL KILL KILL KILL KILL KILL KILL **KILL YOU**
NOT GIVING UP.
WHAT THE HELL--?
NEVER LETTING ANYONE DOWN, NO MATTER WHAT IT COST HIM.
ROVER, ARE YOU--
WHAT? SHIT! NO!
THAT WASN'T RED...

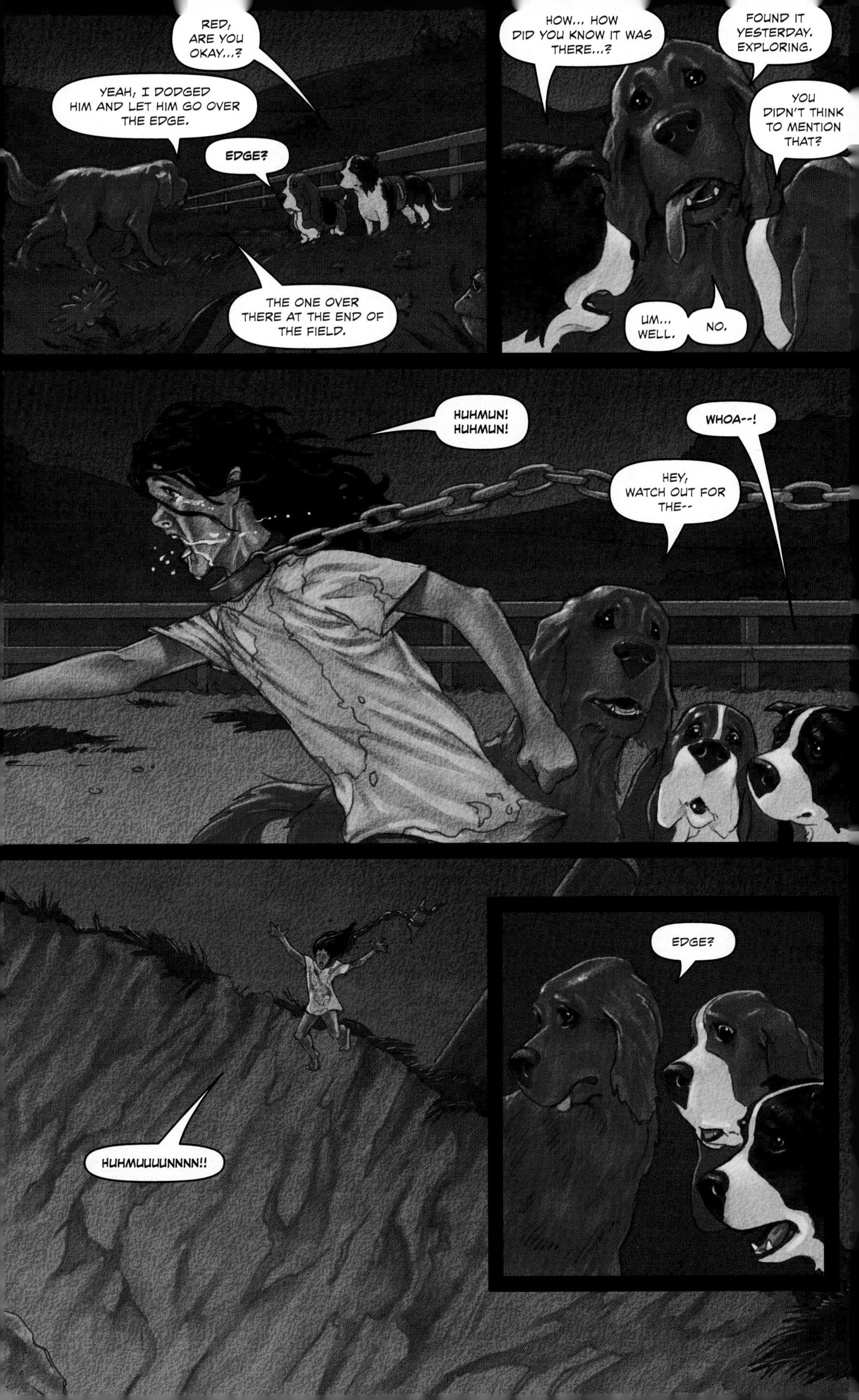
RED, ARE YOU OKAY...?
YEAH, I DODGED HIM AND LET HIM GO OVER THE EDGE.
EDGE?
THE ONE OVER THERE AT THE END OF THE FIELD.
HOW... HOW DID YOU KNOW IT WAS THERE...?
FOUND IT YESTERDAY. EXPLORING.
YOU DIDN'T THINK TO MENTION THAT?
UM... WELL.
NO.
HUHMUN! HUHMUN!
HEY, WATCH OUT FOR THE--
WHOA--!
HUHMUUUUNNNN!!
EDGE?

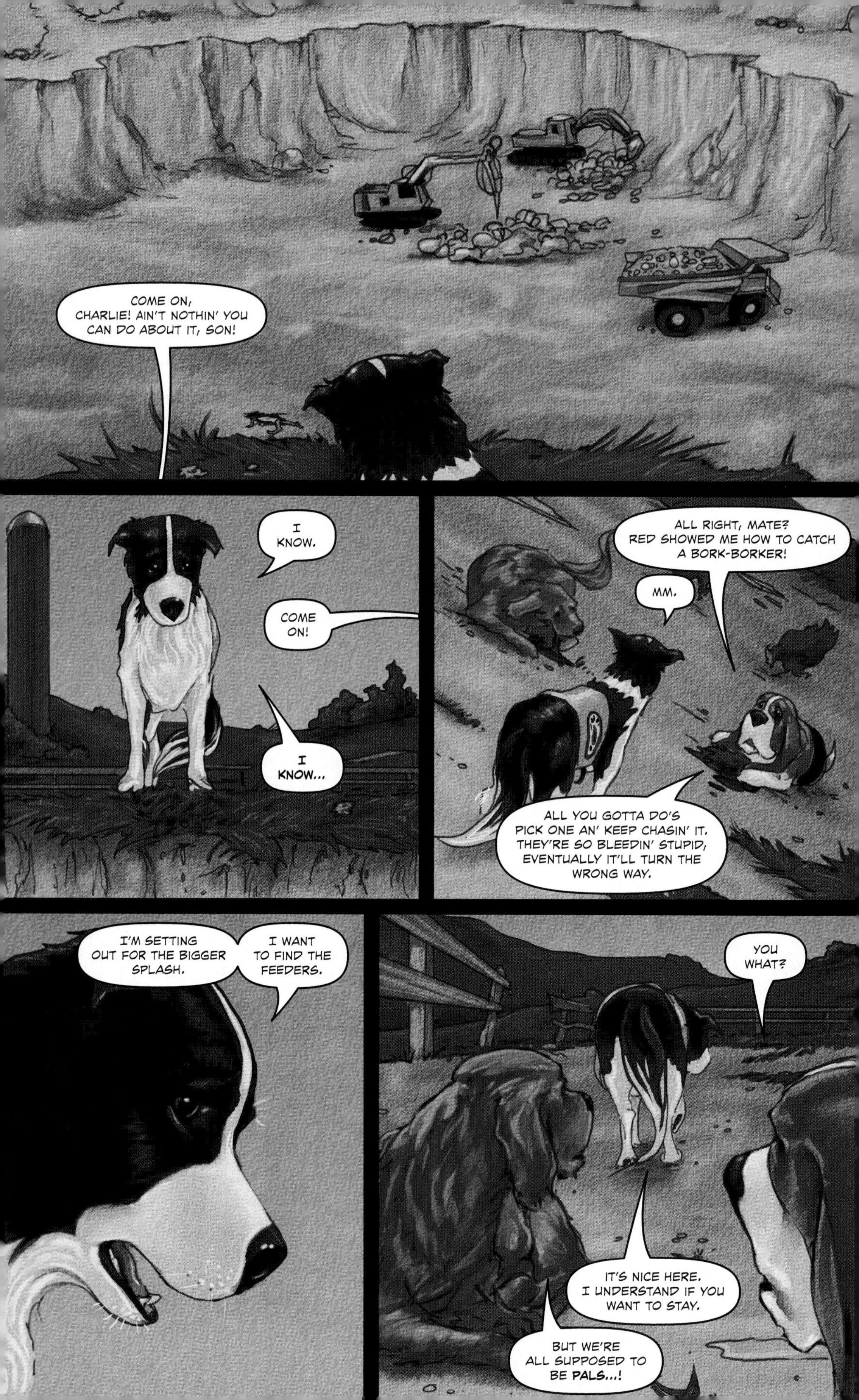
COME ON, CHARLIE! AIN'T NOTHIN' YOU CAN DO ABOUT IT, SON!
I KNOW.
COME ON!
I KNOW...
ALL RIGHT, MATE? RED SHOWED ME HOW TO CATCH A BORK-BORKER!
MM.
ALL YOU GOTTA DO'S PICK ONE AN' KEEP CHASIN' IT. THEY'RE SO BLEEDIN' STUPID, EVENTUALLY IT'LL TURN THE WRONG WAY.
I'M SETTING OUT FOR THE BIGGER SPLASH.
I WANT TO FIND THE FEEDERS.
YOU WHAT?
IT'S NICE HERE. I UNDERSTAND IF YOU WANT TO STAY.
BUT WE'RE ALL SUPPOSED TO BE PALS...!

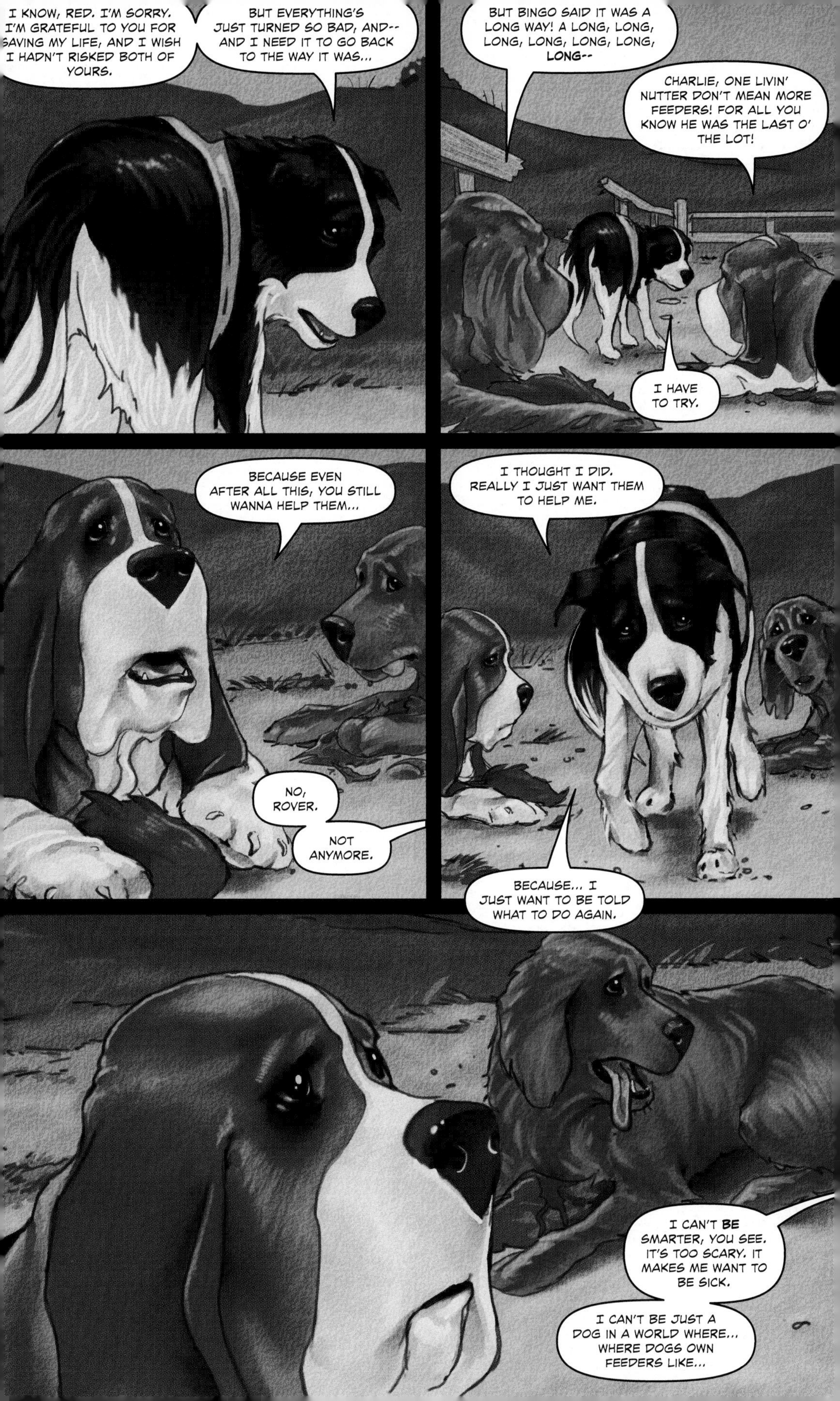

I KNOW, RED. I'M SORRY. I'M GRATEFUL TO YOU FOR SAVING MY LIFE, AND I WISH I HADN'T RISKED BOTH OF YOURS.
BUT EVERYTHING'S JUST TURNED SO BAD, AND-- AND I NEED IT TO GO BACK TO THE WAY IT WAS...
BUT BINGO SAID IT WAS A LONG WAY! A LONG, LONG, LONG, LONG, LONG, LONG, LONG--
CHARLIE, ONE LIVIN' NUTTER DON'T MEAN MORE FEEDERS! FOR ALL YOU KNOW HE WAS THE LAST O' THE LOT!
I HAVE TO TRY.
BECAUSE EVEN AFTER ALL THIS, YOU STILL WANNA HELP THEM...
NO, ROVER.
NOT ANYMORE.
I THOUGHT I DID. REALLY I JUST WANT THEM TO HELP ME.
BECAUSE... I JUST WANT TO BE TOLD WHAT TO DO AGAIN.
I CAN'T **BE** SMARTER, YOU SEE. IT'S TOO SCARY. IT MAKES ME WANT TO BE SICK.
I CAN'T BE JUST A DOG IN A WORLD WHERE... WHERE DOGS OWN FEEDERS LIKE...

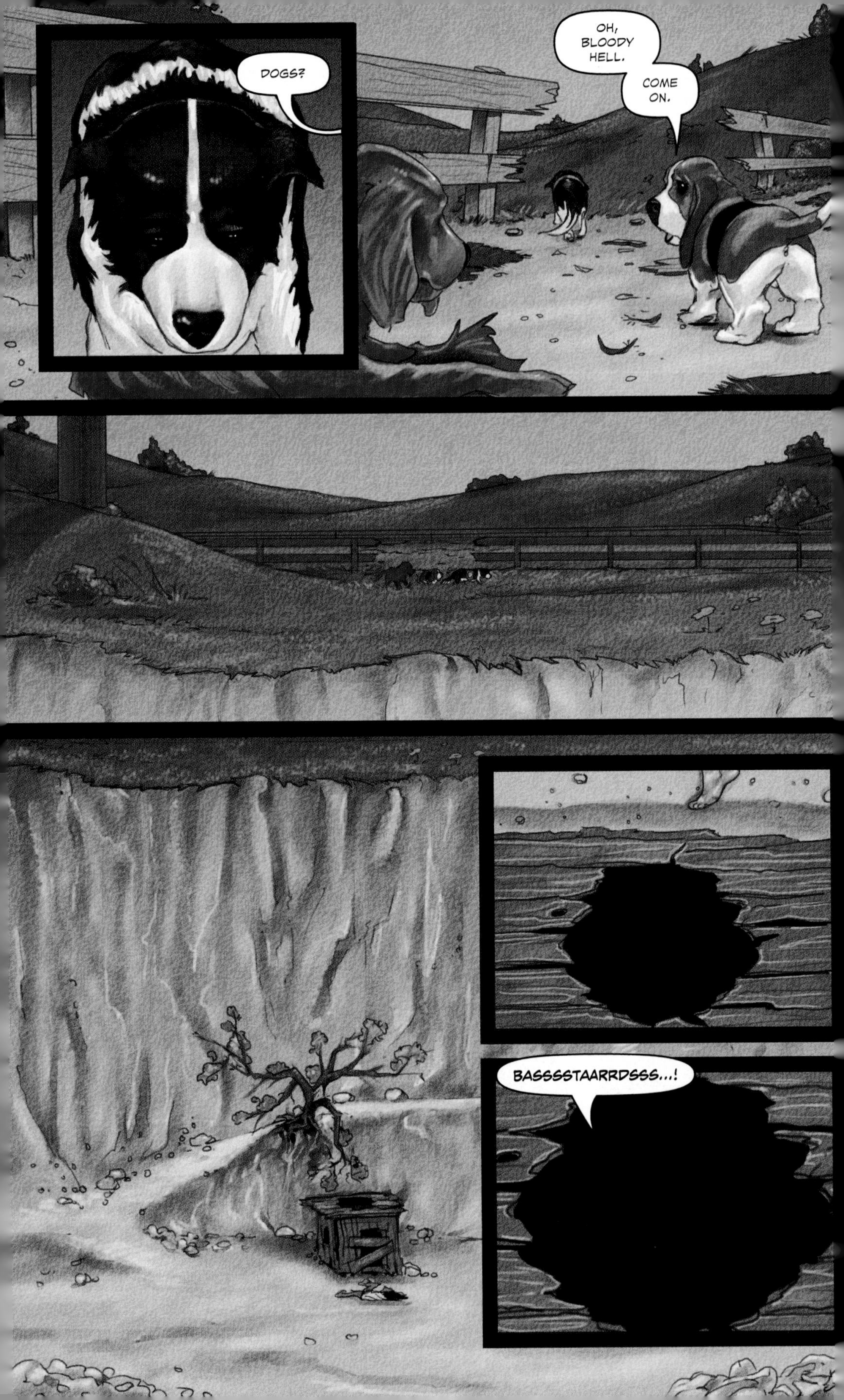
DOGS?
OH, BLOODY HELL.
COME ON.
BASSSSTAARRDSSS...!

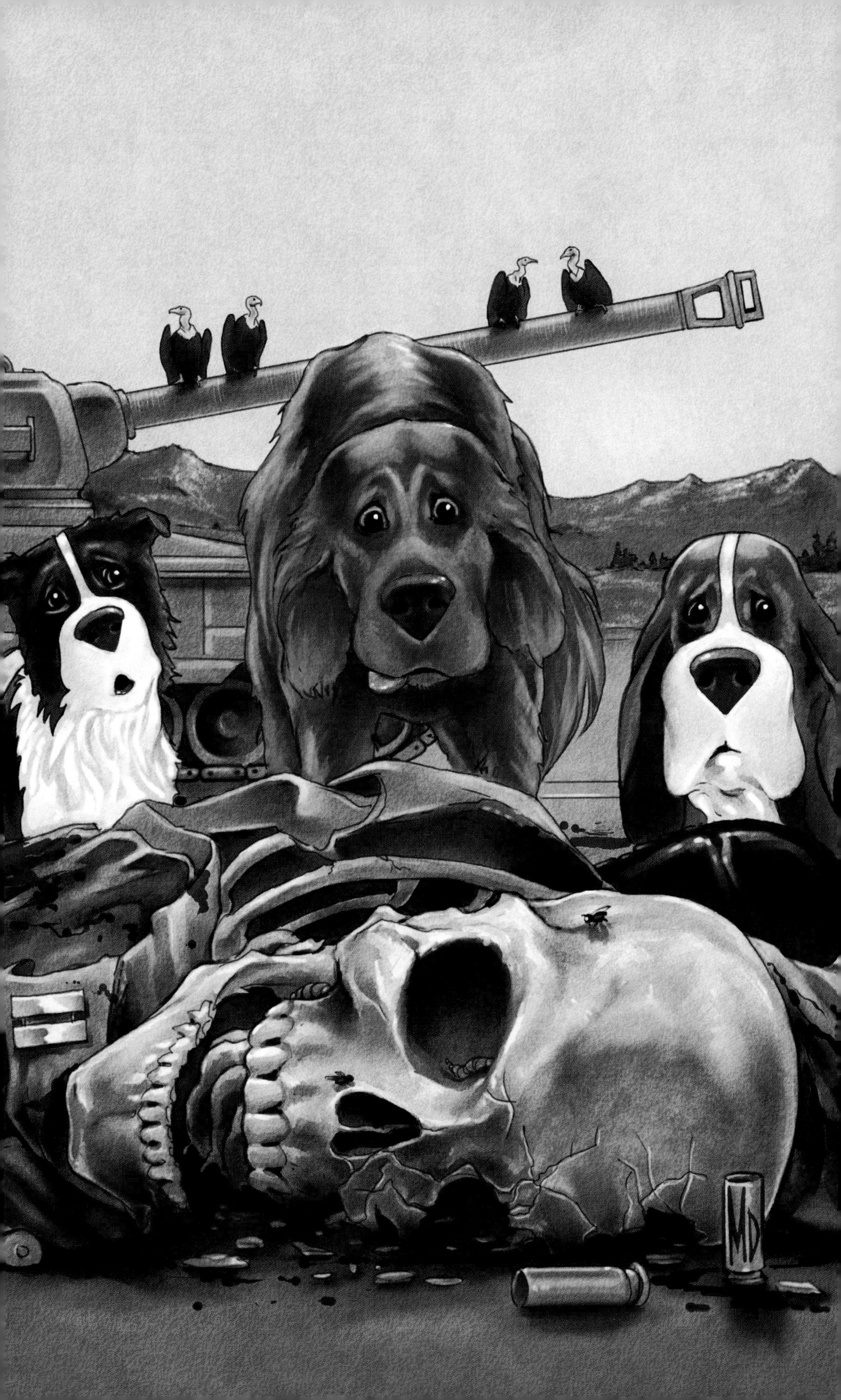
MD

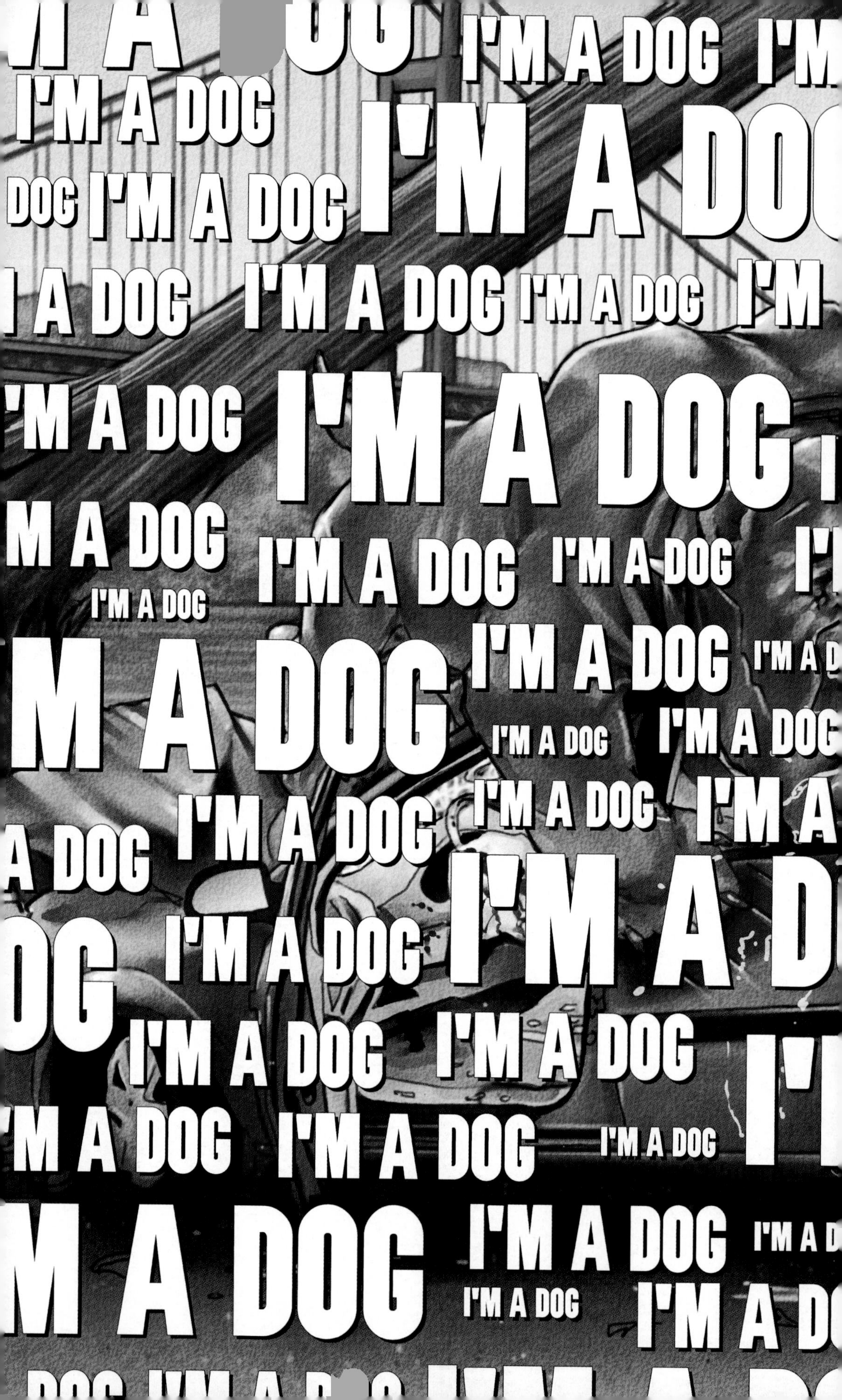

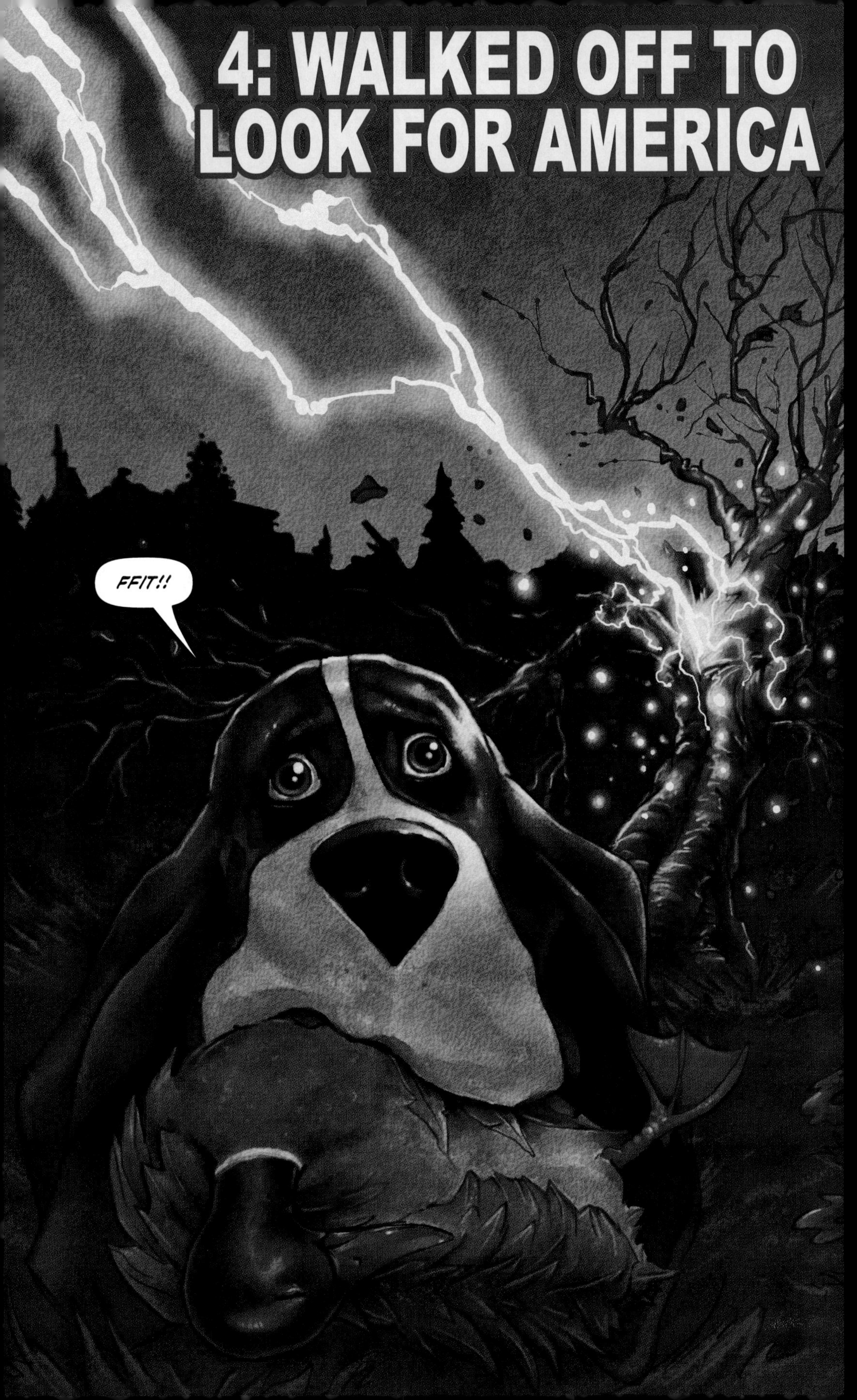
4: WALKED OFF TO LOOK FOR AMERICA
FFIT!!

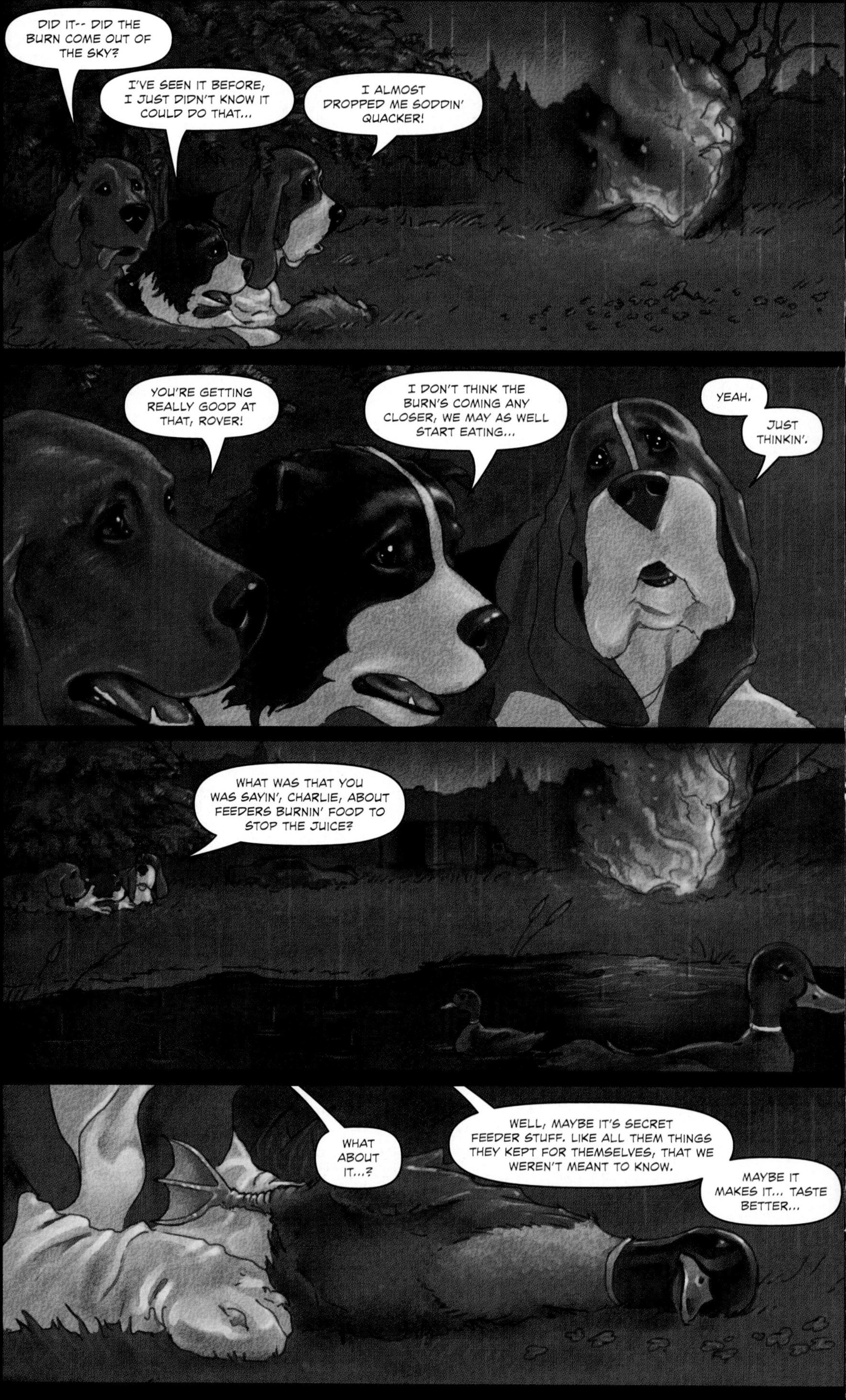
DID IT-- DID THE BURN COME OUT OF THE SKY?
I'VE SEEN IT BEFORE, I JUST DIDN'T KNOW IT COULD DO THAT...
I ALMOST DROPPED ME SODDIN' QUACKER!
YOU'RE GETTING REALLY GOOD AT THAT, ROVER!
I DON'T THINK THE BURN'S COMING ANY CLOSER, WE MAY AS WELL START EATING...
YEAH.
JUST THINKIN'.
WHAT WAS THAT YOU WAS SAYIN', CHARLIE, ABOUT FEEDERS BURNIN' FOOD TO STOP THE JUICE?
WHAT ABOUT IT...?
WELL, MAYBE IT'S SECRET FEEDER STUFF. LIKE ALL THEM THINGS THEY KEPT FOR THEMSELVES, THAT WE WEREN'T MEANT TO KNOW.
MAYBE IT MAKES IT... TASTE BETTER...

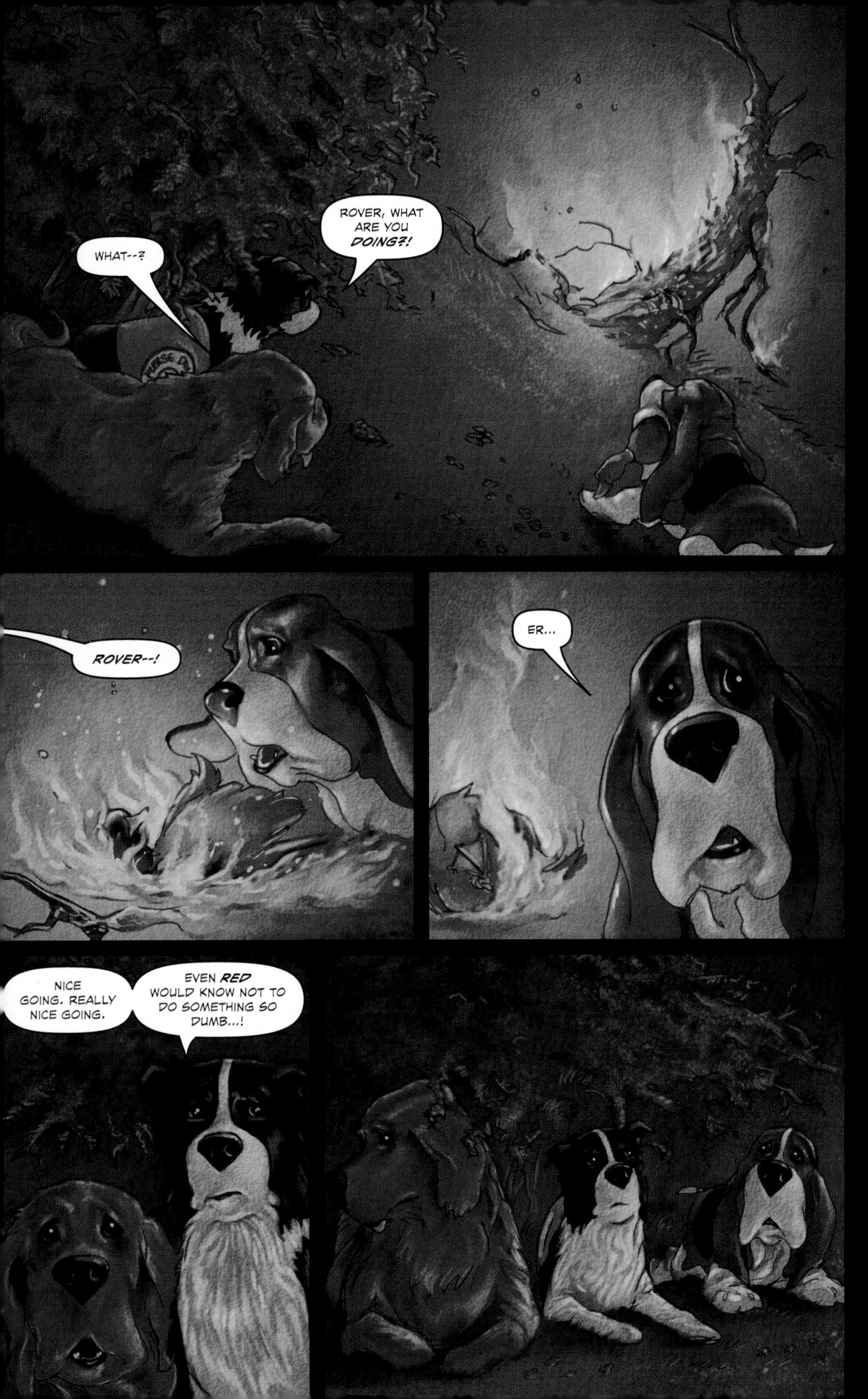
WHAT--?
ROVER, WHAT ARE YOU *DOING?!*
ROVER--!
ER...
NICE GOING. REALLY NICE GOING.
EVEN *RED* WOULD KNOW NOT TO DO SOMETHING SO DUMB...!

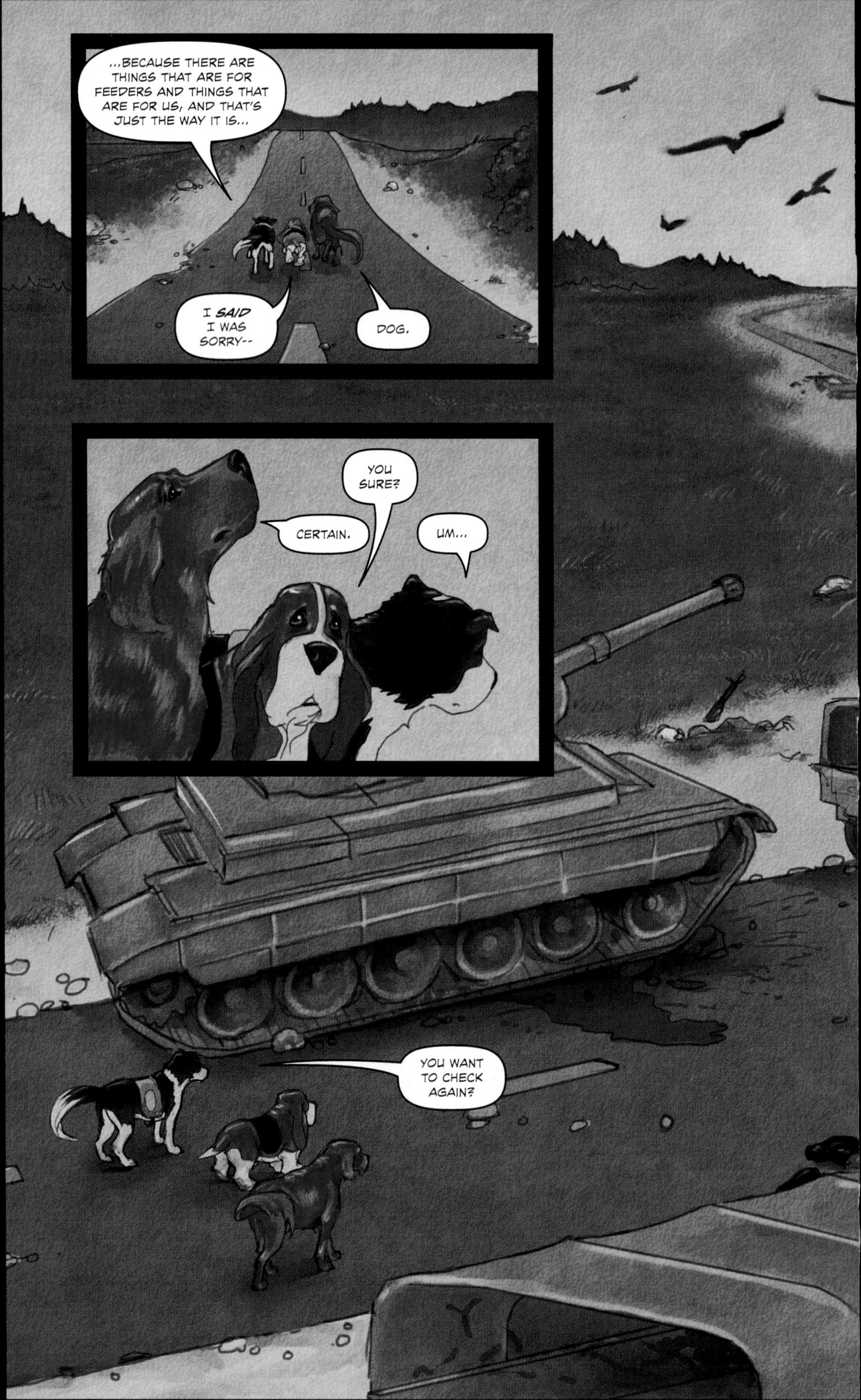
...BECAUSE THERE ARE THINGS THAT ARE FOR FEEDERS AND THINGS THAT ARE FOR US, AND THAT'S JUST THE WAY IT IS...
I *SAID* I WAS SORRY--
DOG.
YOU SURE?
CERTAIN.
UM...
YOU WANT TO CHECK AGAIN?

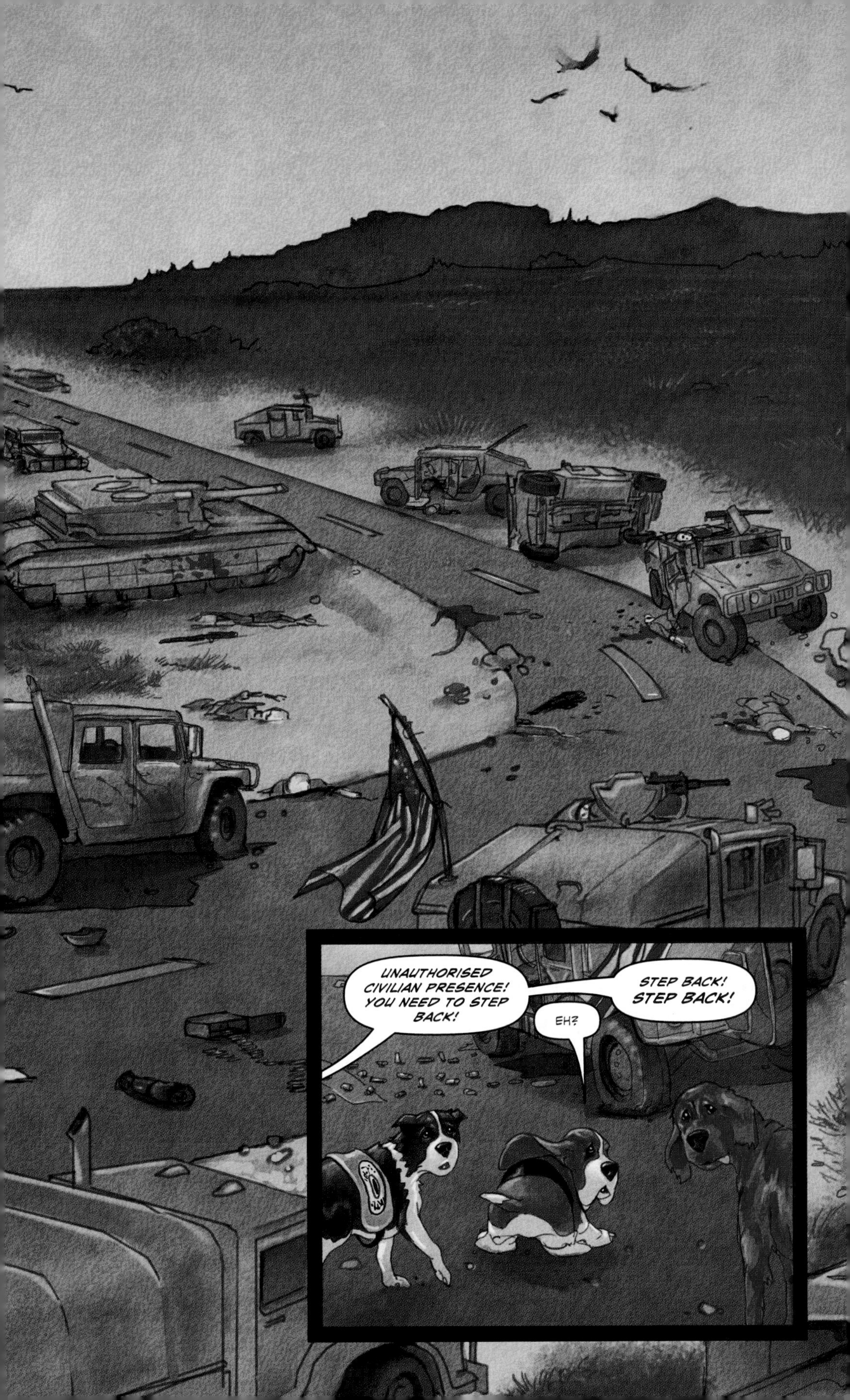
UNAUTHORISED CIVILIAN PRESENCE! YOU NEED TO STEP BACK!
STEP BACK! STEP BACK!
EH?

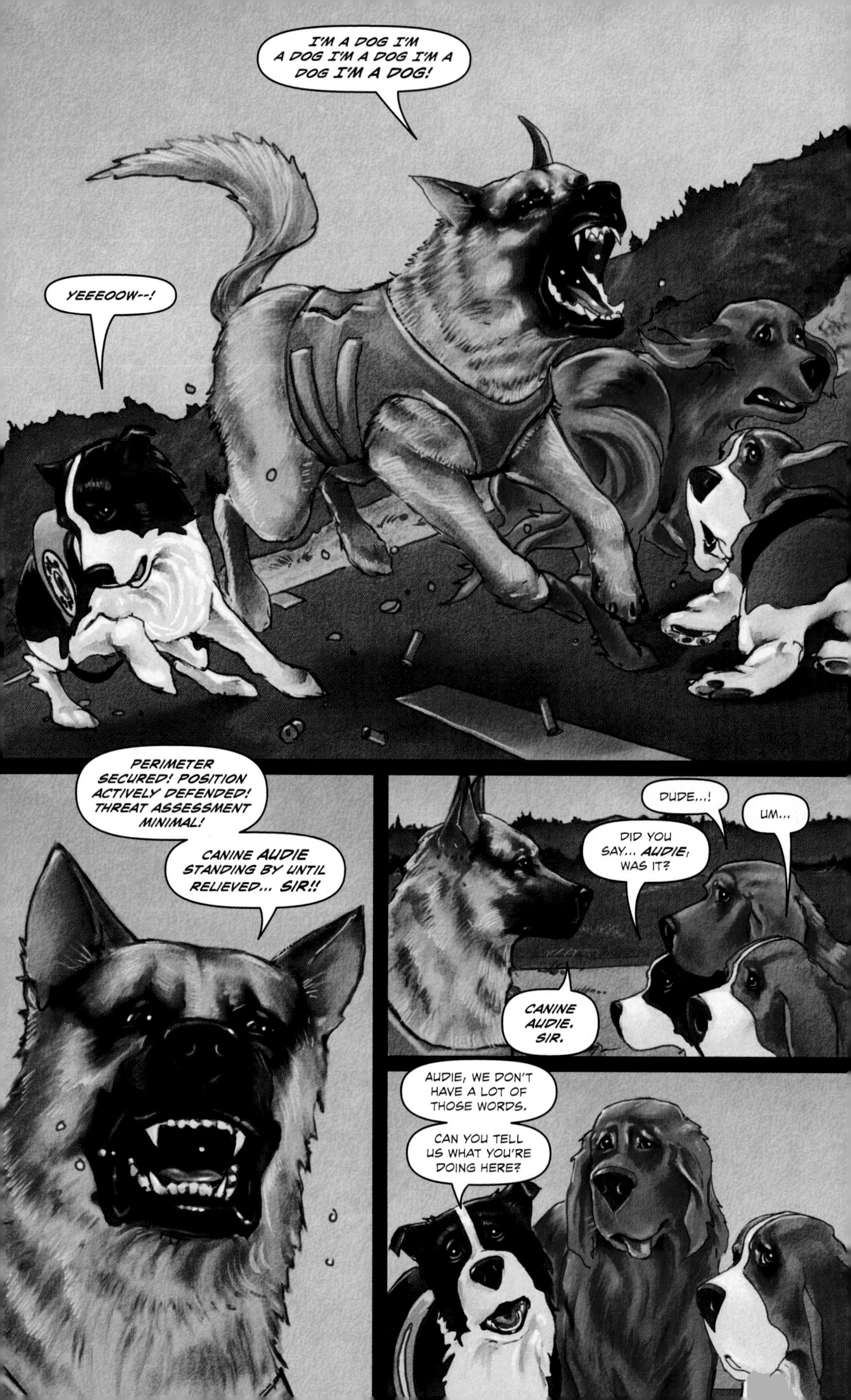
I'M A DOG I'M A DOG I'M A DOG I'M A DOG I'M A DOG!
YEEEOOW--!
PERIMETER SECURED! POSITION ACTIVELY DEFENDED! THREAT ASSESSMENT MINIMAL!
CANINE AUDIE STANDING BY UNTIL RELIEVED... SIR!!
DUDE...!
UM...
DID YOU SAY... AUDIE, WAS IT?
CANINE AUDIE. SIR.
AUDIE, WE DON'T HAVE A LOT OF THOSE WORDS.
CAN YOU TELL US WHAT YOU'RE DOING HERE?

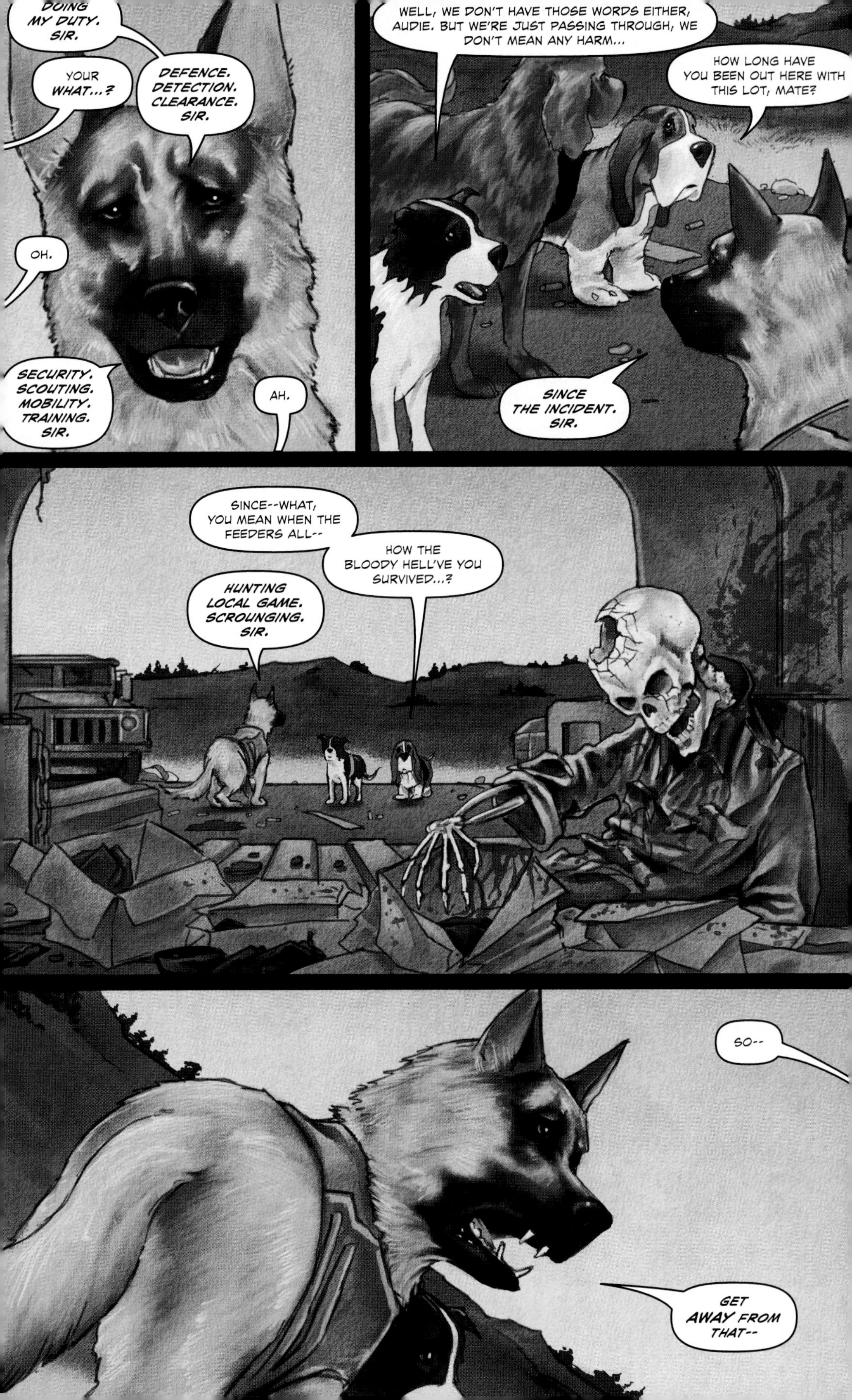
DOING MY DUTY. SIR.
YOUR WHAT...?
DEFENCE. DETECTION. CLEARANCE. SIR.
OH.
SECURITY. SCOUTING. MOBILITY. TRAINING. SIR.
AH.
WELL, WE DON'T HAVE THOSE WORDS EITHER, AUDIE. BUT WE'RE JUST PASSING THROUGH, WE DON'T MEAN ANY HARM...
HOW LONG HAVE YOU BEEN OUT HERE WITH THIS LOT, MATE?
SINCE THE INCIDENT. SIR.
SINCE--WHAT, YOU MEAN WHEN THE FEEDERS ALL--
HOW THE BLOODY HELL'VE YOU SURVIVED...?
HUNTING LOCAL GAME. SCROUNGING. SIR.
SO--
GET AWAY FROM THAT--

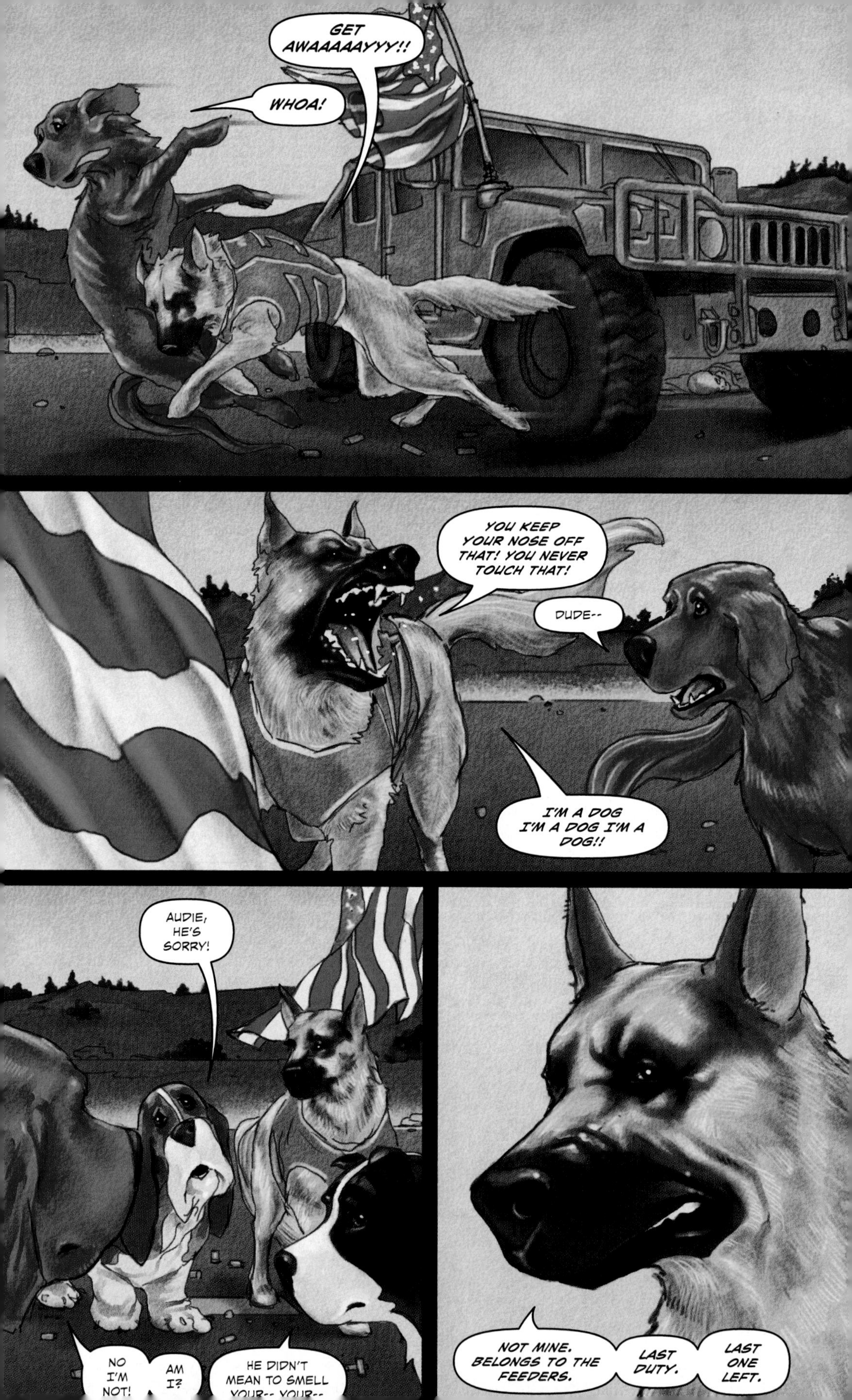

GET AWAAAAAAYYY!!
WHOA!
YOU KEEP YOUR NOSE OFF THAT! YOU NEVER TOUCH THAT!
DUDE--
I'M A DOG I'M A DOG I'M A DOG!!
AUDIE, HE'S SORRY!
NO I'M NOT!
AM I?
HE DIDN'T MEAN TO SMELL
NOT MINE. BELONGS TO THE FEEDERS.
LAST DUTY.
LAST ONE LEFT.

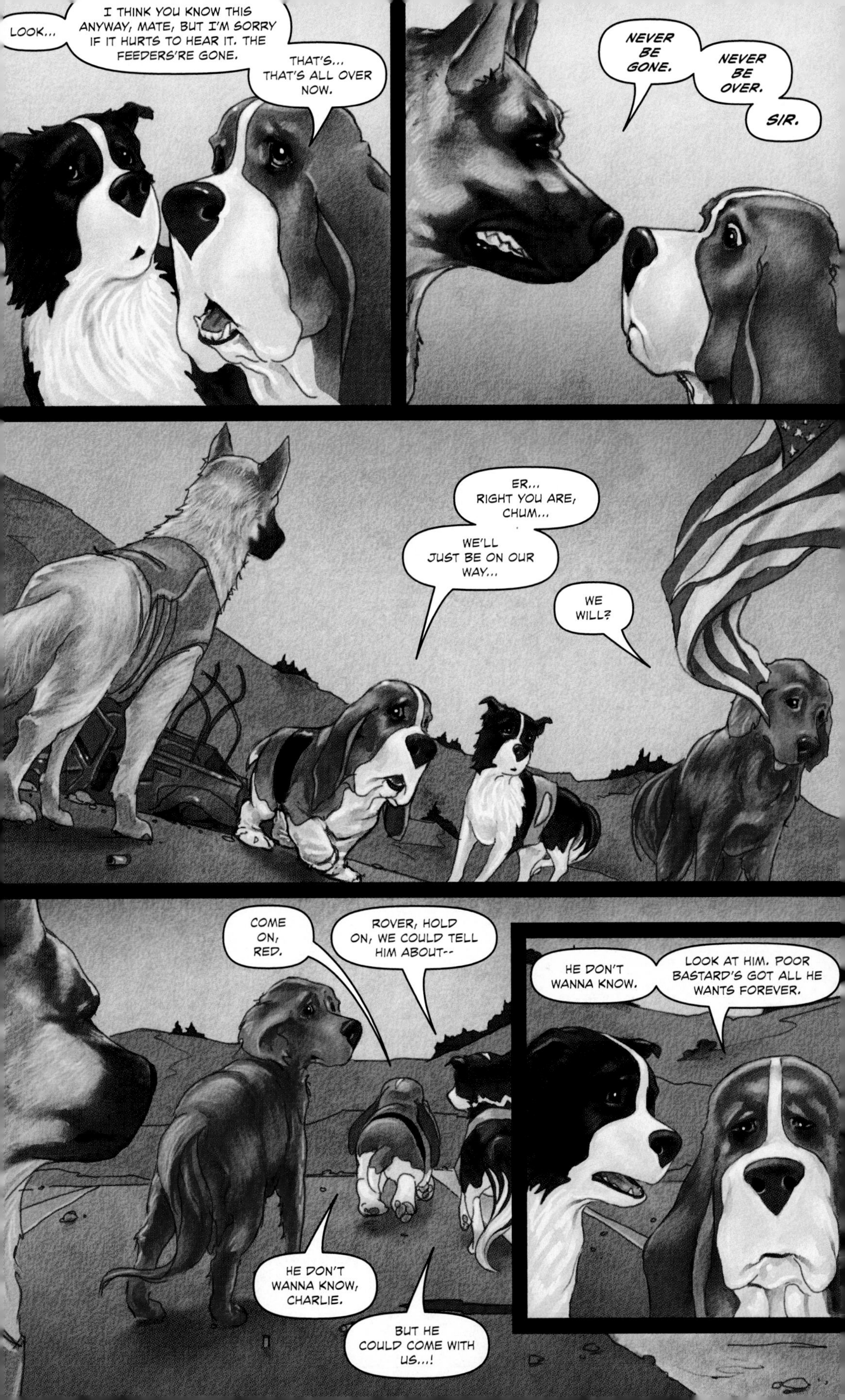
LOOK...
I THINK YOU KNOW THIS ANYWAY, MATE, BUT I'M SORRY IF IT HURTS TO HEAR IT. THE FEEDERS'RE GONE.
THAT'S... THAT'S ALL OVER NOW.
NEVER BE GONE.
NEVER BE OVER.
SIR.
ER... RIGHT YOU ARE, CHUM...
WE'LL JUST BE ON OUR WAY...
WE WILL?
COME ON, RED.
ROVER, HOLD ON, WE COULD TELL HIM ABOUT--
HE DON'T WANNA KNOW, CHARLIE.
BUT HE COULD COME WITH US...!
HE DON'T WANNA KNOW.
LOOK AT HIM. POOR BASTARD'S GOT ALL HE WANTS FOREVER.

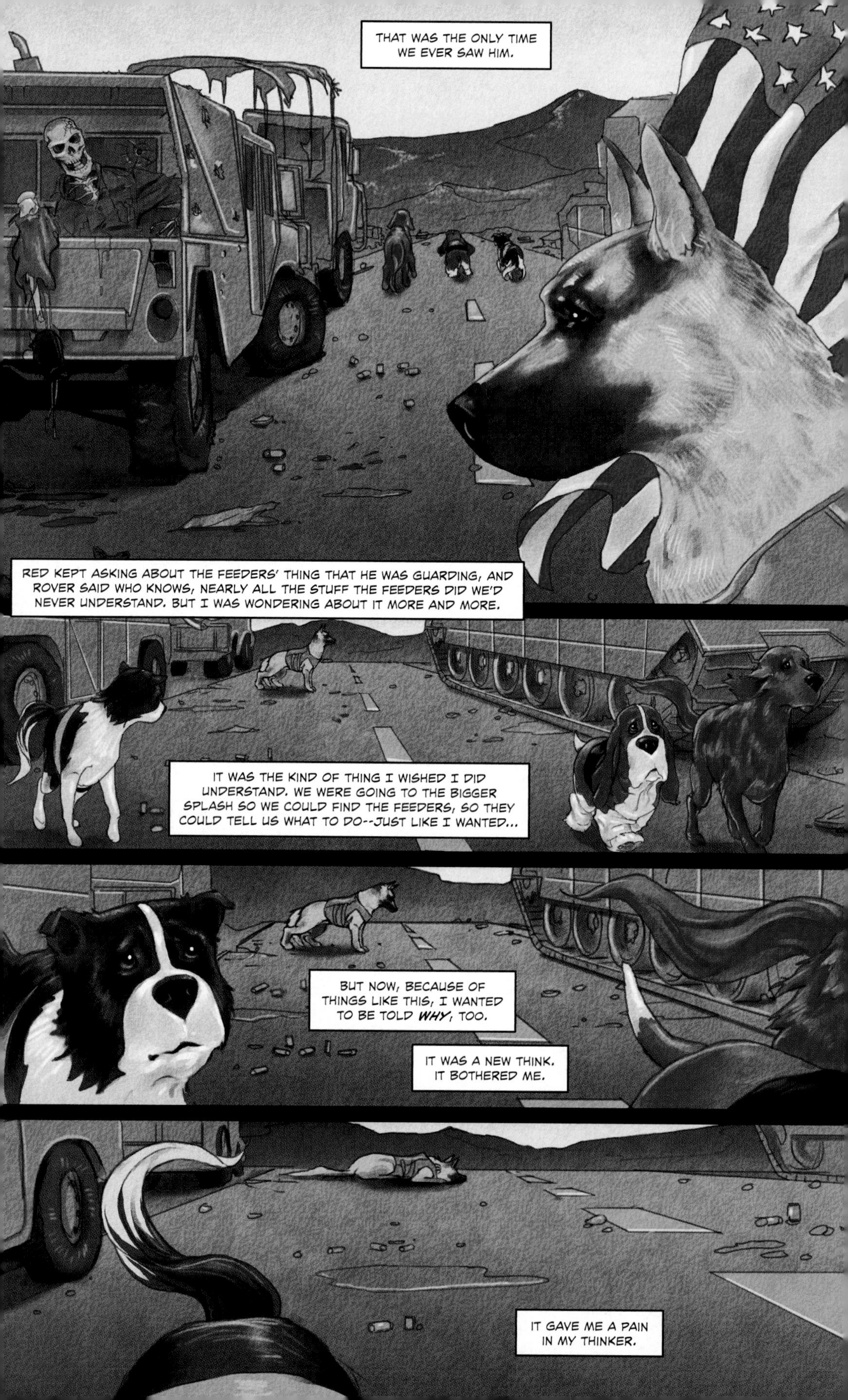
THAT WAS THE ONLY TIME WE EVER SAW HIM.
RED KEPT ASKING ABOUT THE FEEDERS' THING THAT HE WAS GUARDING, AND ROVER SAID WHO KNOWS, NEARLY ALL THE STUFF THE FEEDERS DID WE'D NEVER UNDERSTAND. BUT I WAS WONDERING ABOUT IT MORE AND MORE.
IT WAS THE KIND OF THING I WISHED I DID UNDERSTAND. WE WERE GOING TO THE BIGGER SPLASH SO WE COULD FIND THE FEEDERS, SO THEY COULD TELL US WHAT TO DO--JUST LIKE I WANTED...
BUT NOW, BECAUSE OF THINGS LIKE THIS, I WANTED TO BE TOLD *WHY*, TOO.
IT WAS A NEW THINK. IT BOTHERED ME.
IT GAVE ME A PAIN IN MY THINKER.

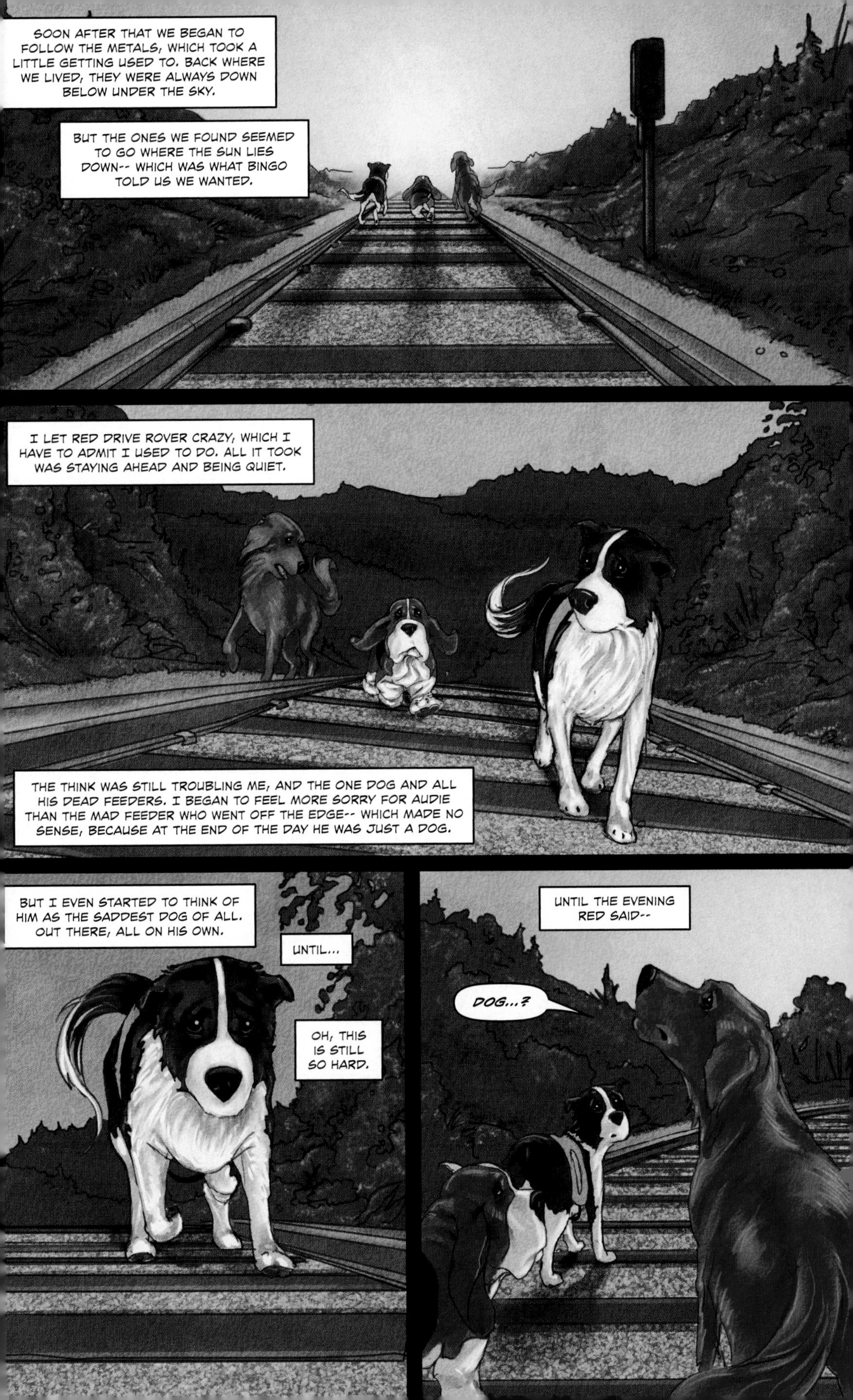
SOON AFTER THAT WE BEGAN TO FOLLOW THE METALS, WHICH TOOK A LITTLE GETTING USED TO. BACK WHERE WE LIVED, THEY WERE ALWAYS DOWN BELOW UNDER THE SKY.
BUT THE ONES WE FOUND SEEMED TO GO WHERE THE SUN LIES DOWN-- WHICH WAS WHAT BINGO TOLD US WE WANTED.
I LET RED DRIVE ROVER CRAZY, WHICH I HAVE TO ADMIT I USED TO DO. ALL IT TOOK WAS STAYING AHEAD AND BEING QUIET.
THE THINK WAS STILL TROUBLING ME, AND THE ONE DOG AND ALL HIS DEAD FEEDERS. I BEGAN TO FEEL MORE SORRY FOR AUDIE THAN THE MAD FEEDER WHO WENT OFF THE EDGE-- WHICH MADE NO SENSE, BECAUSE AT THE END OF THE DAY HE WAS JUST A DOG.
BUT I EVEN STARTED TO THINK OF HIM AS THE SADDEST DOG OF ALL. OUT THERE, ALL ON HIS OWN.
UNTIL...
OH, THIS IS STILL SO HARD.
UNTIL THE EVENING RED SAID--
DOG...?

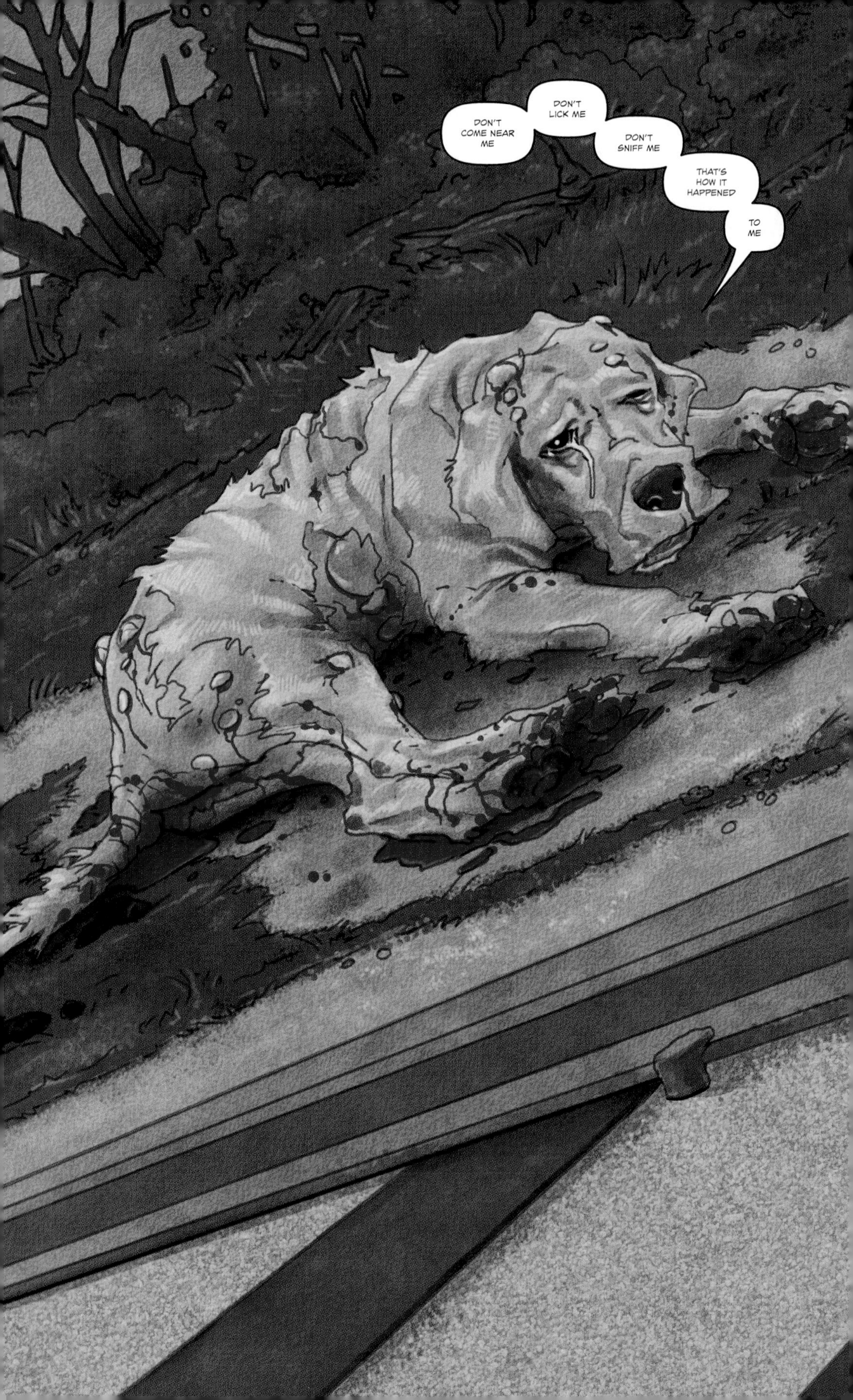
DON'T COME NEAR ME
DON'T LICK ME
DON'T SNIFF ME
THAT'S HOW IT HAPPENED
TO ME

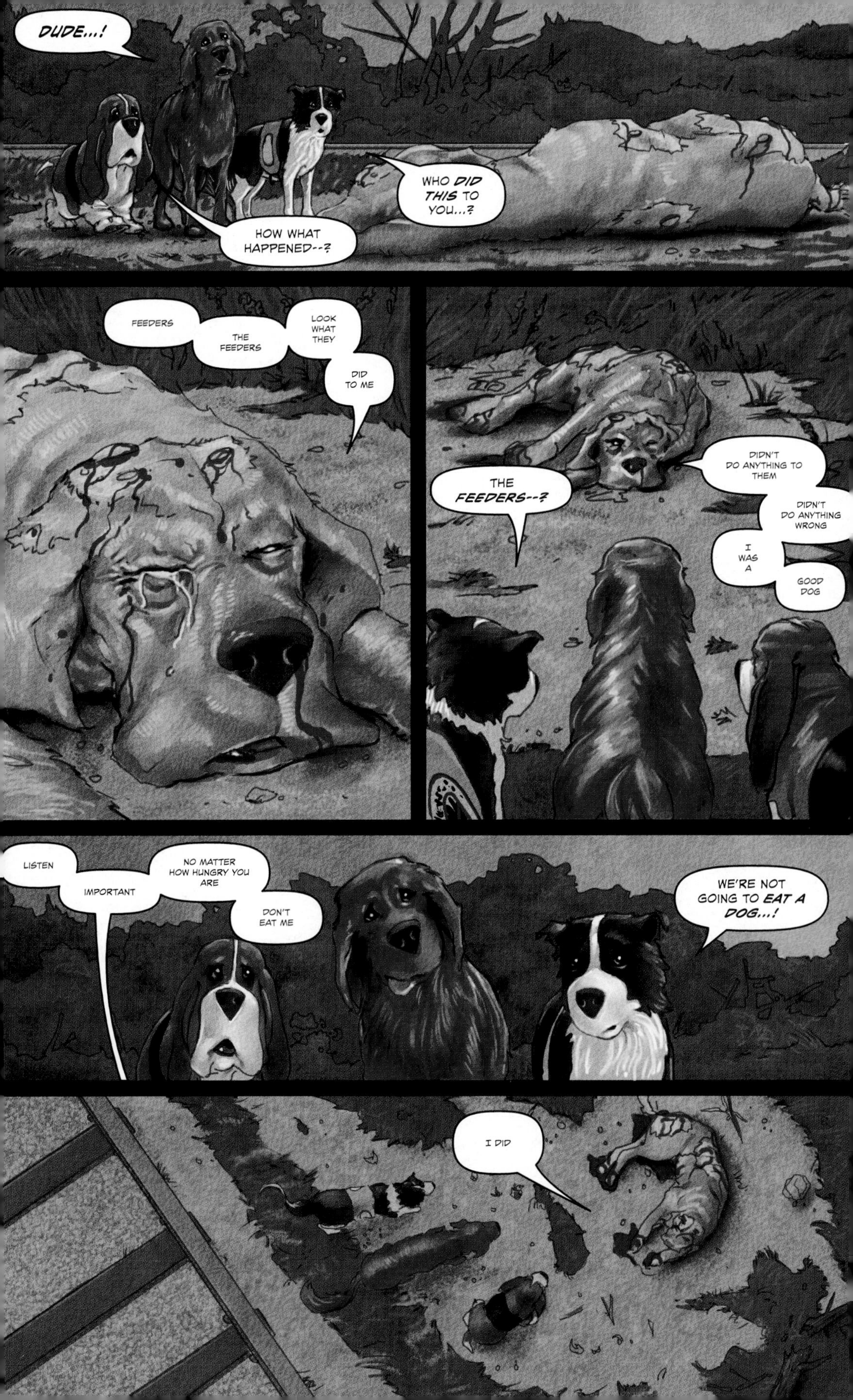

DUDE...!
HOW WHAT HAPPENED--?
WHO DID THIS TO YOU...?
FEEDERS
THE FEEDERS
LOOK WHAT THEY
DID TO ME
THE FEEDERS--?
DIDN'T DO ANYTHING TO THEM
DIDN'T DO ANYTHING WRONG
I WAS A
GOOD DOG
LISTEN
IMPORTANT
NO MATTER HOW HUNGRY YOU ARE
DON'T EAT ME
WE'RE NOT GOING TO EAT A DOG...!
I DID

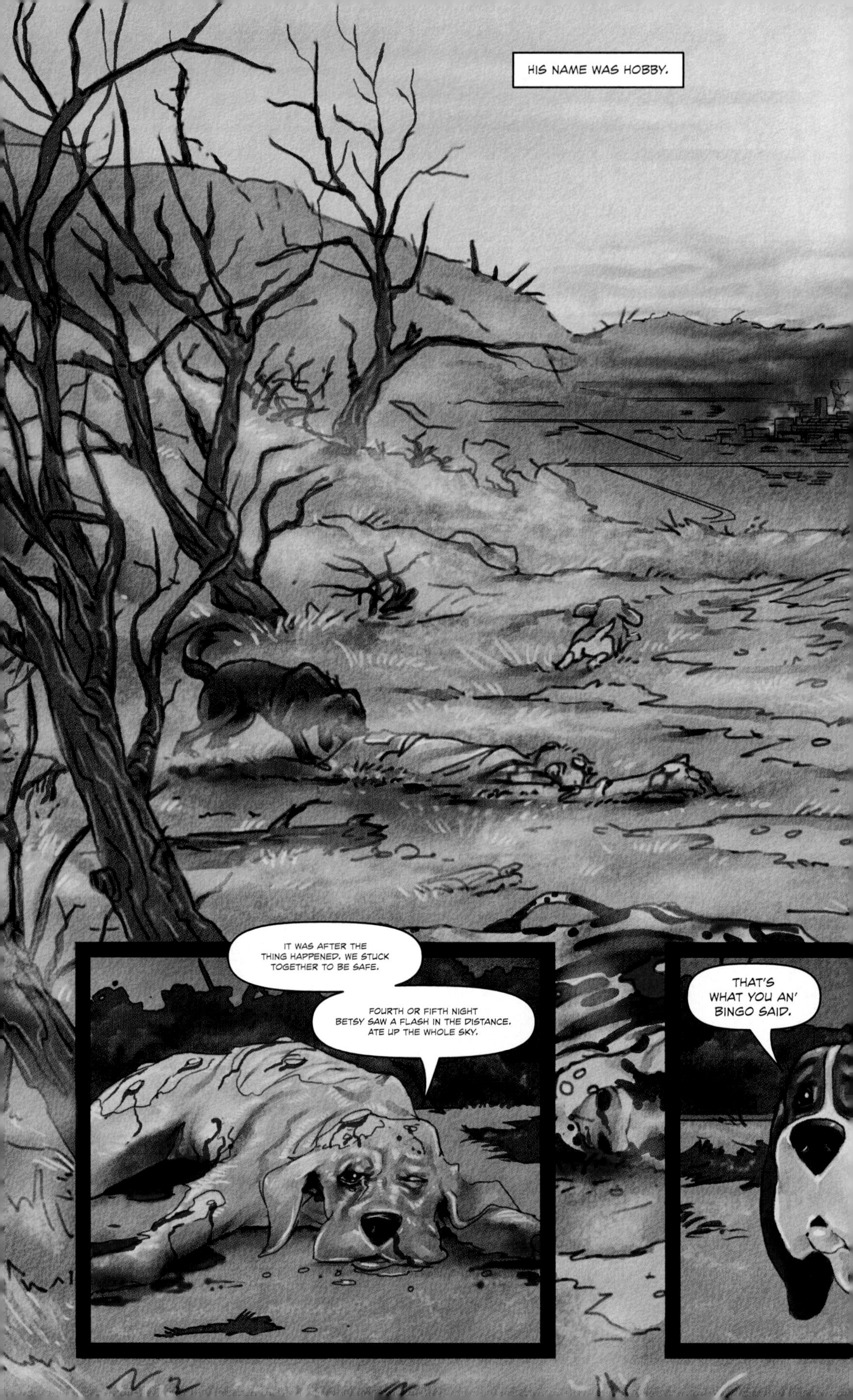
HIS NAME WAS HOBBY.
IT WAS AFTER THE THING HAPPENED. WE STUCK TOGETHER TO BE SAFE.
FOURTH OR FIFTH NIGHT BETSY SAW A FLASH IN THE DISTANCE. ATE UP THE WHOLE SKY.
THAT'S WHAT YOU AN' BINGO SAID.

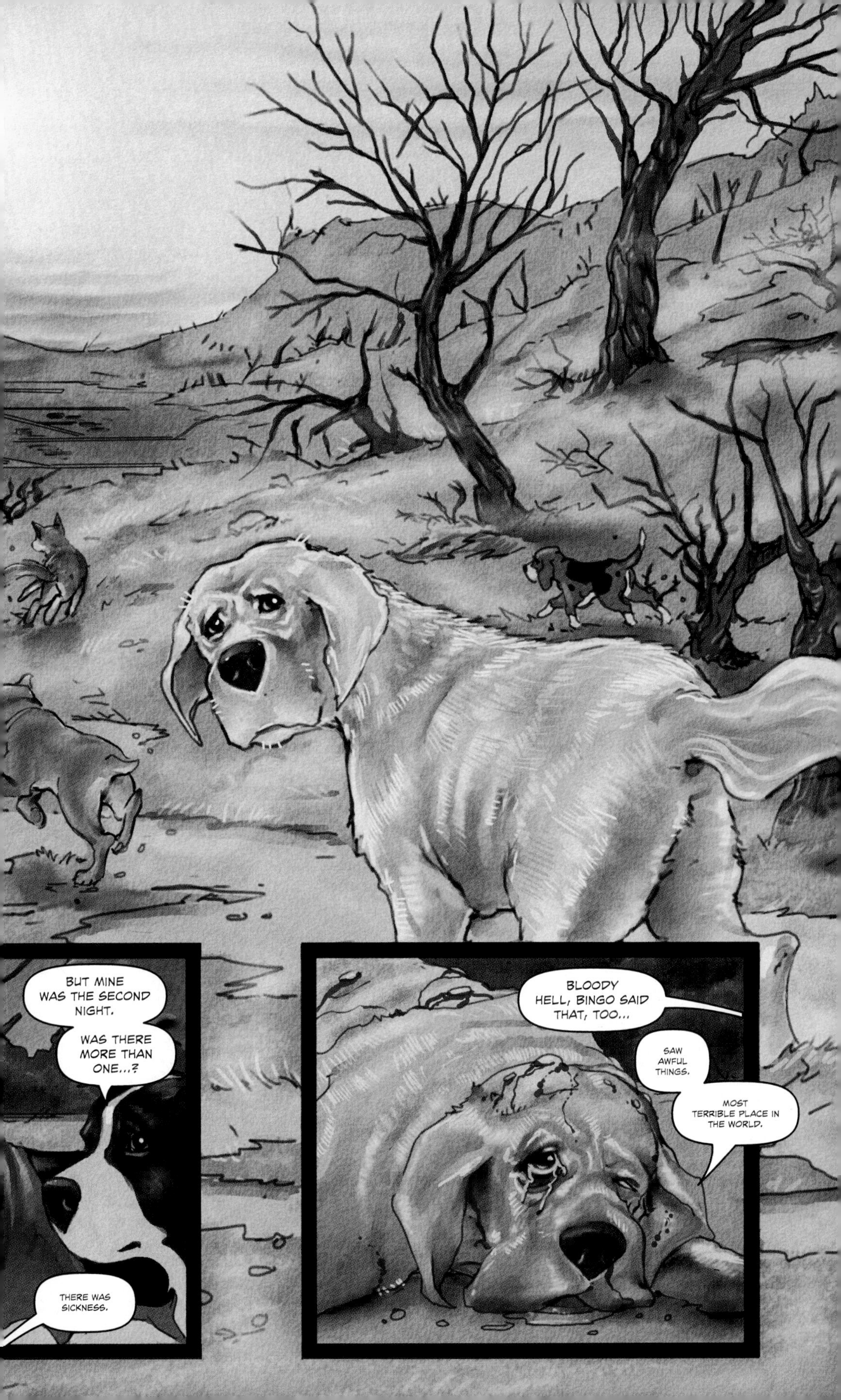
BUT MINE WAS THE SECOND NIGHT.
WAS THERE MORE THAN ONE...?
THERE WAS SICKNESS.
BLOODY HELL, BINGO SAID THAT, TOO...
SAW AWFUL THINGS.
MOST TERRIBLE PLACE IN THE WORLD.

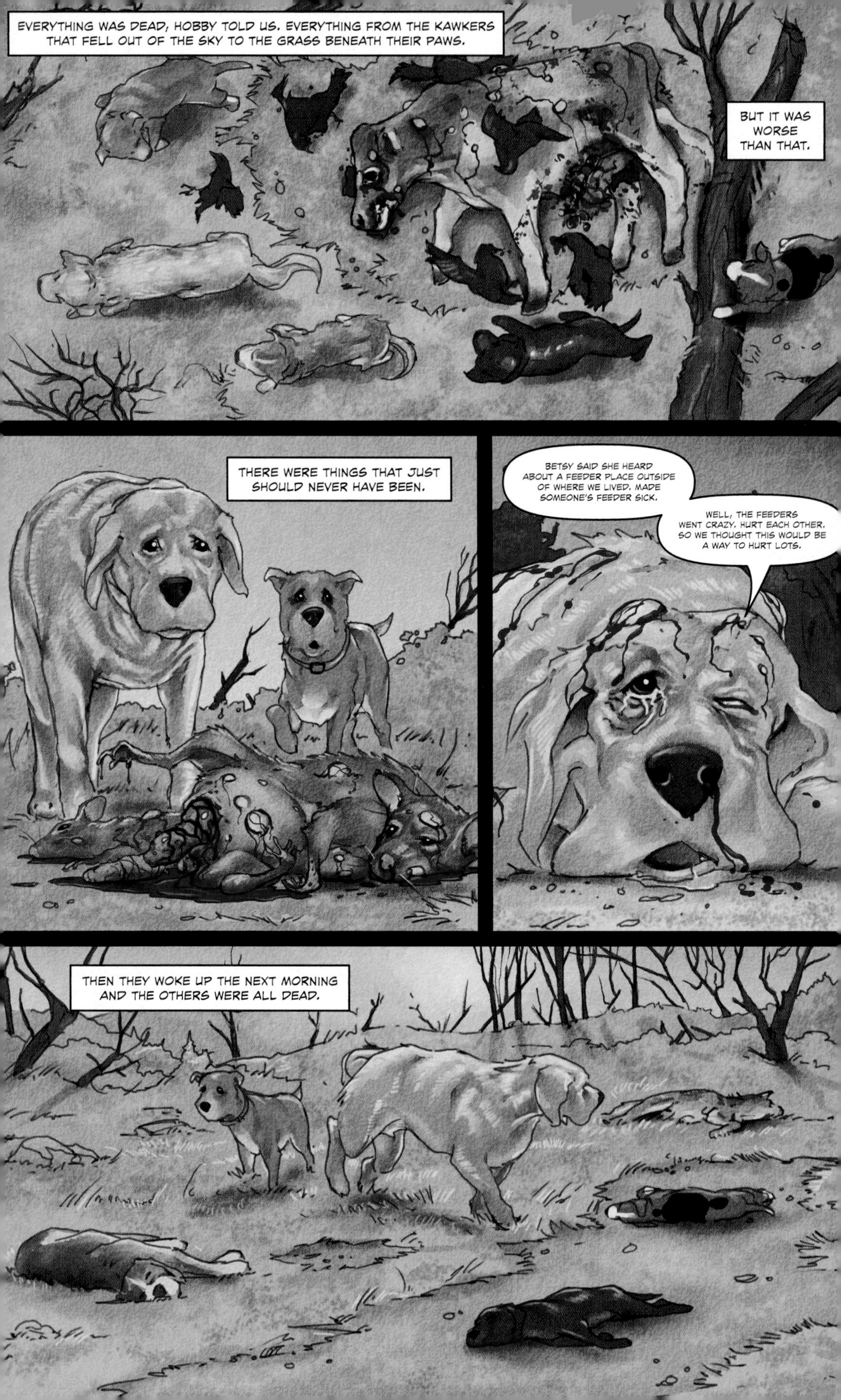
EVERYTHING WAS DEAD, HOBBY TOLD US. EVERYTHING FROM THE KAWKERS THAT FELL OUT OF THE SKY TO THE GRASS BENEATH THEIR PAWS.
BUT IT WAS WORSE THAN THAT.
THERE WERE THINGS THAT JUST SHOULD NEVER HAVE BEEN.
BETSY SAID SHE HEARD ABOUT A FEEDER PLACE OUTSIDE OF WHERE WE LIVED. MADE SOMEONE'S FEEDER SICK.
WELL, THE FEEDERS WENT CRAZY. HURT EACH OTHER. SO WE THOUGHT THIS WOULD BE A WAY TO HURT LOTS.
THEN THEY WOKE UP THE NEXT MORNING AND THE OTHERS WERE ALL DEAD.

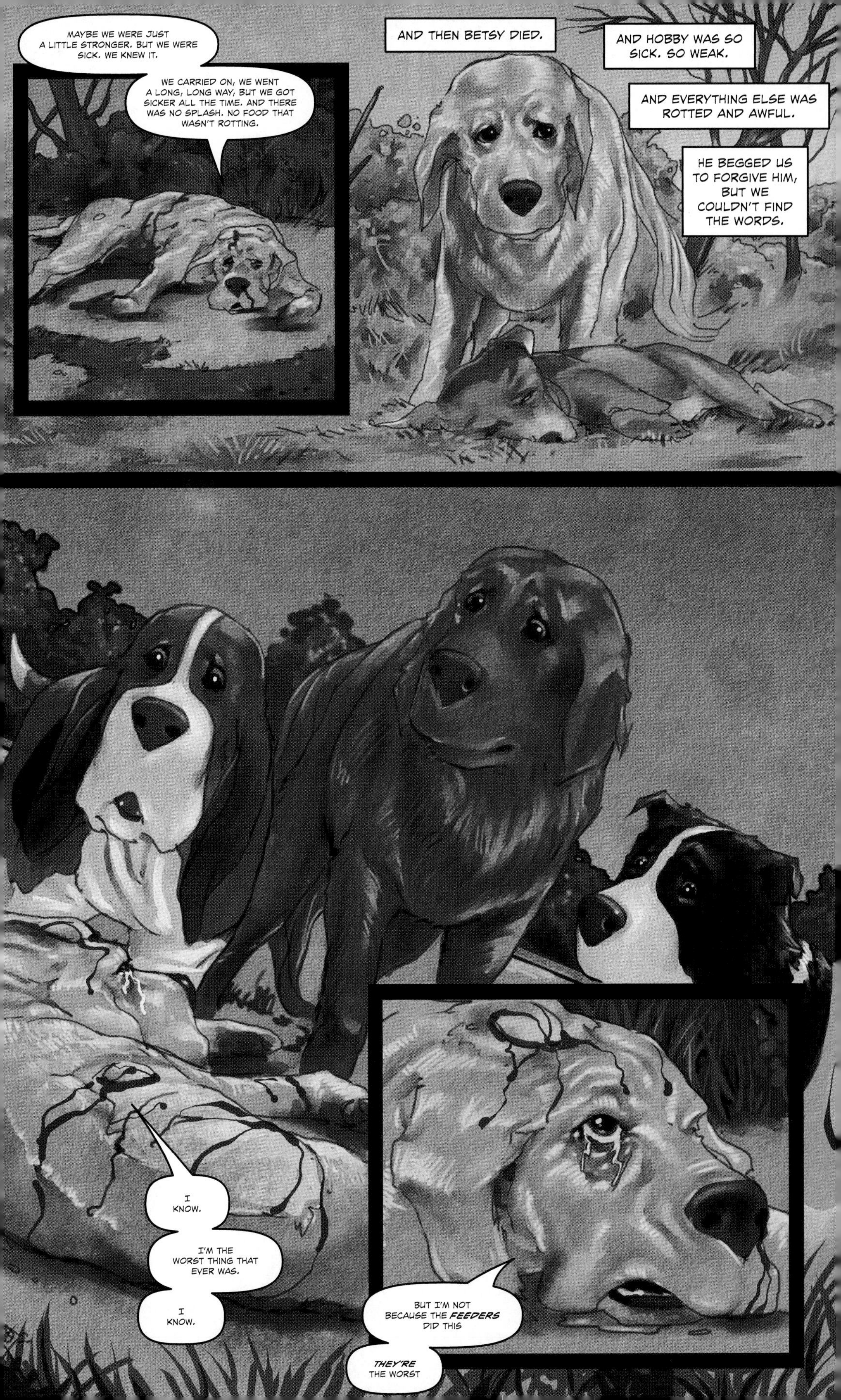

MAYBE WE WERE JUST A LITTLE STRONGER. BUT WE WERE SICK. WE KNEW IT.
WE CARRIED ON, WE WENT A LONG, LONG WAY, BUT WE GOT SICKER ALL THE TIME. AND THERE WAS NO SPLASH. NO FOOD THAT WASN'T ROTTING.
AND THEN BETSY DIED.
AND HOBBY WAS SO SICK. SO WEAK.
AND EVERYTHING ELSE WAS ROTTED AND AWFUL.
HE BEGGED US TO FORGIVE HIM, BUT WE COULDN'T FIND THE WORDS.
I KNOW.
I'M THE WORST THING THAT EVER WAS.
I KNOW.
BUT I'M NOT BECAUSE THE *FEEDERS* DID THIS
THEY'RE THE WORST

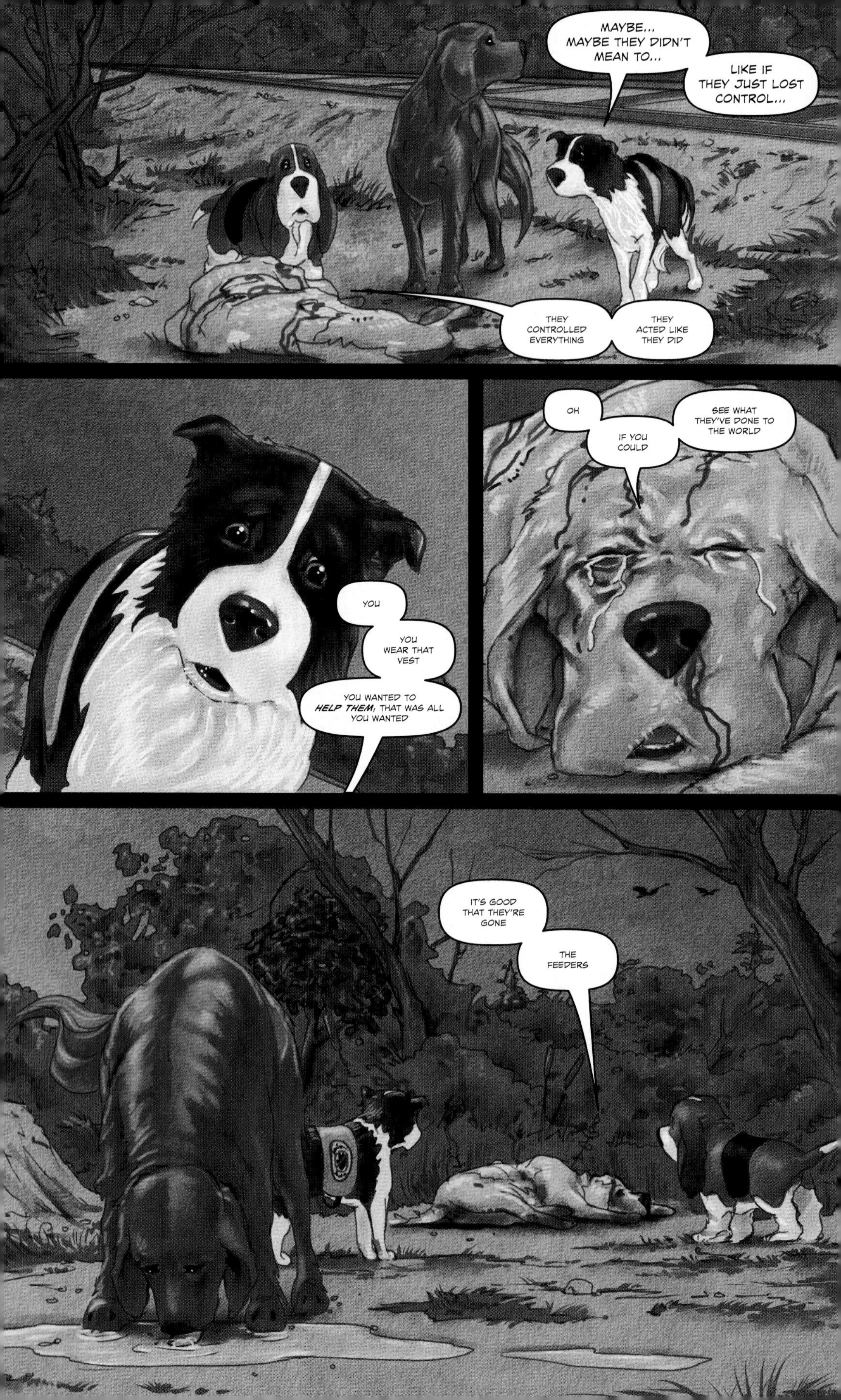
MAYBE... MAYBE THEY DIDN'T MEAN TO...
LIKE IF THEY JUST LOST CONTROL...
THEY CONTROLLED EVERYTHING
THEY ACTED LIKE THEY DID
YOU
YOU WEAR THAT VEST
YOU WANTED TO *HELP THEM*; THAT WAS ALL YOU WANTED
OH
IF YOU COULD
SEE WHAT THEY'VE DONE TO THE WORLD
IT'S GOOD THAT THEY'RE GONE
THE FEEDERS

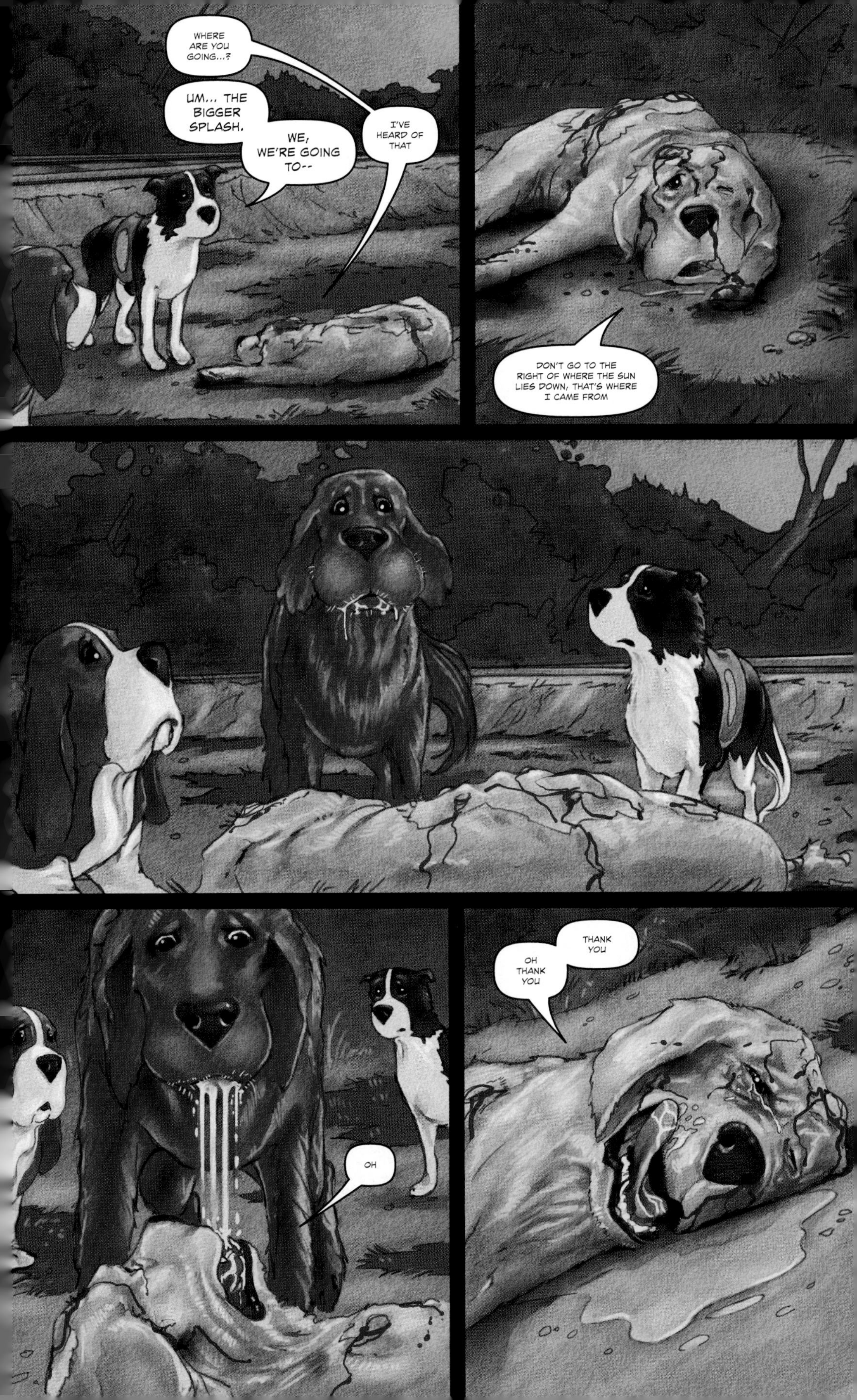
WHERE ARE YOU GOING...?
UM... THE BIGGER SPLASH.
WE, WE'RE GOING TO--
I'VE HEARD OF THAT
DON'T GO TO THE RIGHT OF WHERE THE SUN LIES DOWN; THAT'S WHERE I CAME FROM
OH
OH THANK YOU
THANK YOU

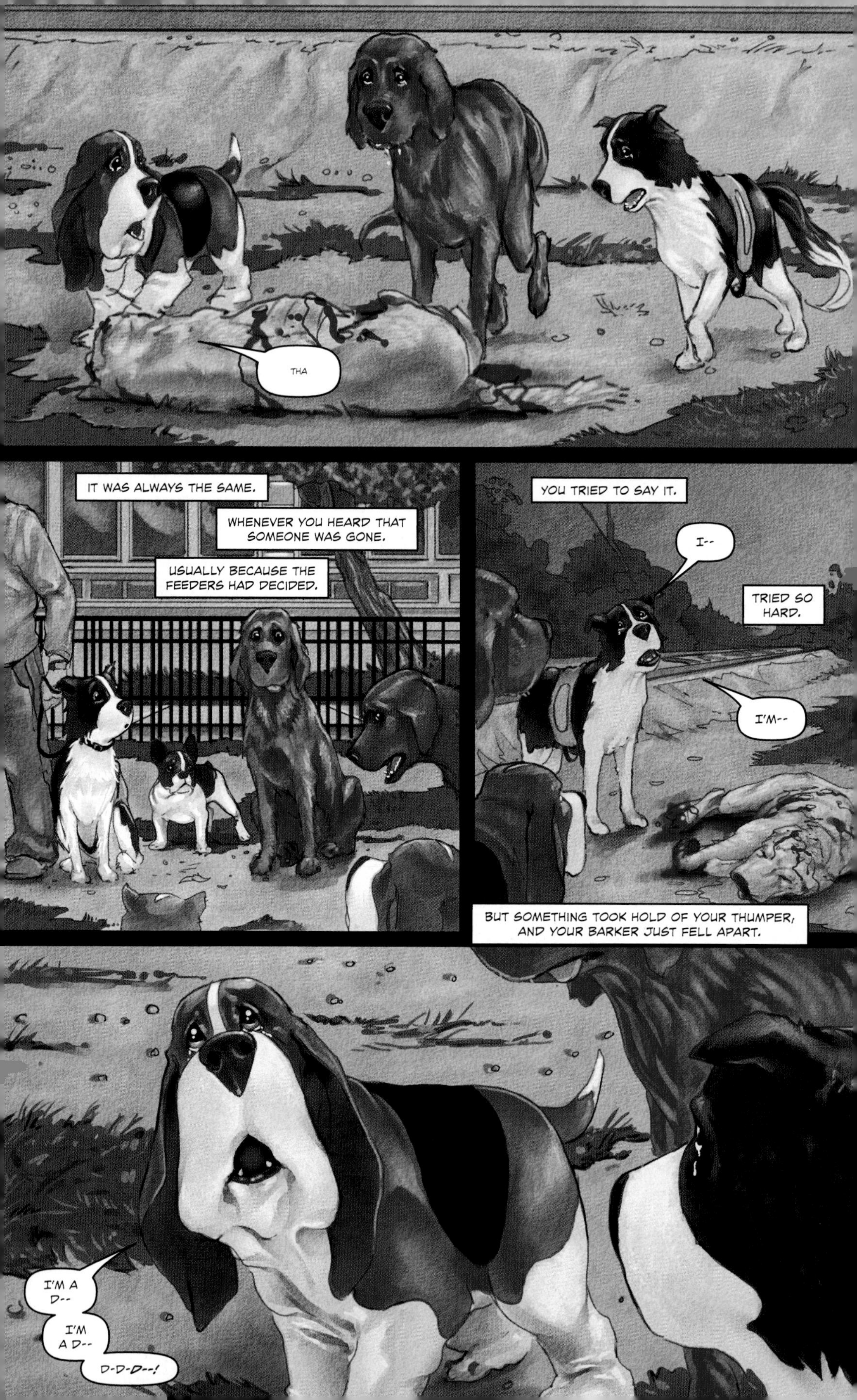
THA
IT WAS ALWAYS THE SAME.
WHENEVER YOU HEARD THAT SOMEONE WAS GONE.
USUALLY BECAUSE THE FEEDERS HAD DECIDED.
YOU TRIED TO SAY IT.
I--
TRIED SO HARD.
I'M--
BUT SOMETHING TOOK HOLD OF YOUR THUMPER, AND YOUR BARKER JUST FELL APART.
I'M A D--
I'M A D--
D-D-D--!

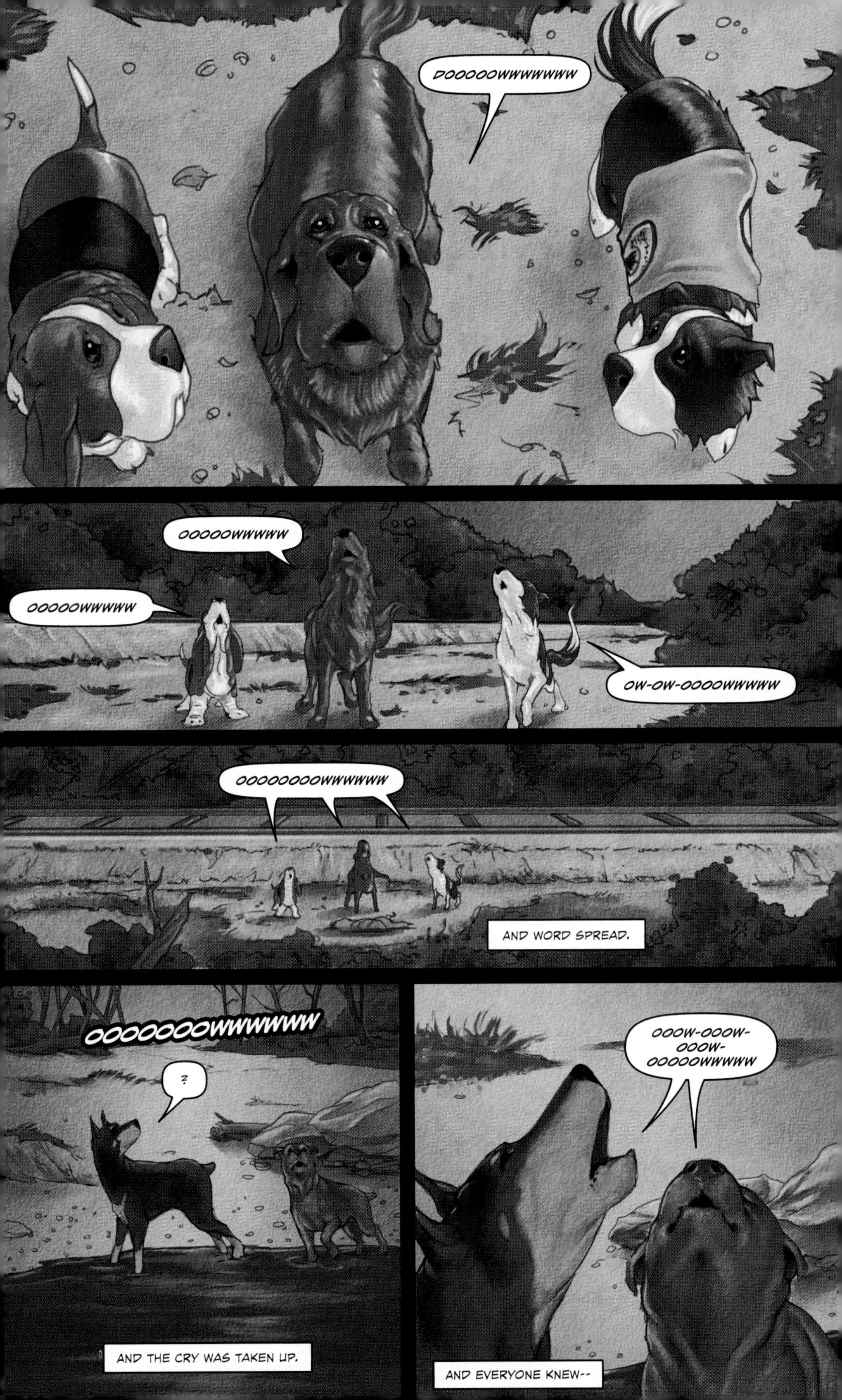
DOOOOOWWWWWW
OOOOOWWWWW
OOOOOWWWWW
OW-OW-OOOOWWWWW
OOOOOOOOWWWWWW
AND WORD SPREAD.
OOOOOOOWWWWWW
?
AND THE CRY WAS TAKEN UP.
OOOW-OOOW-
OOOW-
OOOOOWWWWW
AND EVERYONE KNEW--

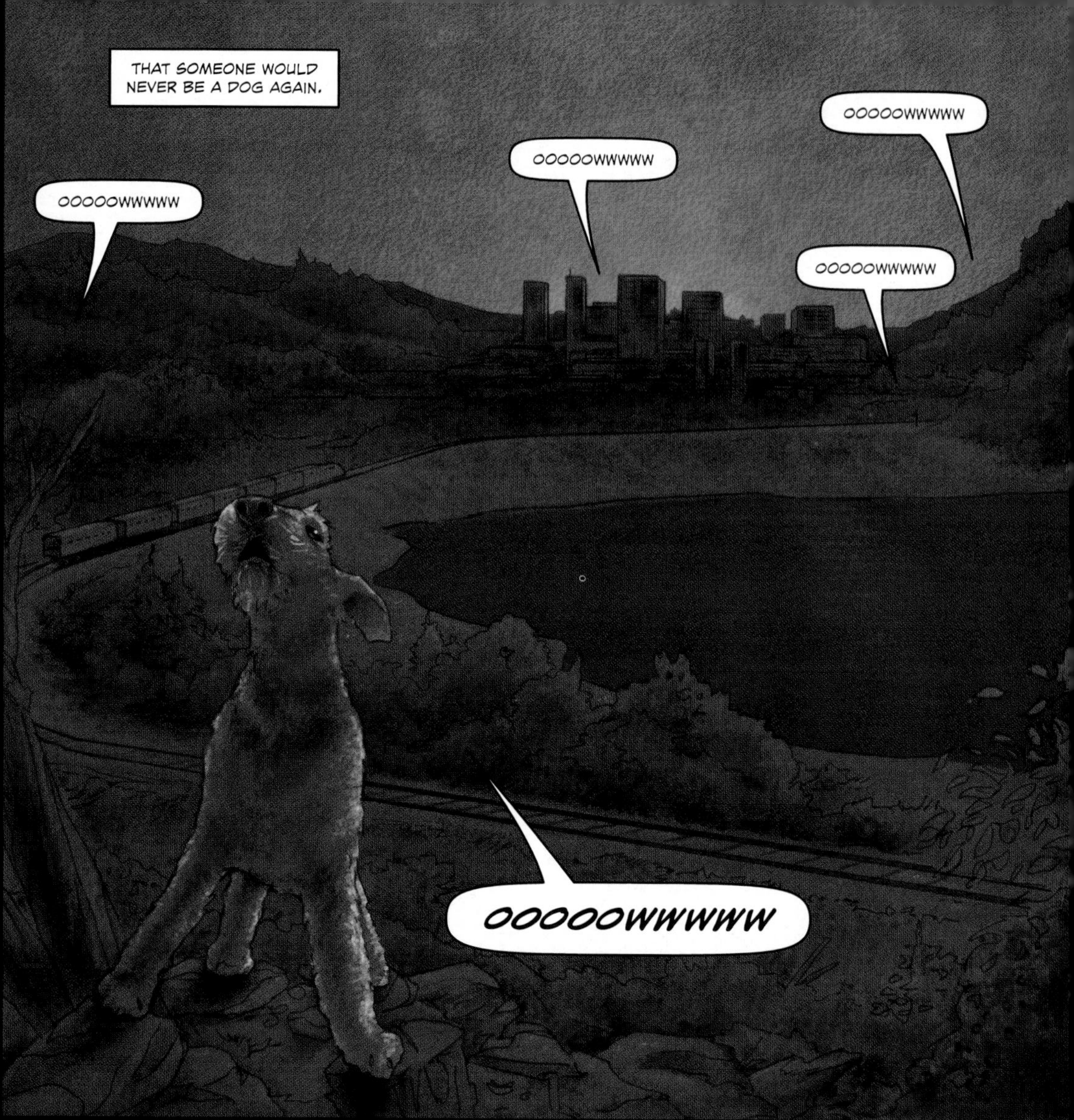
THAT SOMEONE WOULD NEVER BE A DOG AGAIN.
OOOOOWWWWW
OOOOOWWWWW
OOOOOWWWWW
OOOOOWWWWW
OOOOOWWWWW

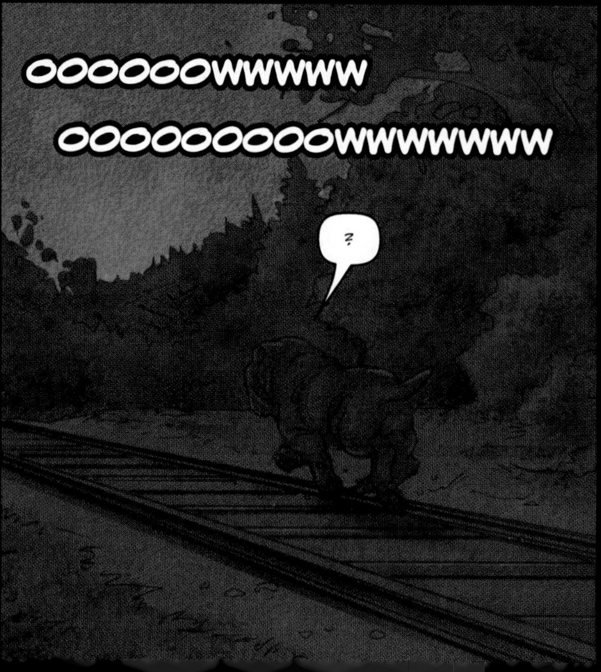
OOOOOOWWWWW
OOOOOOOOOOWWWWWWWW
?

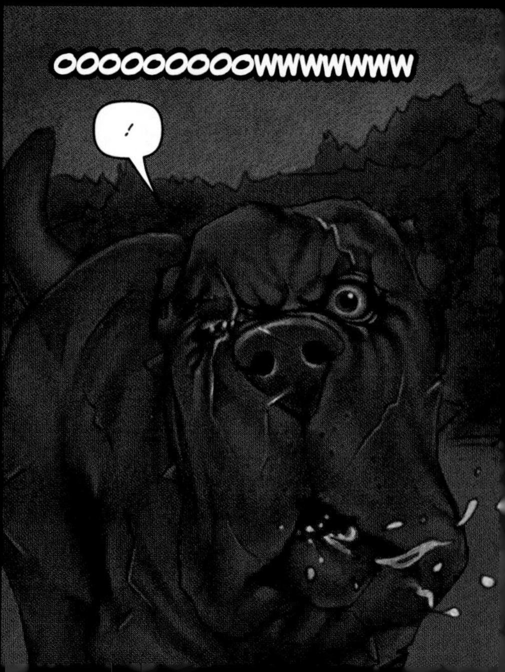
OOOOOOOOOWWWWWWW
!

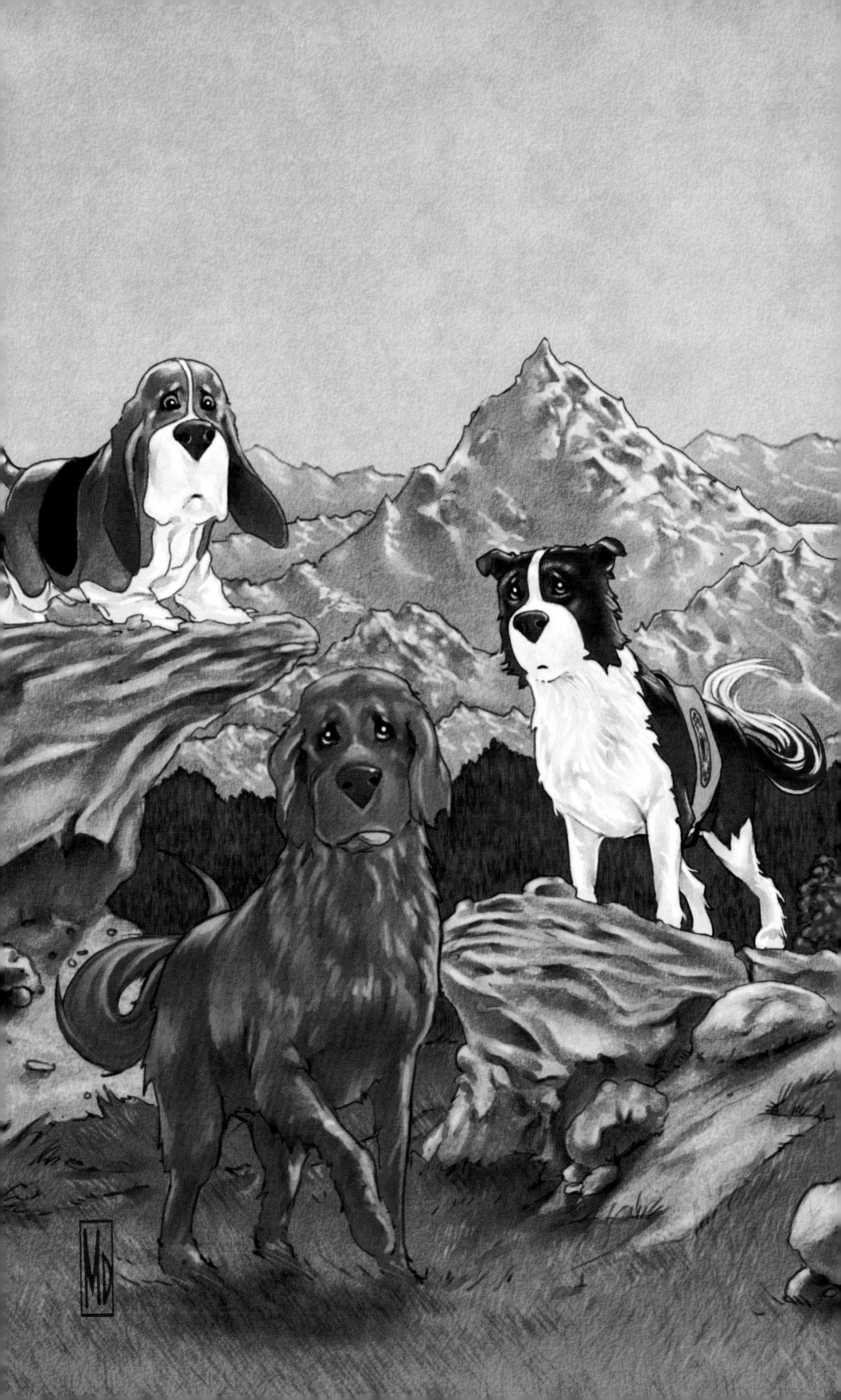

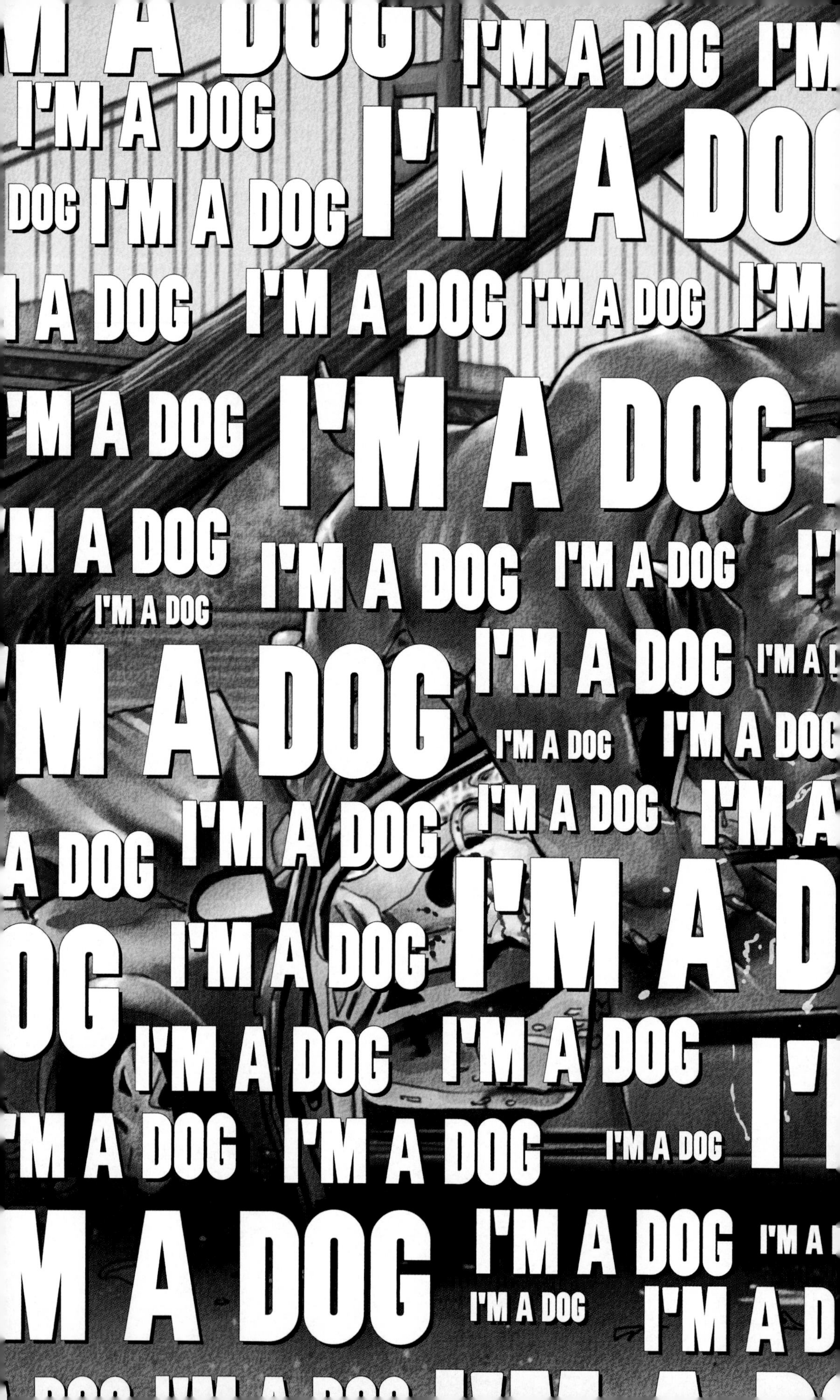

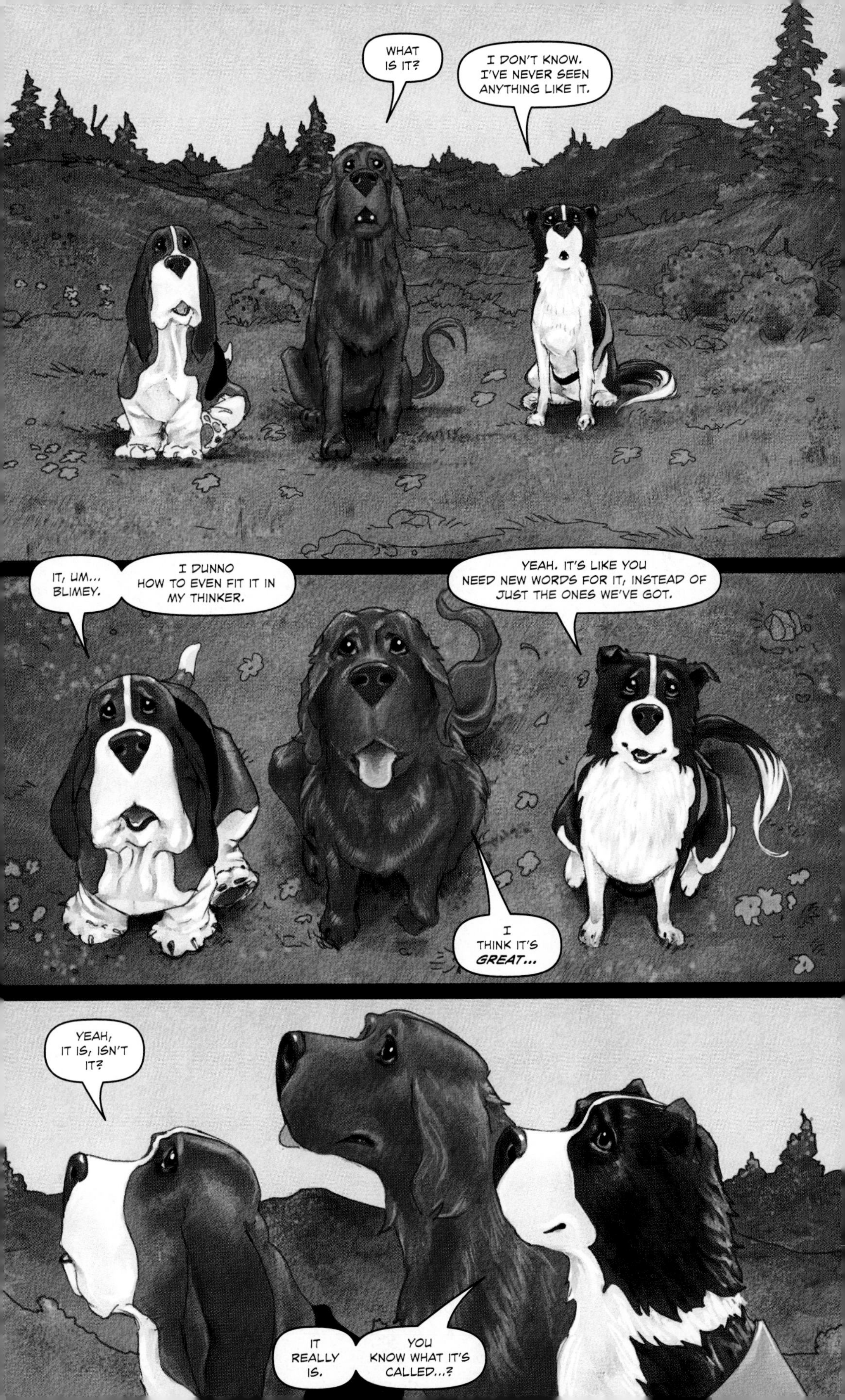
WHAT IS IT?
I DON'T KNOW. I'VE NEVER SEEN ANYTHING LIKE IT.
IT, UM... BLIMEY.
I DUNNO HOW TO EVEN FIT IT IN MY THINKER.
YEAH. IT'S LIKE YOU NEED NEW WORDS FOR IT, INSTEAD OF JUST THE ONES WE'VE GOT.
I THINK IT'S *GREAT...*
YEAH, IT IS, ISN'T IT?
IT REALLY IS.
YOU KNOW WHAT IT'S CALLED...?

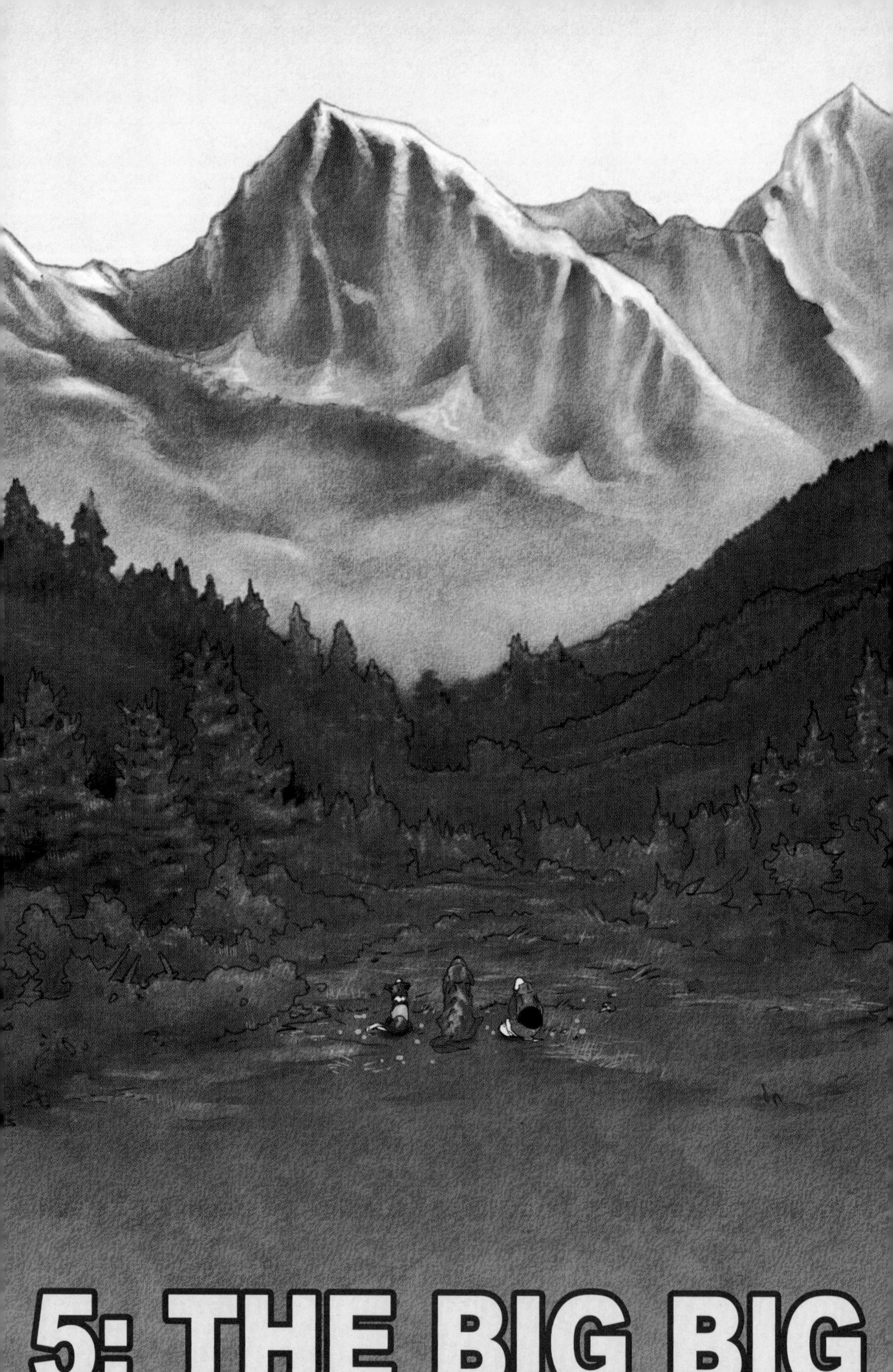

5: THE BIG BIG

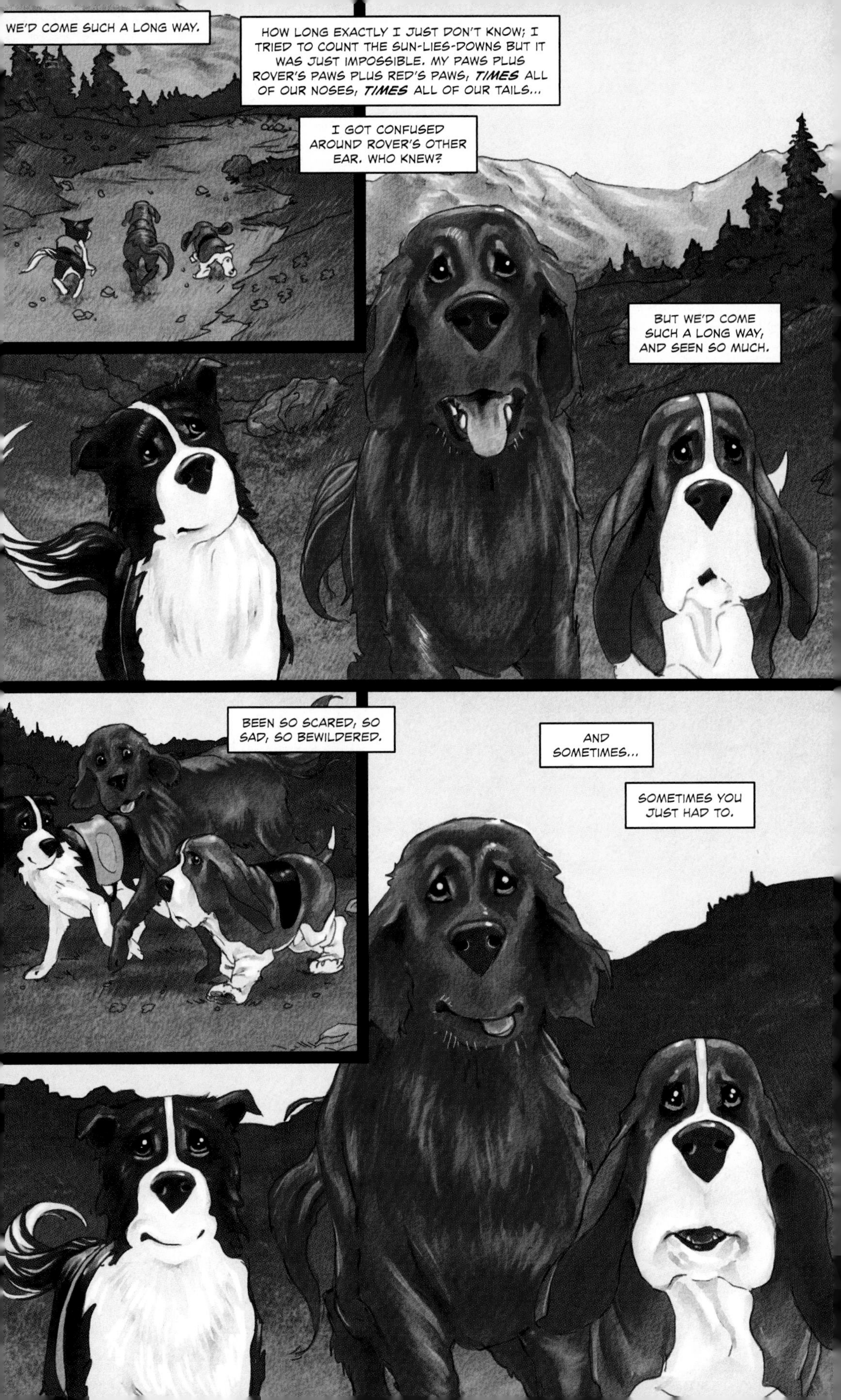
WE'D COME SUCH A LONG WAY.
HOW LONG EXACTLY I JUST DON'T KNOW; I TRIED TO COUNT THE SUN-LIES-DOWNS BUT IT WAS JUST IMPOSSIBLE. MY PAWS PLUS ROVER'S PAWS PLUS RED'S PAWS, ***TIMES*** ALL OF OUR NOSES, ***TIMES*** ALL OF OUR TAILS...
I GOT CONFUSED AROUND ROVER'S OTHER EAR. WHO KNEW?
BUT WE'D COME SUCH A LONG WAY, AND SEEN SO MUCH.
BEEN SO SCARED, SO SAD, SO BEWILDERED.
AND SOMETIMES...
SOMETIMES YOU JUST HAD TO.

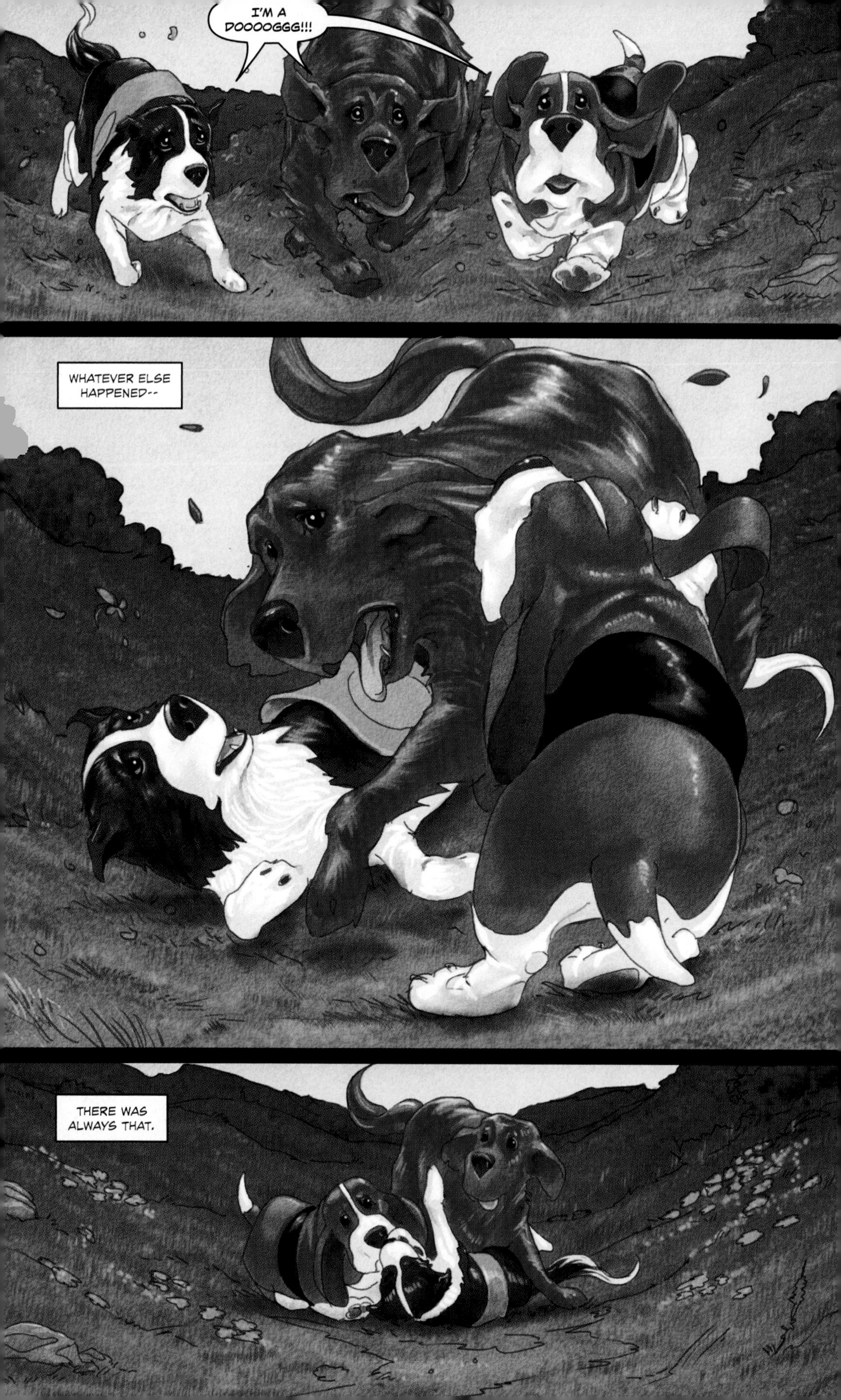
I'M A DOOOOGGG!!!
WHATEVER ELSE HAPPENED--
THERE WAS ALWAYS THAT.

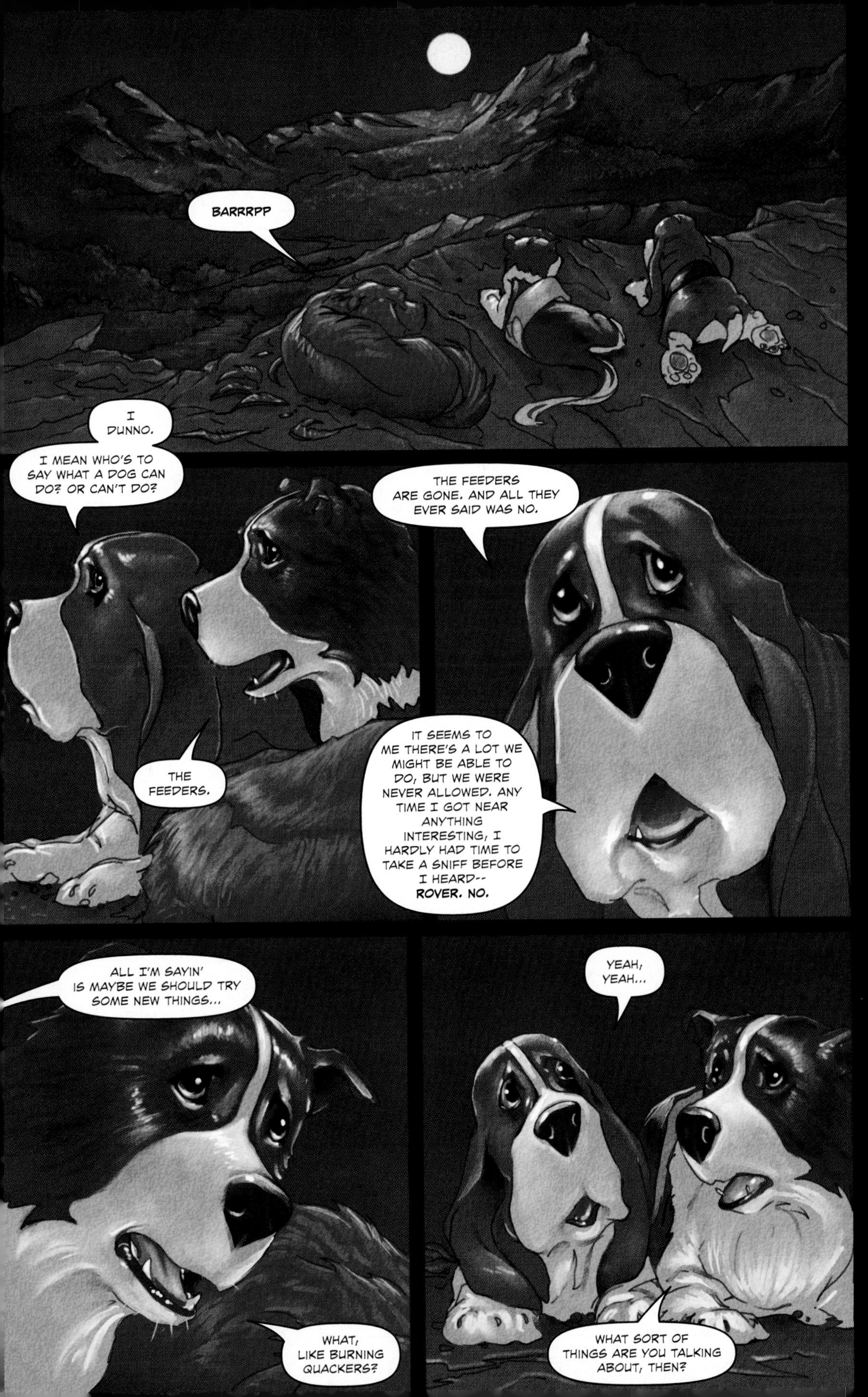
BARRRPP
I DUNNO.
I MEAN WHO'S TO SAY WHAT A DOG CAN DO? OR CAN'T DO?
THE FEEDERS.
THE FEEDERS ARE GONE. AND ALL THEY EVER SAID WAS NO.
IT SEEMS TO ME THERE'S A LOT WE MIGHT BE ABLE TO DO, BUT WE WERE NEVER ALLOWED. ANY TIME I GOT NEAR ANYTHING INTERESTING, I HARDLY HAD TIME TO TAKE A SNIFF BEFORE I HEARD-- **ROVER. NO.**
ALL I'M SAYIN' IS MAYBE WE SHOULD TRY SOME NEW THINGS...
WHAT, LIKE BURNING QUACKERS?
YEAH, YEAH...
WHAT SORT OF THINGS ARE YOU TALKING ABOUT, THEN?

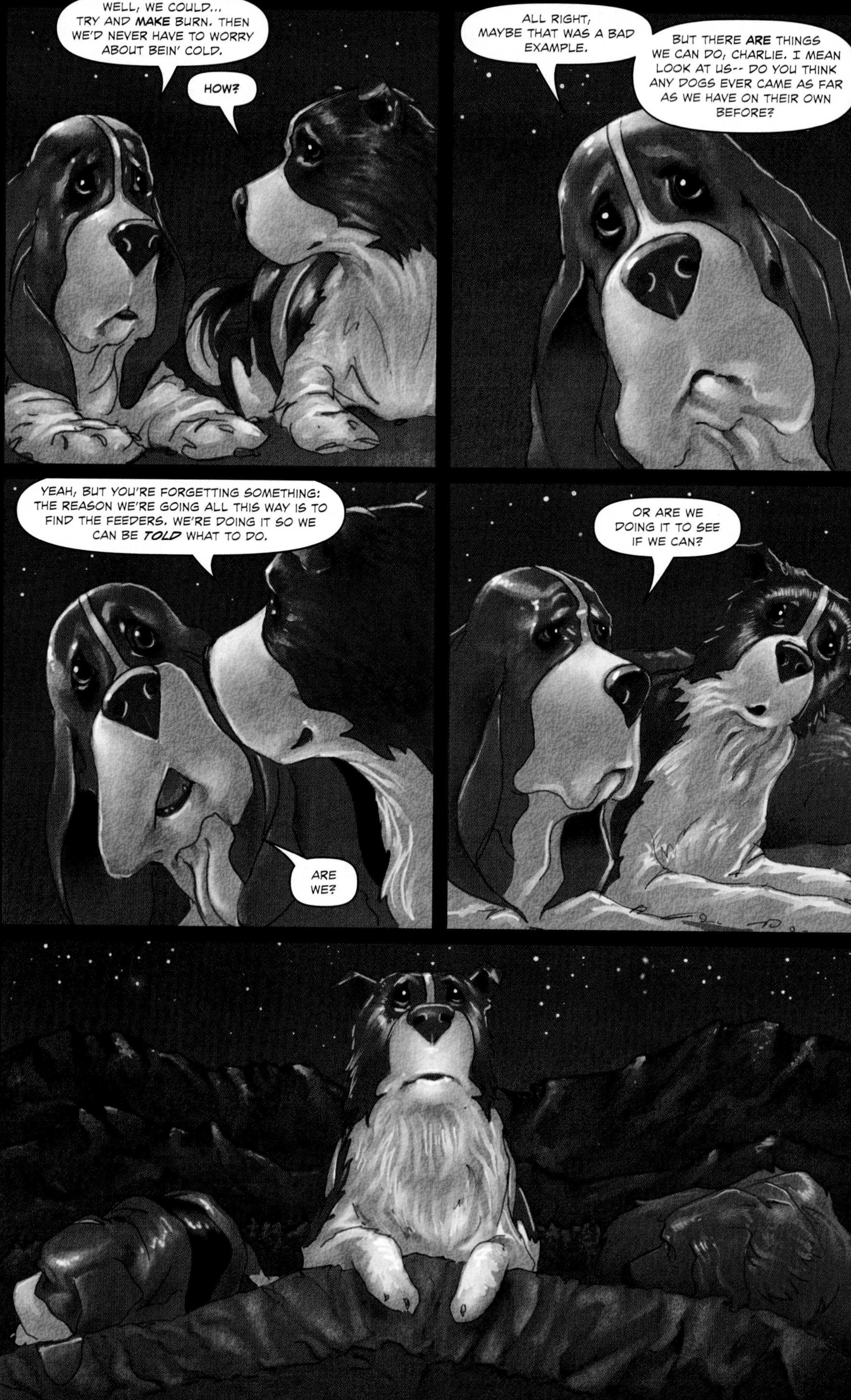

WELL, WE COULD... TRY AND **MAKE** BURN. THEN WE'D NEVER HAVE TO WORRY ABOUT BEIN' COLD.
HOW?
ALL RIGHT, MAYBE THAT WAS A BAD EXAMPLE.
BUT THERE **ARE** THINGS WE CAN DO, CHARLIE. I MEAN LOOK AT US-- DO YOU THINK ANY DOGS EVER CAME AS FAR AS WE HAVE ON THEIR OWN BEFORE?
YEAH, BUT YOU'RE FORGETTING SOMETHING: THE REASON WE'RE GOING ALL THIS WAY IS TO FIND THE FEEDERS. WE'RE DOING IT SO WE CAN BE ***TOLD*** WHAT TO DO.
ARE WE?
OR ARE WE DOING IT TO SEE IF WE CAN?

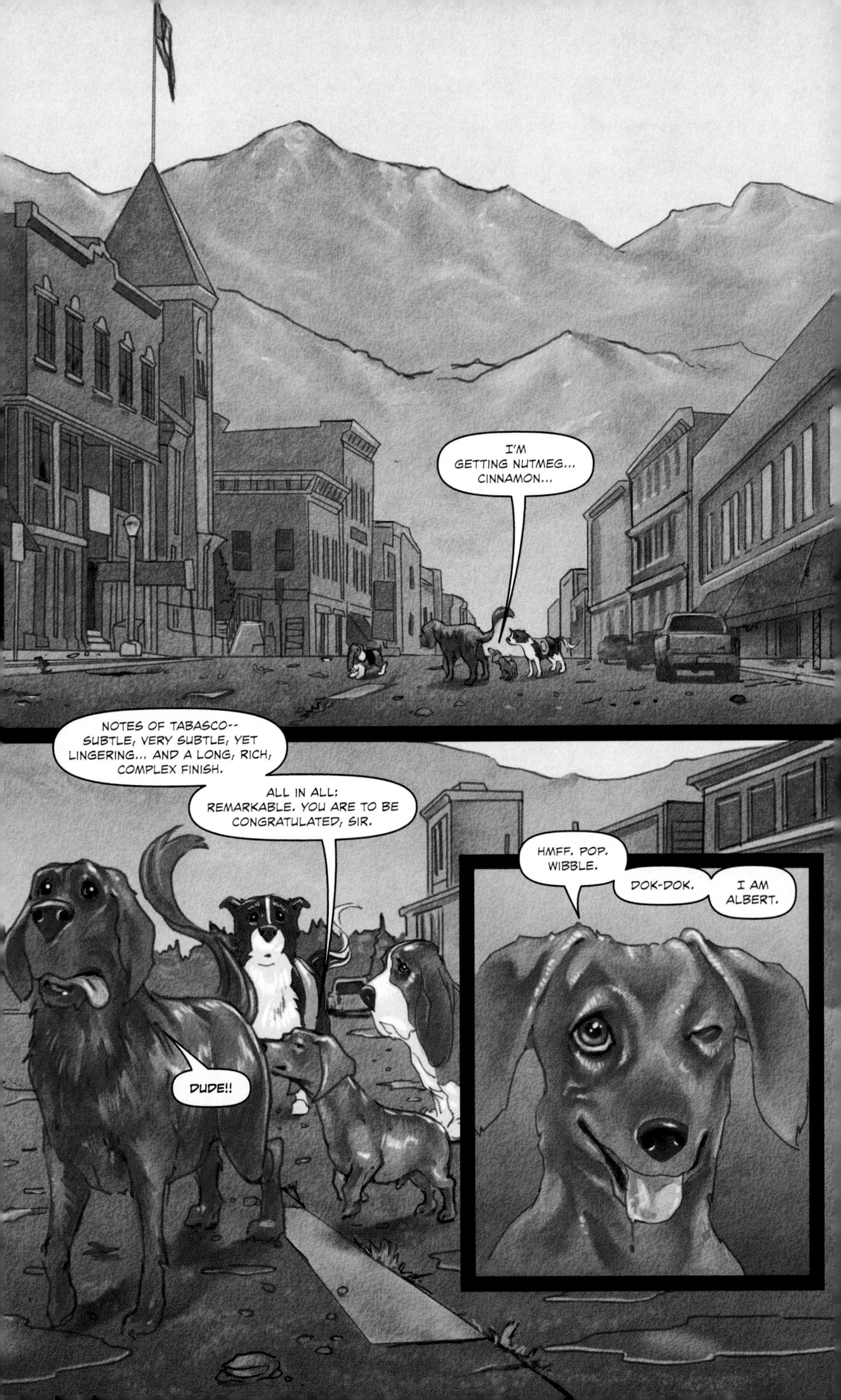
I'M GETTING NUTMEG... CINNAMON...
NOTES OF TABASCO-- SUBTLE, VERY SUBTLE, YET LINGERING... AND A LONG, RICH, COMPLEX FINISH.
ALL IN ALL: REMARKABLE. YOU ARE TO BE CONGRATULATED, SIR.
DUDE!!
HMFF. POP. WIBBLE.
DOK-DOK.
I AM ALBERT.

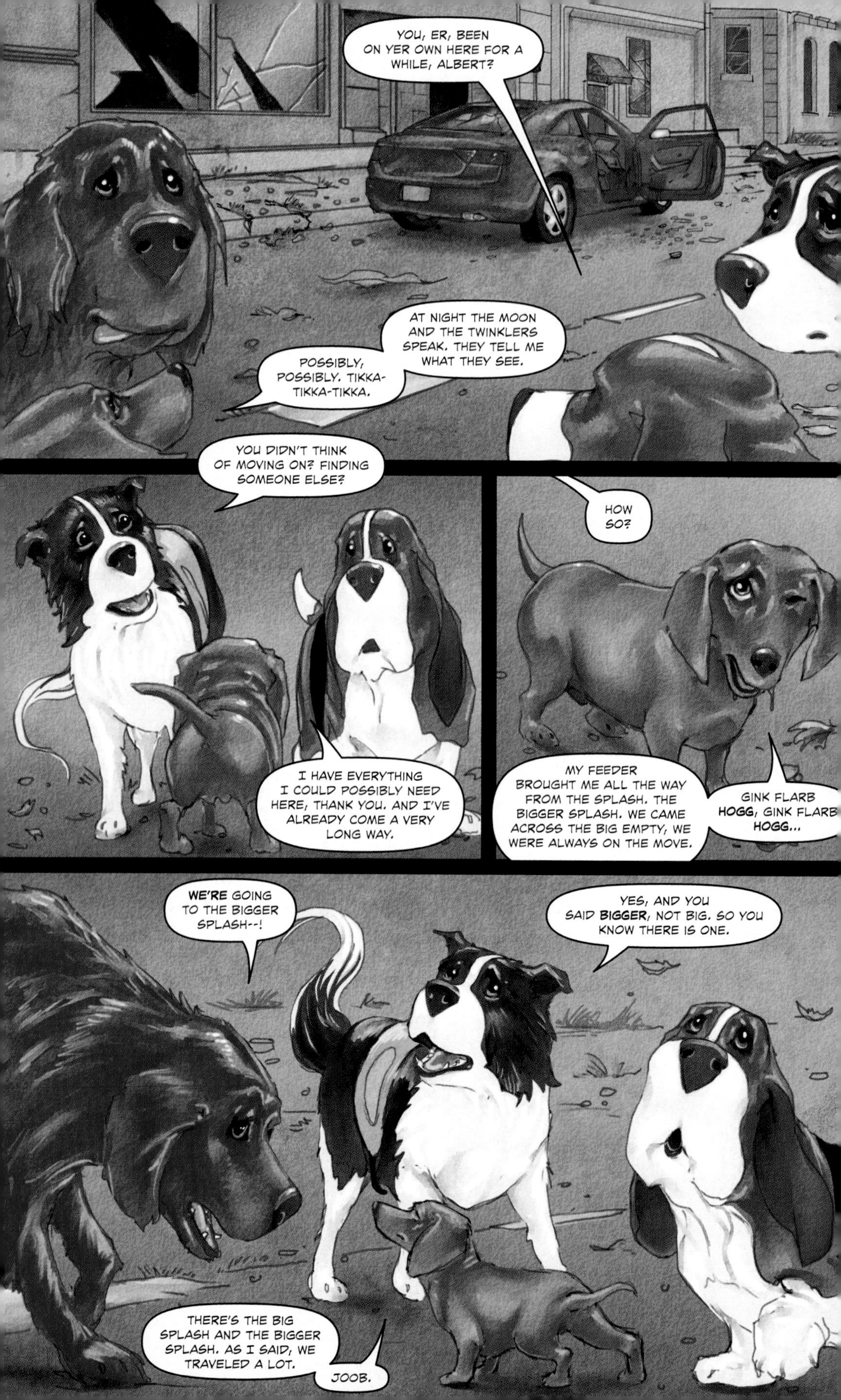

YOU, ER, BEEN ON YER OWN HERE FOR A WHILE, ALBERT?
POSSIBLY, POSSIBLY. TIKKA-TIKKA-TIKKA.
AT NIGHT THE MOON AND THE TWINKLERS SPEAK. THEY TELL ME WHAT THEY SEE.
YOU DIDN'T THINK OF MOVING ON? FINDING SOMEONE ELSE?
I HAVE EVERYTHING I COULD POSSIBLY NEED HERE, THANK YOU. AND I'VE ALREADY COME A VERY LONG WAY.
HOW SO?
MY FEEDER BROUGHT ME ALL THE WAY FROM THE SPLASH. THE BIGGER SPLASH. WE CAME ACROSS THE BIG EMPTY, WE WERE ALWAYS ON THE MOVE.
GINK FLARB **HOGG**, GINK FLARB **HOGG**...
WE'RE GOING TO THE BIGGER SPLASH--!
YES, AND YOU SAID **BIGGER**, NOT BIG. SO YOU KNOW THERE IS ONE.
THERE'S THE BIG SPLASH AND THE BIGGER SPLASH. AS I SAID, WE TRAVELED A LOT.
JOOB.

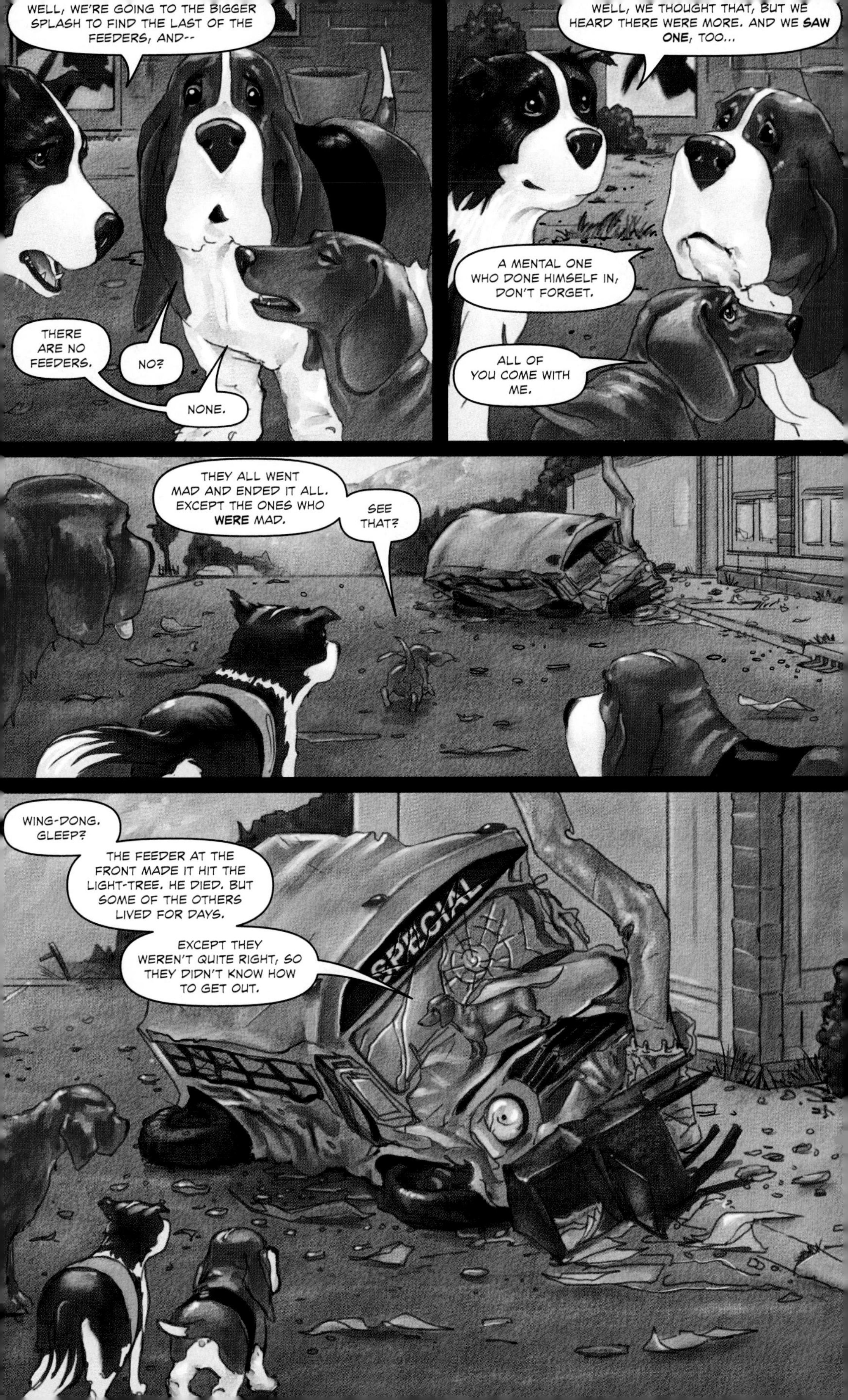
WELL, WE'RE GOING TO THE BIGGER SPLASH TO FIND THE LAST OF THE FEEDERS, AND--
THERE ARE NO FEEDERS.
NO?
NONE.
WELL, WE THOUGHT THAT, BUT WE HEARD THERE WERE MORE. AND WE **SAW ONE**, TOO...
A MENTAL ONE WHO DONE HIMSELF IN, DON'T FORGET.
ALL OF YOU COME WITH ME.
THEY ALL WENT MAD AND ENDED IT ALL. EXCEPT THE ONES WHO **WERE** MAD.
SEE THAT?
WING-DONG. GLEEP?
THE FEEDER AT THE FRONT MADE IT HIT THE LIGHT-TREE. HE DIED. BUT SOME OF THE OTHERS LIVED FOR DAYS.
EXCEPT THEY WEREN'T QUITE RIGHT, SO THEY DIDN'T KNOW HOW TO GET OUT.
SPECIAL

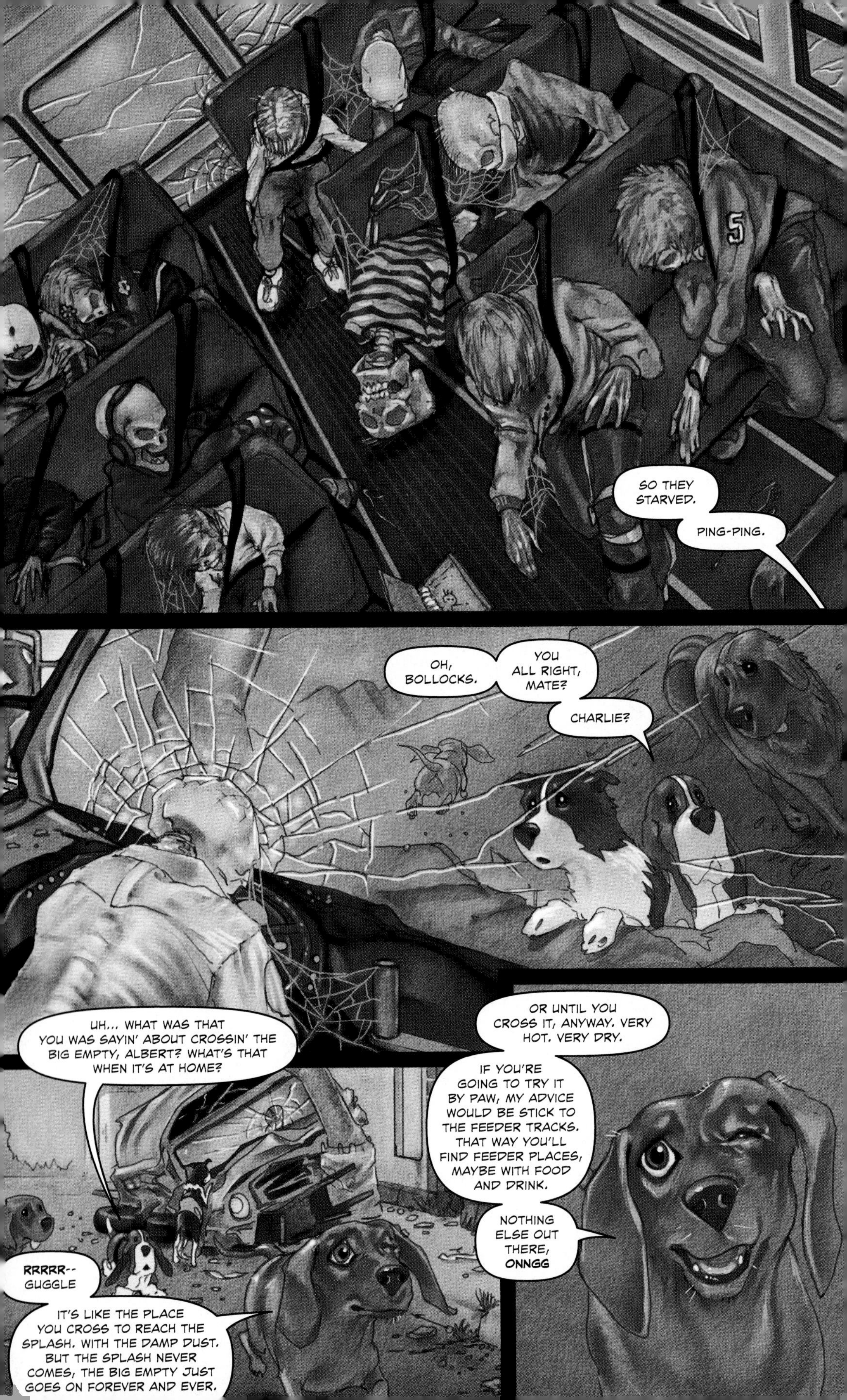
SO THEY STARVED.
PING-PING.
OH, BOLLOCKS.
YOU ALL RIGHT, MATE?
CHARLIE?
UH... WHAT WAS THAT YOU WAS SAYIN' ABOUT CROSSIN' THE BIG EMPTY, ALBERT? WHAT'S THAT WHEN IT'S AT HOME?
RRRRR--GUGGLE
IT'S LIKE THE PLACE YOU CROSS TO REACH THE SPLASH. WITH THE DAMP DUST. BUT THE SPLASH NEVER COMES; THE BIG EMPTY JUST GOES ON FOREVER AND EVER.
OR UNTIL YOU CROSS IT, ANYWAY. VERY HOT. VERY DRY.
IF YOU'RE GOING TO TRY IT BY PAW, MY ADVICE WOULD BE STICK TO THE FEEDER TRACKS. THAT WAY YOU'LL FIND FEEDER PLACES, MAYBE WITH FOOD AND DRINK.
NOTHING ELSE OUT THERE, **ONNGG**

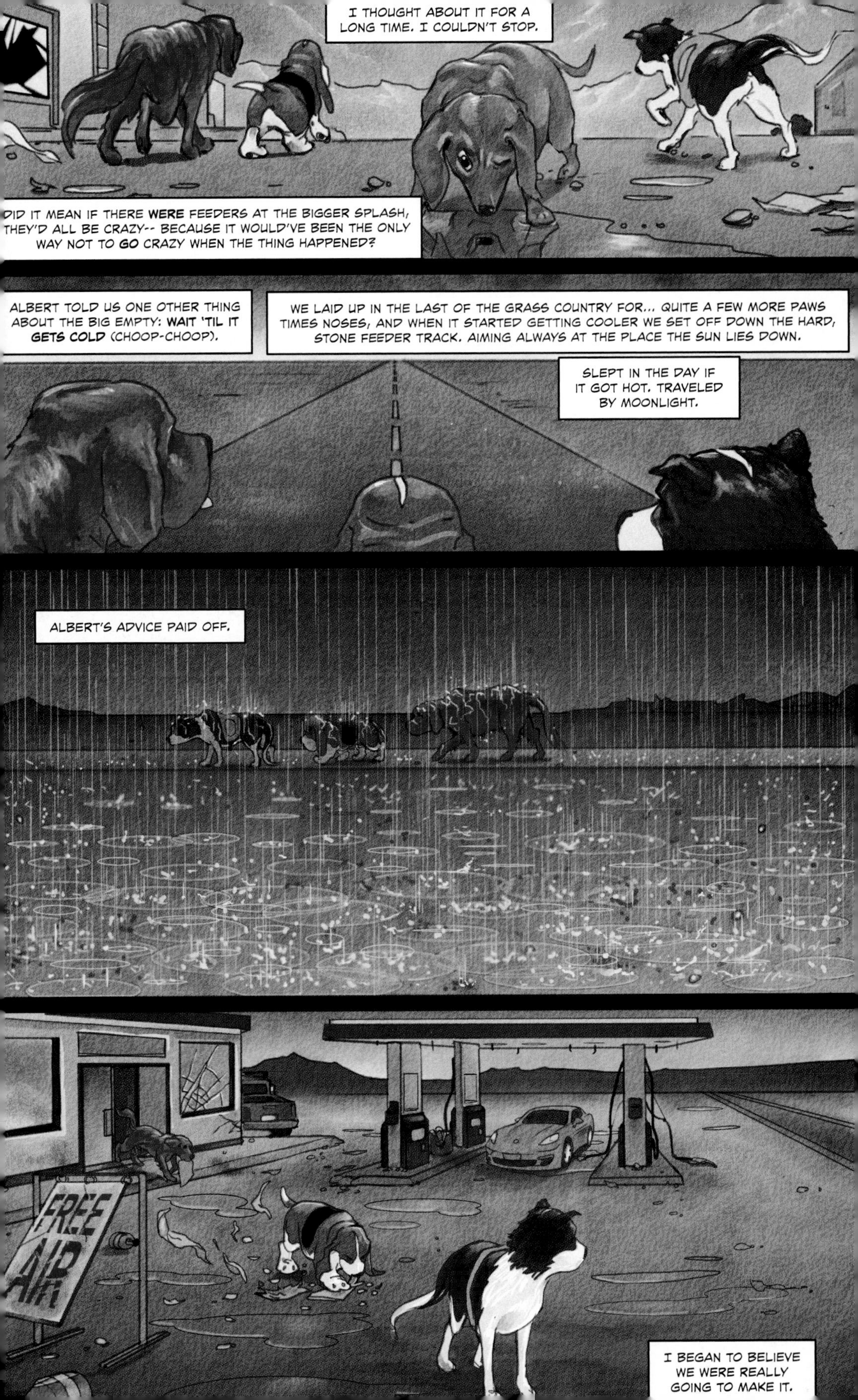
I THOUGHT ABOUT IT FOR A LONG TIME. I COULDN'T STOP.
DID IT MEAN IF THERE **WERE** FEEDERS AT THE BIGGER SPLASH, THEY'D ALL BE CRAZY-- BECAUSE IT WOULD'VE BEEN THE ONLY WAY NOT TO **GO** CRAZY WHEN THE THING HAPPENED?
ALBERT TOLD US ONE OTHER THING ABOUT THE BIG EMPTY: **WAIT 'TIL IT GETS COLD** (CHOOP-CHOOP).
WE LAID UP IN THE LAST OF THE GRASS COUNTRY FOR... QUITE A FEW MORE PAWS TIMES NOSES, AND WHEN IT STARTED GETTING COOLER WE SET OFF DOWN THE HARD, STONE FEEDER TRACK. AIMING ALWAYS AT THE PLACE THE SUN LIES DOWN.
SLEPT IN THE DAY IF IT GOT HOT. TRAVELED BY MOONLIGHT.
ALBERT'S ADVICE PAID OFF.
FREE AIR
I BEGAN TO BELIEVE WE WERE REALLY GOING TO MAKE IT.

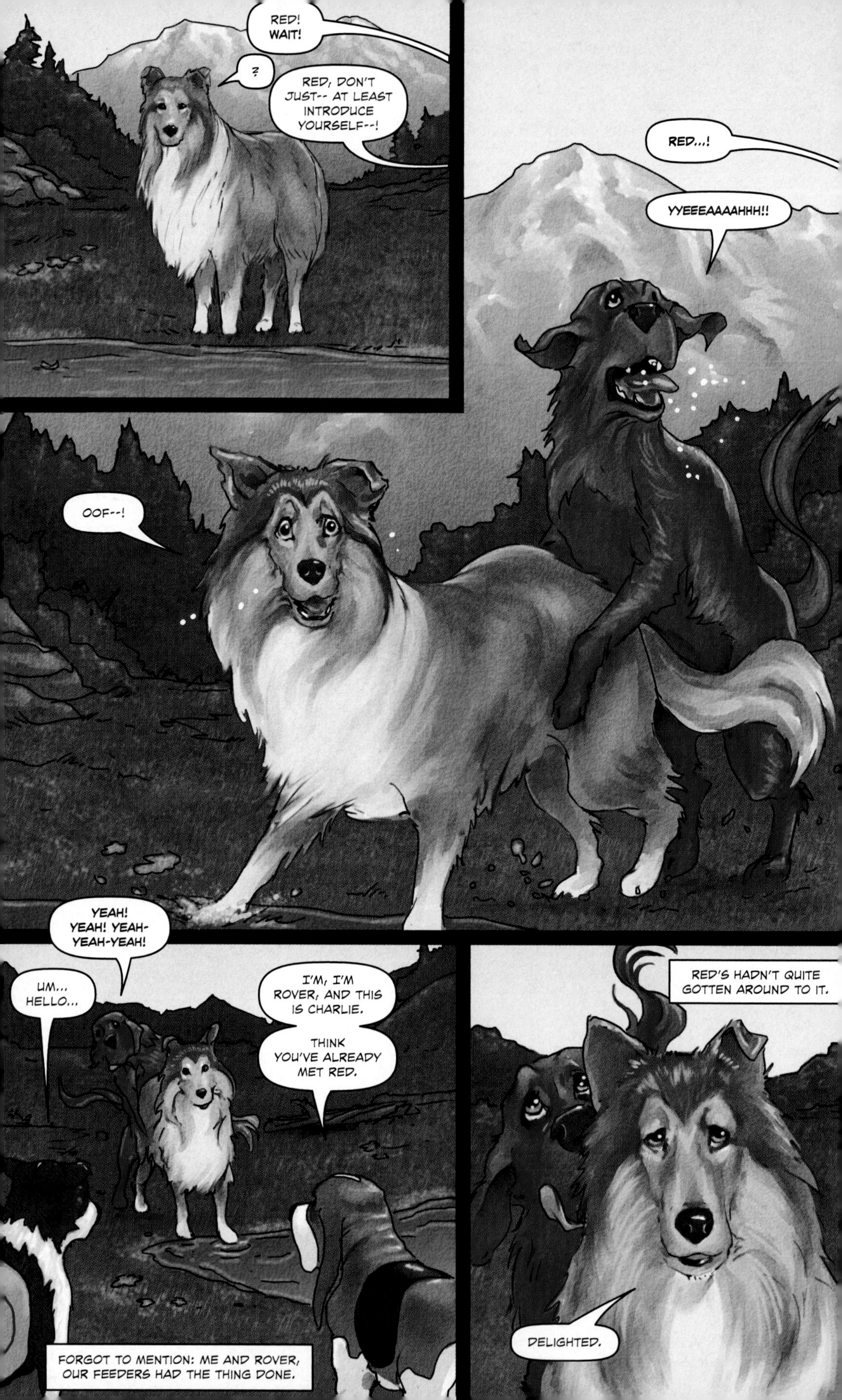
RED! WAIT!
?
RED, DON'T JUST-- AT LEAST INTRODUCE YOURSELF--!
RED...!
YYEEEAAAAHHH!!
OOF--!
YEAH! YEAH! YEAH-YEAH-YEAH!
UM... HELLO...
I'M, I'M ROVER, AND THIS IS CHARLIE.
THINK YOU'VE ALREADY MET RED.
FORGOT TO MENTION: ME AND ROVER, OUR FEEDERS HAD THE THING DONE.
RED'S HADN'T QUITE GOTTEN AROUND TO IT.
DELIGHTED.

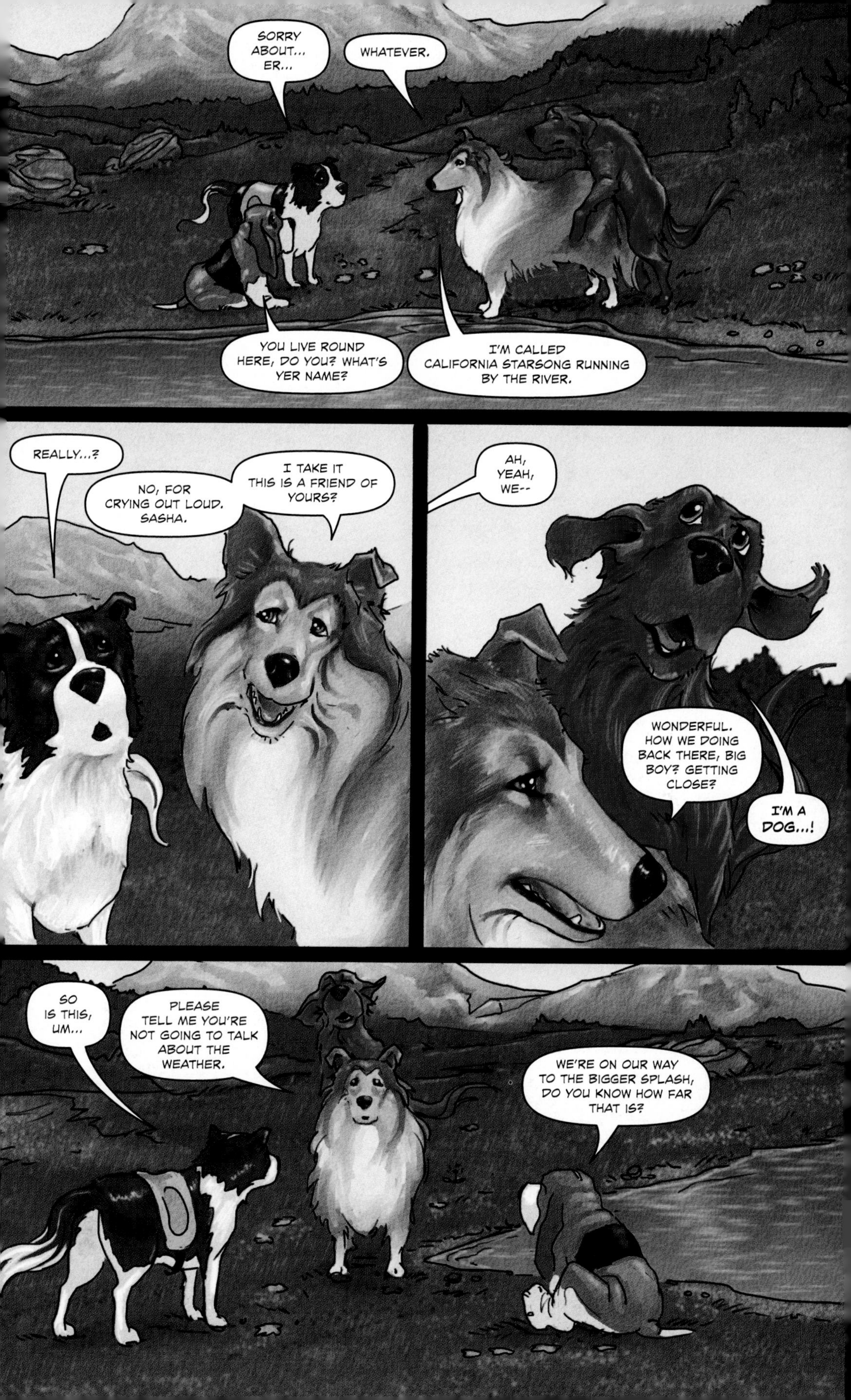
SORRY ABOUT... ER...
WHATEVER.
YOU LIVE ROUND HERE, DO YOU? WHAT'S YER NAME?
I'M CALLED CALIFORNIA STARSONG RUNNING BY THE RIVER.
REALLY...?
NO, FOR CRYING OUT LOUD. SASHA.
I TAKE IT THIS IS A FRIEND OF YOURS?
AH, YEAH, WE--
WONDERFUL. HOW WE DOING BACK THERE, BIG BOY? GETTING CLOSE?
I'M A DOG...!
SO IS THIS, UM...
PLEASE TELL ME YOU'RE NOT GOING TO TALK ABOUT THE WEATHER.
WE'RE ON OUR WAY TO THE BIGGER SPLASH, DO YOU KNOW HOW FAR THAT IS?

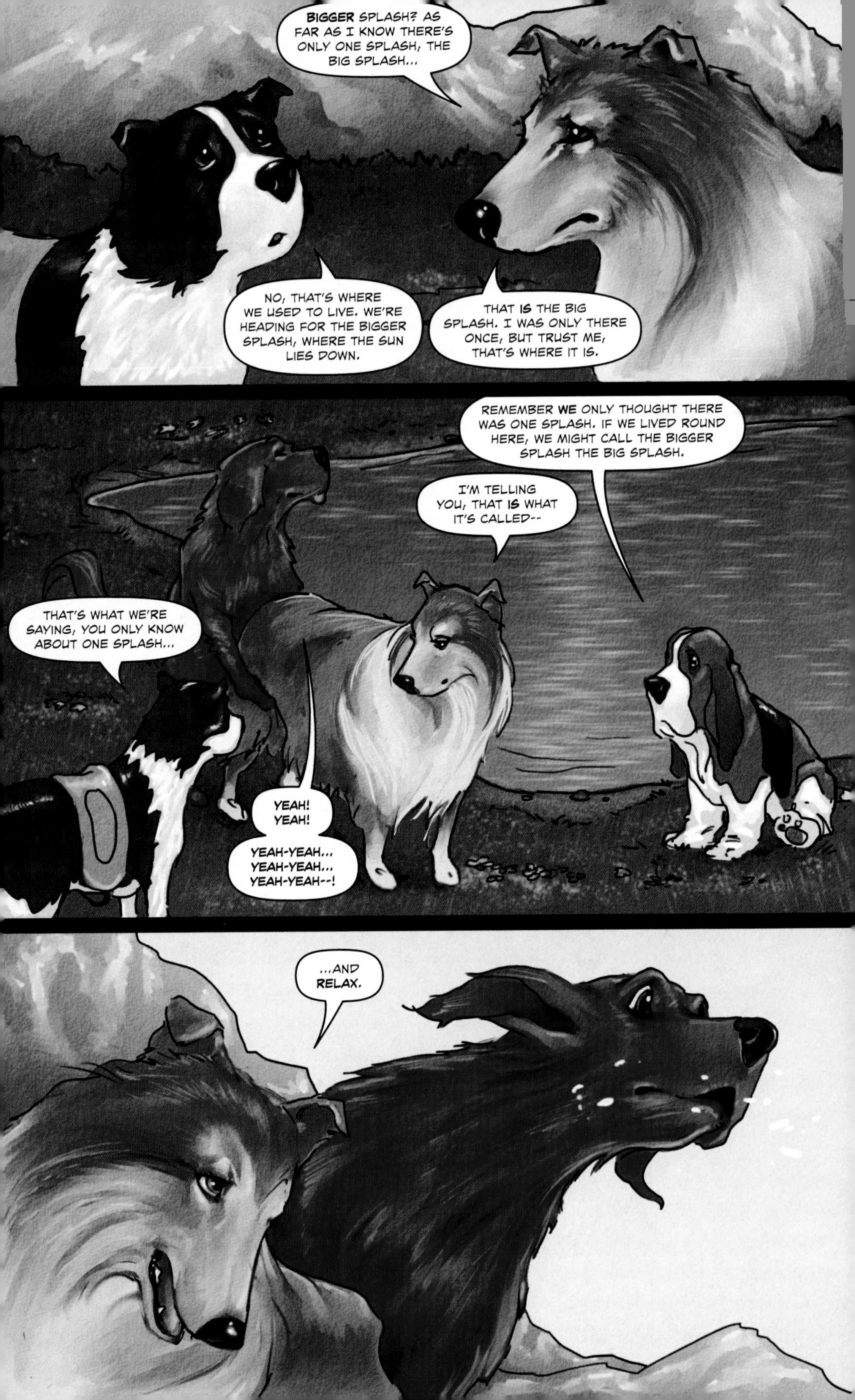
BIGGER SPLASH? AS FAR AS I KNOW THERE'S ONLY ONE SPLASH, THE BIG SPLASH...
NO, THAT'S WHERE WE USED TO LIVE. WE'RE HEADING FOR THE BIGGER SPLASH, WHERE THE SUN LIES DOWN.
THAT IS THE BIG SPLASH. I WAS ONLY THERE ONCE, BUT TRUST ME, THAT'S WHERE IT IS.
REMEMBER WE ONLY THOUGHT THERE WAS ONE SPLASH. IF WE LIVED ROUND HERE, WE MIGHT CALL THE BIGGER SPLASH THE BIG SPLASH.
I'M TELLING YOU, THAT IS WHAT IT'S CALLED--
THAT'S WHAT WE'RE SAYING, YOU ONLY KNOW ABOUT ONE SPLASH...
YEAH! YEAH!
YEAH-YEAH... YEAH-YEAH... YEAH-YEAH--!
...AND RELAX.

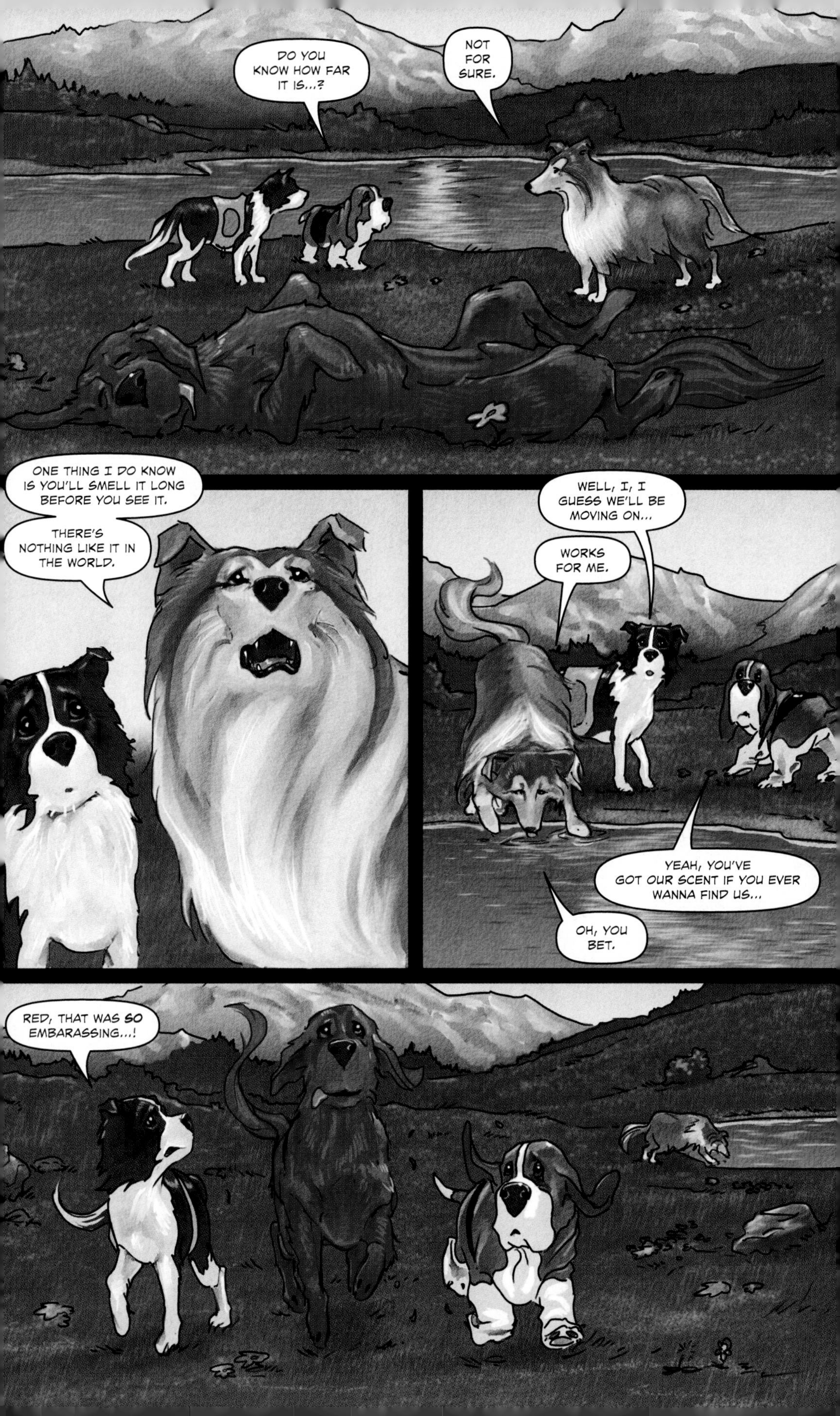
DO YOU KNOW HOW FAR IT IS...?
NOT FOR SURE.
ONE THING I DO KNOW IS YOU'LL SMELL IT LONG BEFORE YOU SEE IT.
THERE'S NOTHING LIKE IT IN THE WORLD.
WELL, I, I GUESS WE'LL BE MOVING ON...
WORKS FOR ME.
YEAH, YOU'VE GOT OUR SCENT IF YOU EVER WANNA FIND US...
OH, YOU BET.
RED, THAT WAS **SO** EMBARASSING...!

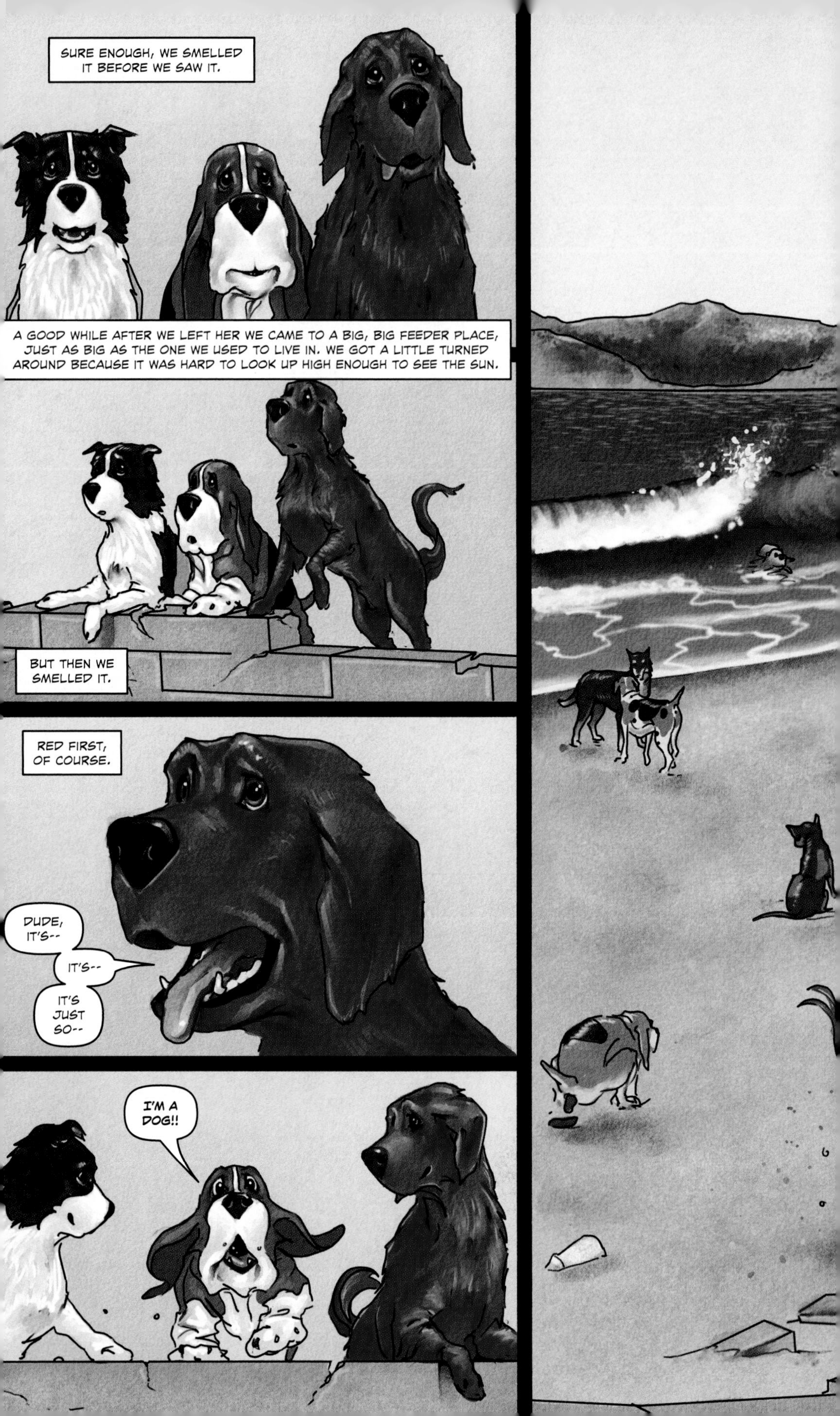
SURE ENOUGH, WE SMELLED IT BEFORE WE SAW IT.
A GOOD WHILE AFTER WE LEFT HER WE CAME TO A BIG, BIG FEEDER PLACE, JUST AS BIG AS THE ONE WE USED TO LIVE IN. WE GOT A LITTLE TURNED AROUND BECAUSE IT WAS HARD TO LOOK UP HIGH ENOUGH TO SEE THE SUN.
BUT THEN WE SMELLED IT.
RED FIRST, OF COURSE.
DUDE, IT'S--
IT'S--
IT'S JUST SO--
I'M A DOG!!

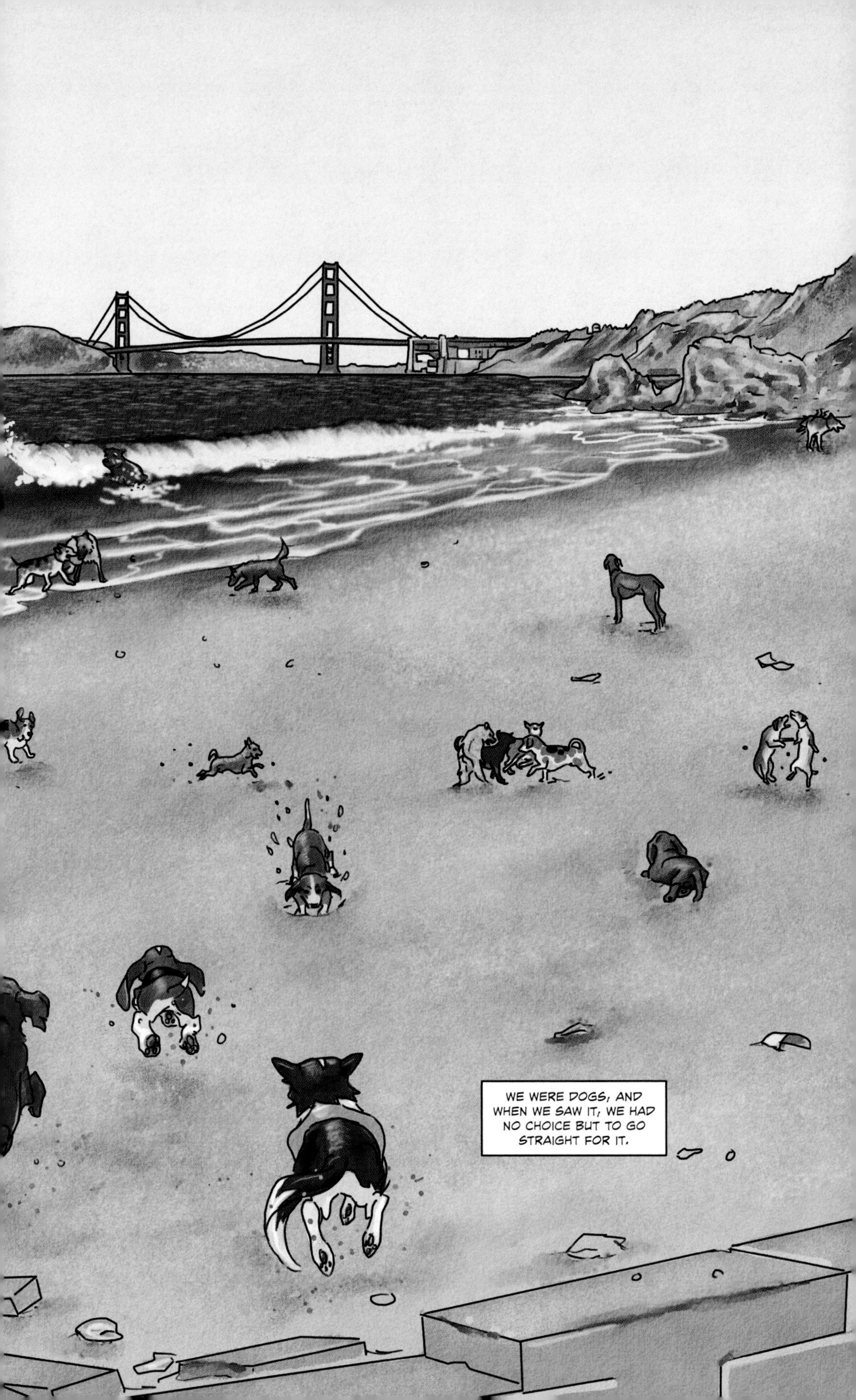
WE WERE DOGS, AND
WHEN WE SAW IT, WE HAD
NO CHOICE BUT TO GO
STRAIGHT FOR IT.

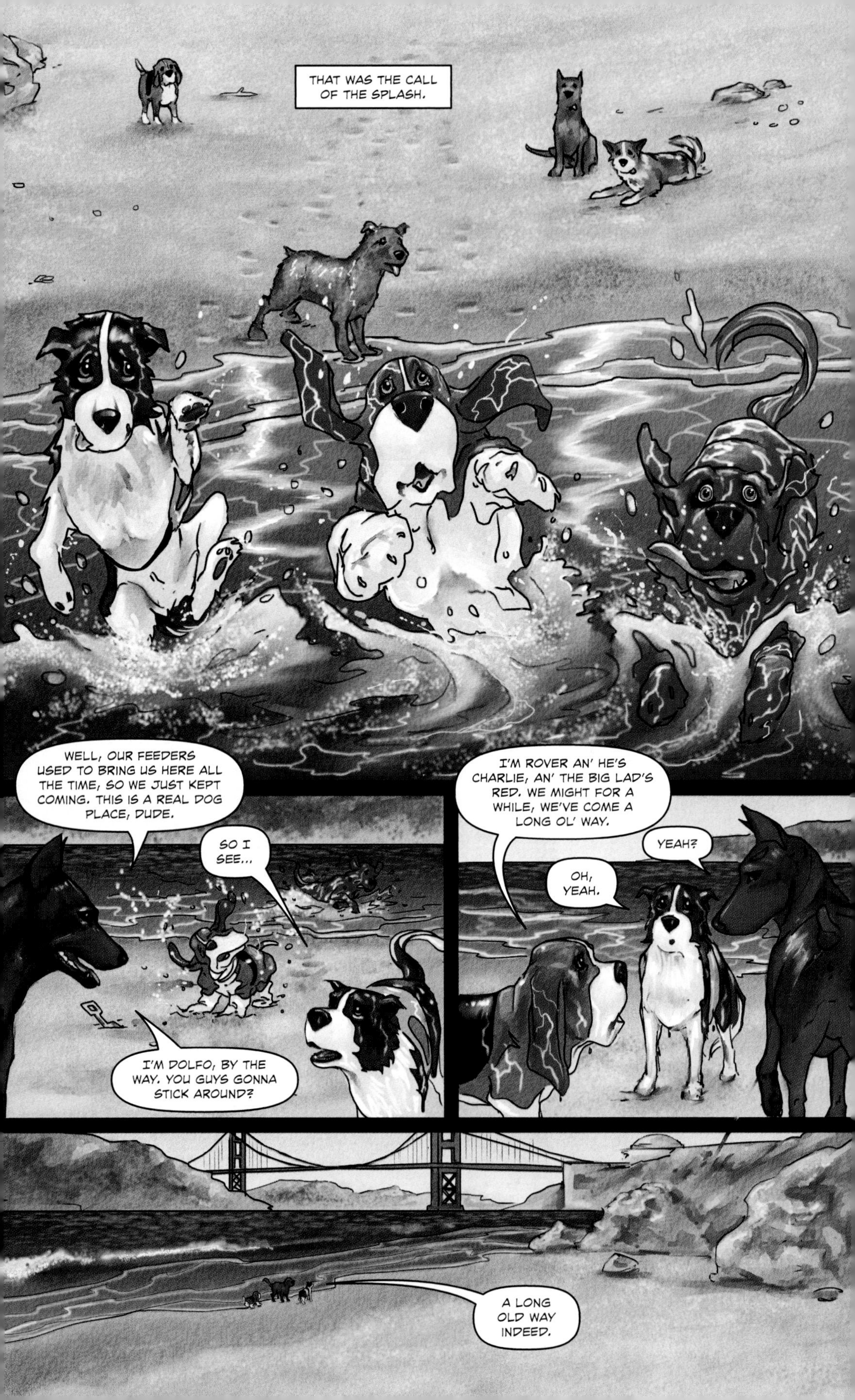
THAT WAS THE CALL OF THE SPLASH.
WELL, OUR FEEDERS USED TO BRING US HERE ALL THE TIME, SO WE JUST KEPT COMING. THIS IS A REAL DOG PLACE, DUDE.
SO I SEE...
I'M DOLFO, BY THE WAY. YOU GUYS GONNA STICK AROUND?
I'M ROVER AN' HE'S CHARLIE, AN' THE BIG LAD'S RED. WE MIGHT FOR A WHILE, WE'VE COME A LONG OL' WAY.
YEAH?
OH, YEAH.
A LONG OLD WAY INDEED.

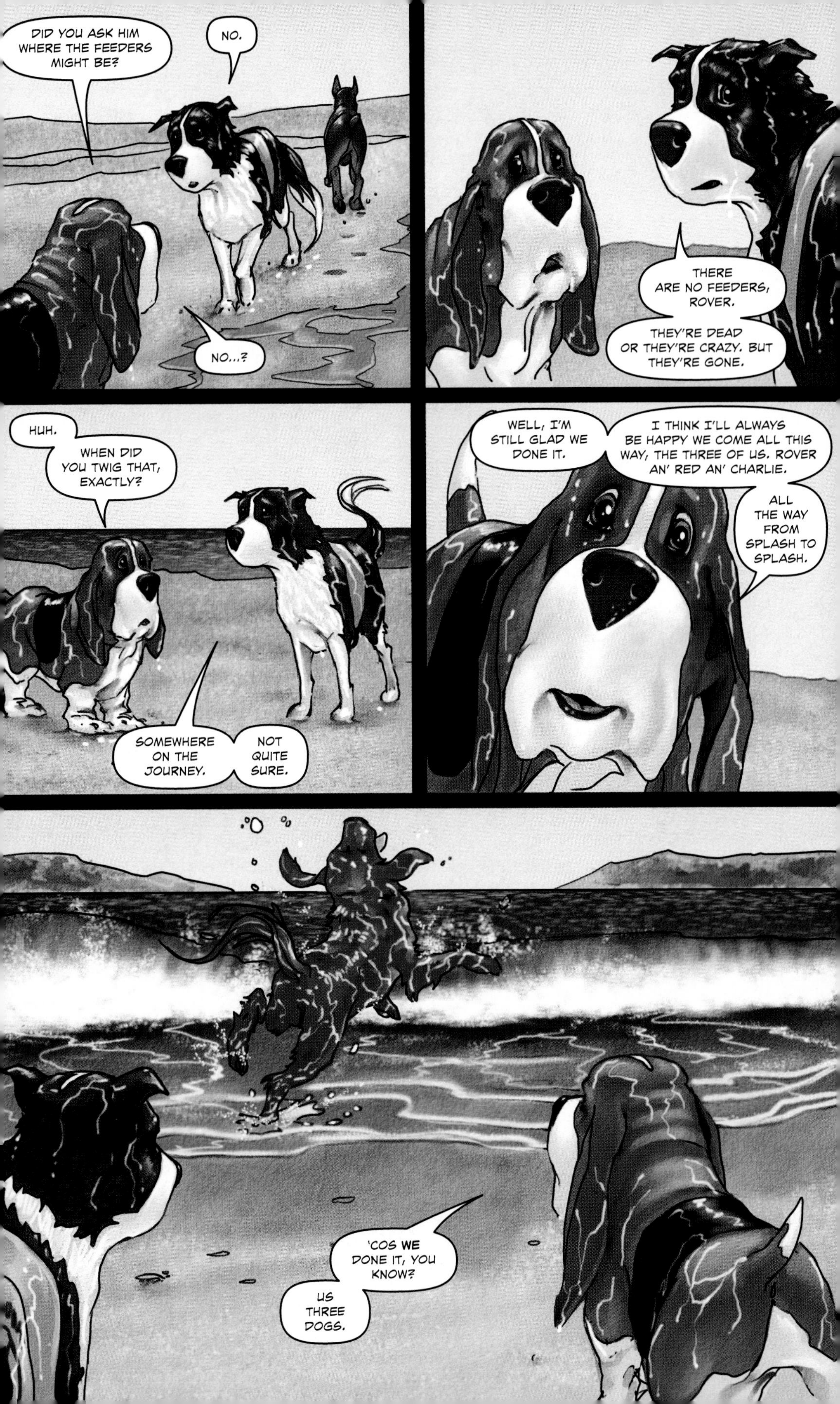
DID YOU ASK HIM WHERE THE FEEDERS MIGHT BE?
NO.
NO...?
THERE ARE NO FEEDERS, ROVER.
THEY'RE DEAD OR THEY'RE CRAZY. BUT THEY'RE GONE.
HUH.
WHEN DID YOU TWIG THAT, EXACTLY?
SOMEWHERE ON THE JOURNEY.
NOT QUITE SURE.
WELL, I'M STILL GLAD WE DONE IT.
I THINK I'LL ALWAYS BE HAPPY WE COME ALL THIS WAY, THE THREE OF US. ROVER AN' RED AN' CHARLIE.
ALL THE WAY FROM SPLASH TO SPLASH.
'COS WE DONE IT, YOU KNOW?
US THREE DOGS.

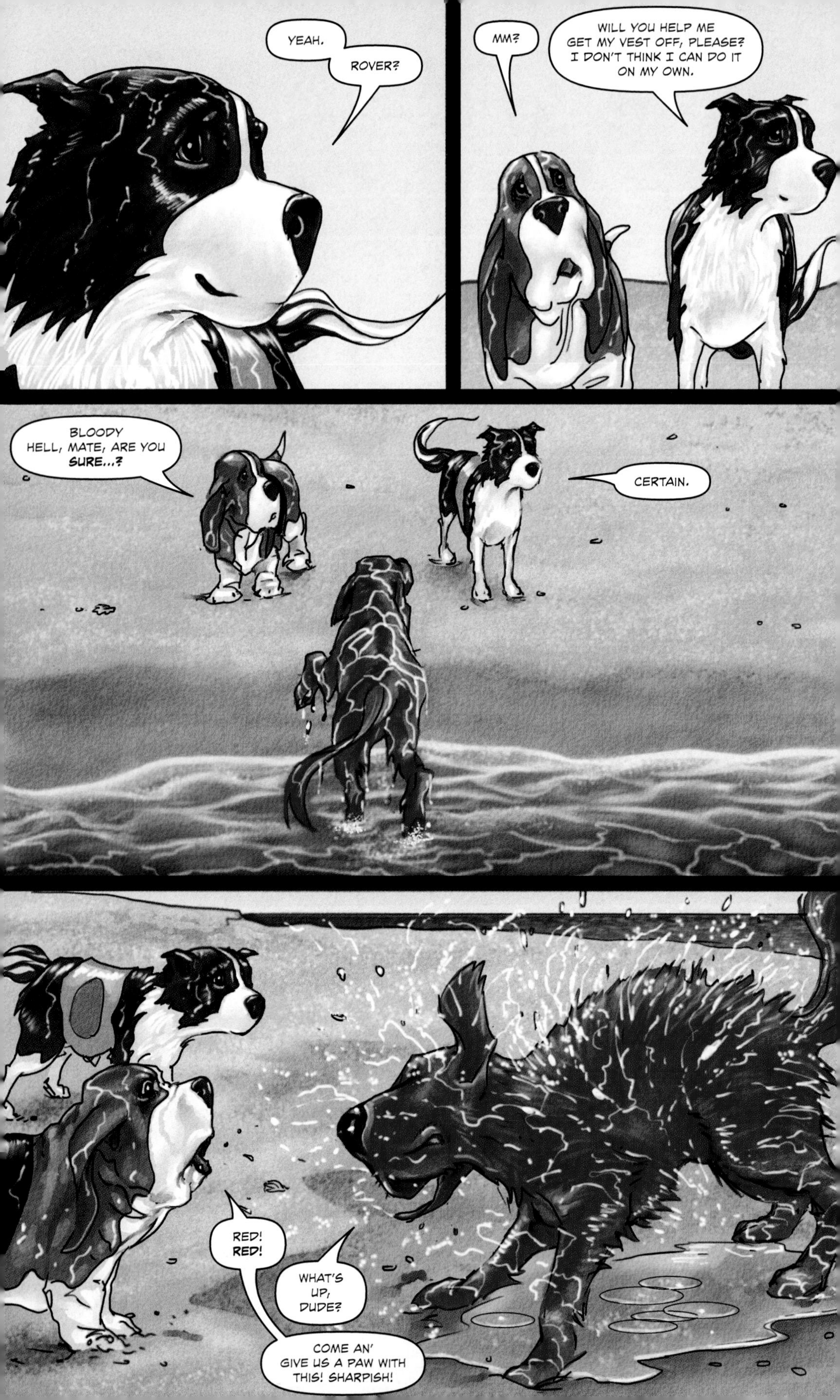
YEAH.
ROVER?
MM?
WILL YOU HELP ME GET MY VEST OFF, PLEASE? I DON'T THINK I CAN DO IT ON MY OWN.
BLOODY HELL, MATE, ARE YOU **SURE...?**
CERTAIN.
RED! **RED!**
WHAT'S UP, DUDE?
COME AN' GIVE US A PAW WITH THIS! SHARPISH!

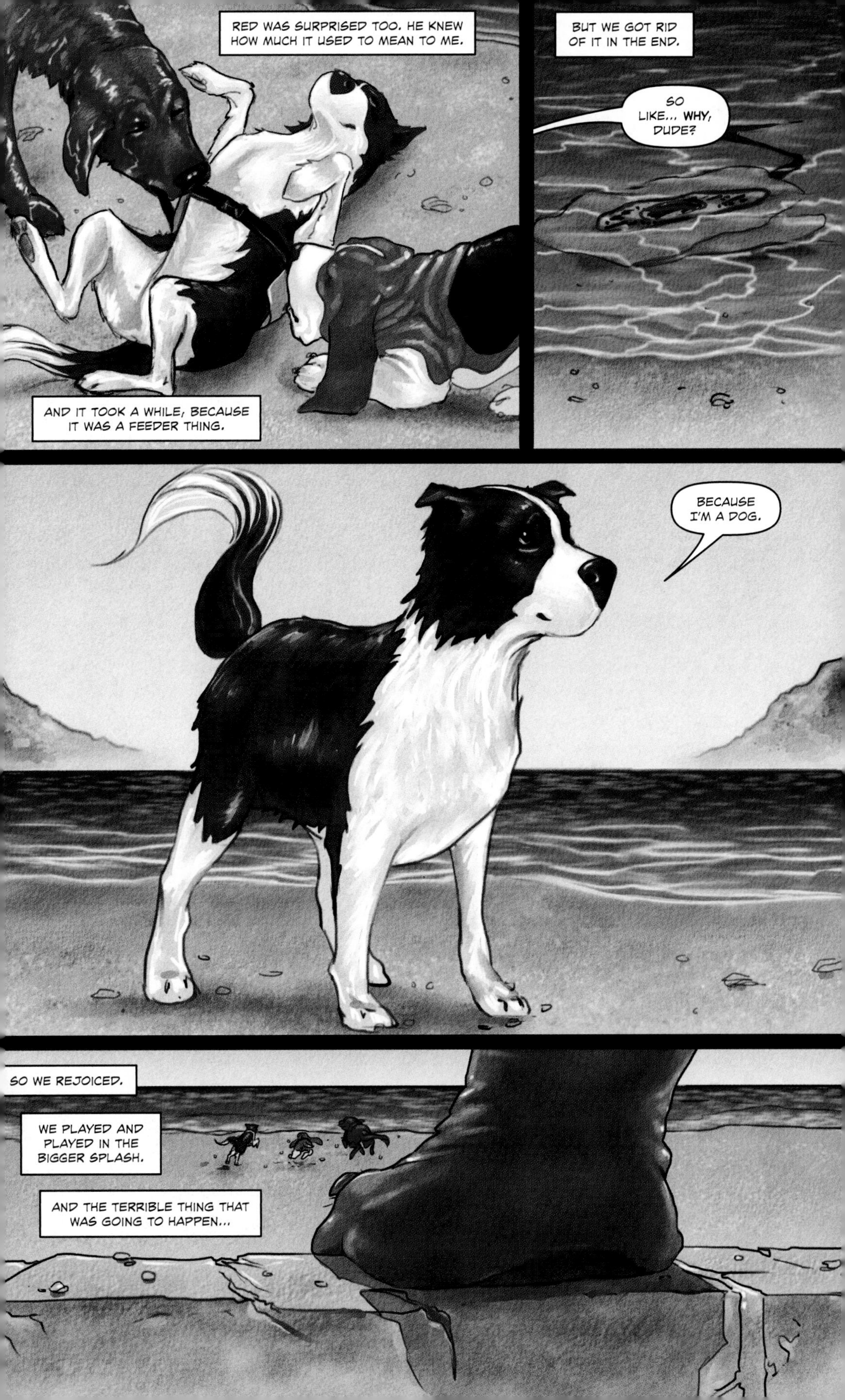
RED WAS SURPRISED TOO. HE KNEW HOW MUCH IT USED TO MEAN TO ME.
AND IT TOOK A WHILE, BECAUSE IT WAS A FEEDER THING.
BUT WE GOT RID OF IT IN THE END.
SO LIKE... WHY, DUDE?
BECAUSE I'M A DOG.
SO WE REJOICED.
WE PLAYED AND PLAYED IN THE BIGGER SPLASH.
AND THE TERRIBLE THING THAT WAS GOING TO HAPPEN...

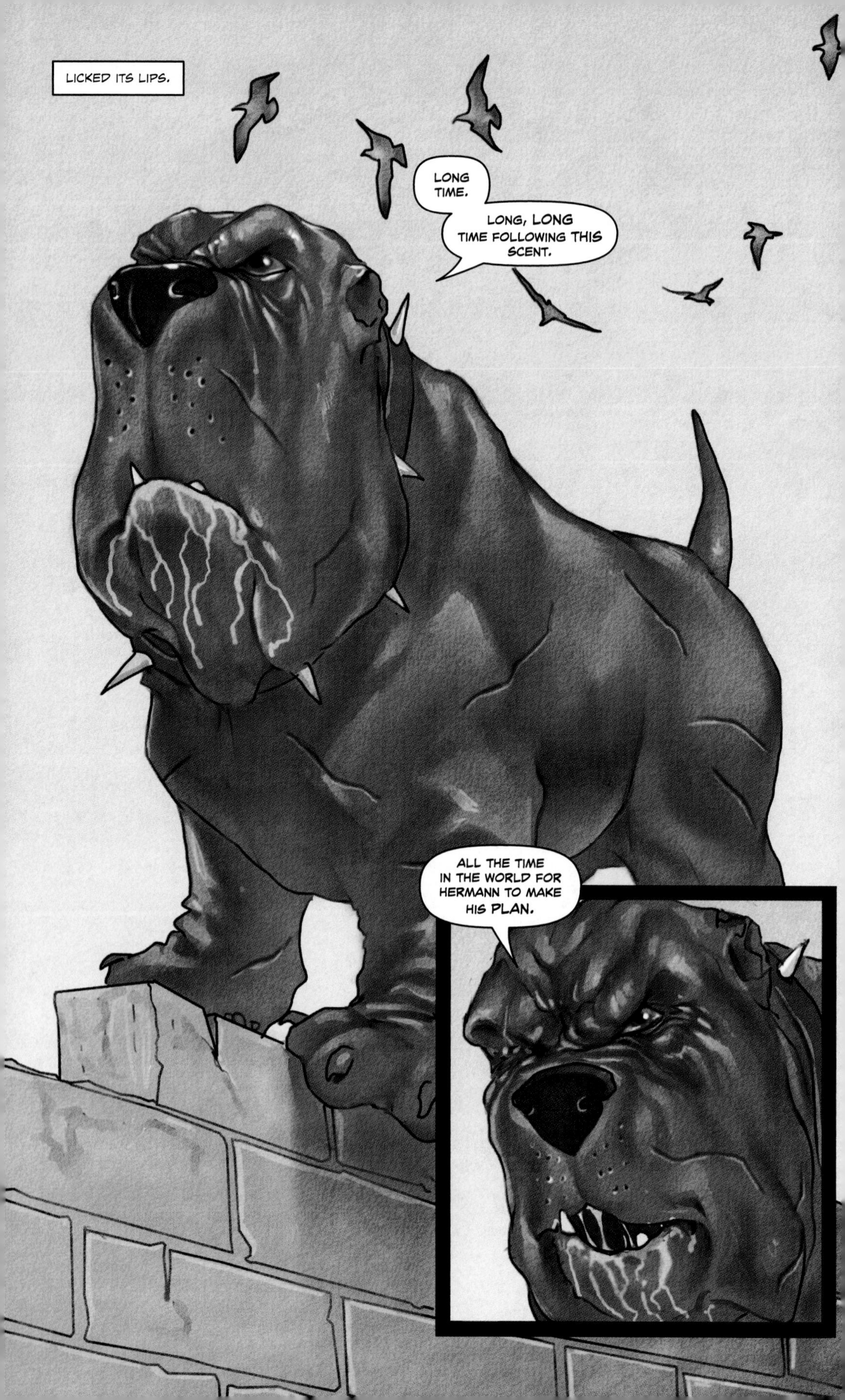
LICKED ITS LIPS.
LONG TIME.
LONG, LONG TIME FOLLOWING THIS SCENT.
ALL THE TIME IN THE WORLD FOR HERMANN TO MAKE HIS PLAN.

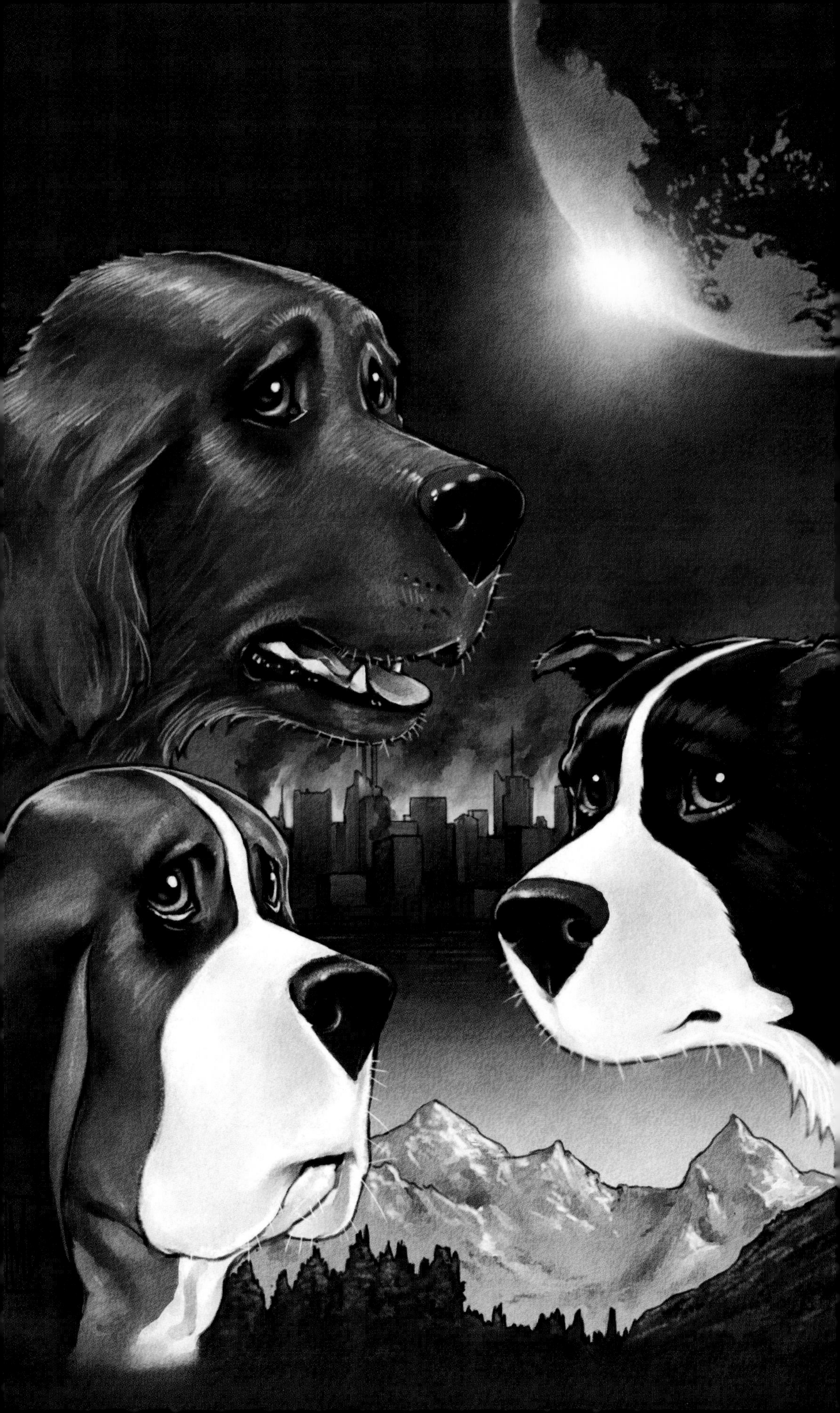

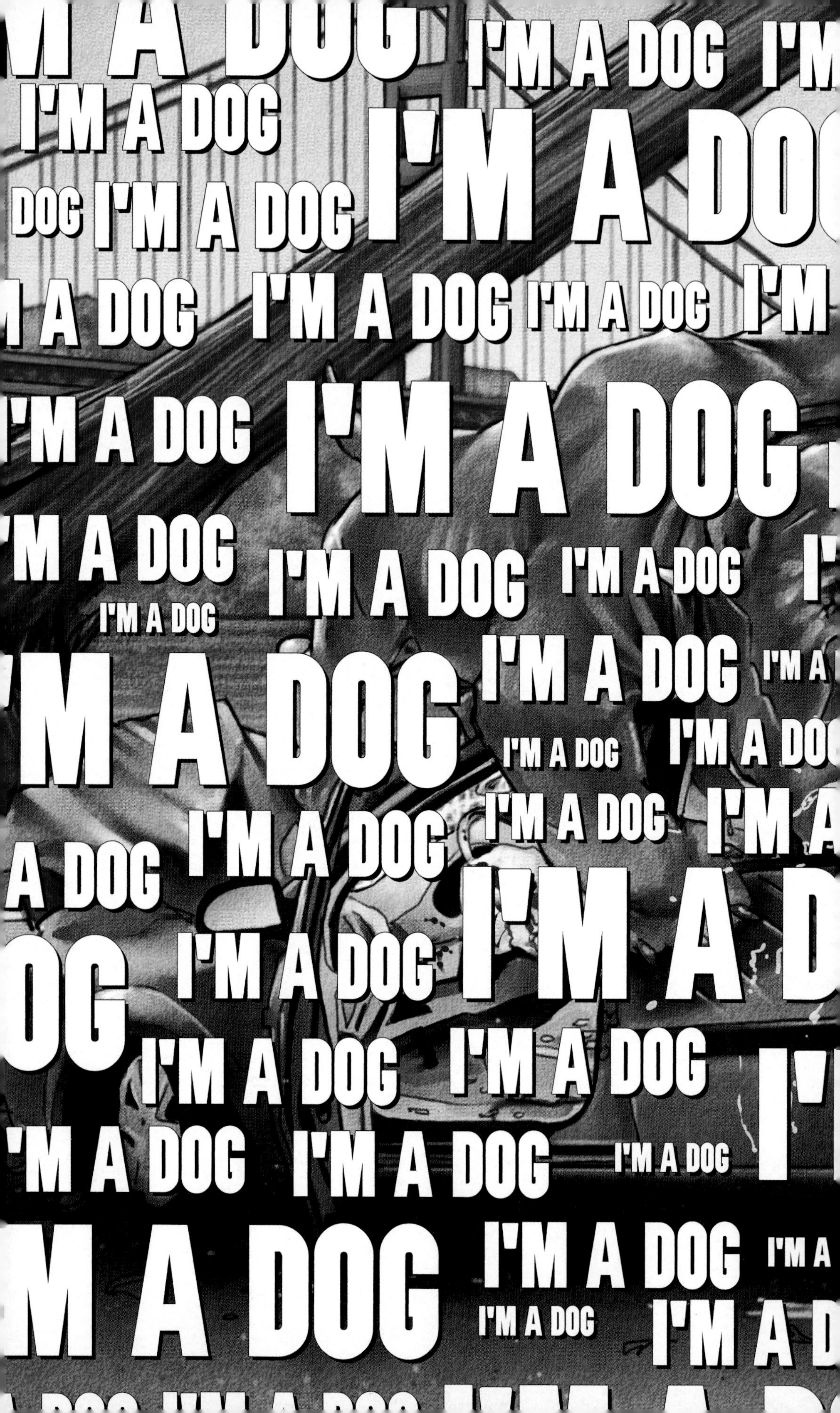

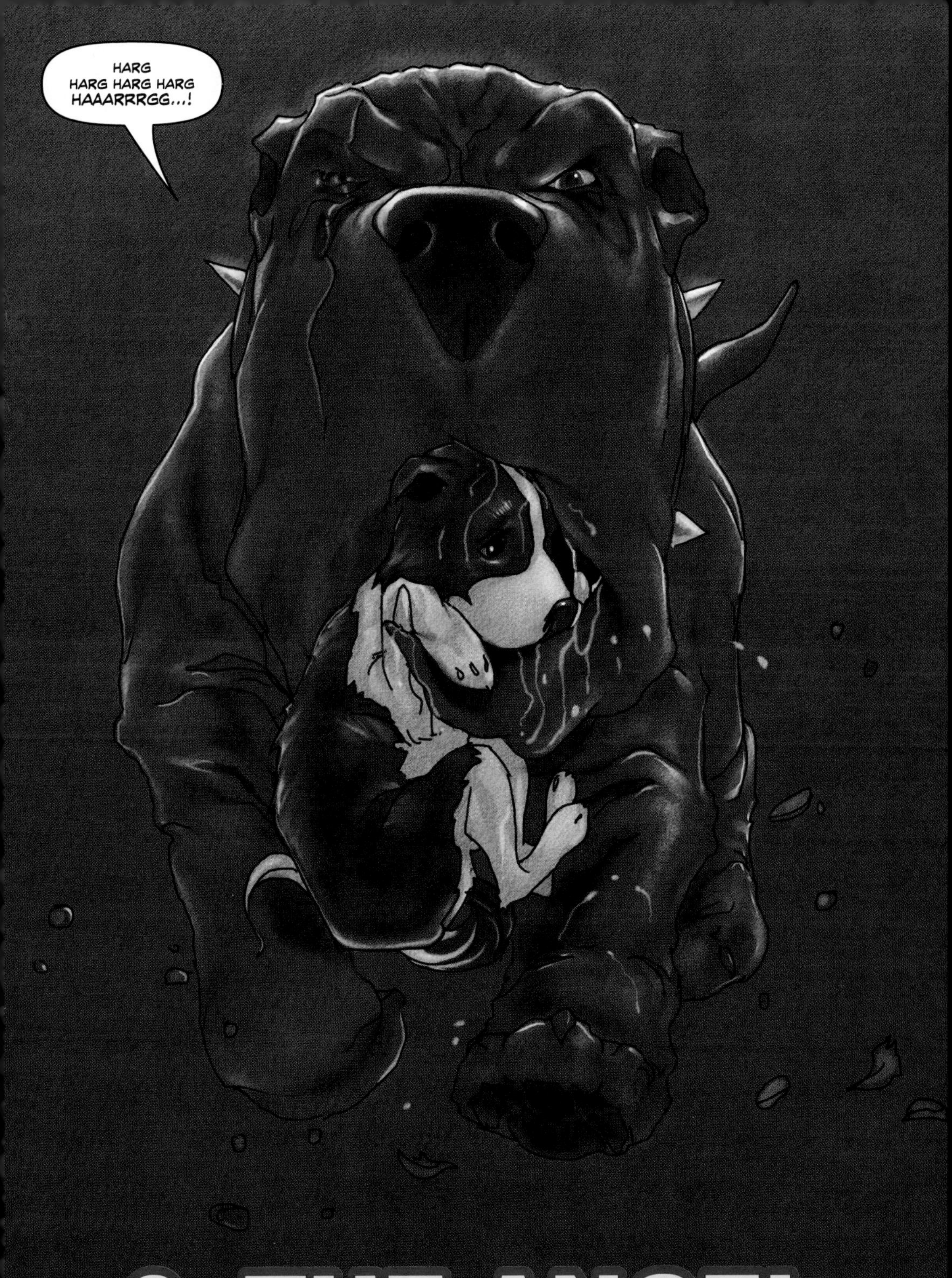
HARG HARG HARG HARG HAAARRRGG...!

6: THE ANGEL WITH HIS DARKER DRAUGHT

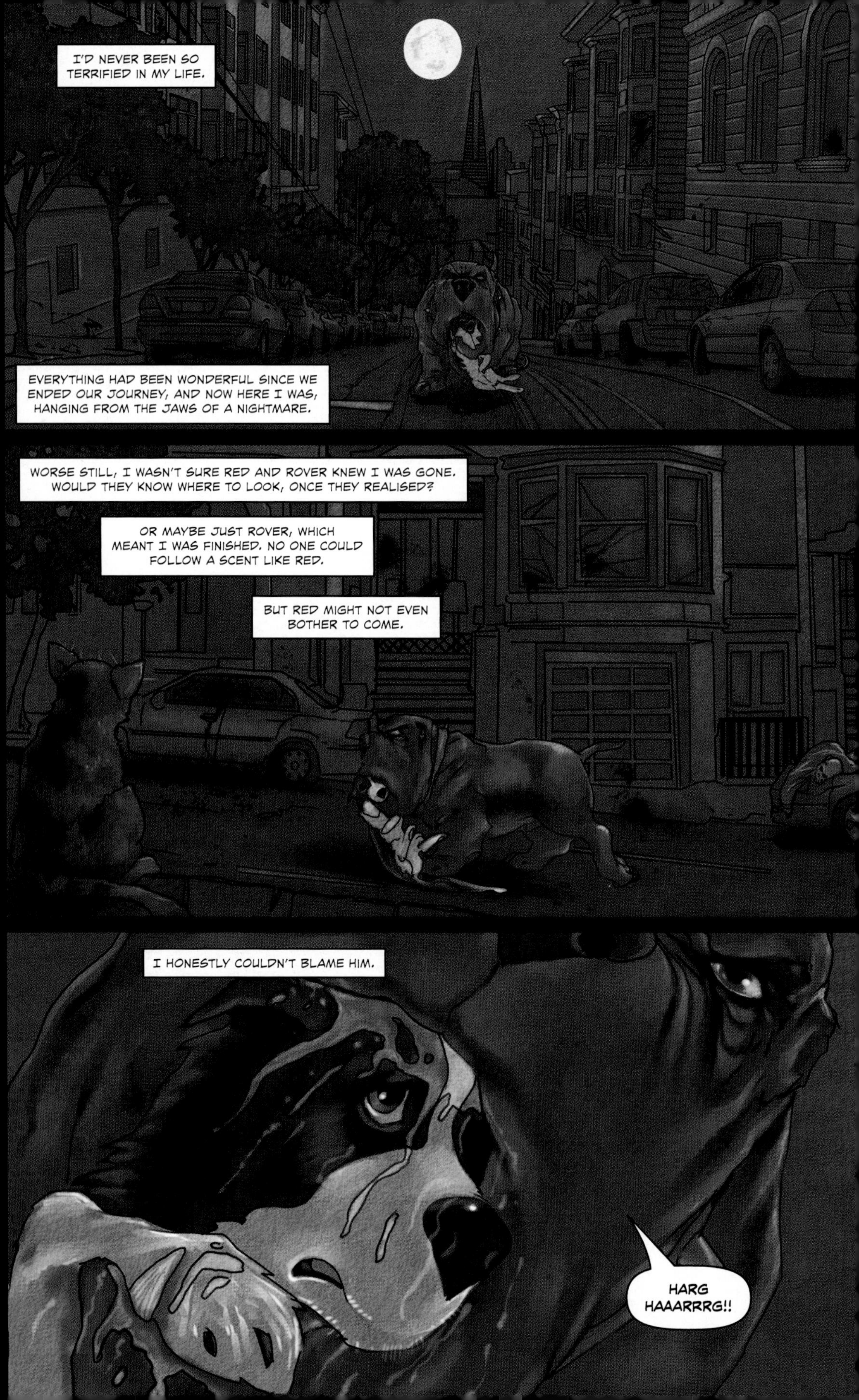
I'D NEVER BEEN SO TERRIFIED IN MY LIFE.
EVERYTHING HAD BEEN WONDERFUL SINCE WE ENDED OUR JOURNEY, AND NOW HERE I WAS, HANGING FROM THE JAWS OF A NIGHTMARE.
WORSE STILL, I WASN'T SURE RED AND ROVER KNEW I WAS GONE. WOULD THEY KNOW WHERE TO LOOK, ONCE THEY REALISED?
OR MAYBE JUST ROVER, WHICH MEANT I WAS FINISHED. NO ONE COULD FOLLOW A SCENT LIKE RED.
BUT RED MIGHT NOT EVEN BOTHER TO COME.
I HONESTLY COULDN'T BLAME HIM.
HARG HAAARRRG!!

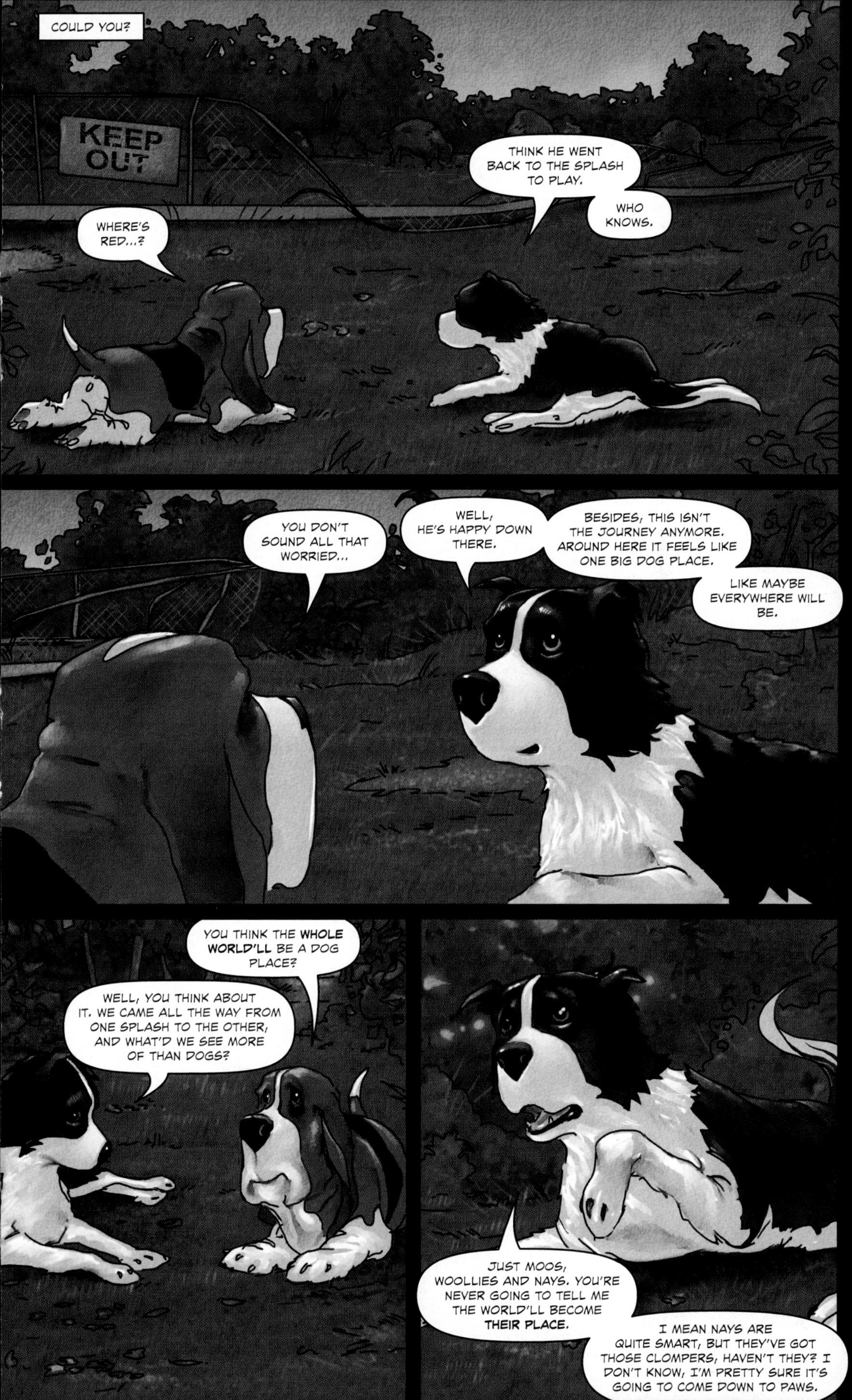
COULD YOU?
KEEP OUT
WHERE'S RED...?
THINK HE WENT BACK TO THE SPLASH TO PLAY.
WHO KNOWS.
YOU DON'T SOUND ALL THAT WORRIED...
WELL, HE'S HAPPY DOWN THERE.
BESIDES, THIS ISN'T THE JOURNEY ANYMORE. AROUND HERE IT FEELS LIKE ONE BIG DOG PLACE.
LIKE MAYBE EVERYWHERE WILL BE.
YOU THINK THE **WHOLE WORLD'LL** BE A DOG PLACE?
WELL, YOU THINK ABOUT IT. WE CAME ALL THE WAY FROM ONE SPLASH TO THE OTHER, AND WHAT'D WE SEE MORE OF THAN DOGS?
JUST MOOS, WOOLLIES AND NAYS. YOU'RE NEVER GOING TO TELL ME THE WORLD'LL BECOME **THEIR PLACE.**
I MEAN NAYS ARE QUITE SMART, BUT THEY'VE GOT THOSE CLOMPERS, HAVEN'T THEY? I DON'T KNOW, I'M PRETTY SURE IT'S GOING TO COME DOWN TO PAWS.

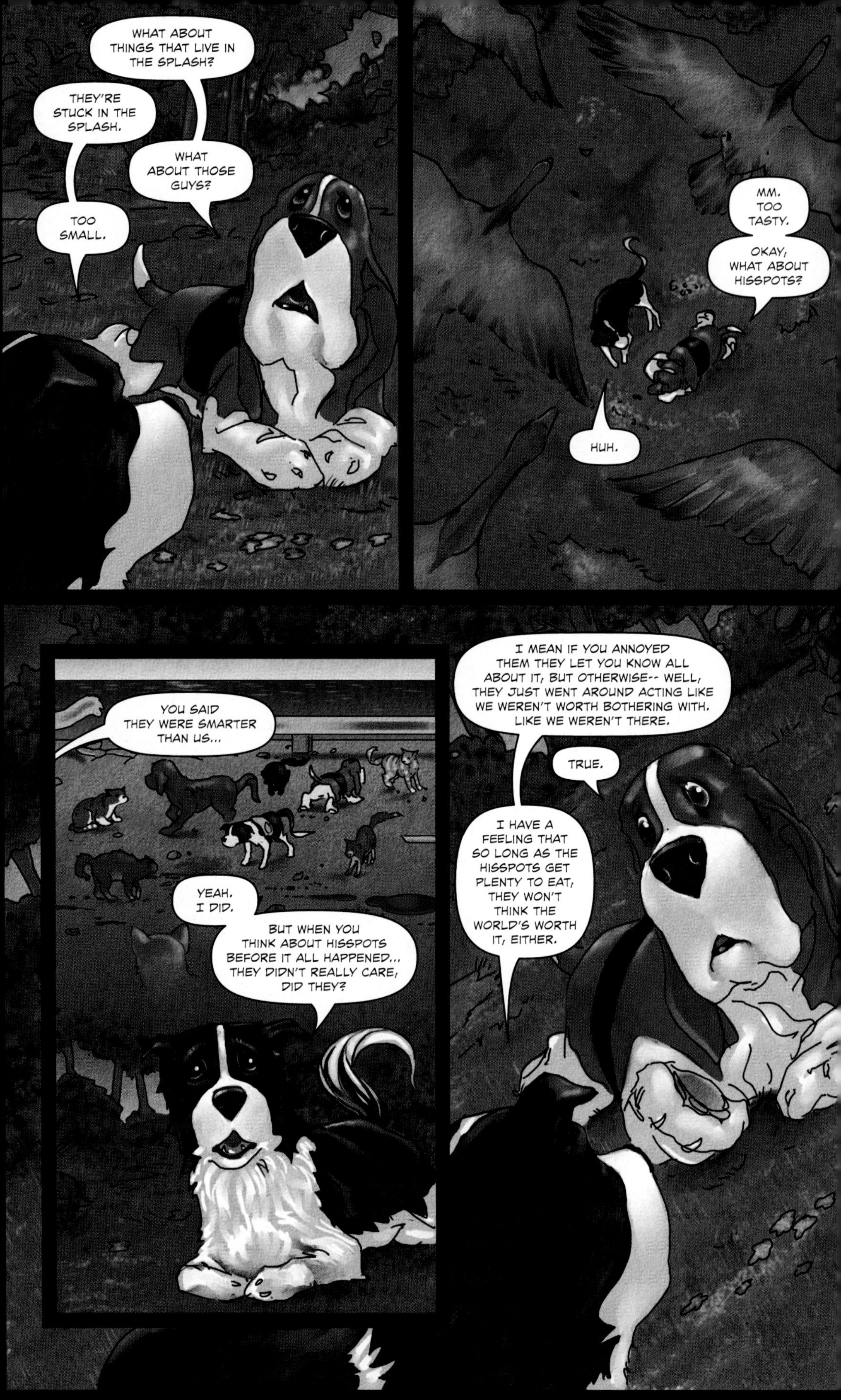
WHAT ABOUT THINGS THAT LIVE IN THE SPLASH?
THEY'RE STUCK IN THE SPLASH.
WHAT ABOUT THOSE GUYS?
TOO SMALL.
MM. TOO TASTY.
OKAY, WHAT ABOUT HISSPOTS?
HUH.
YOU SAID THEY WERE SMARTER THAN US...
YEAH. I DID.
BUT WHEN YOU THINK ABOUT HISSPOTS BEFORE IT ALL HAPPENED... THEY DIDN'T REALLY CARE, DID THEY?
I MEAN IF YOU ANNOYED THEM THEY LET YOU KNOW ALL ABOUT IT, BUT OTHERWISE-- WELL, THEY JUST WENT AROUND ACTING LIKE WE WEREN'T WORTH BOTHERING WITH. LIKE WE WEREN'T THERE.
TRUE.
I HAVE A FEELING THAT SO LONG AS THE HISSPOTS GET PLENTY TO EAT, THEY WON'T THINK THE WORLD'S WORTH IT, EITHER.

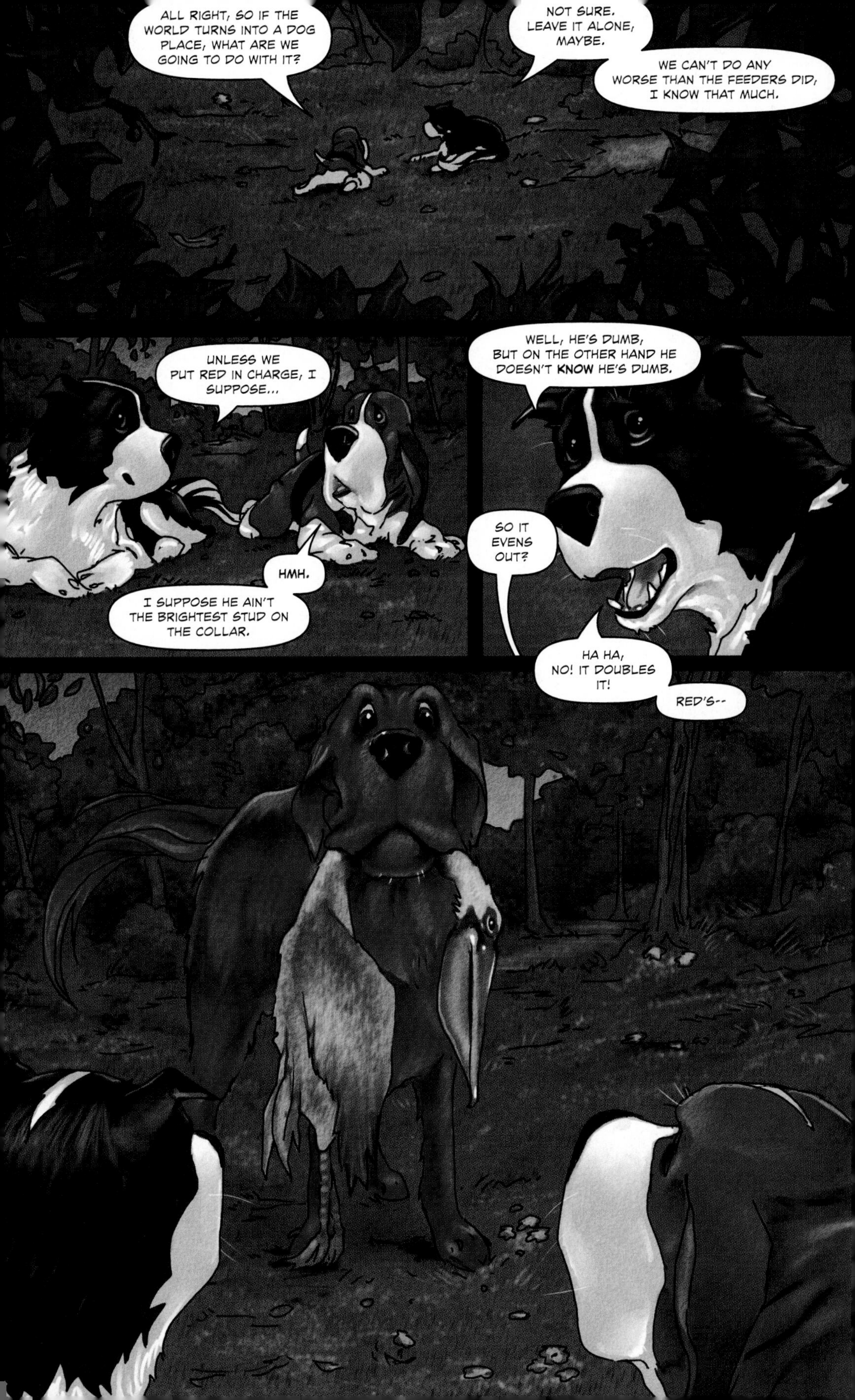
ALL RIGHT, SO IF THE WORLD TURNS INTO A DOG PLACE, WHAT ARE WE GOING TO DO WITH IT?
NOT SURE. LEAVE IT ALONE, MAYBE.
WE CAN'T DO ANY WORSE THAN THE FEEDERS DID, I KNOW THAT MUCH.
UNLESS WE PUT RED IN CHARGE, I SUPPOSE...
HMH.
I SUPPOSE HE AIN'T THE BRIGHTEST STUD ON THE COLLAR.
WELL, HE'S DUMB, BUT ON THE OTHER HAND HE DOESN'T **KNOW** HE'S DUMB.
SO IT EVENS OUT?
HA HA, NO! IT DOUBLES IT!
RED'S--

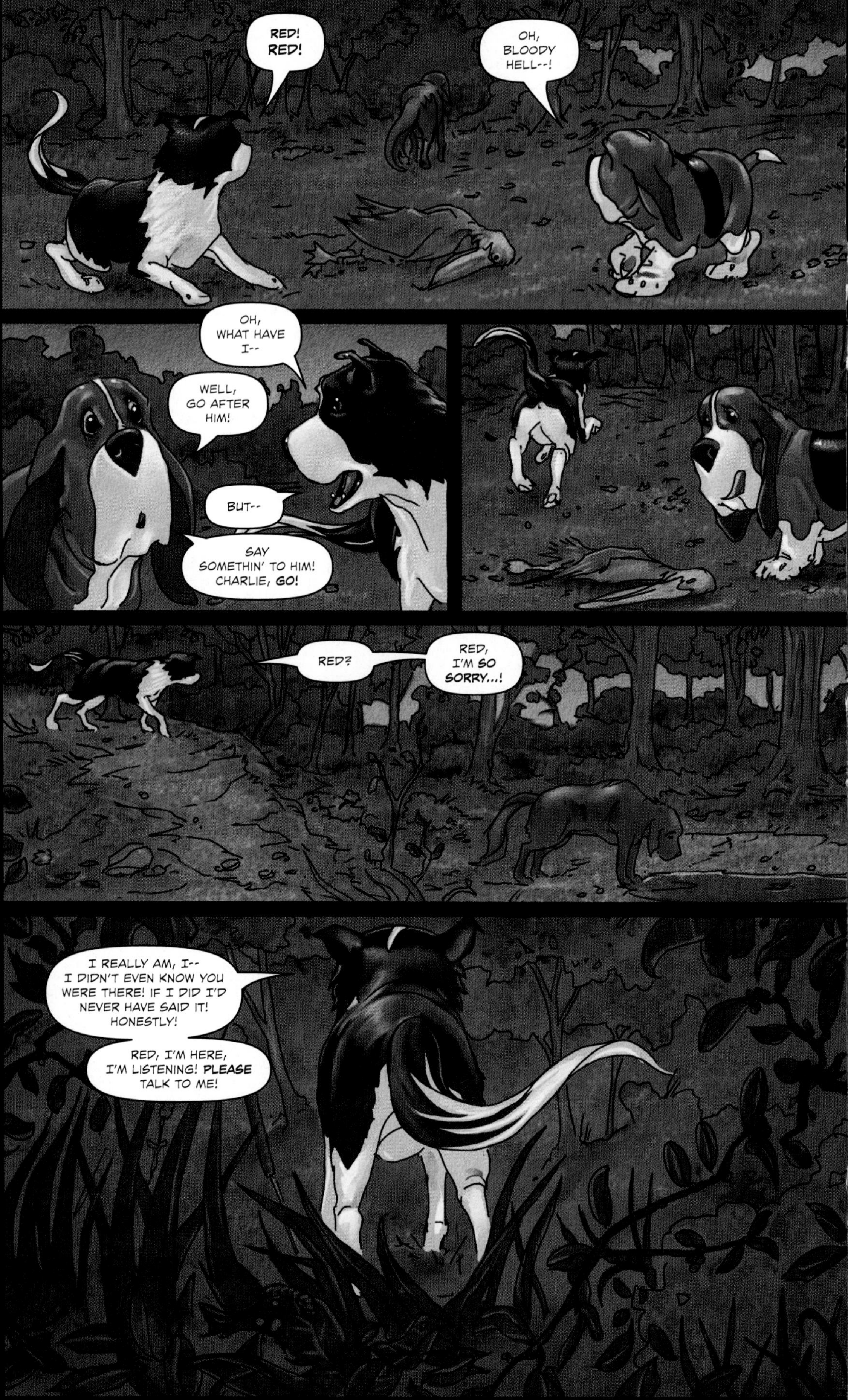
RED!
RED!
OH, BLOODY HELL--!
OH, WHAT HAVE I--
WELL, GO AFTER HIM!
BUT--
SAY SOMETHIN' TO HIM! CHARLIE, GO!
RED?
RED, I'M SO SORRY...!
I REALLY AM, I-- I DIDN'T EVEN KNOW YOU WERE THERE! IF I DID I'D NEVER HAVE SAID IT! HONESTLY!
RED, I'M HERE, I'M LISTENING! PLEASE TALK TO ME!

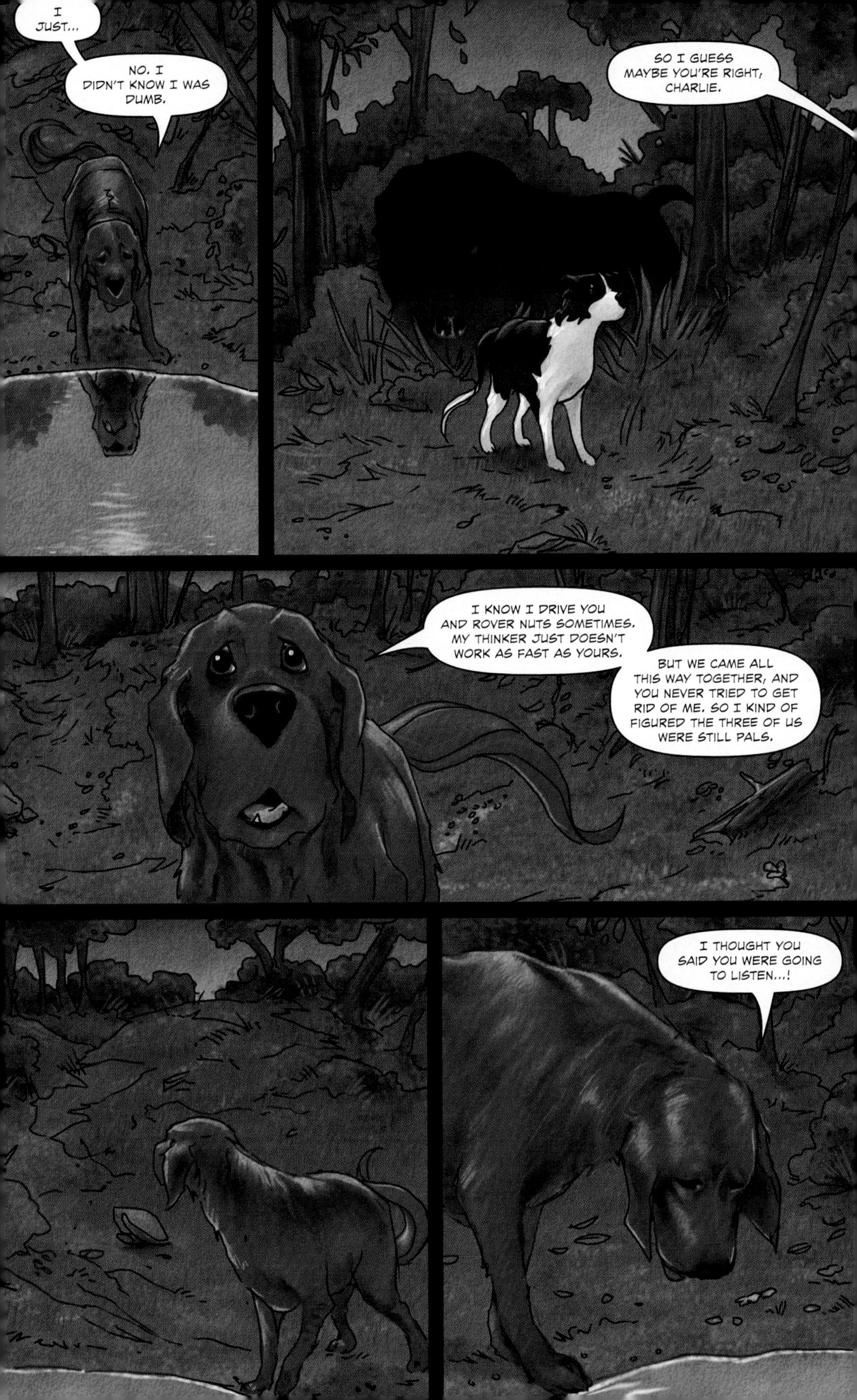
I JUST...
NO. I DIDN'T KNOW I WAS DUMB.
SO I GUESS MAYBE YOU'RE RIGHT, CHARLIE.
I KNOW I DRIVE YOU AND ROVER NUTS SOMETIMES. MY THINKER JUST DOESN'T WORK AS FAST AS YOURS.
BUT WE CAME ALL THIS WAY TOGETHER, AND YOU NEVER TRIED TO GET RID OF ME. SO I KIND OF FIGURED THE THREE OF US WERE STILL PALS.
I THOUGHT YOU SAID YOU WERE GOING TO LISTEN...!

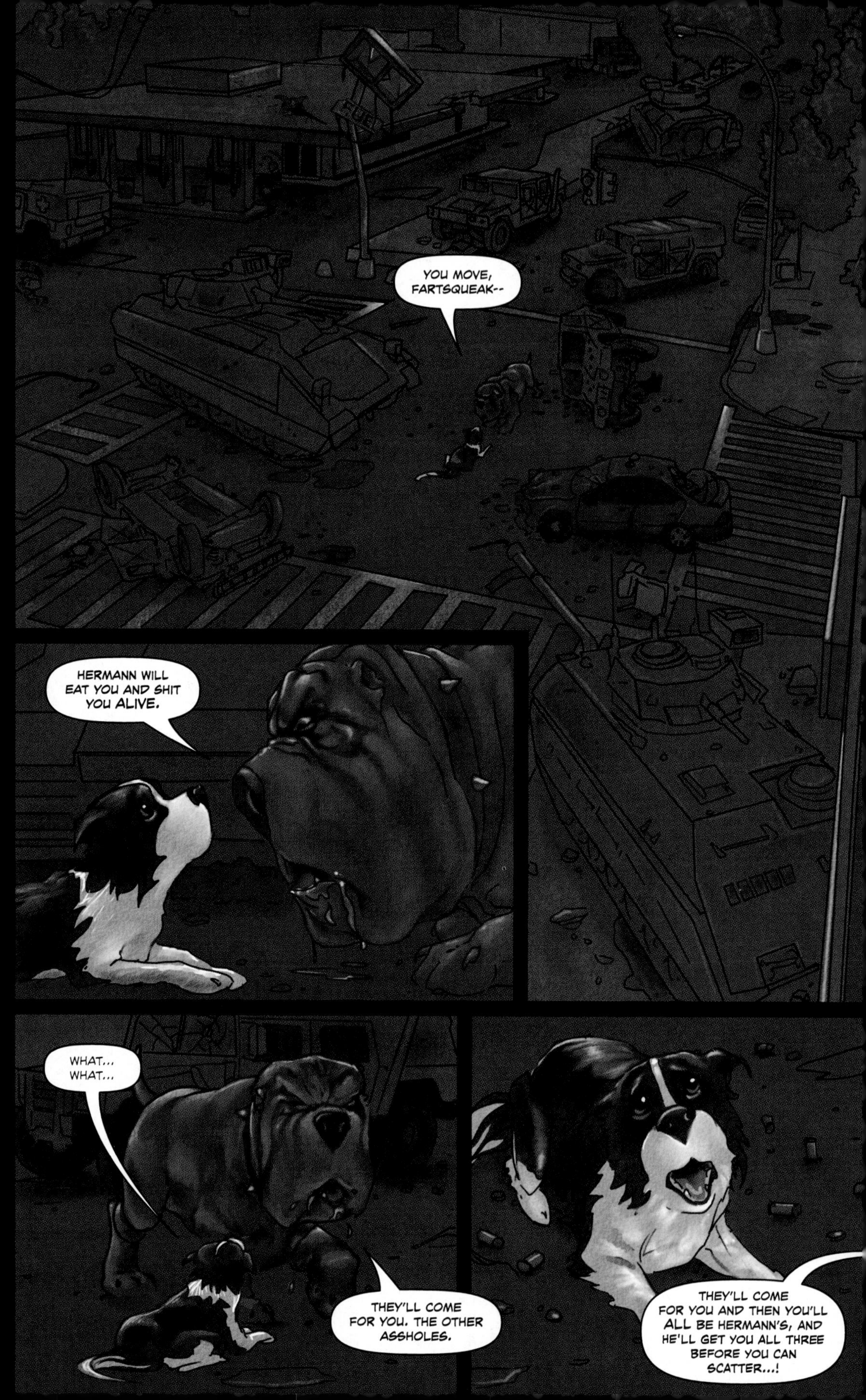
YOU MOVE, FARTSQUEAK--
HERMANN WILL EAT YOU AND SHIT YOU ALIVE.
WHAT... WHAT...
THEY'LL COME FOR YOU. THE OTHER ASSHOLES.
THEY'LL COME FOR YOU AND THEN YOU'LL ALL BE HERMANN'S, AND HE'LL GET YOU ALL THREE BEFORE YOU CAN SCATTER...!

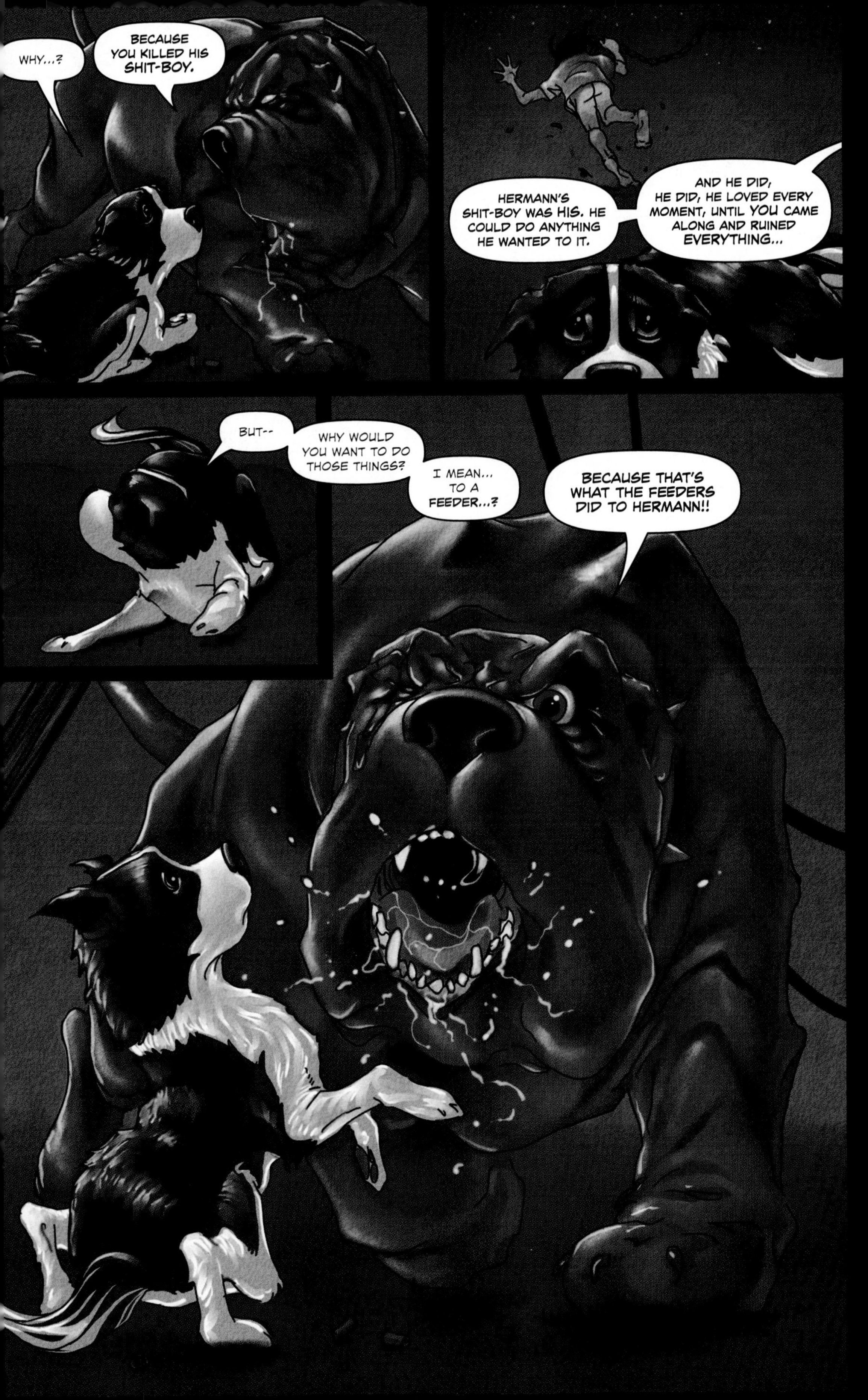
WHY...?
BECAUSE YOU KILLED HIS SHIT-BOY.
HERMANN'S SHIT-BOY WAS HIS. HE COULD DO ANYTHING HE WANTED TO IT.
AND HE DID, HE DID, HE LOVED EVERY MOMENT, UNTIL YOU CAME ALONG AND RUINED EVERYTHING...
BUT--
WHY WOULD YOU WANT TO DO THOSE THINGS?
I MEAN... TO A FEEDER...?
BECAUSE THAT'S WHAT THE FEEDERS DID TO HERMANN!!

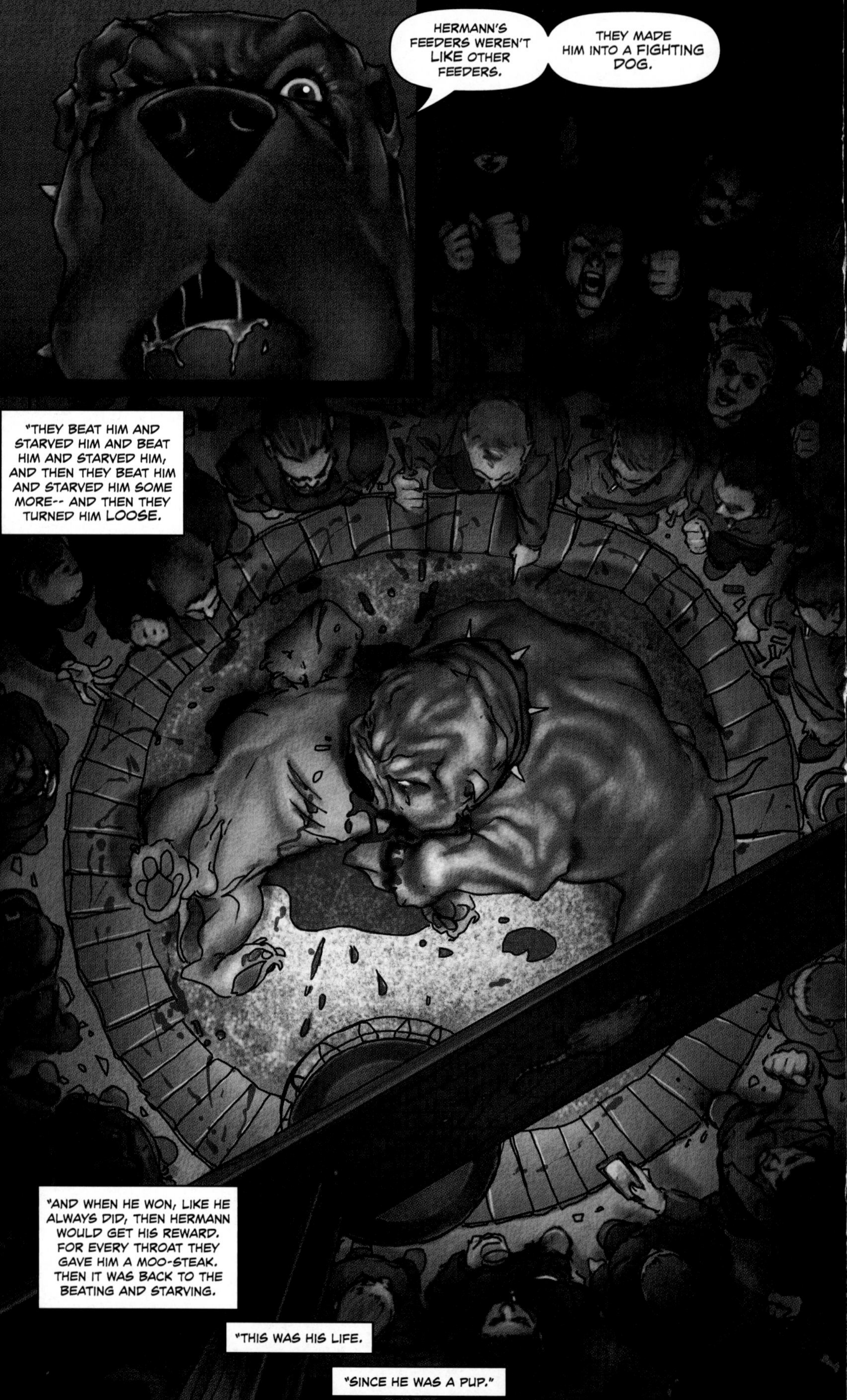
HERMANN'S FEEDERS WEREN'T LIKE OTHER FEEDERS.
THEY MADE HIM INTO A FIGHTING DOG.
"THEY BEAT HIM AND STARVED HIM AND BEAT HIM AND STARVED HIM, AND THEN THEY BEAT HIM AND STARVED HIM SOME MORE-- AND THEN THEY TURNED HIM LOOSE.
"AND WHEN HE WON, LIKE HE ALWAYS DID, THEN HERMANN WOULD GET HIS REWARD. FOR EVERY THROAT THEY GAVE HIM A MOO-STEAK. THEN IT WAS BACK TO THE BEATING AND STARVING.
"THIS WAS HIS LIFE.
"SINCE HE WAS A PUP."

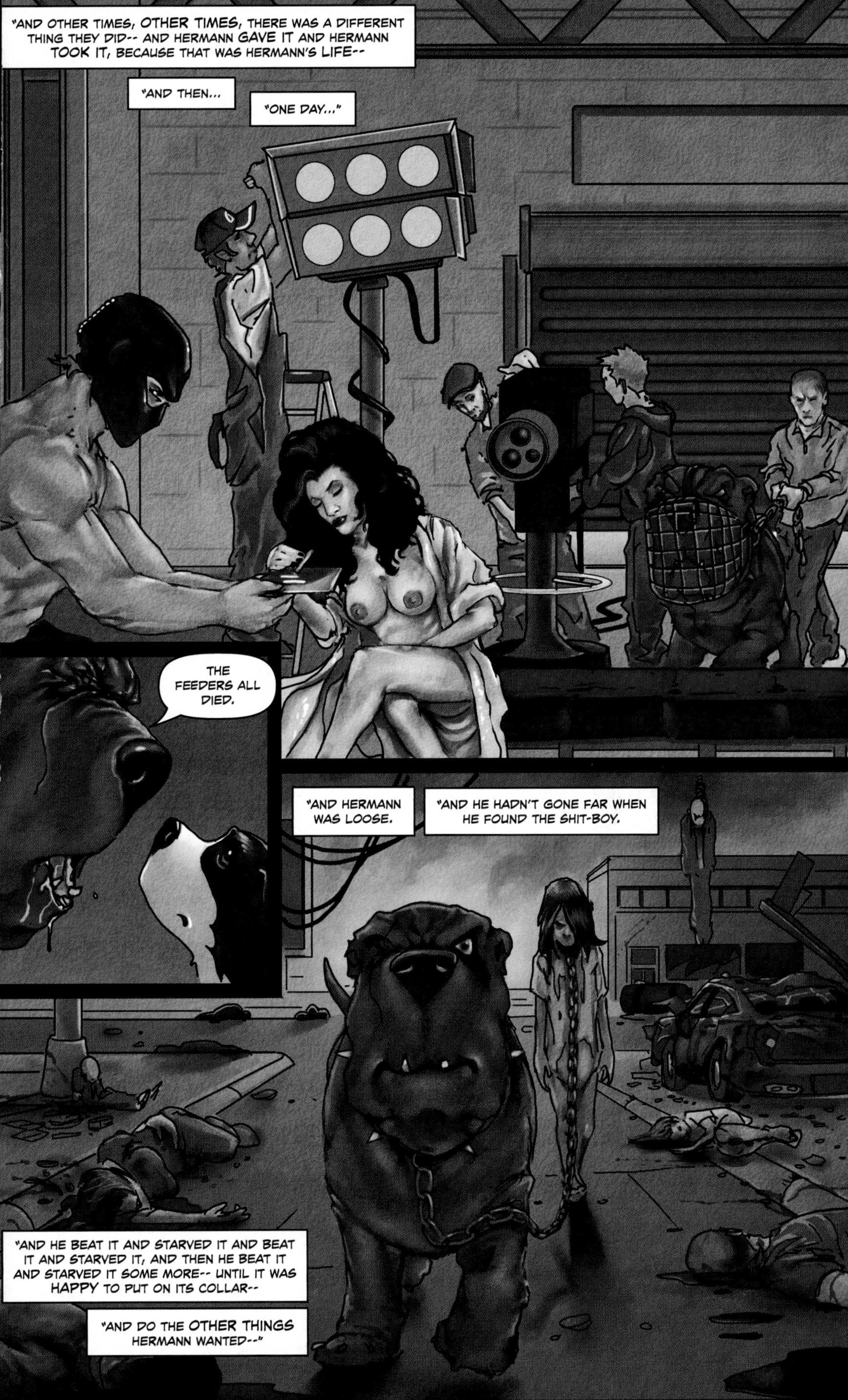

"AND OTHER TIMES, OTHER TIMES, THERE WAS A DIFFERENT THING THEY DID-- AND HERMANN GAVE IT AND HERMANN TOOK IT, BECAUSE THAT WAS HERMANN'S LIFE--
"AND THEN...
"ONE DAY..."
THE FEEDERS ALL DIED.
"AND HERMANN WAS LOOSE.
"AND HE HADN'T GONE FAR WHEN HE FOUND THE SHIT-BOY.
"AND HE BEAT IT AND STARVED IT AND BEAT IT AND STARVED IT, AND THEN HE BEAT IT AND STARVED IT SOME MORE-- UNTIL IT WAS HAPPY TO PUT ON ITS COLLAR--
"AND DO THE OTHER THINGS HERMANN WANTED--"

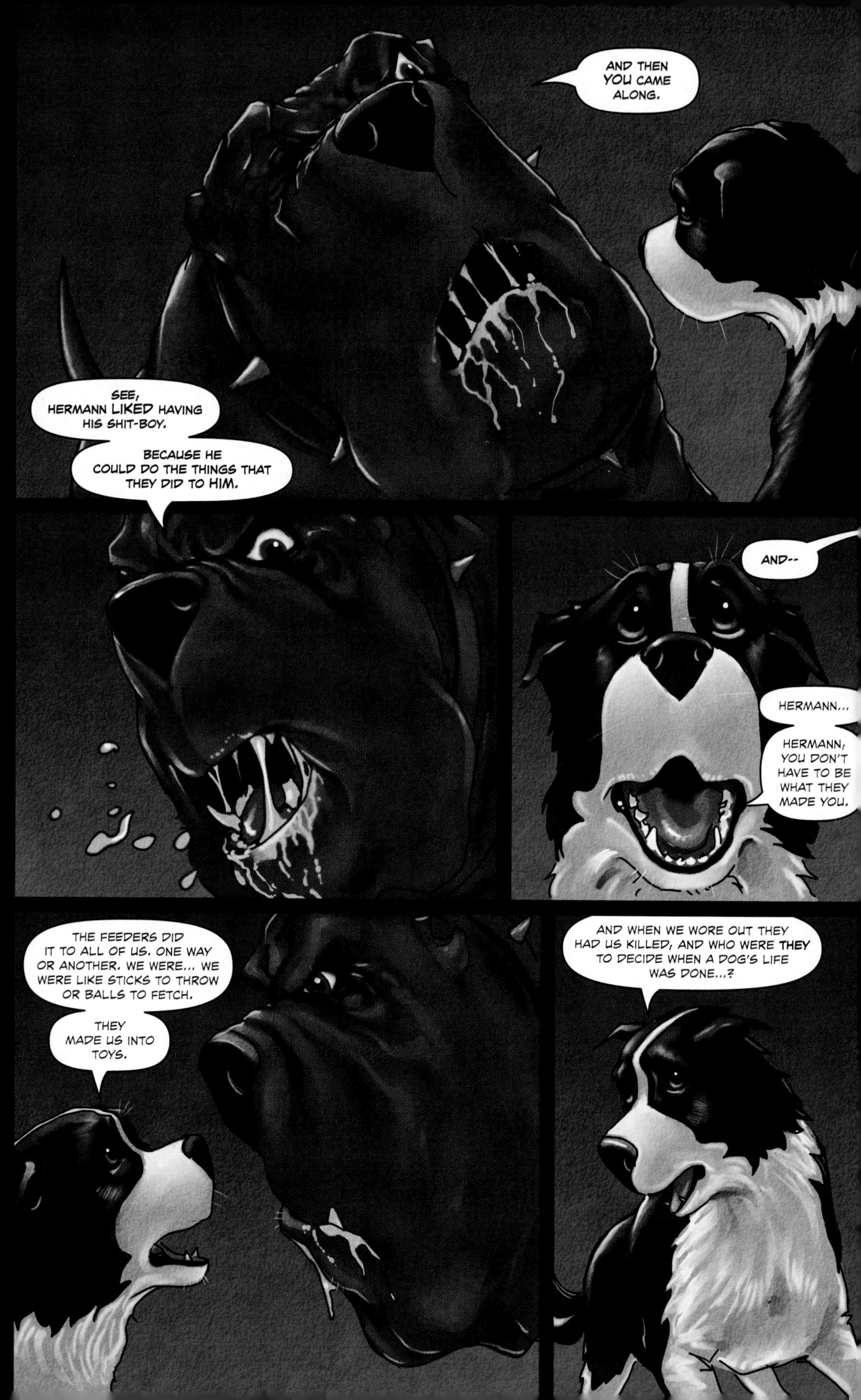
AND THEN YOU CAME ALONG.
SEE, HERMANN LIKED HAVING HIS SHIT-BOY.
BECAUSE HE COULD DO THE THINGS THAT THEY DID TO HIM.
AND--
HERMANN...
HERMANN, YOU DON'T HAVE TO BE WHAT THEY MADE YOU.
THE FEEDERS DID IT TO ALL OF US. ONE WAY OR ANOTHER. WE WERE... WE WERE LIKE STICKS TO THROW OR BALLS TO FETCH.
THEY MADE US INTO TOYS.
AND WHEN WE WORE OUT THEY HAD US KILLED, AND WHO WERE THEY TO DECIDE WHEN A DOG'S LIFE WAS DONE...?

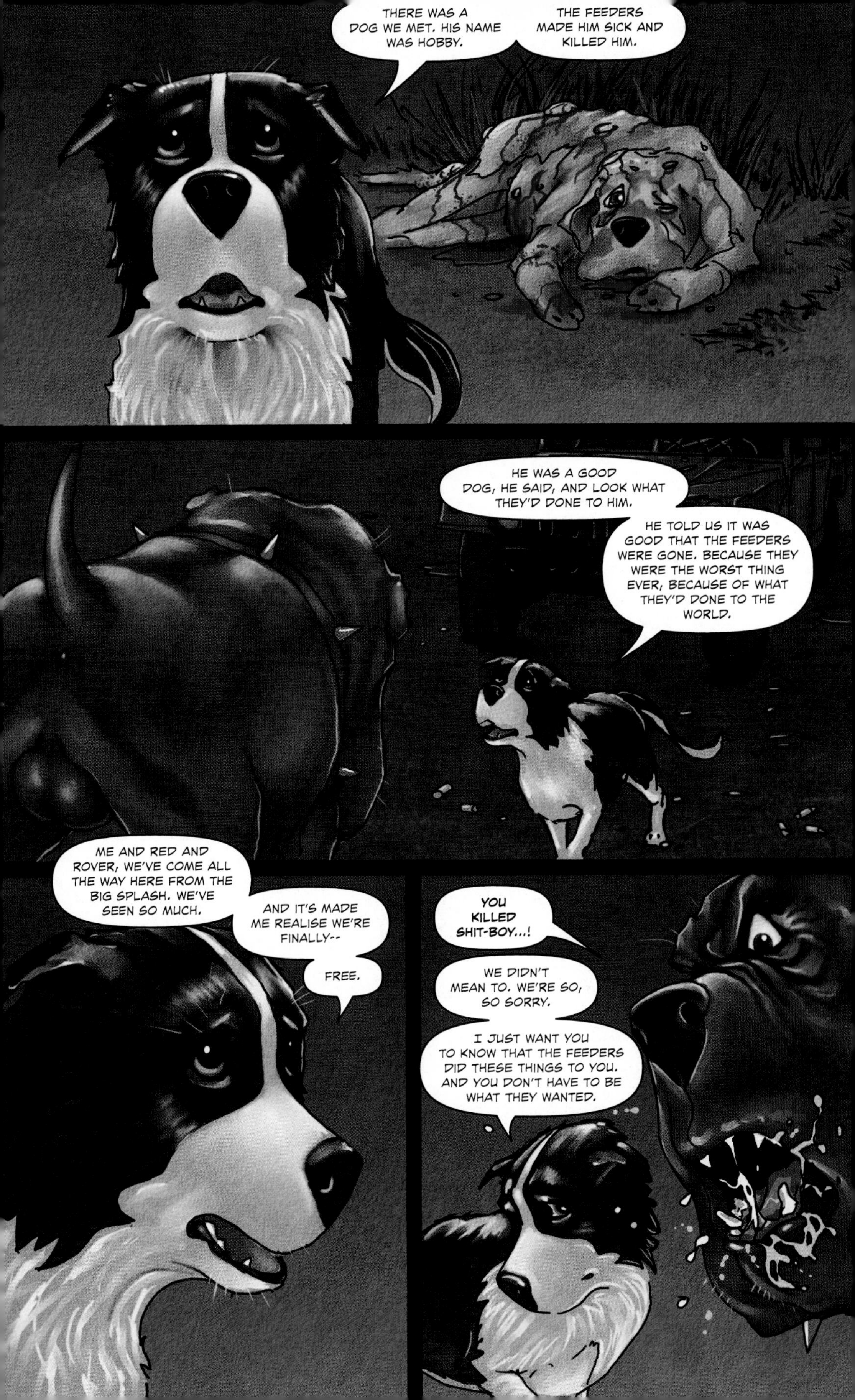
THERE WAS A DOG WE MET. HIS NAME WAS HOBBY.
THE FEEDERS MADE HIM SICK AND KILLED HIM.
HE WAS A GOOD DOG, HE SAID, AND LOOK WHAT THEY'D DONE TO HIM.
HE TOLD US IT WAS GOOD THAT THE FEEDERS WERE GONE. BECAUSE THEY WERE THE WORST THING EVER, BECAUSE OF WHAT THEY'D DONE TO THE WORLD.
ME AND RED AND ROVER, WE'VE COME ALL THE WAY HERE FROM THE BIG SPLASH. WE'VE SEEN SO MUCH.
AND IT'S MADE ME REALISE WE'RE FINALLY--
FREE.
YOU KILLED SHIT-BOY...!
WE DIDN'T MEAN TO. WE'RE SO, SO SORRY.
I JUST WANT YOU TO KNOW THAT THE FEEDERS DID THESE THINGS TO YOU. AND YOU DON'T HAVE TO BE WHAT THEY WANTED.

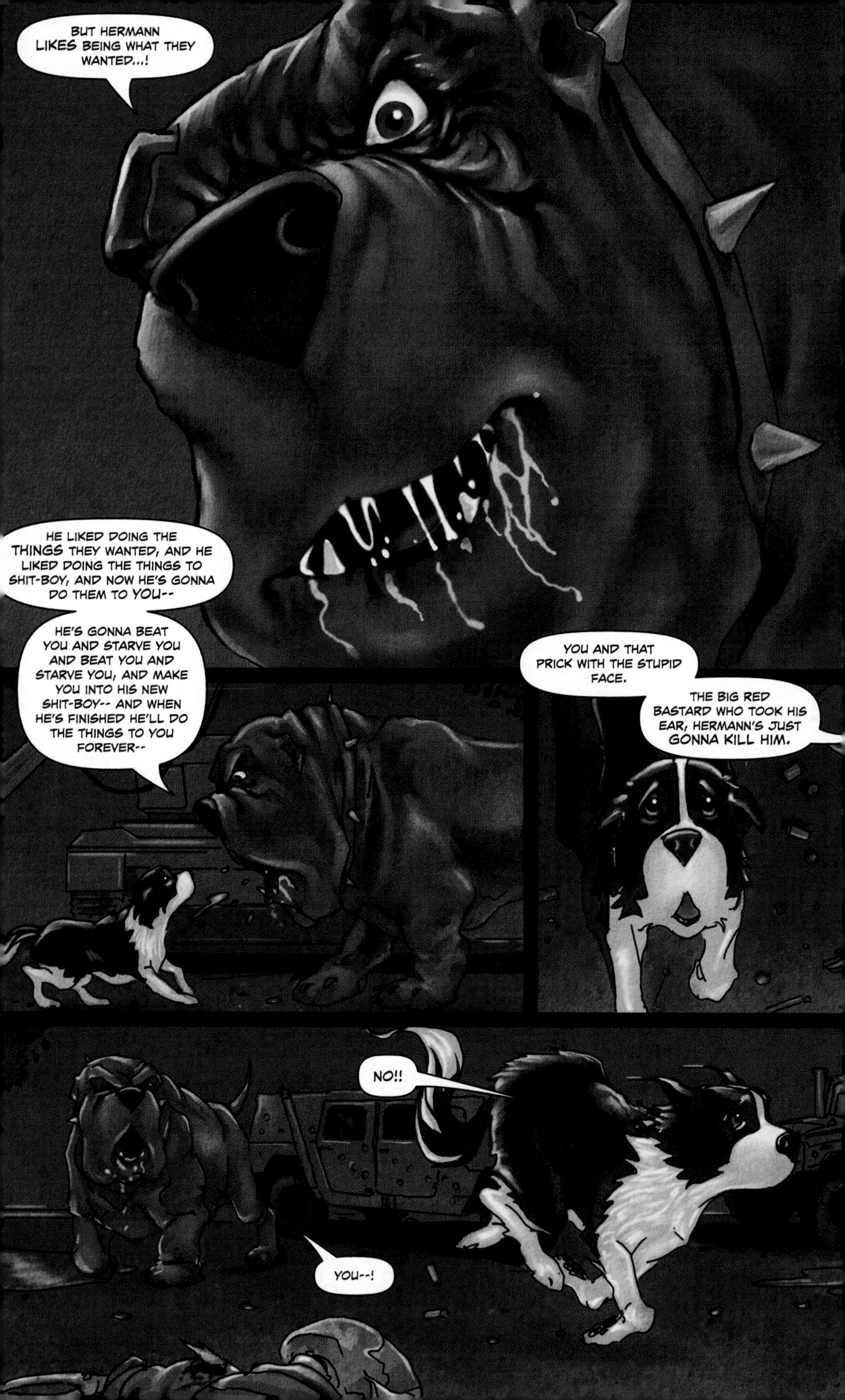
BUT HERMANN LIKES BEING WHAT THEY WANTED...!
HE LIKED DOING THE THINGS THEY WANTED, AND HE LIKED DOING THE THINGS TO SHIT-BOY, AND NOW HE'S GONNA DO THEM TO YOU--
HE'S GONNA BEAT YOU AND STARVE YOU AND BEAT YOU AND STARVE YOU, AND MAKE YOU INTO HIS NEW SHIT-BOY-- AND WHEN HE'S FINISHED HE'LL DO THE THINGS TO YOU FOREVER--
YOU AND THAT PRICK WITH THE STUPID FACE.
THE BIG RED BASTARD WHO TOOK HIS EAR, HERMANN'S JUST GONNA KILL HIM.
NO!!
YOU--!

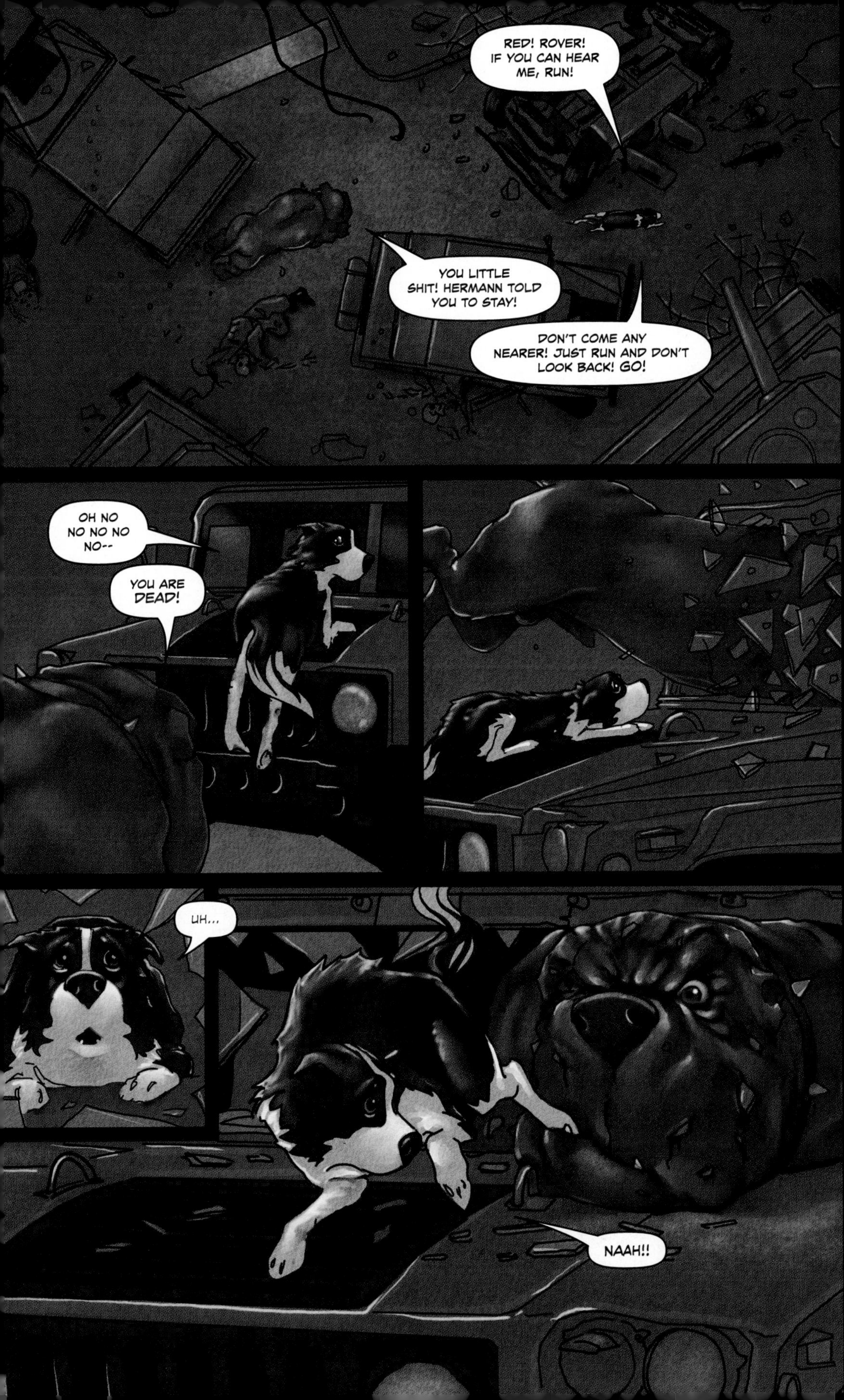
RED! ROVER!
IF YOU CAN HEAR ME, RUN!
YOU LITTLE SHIT! HERMANN TOLD YOU TO STAY!
DON'T COME ANY NEARER! JUST RUN AND DON'T LOOK BACK! GO!
OH NO NO NO NO NO--
YOU ARE DEAD!
UH...
NAAH!!

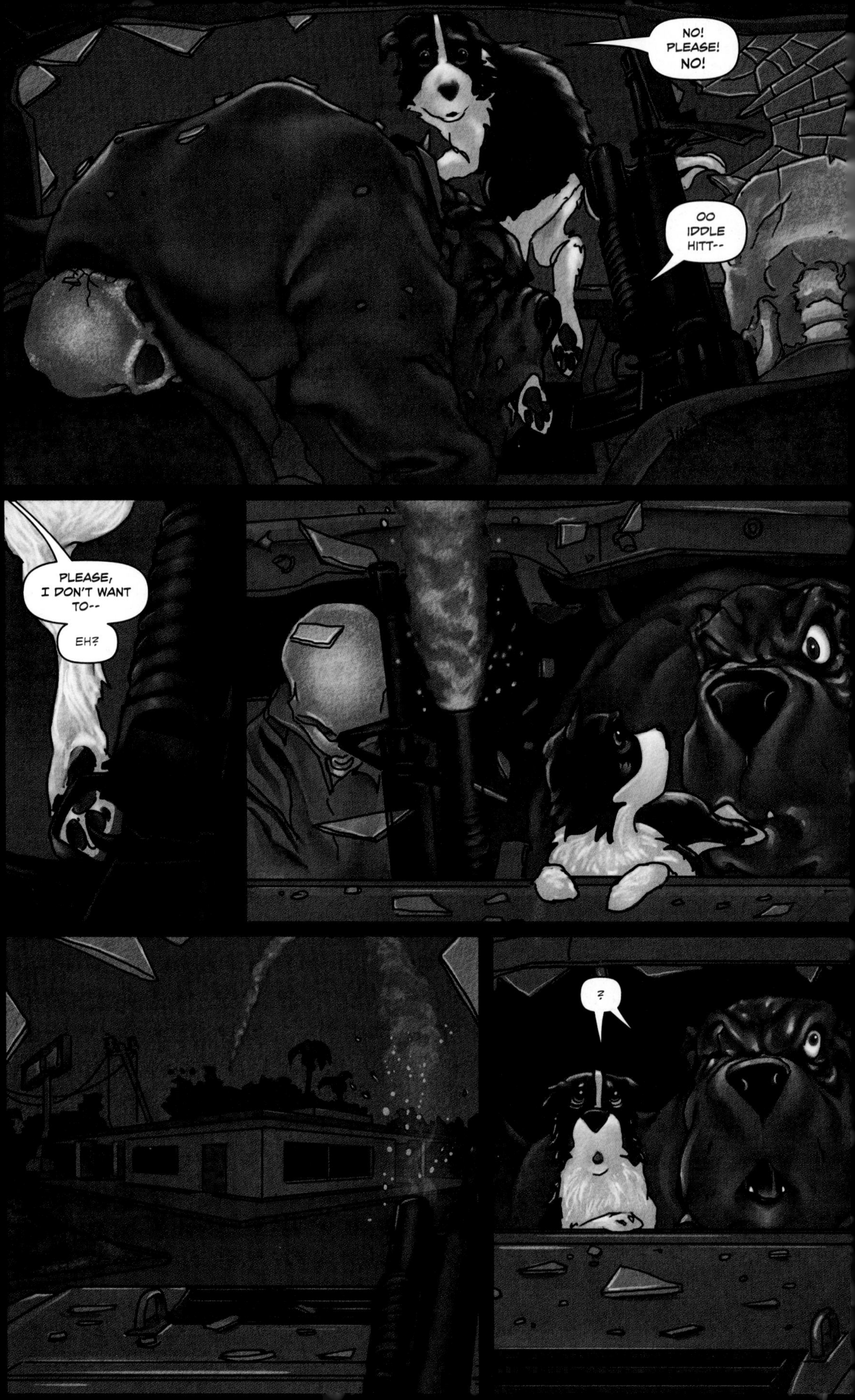
NO! PLEASE! NO!
OO IDDLE HITT--
PLEASE, I DON'T WANT TO--
EH?
?

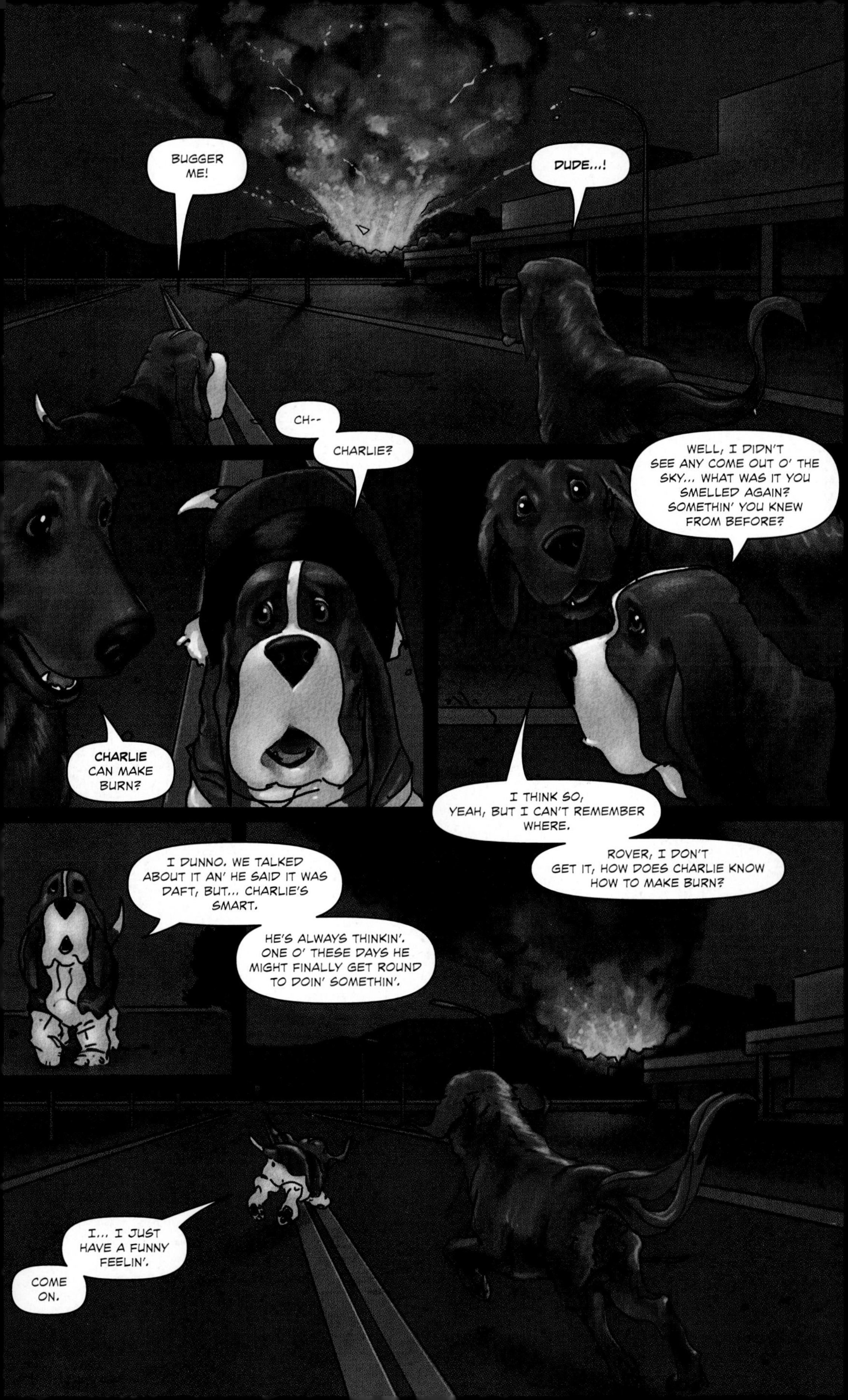
BUGGER ME!
DUDE...!
CH--
CHARLIE?
CHARLIE CAN MAKE BURN?
WELL, I DIDN'T SEE ANY COME OUT O' THE SKY... WHAT WAS IT YOU SMELLED AGAIN? SOMETHIN' YOU KNEW FROM BEFORE?
I THINK SO, YEAH, BUT I CAN'T REMEMBER WHERE.
ROVER, I DON'T GET IT, HOW DOES CHARLIE KNOW HOW TO MAKE BURN?
I DUNNO. WE TALKED ABOUT IT AN' HE SAID IT WAS DAFT, BUT... CHARLIE'S SMART.
HE'S ALWAYS THINKIN'. ONE O' THESE DAYS HE MIGHT FINALLY GET ROUND TO DOIN' SOMETHIN'.
I... I JUST HAVE A FUNNY FEELIN'.
COME ON.

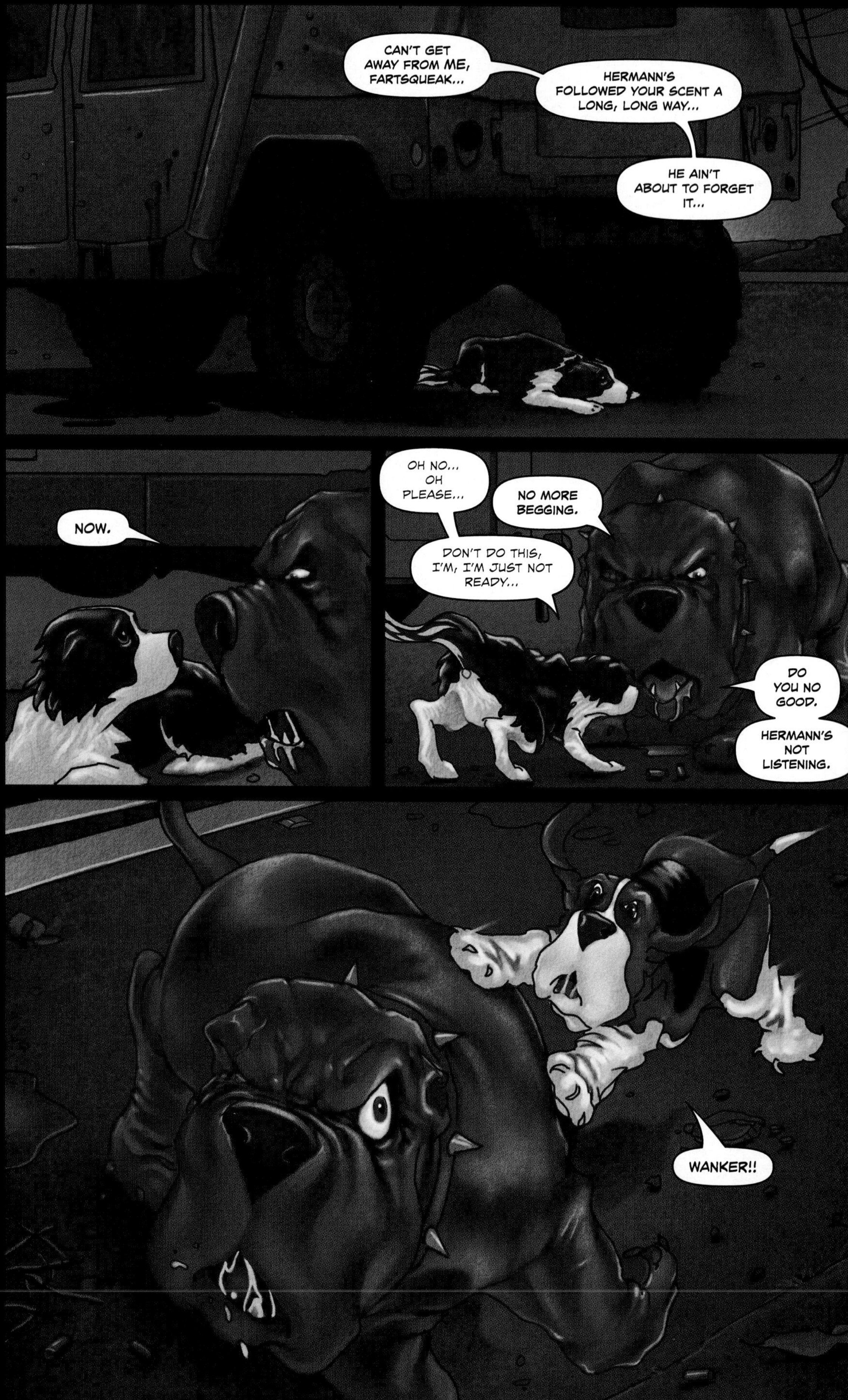
CAN'T GET AWAY FROM ME, FARTSQUEAK...
HERMANN'S FOLLOWED YOUR SCENT A LONG, LONG WAY...
HE AIN'T ABOUT TO FORGET IT...
NOW.
OH NO... OH PLEASE...
DON'T DO THIS, I'M, I'M JUST NOT READY...
NO MORE BEGGING.
DO YOU NO GOOD.
HERMANN'S NOT LISTENING.
WANKER!!

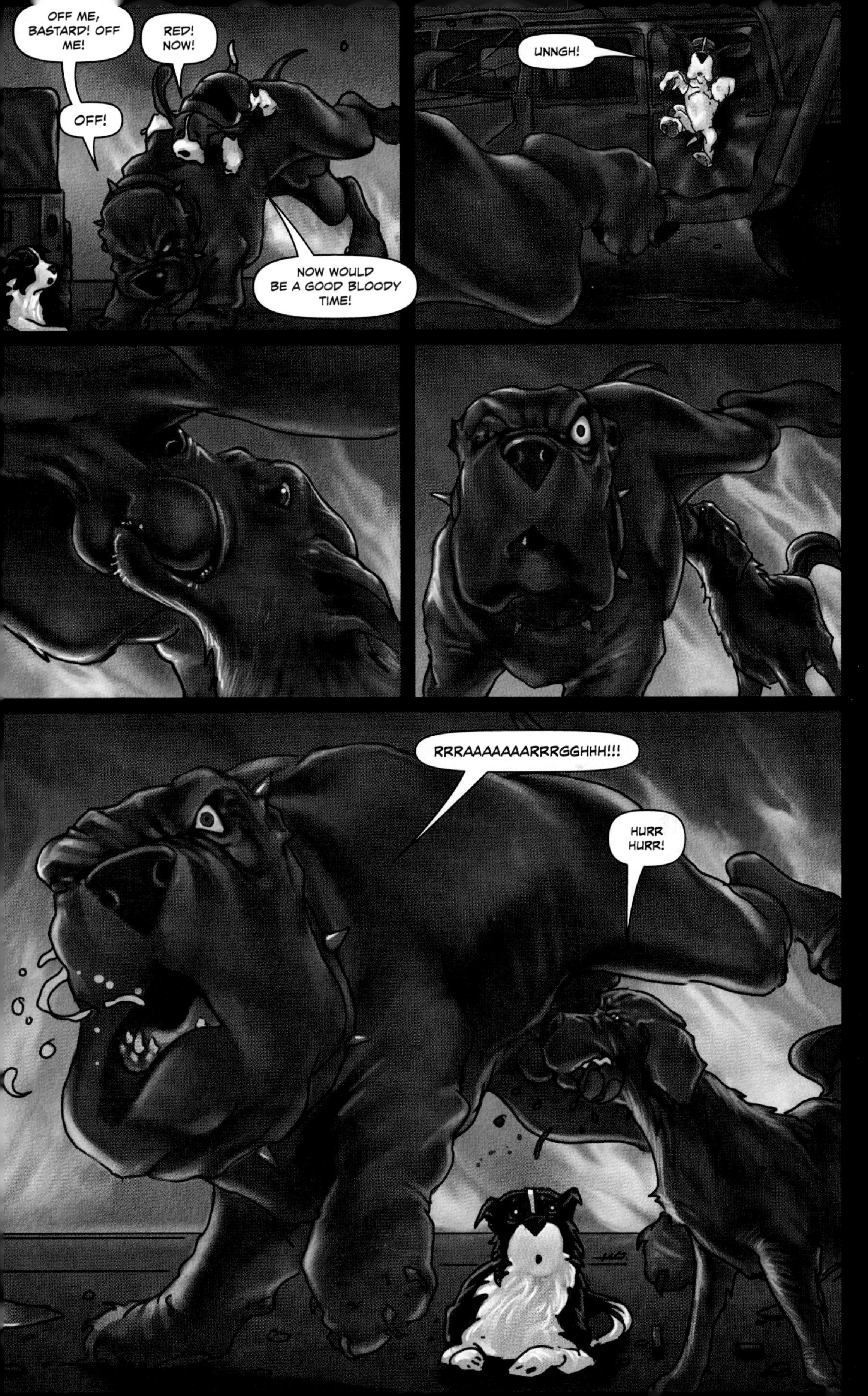
OFF ME, BASTARD! OFF ME!
RED! NOW!
OFF!
NOW WOULD BE A GOOD BLOODY TIME!
UNNGH!
RRRAAAAAAAARRRGGHHH!!!
HURR HURR!

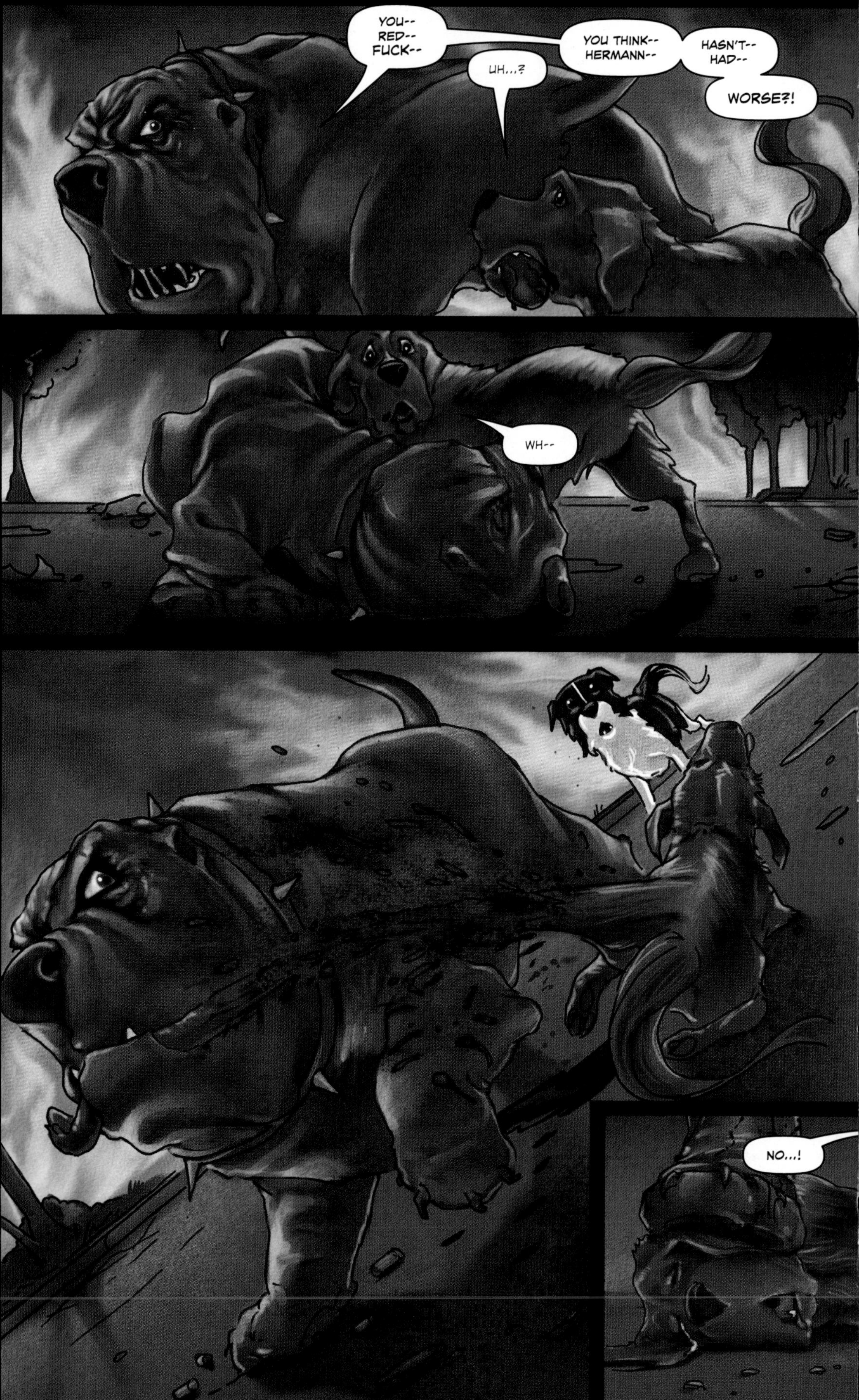
YOU-- RED-- FUCK--
UH...?
YOU THINK-- HERMANN--
HASN'T-- HAD--
WORSE?!
WH--
NO...!

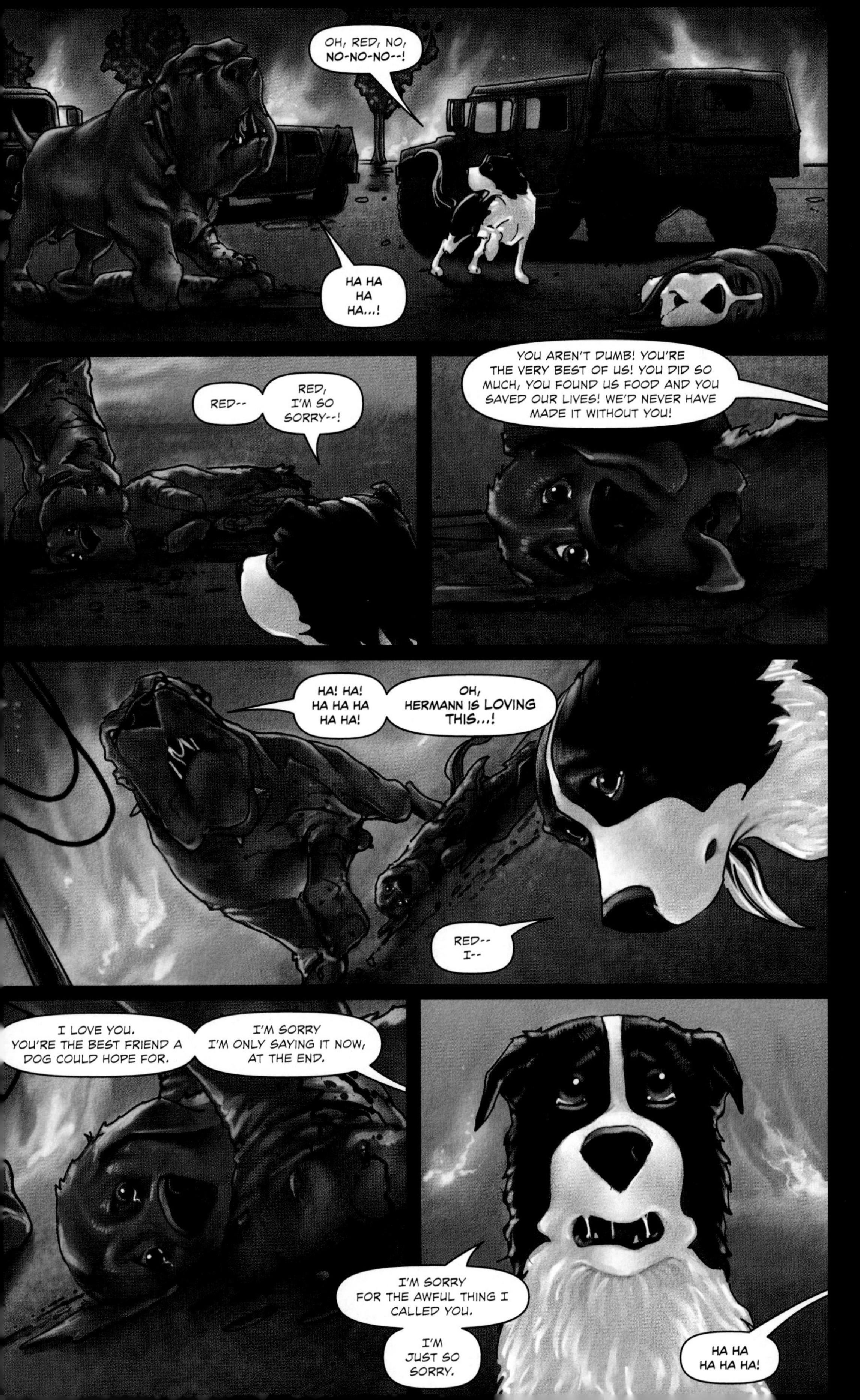
OH, RED, NO, NO-NO-NO--!
HA HA HA HA...!
RED--
RED, I'M SO SORRY--!
YOU AREN'T DUMB! YOU'RE THE VERY BEST OF US! YOU DID SO MUCH, YOU FOUND US FOOD AND YOU SAVED OUR LIVES! WE'D NEVER HAVE MADE IT WITHOUT YOU!
HA! HA! HA HA HA HA HA!
OH, HERMANN IS LOVING THIS...!
RED-- I--
I LOVE YOU. YOU'RE THE BEST FRIEND A DOG COULD HOPE FOR.
I'M SORRY I'M ONLY SAYING IT NOW, AT THE END.
I'M SORRY FOR THE AWFUL THING I CALLED YOU.
I'M JUST SO SORRY.
HA HA HA HA HA!

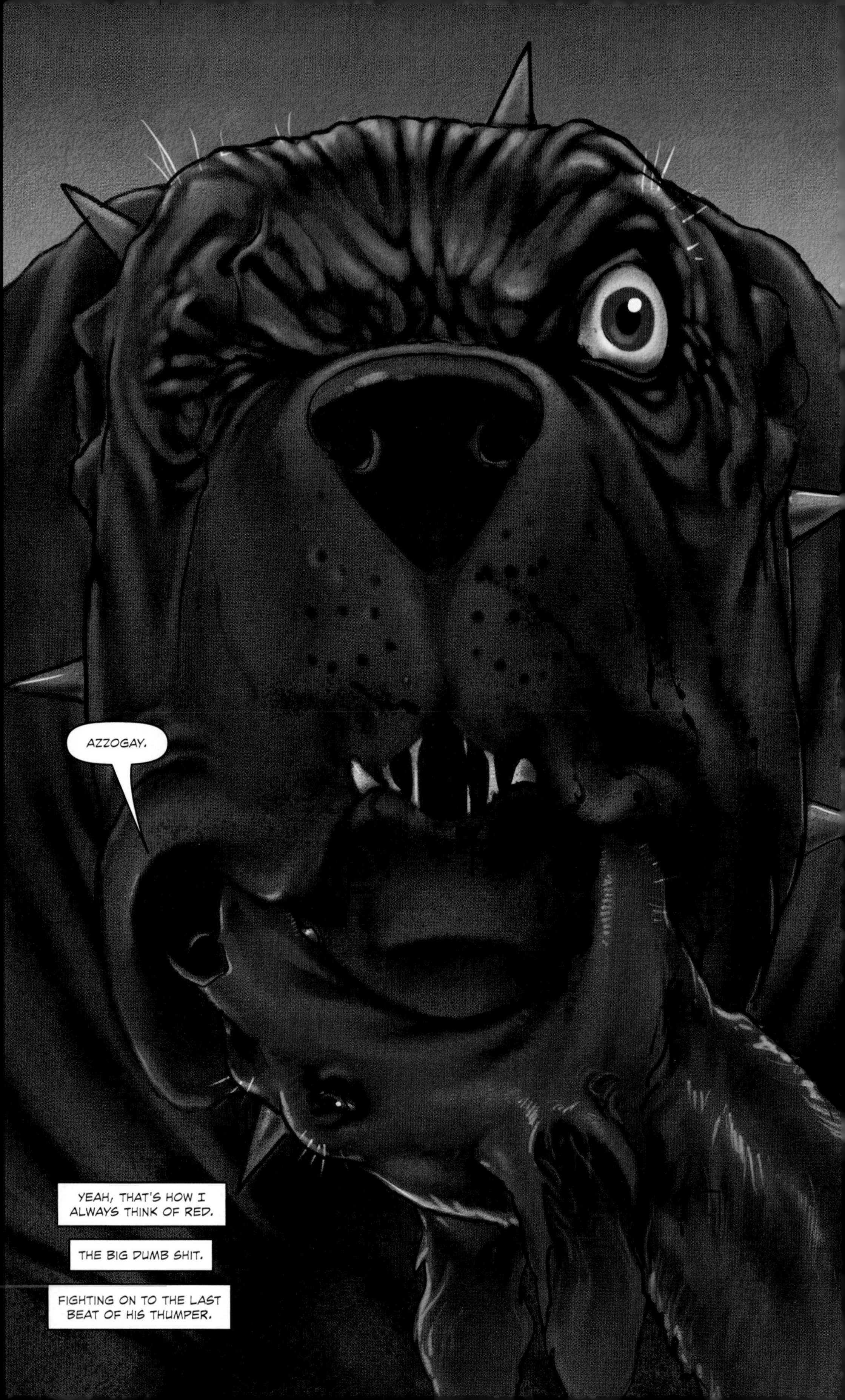
AZZOGAY.
YEAH, THAT'S HOW I ALWAYS THINK OF RED.
THE BIG DUMB SHIT.
FIGHTING ON TO THE LAST BEAT OF HIS THUMPER.

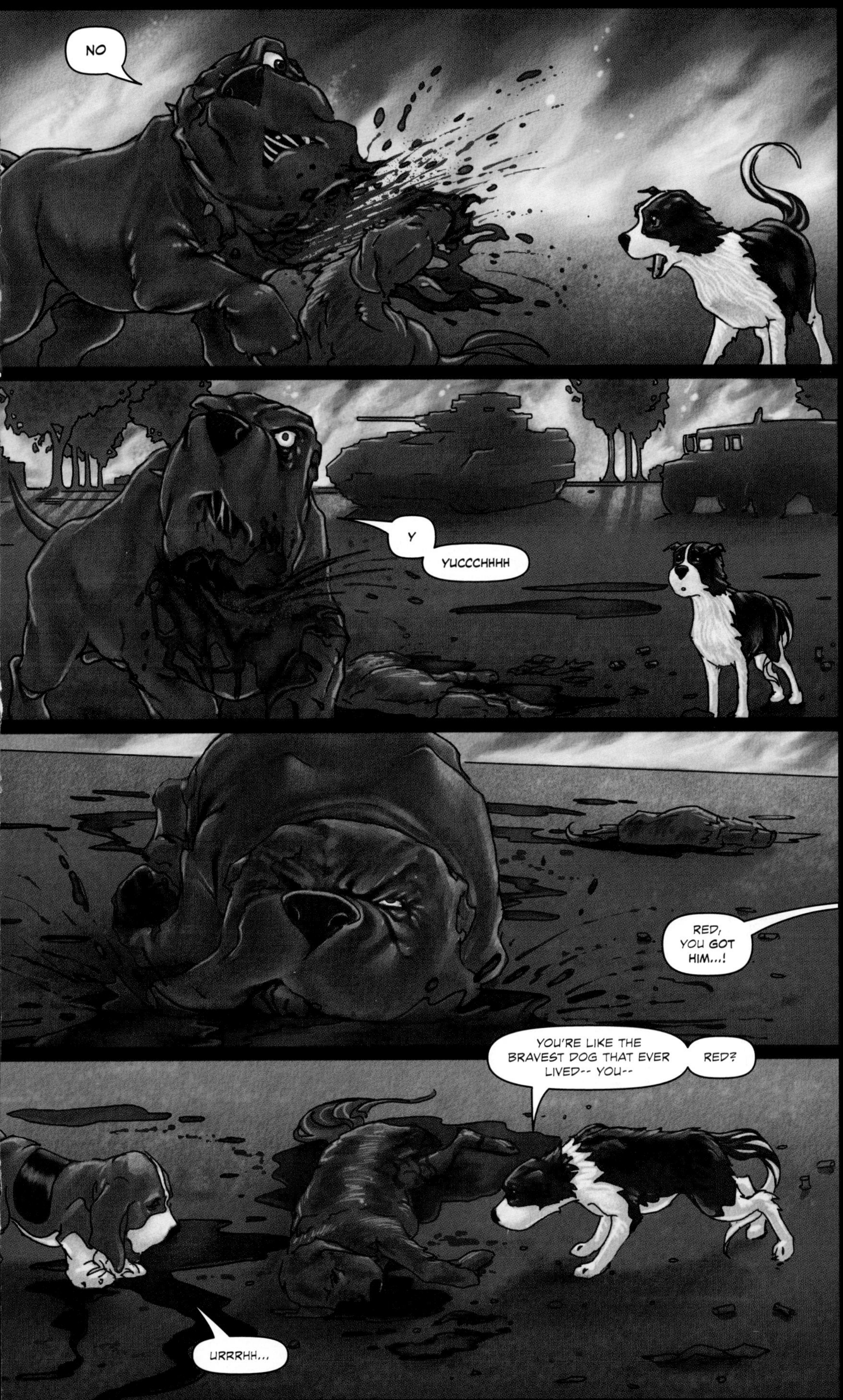
NO
Y
YUCCCHHHH
RED, YOU GOT HIM...!
YOU'RE LIKE THE BRAVEST DOG THAT EVER LIVED-- YOU--
RED?
URRRHH...

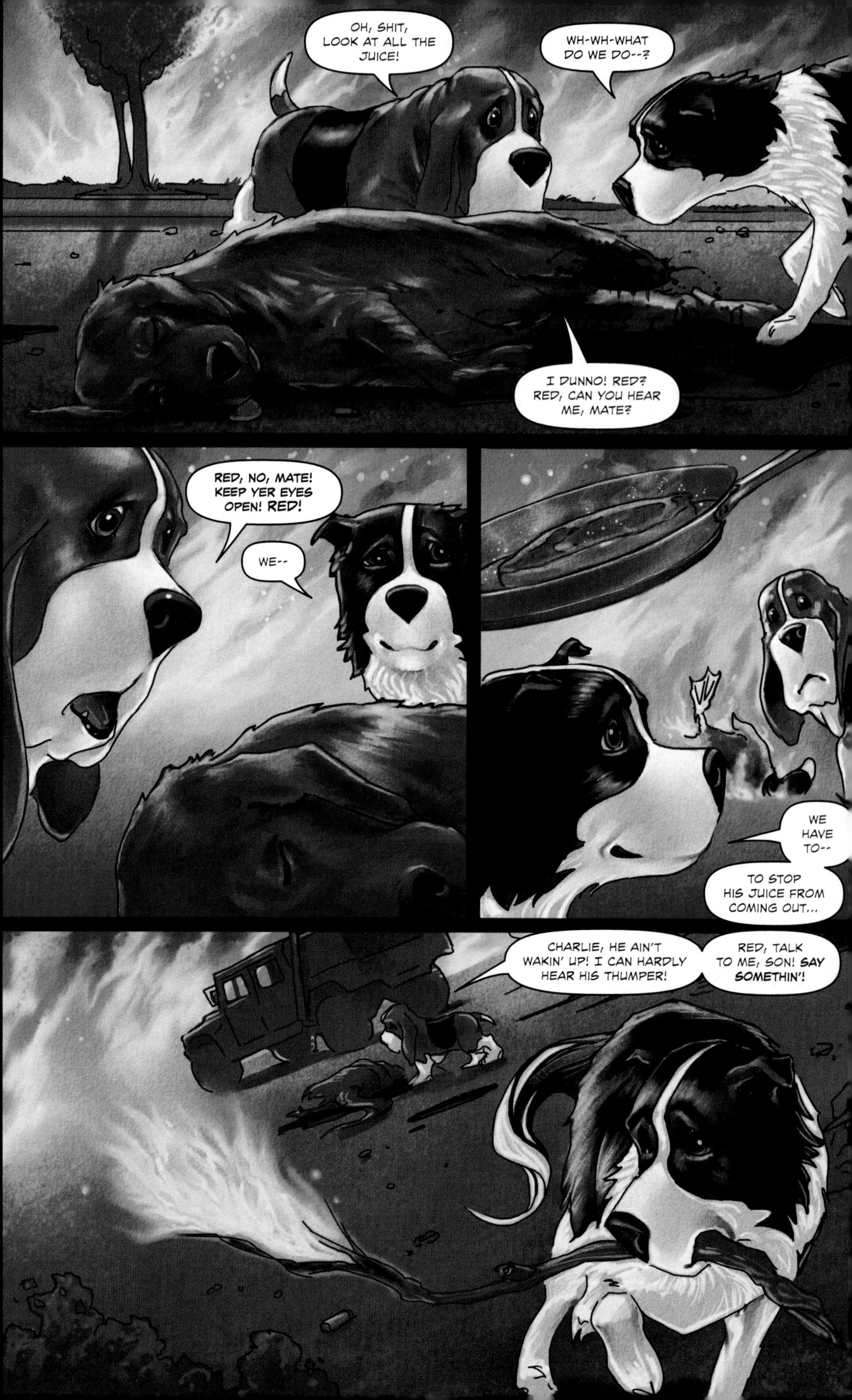
OH, SHIT, LOOK AT ALL THE JUICE!
WH-WH-WHAT DO WE DO--?
I DUNNO! RED? RED, CAN YOU HEAR ME, MATE?
RED, NO, MATE! KEEP YER EYES OPEN! RED!
WE--
WE HAVE TO--
TO STOP HIS JUICE FROM COMING OUT...
CHARLIE, HE AIN'T WAKIN' UP! I CAN HARDLY HEAR HIS THUMPER!
RED, TALK TO ME, SON! SAY SOMETHIN'!

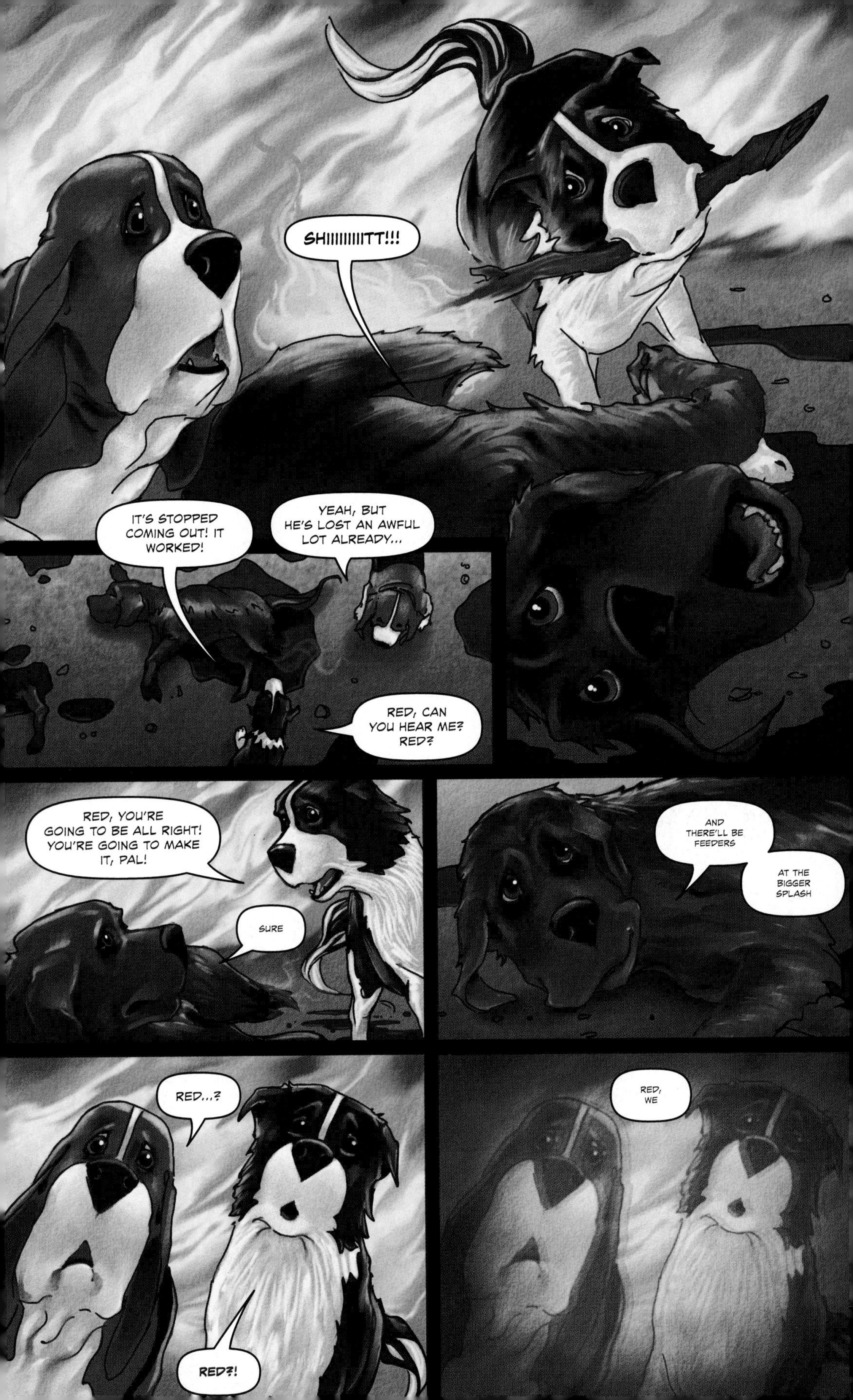
SHIIIIIIIIITT!!!
IT'S STOPPED COMING OUT! IT WORKED!
YEAH, BUT HE'S LOST AN AWFUL LOT ALREADY...
RED, CAN YOU HEAR ME? RED?
RED, YOU'RE GOING TO BE ALL RIGHT! YOU'RE GOING TO MAKE IT, PAL!
SURE
AND THERE'LL BE FEEDERS
AT THE BIGGER SPLASH
RED...?
RED?!
RED, WE

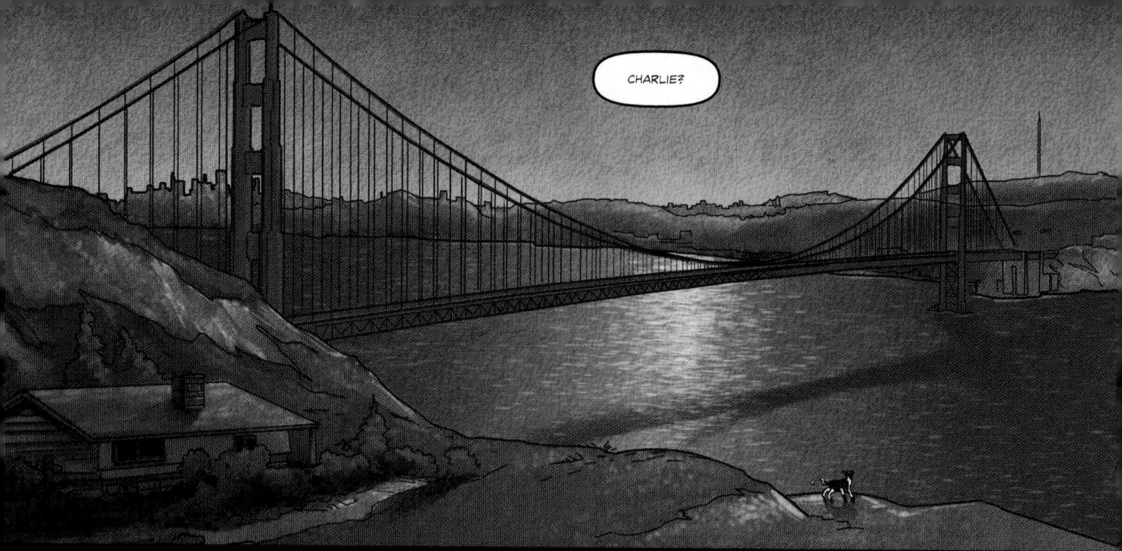
CHARLIE?

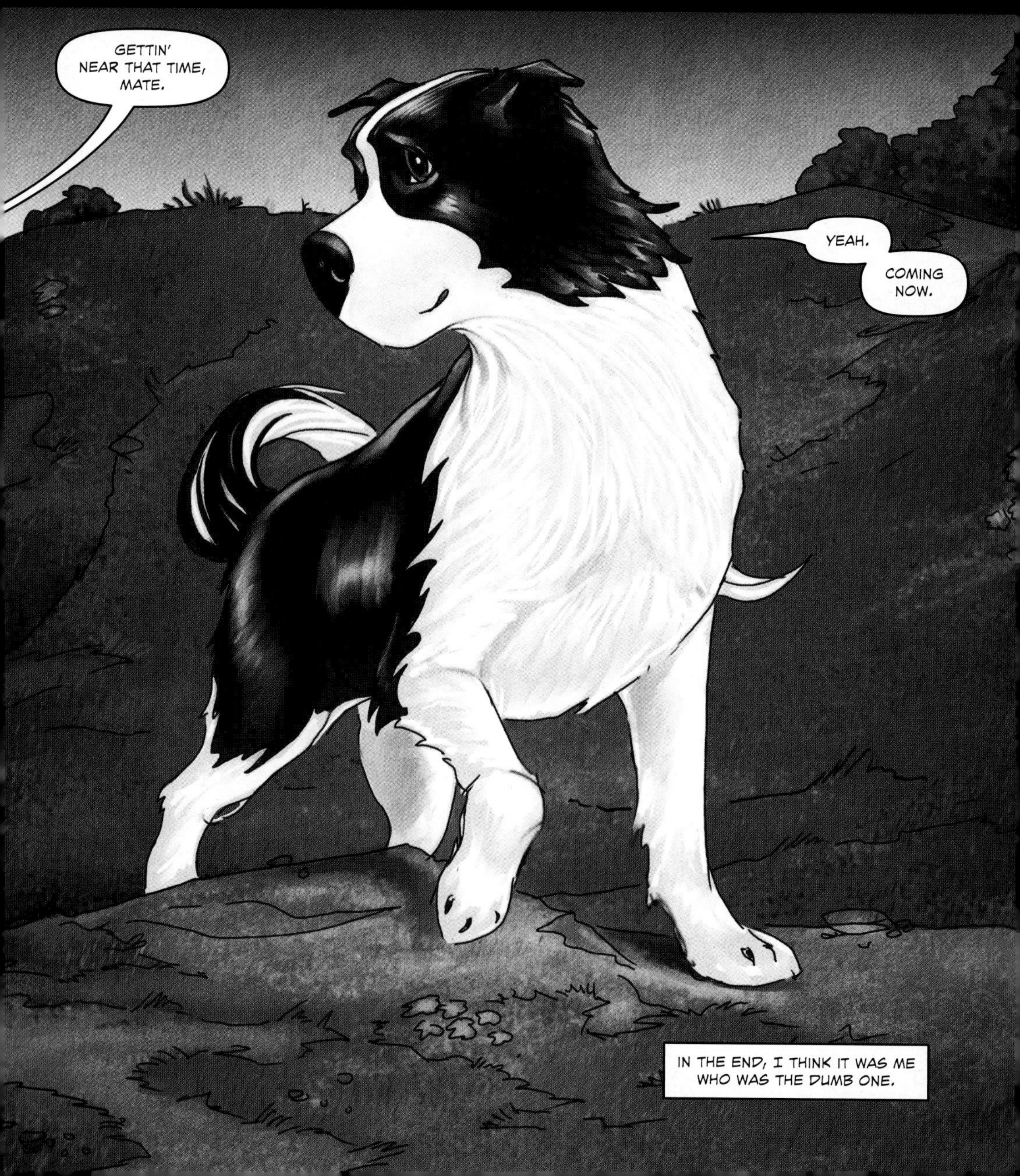
GETTIN' NEAR THAT TIME, MATE.
YEAH.
COMING NOW.
IN THE END, I THINK IT WAS ME WHO WAS THE DUMB ONE.

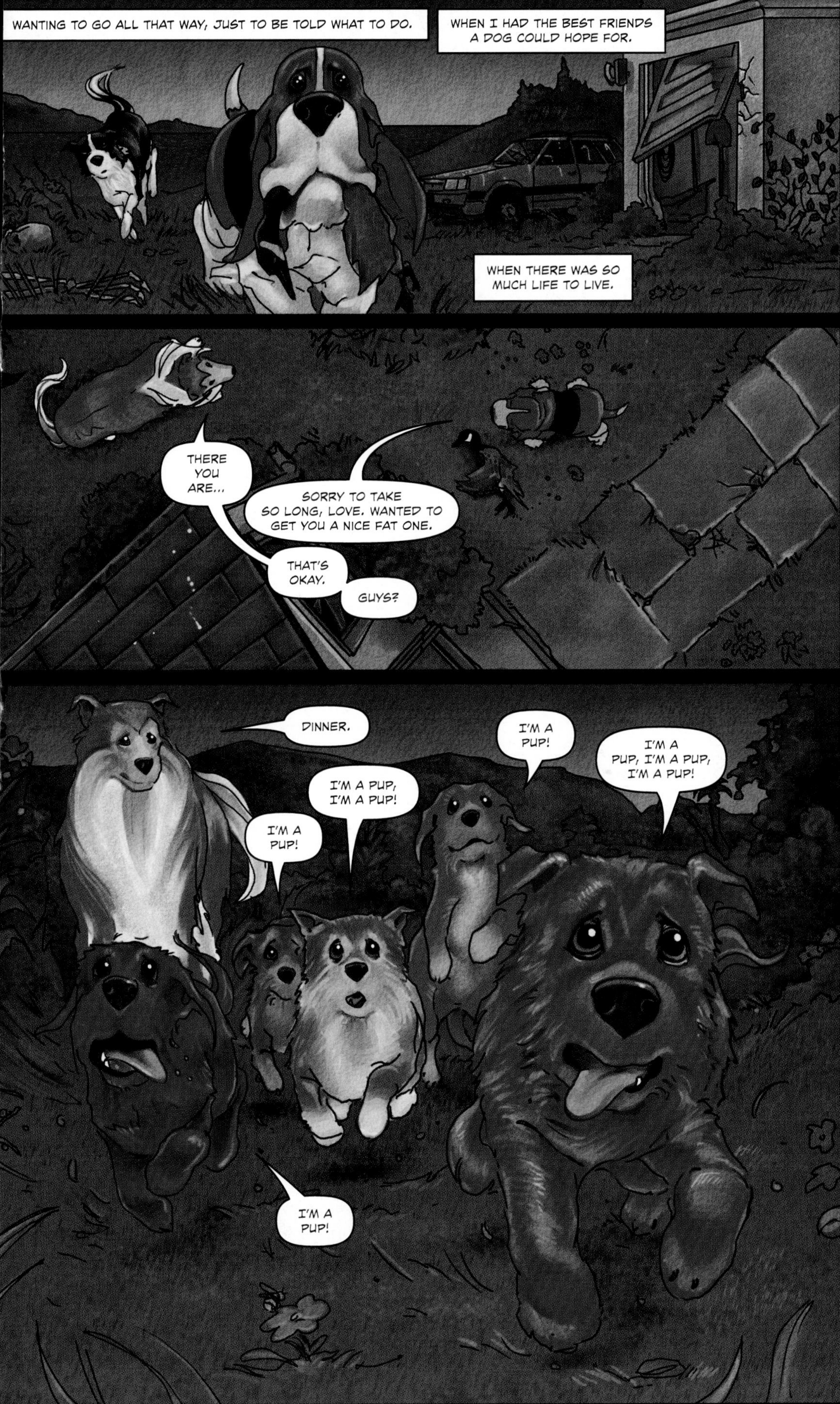
WANTING TO GO ALL THAT WAY, JUST TO BE TOLD WHAT TO DO.
WHEN I HAD THE BEST FRIENDS A DOG COULD HOPE FOR.
WHEN THERE WAS SO MUCH LIFE TO LIVE.
THERE YOU ARE...
SORRY TO TAKE SO LONG, LOVE. WANTED TO GET YOU A NICE FAT ONE.
THAT'S OKAY.
GUYS?
DINNER.
I'M A PUP!
I'M A PUP, I'M A PUP, I'M A PUP!
I'M A PUP, I'M A PUP!
I'M A PUP!
I'M A PUP!

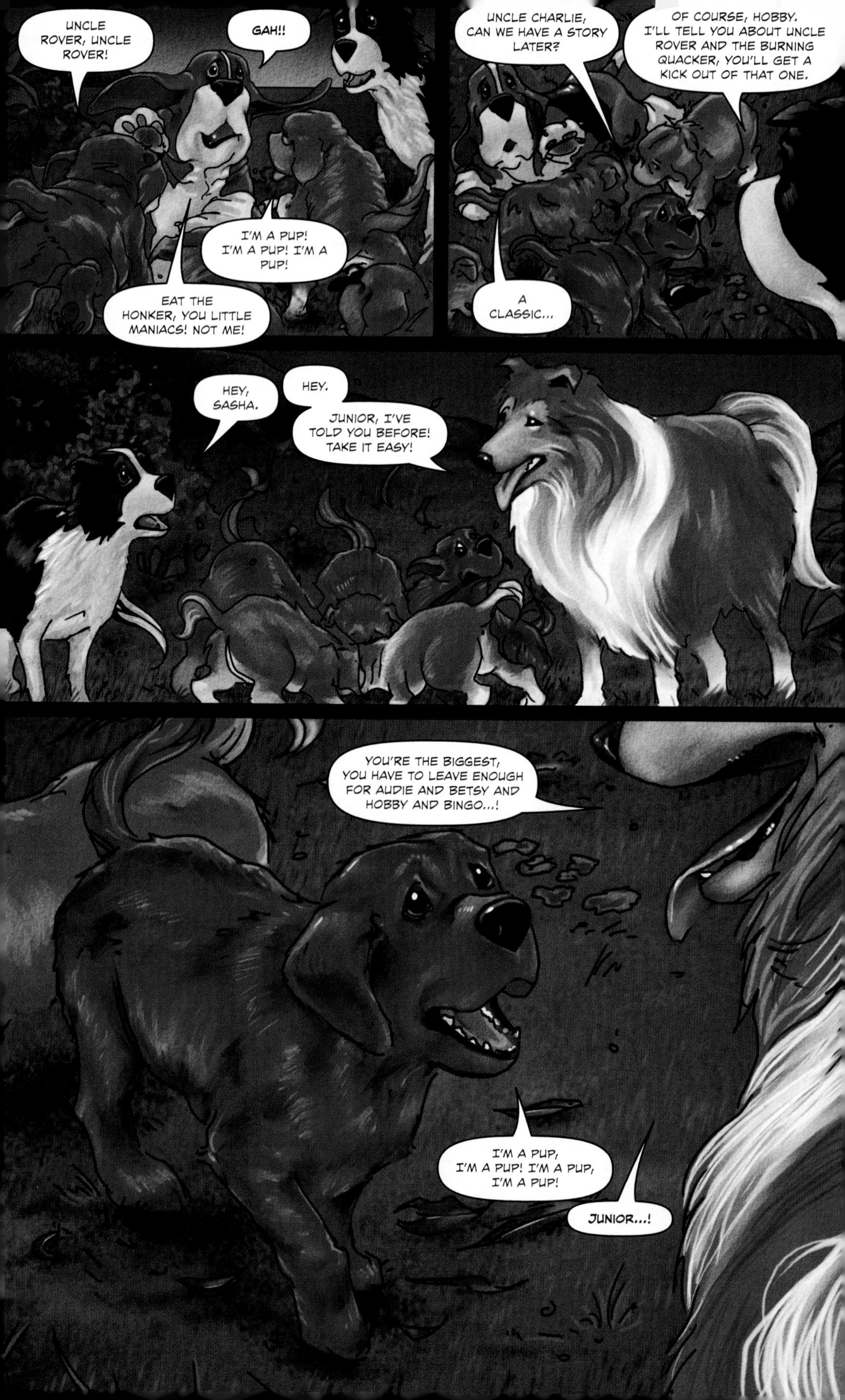
UNCLE ROVER, UNCLE ROVER!
GAH!!
I'M A PUP! I'M A PUP! I'M A PUP!
EAT THE HONKER, YOU LITTLE MANIACS! NOT ME!
UNCLE CHARLIE, CAN WE HAVE A STORY LATER?
OF COURSE, HOBBY. I'LL TELL YOU ABOUT UNCLE ROVER AND THE BURNING QUACKER, YOU'LL GET A KICK OUT OF THAT ONE.
A CLASSIC...
HEY, SASHA.
HEY.
JUNIOR, I'VE TOLD YOU BEFORE! TAKE IT EASY!
YOU'RE THE BIGGEST, YOU HAVE TO LEAVE ENOUGH FOR AUDIE AND BETSY AND HOBBY AND BINGO...!
I'M A PUP, I'M A PUP! I'M A PUP, I'M A PUP!
JUNIOR...!

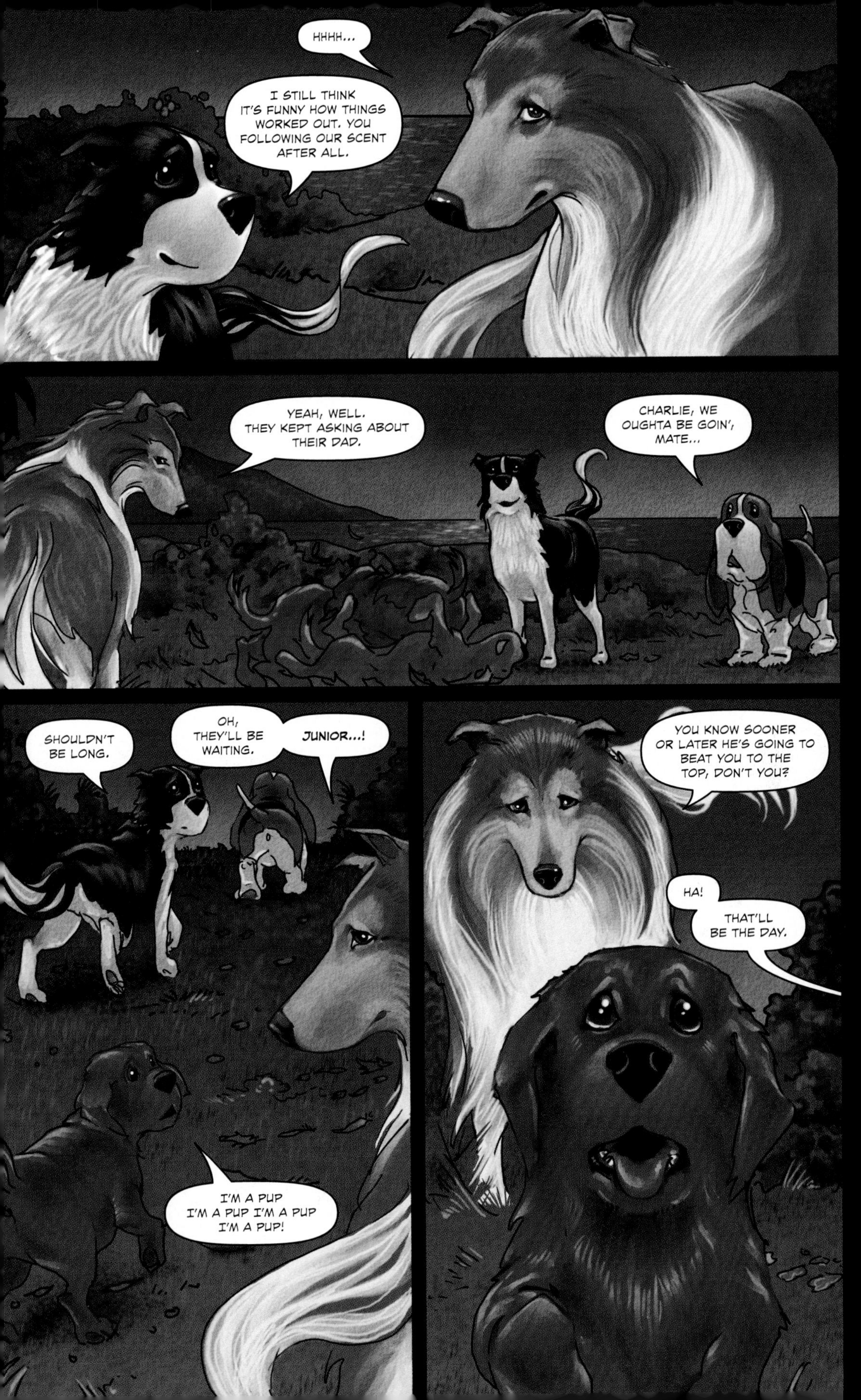
HHHH...
I STILL THINK IT'S FUNNY HOW THINGS WORKED OUT. YOU FOLLOWING OUR SCENT AFTER ALL.
YEAH, WELL. THEY KEPT ASKING ABOUT THEIR DAD.
CHARLIE, WE OUGHTA BE GOIN', MATE...
SHOULDN'T BE LONG.
OH, THEY'LL BE WAITING.
JUNIOR...!
I'M A PUP I'M A PUP I'M A PUP I'M A PUP!
YOU KNOW SOONER OR LATER HE'S GOING TO BEAT YOU TO THE TOP, DON'T YOU?
HA!
THAT'LL BE THE DAY.

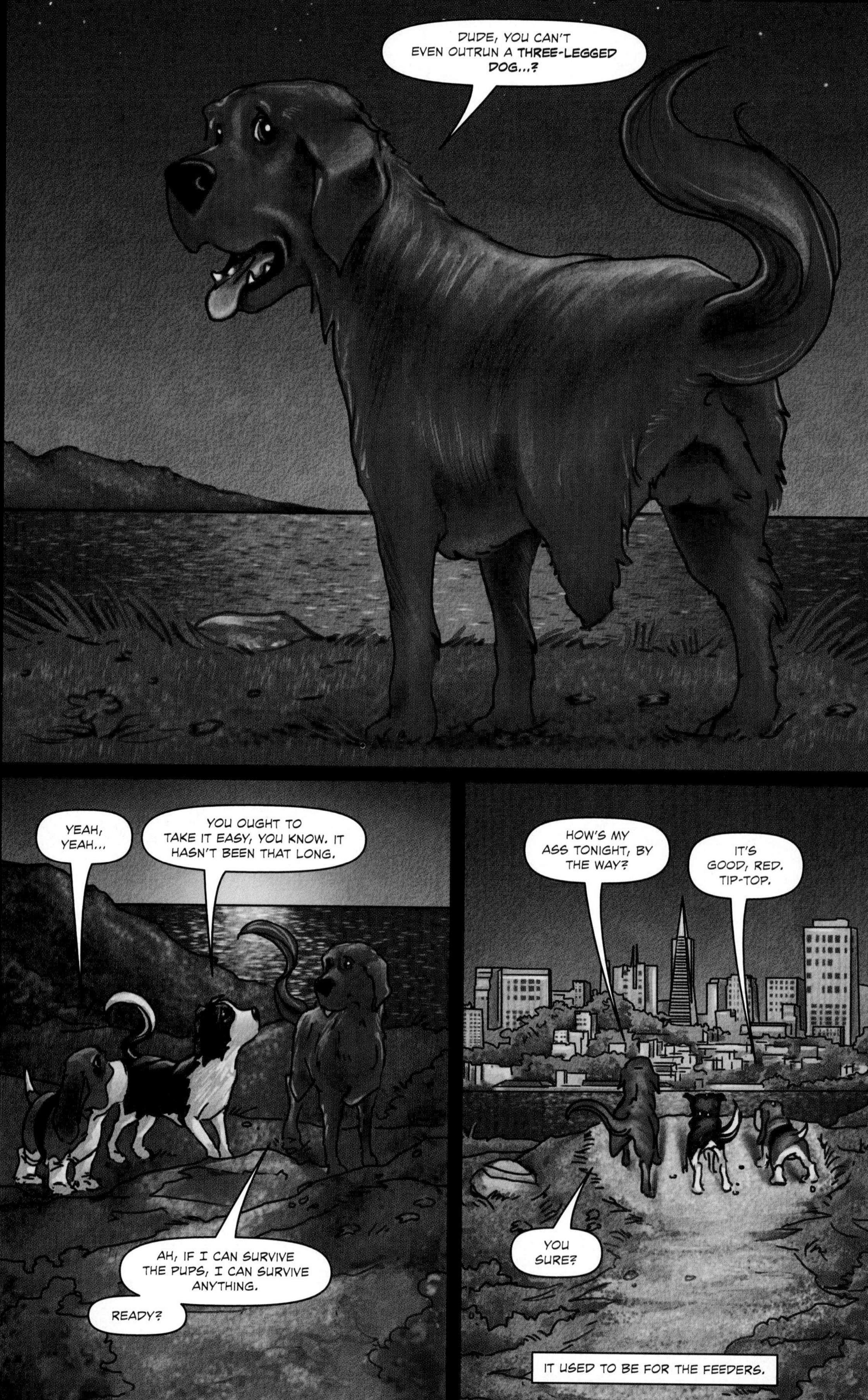
DUDE, YOU CAN'T EVEN OUTRUN A THREE-LEGGED DOG...?
YEAH, YEAH...
YOU OUGHT TO TAKE IT EASY, YOU KNOW. IT HASN'T BEEN THAT LONG.
AH, IF I CAN SURVIVE THE PUPS, I CAN SURVIVE ANYTHING.
READY?
HOW'S MY ASS TONIGHT, BY THE WAY?
IT'S GOOD, RED. TIP-TOP.
YOU SURE?
IT USED TO BE FOR THE FEEDERS.

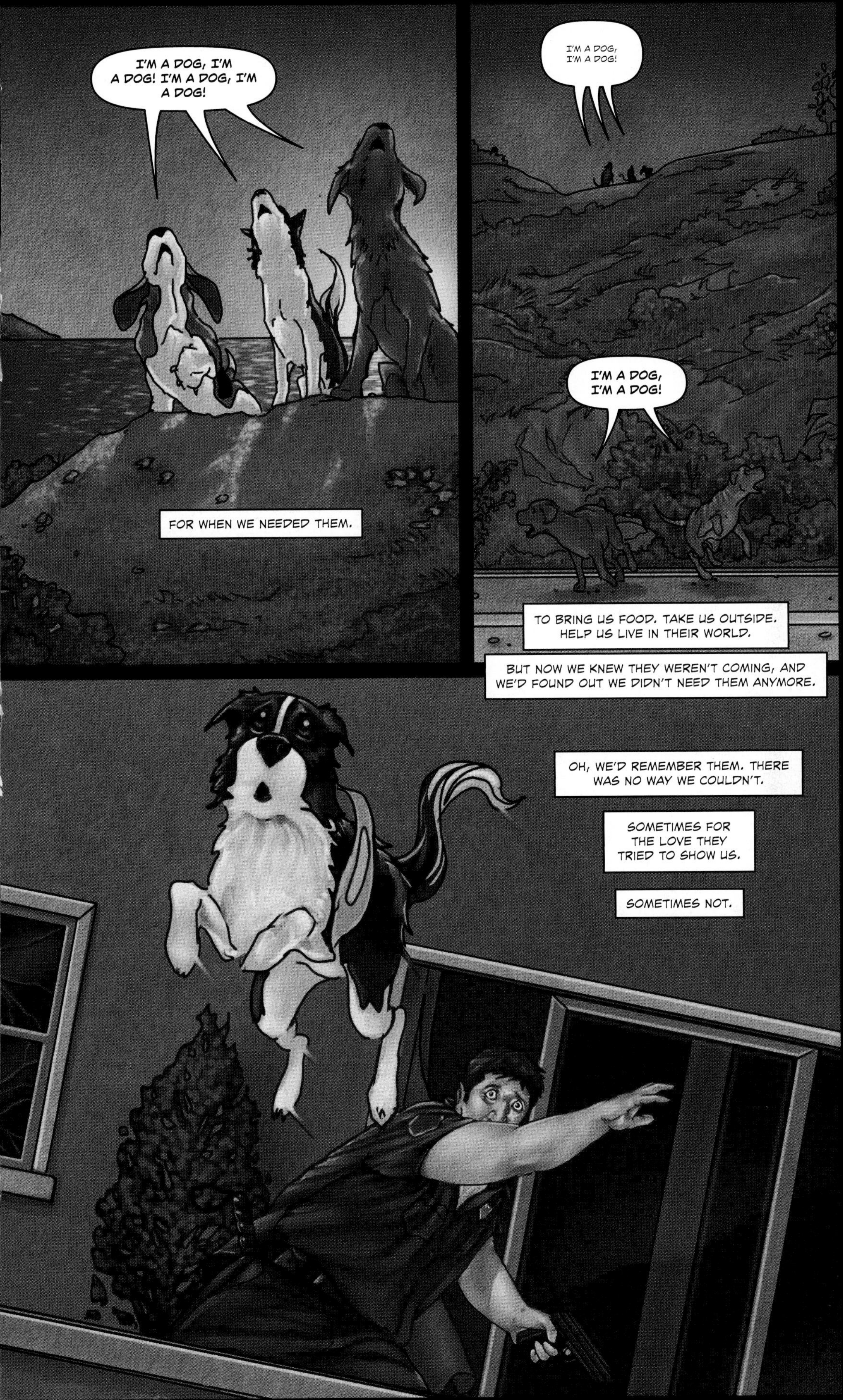
I'M A DOG, I'M A DOG! I'M A DOG, I'M A DOG!
FOR WHEN WE NEEDED THEM.
I'M A DOG, I'M A DOG!
I'M A DOG, I'M A DOG!
TO BRING US FOOD. TAKE US OUTSIDE. HELP US LIVE IN THEIR WORLD.
BUT NOW WE KNEW THEY WEREN'T COMING, AND WE'D FOUND OUT WE DIDN'T NEED THEM ANYMORE.
OH, WE'D REMEMBER THEM. THERE WAS NO WAY WE COULDN'T.
SOMETIMES FOR THE LOVE THEY TRIED TO SHOW US.
SOMETIMES NOT.

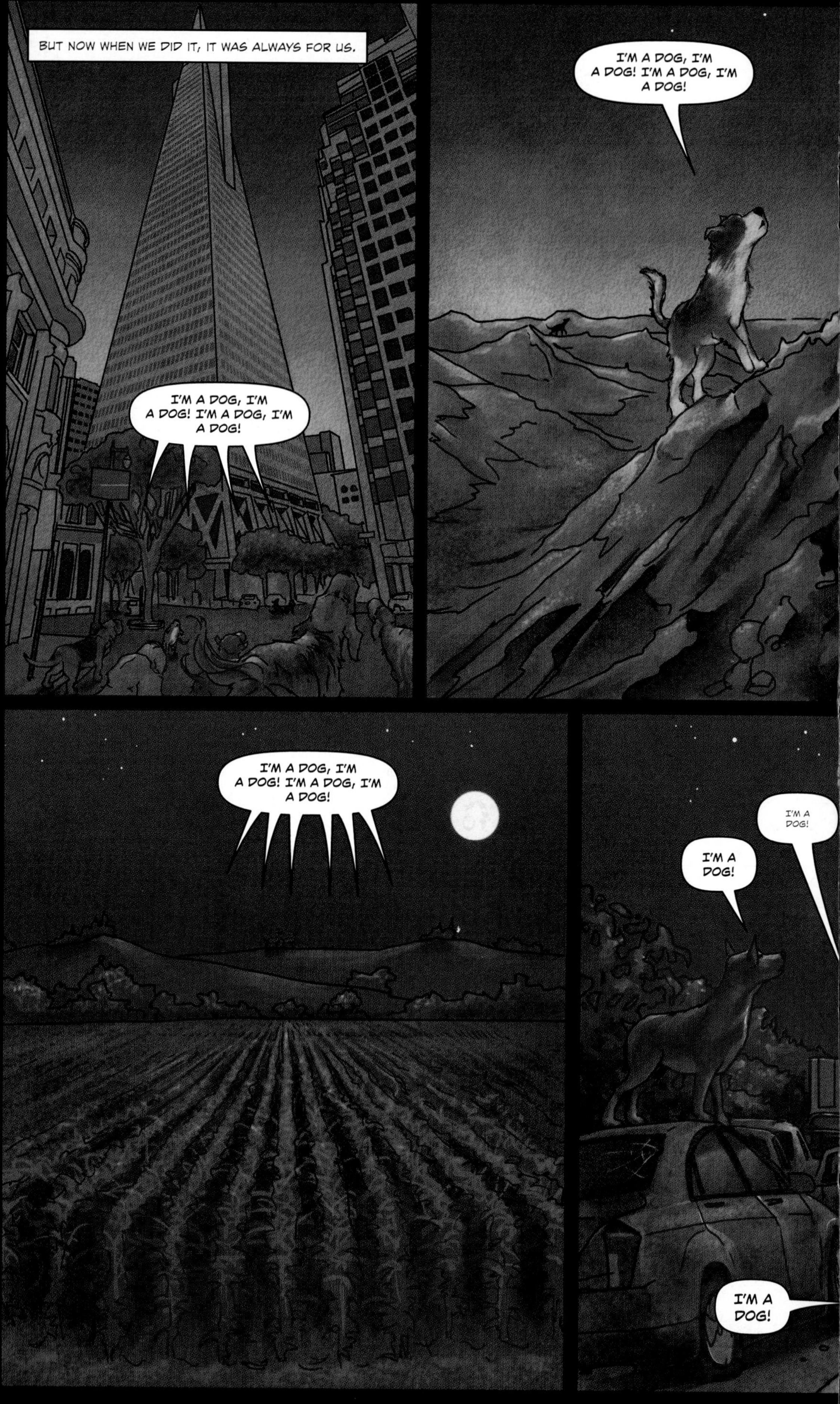
BUT NOW WHEN WE DID IT, IT WAS ALWAYS FOR US.
I'M A DOG, I'M A DOG! I'M A DOG, I'M A DOG!
I'M A DOG, I'M A DOG! I'M A DOG, I'M A DOG!
I'M A DOG, I'M A DOG! I'M A DOG, I'M A DOG!
I'M A DOG!
I'M A DOG!
I'M A DOG!

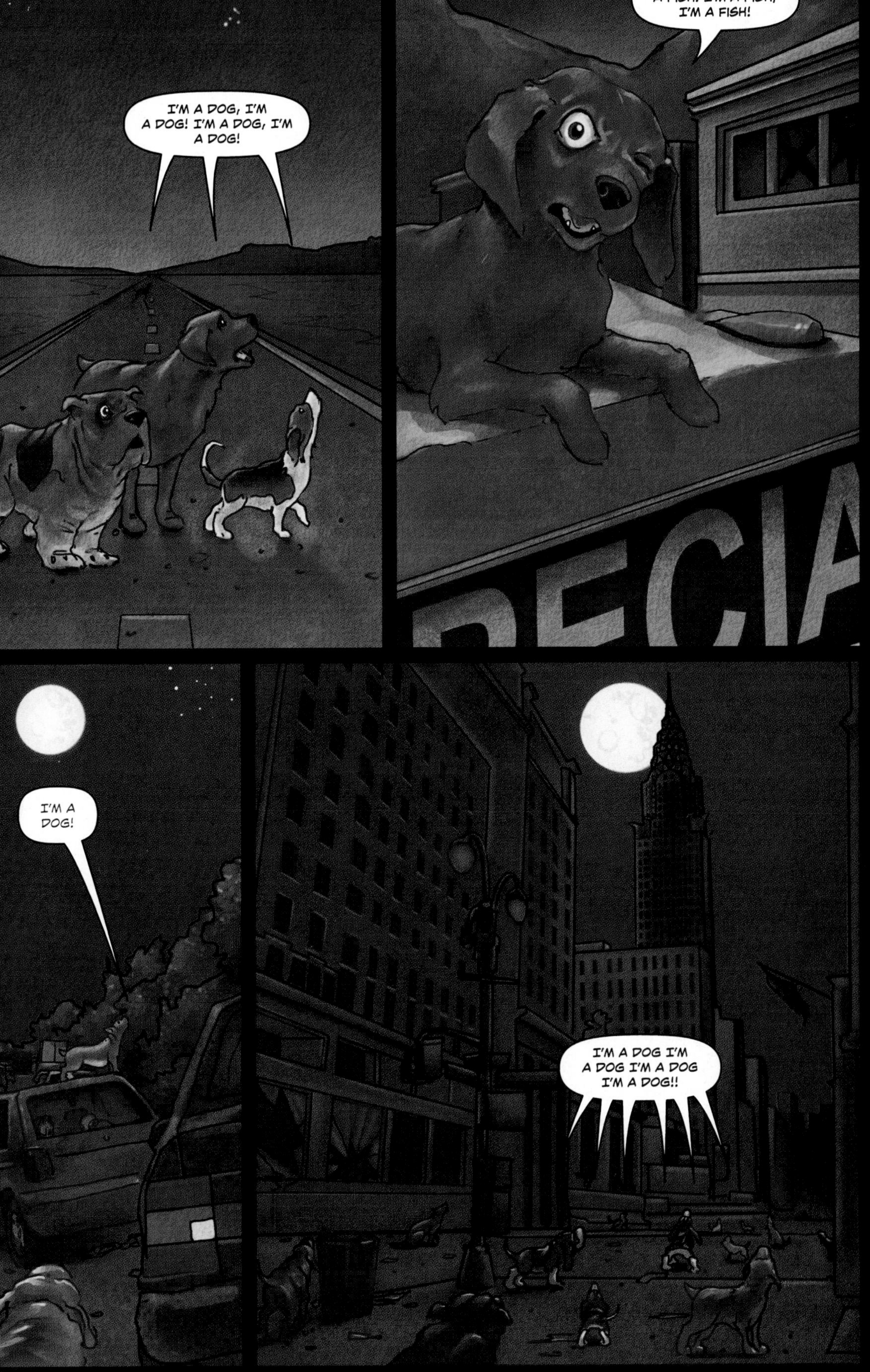
I'M A DOG, I'M A DOG! I'M A DOG, I'M A DOG!
I'M A FISH!
I'M A DOG!
I'M A DOG I'M A DOG I'M A DOG I'M A DOG!!

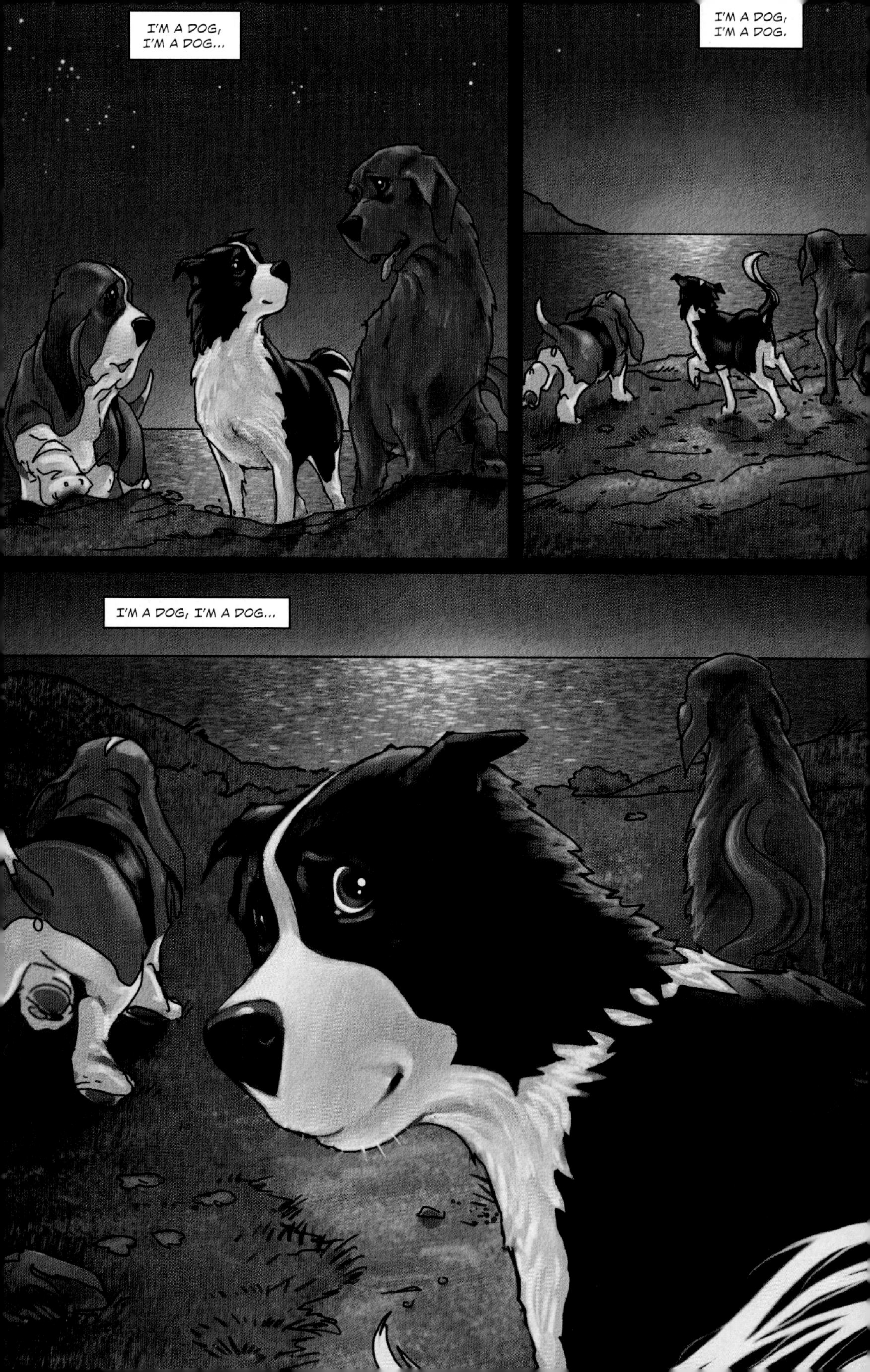
I'M A DOG,
I'M A DOG...
I'M A DOG,
I'M A DOG.
I'M A DOG, I'M A DOG...

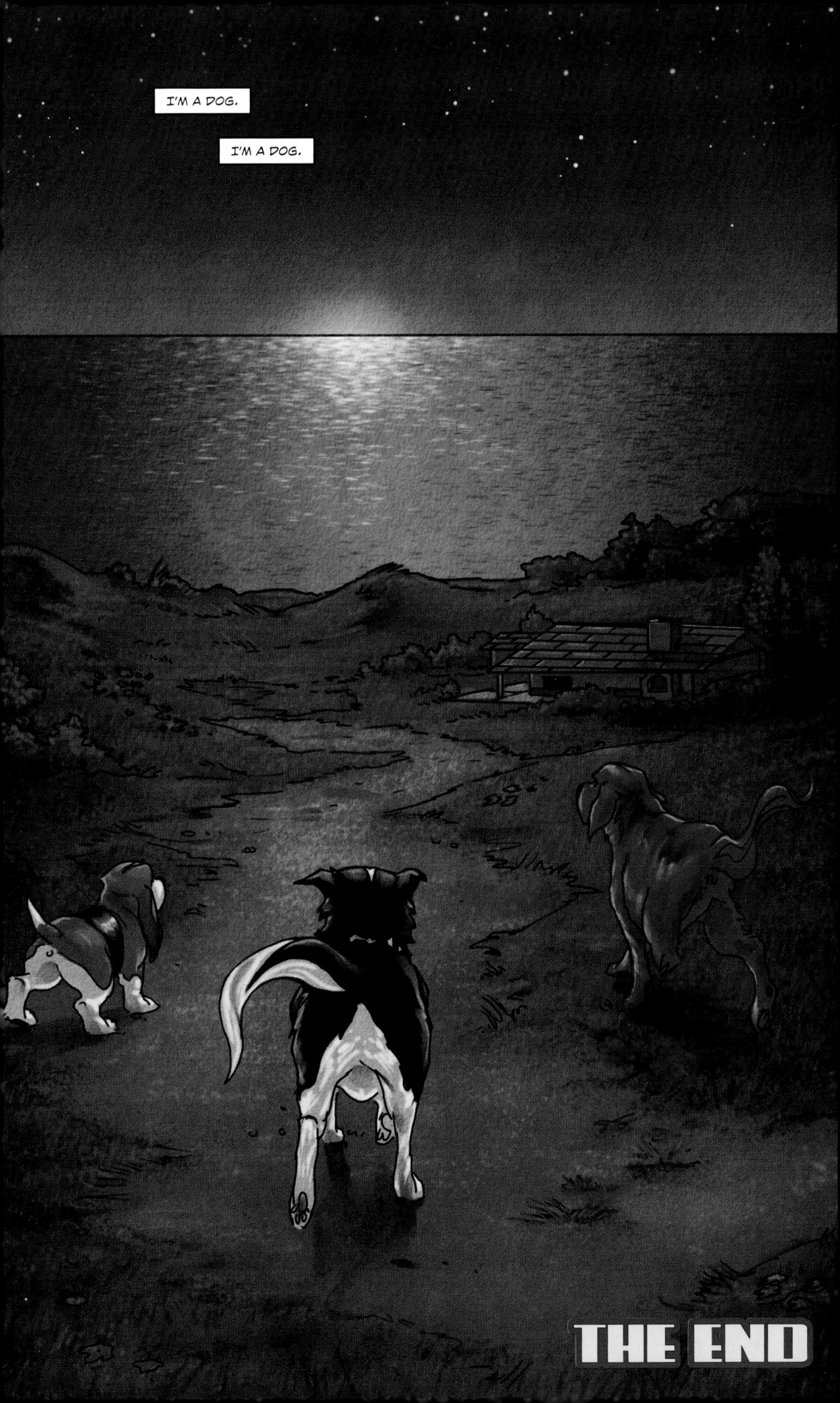
I'M A DOG.
I'M A DOG.
THE END

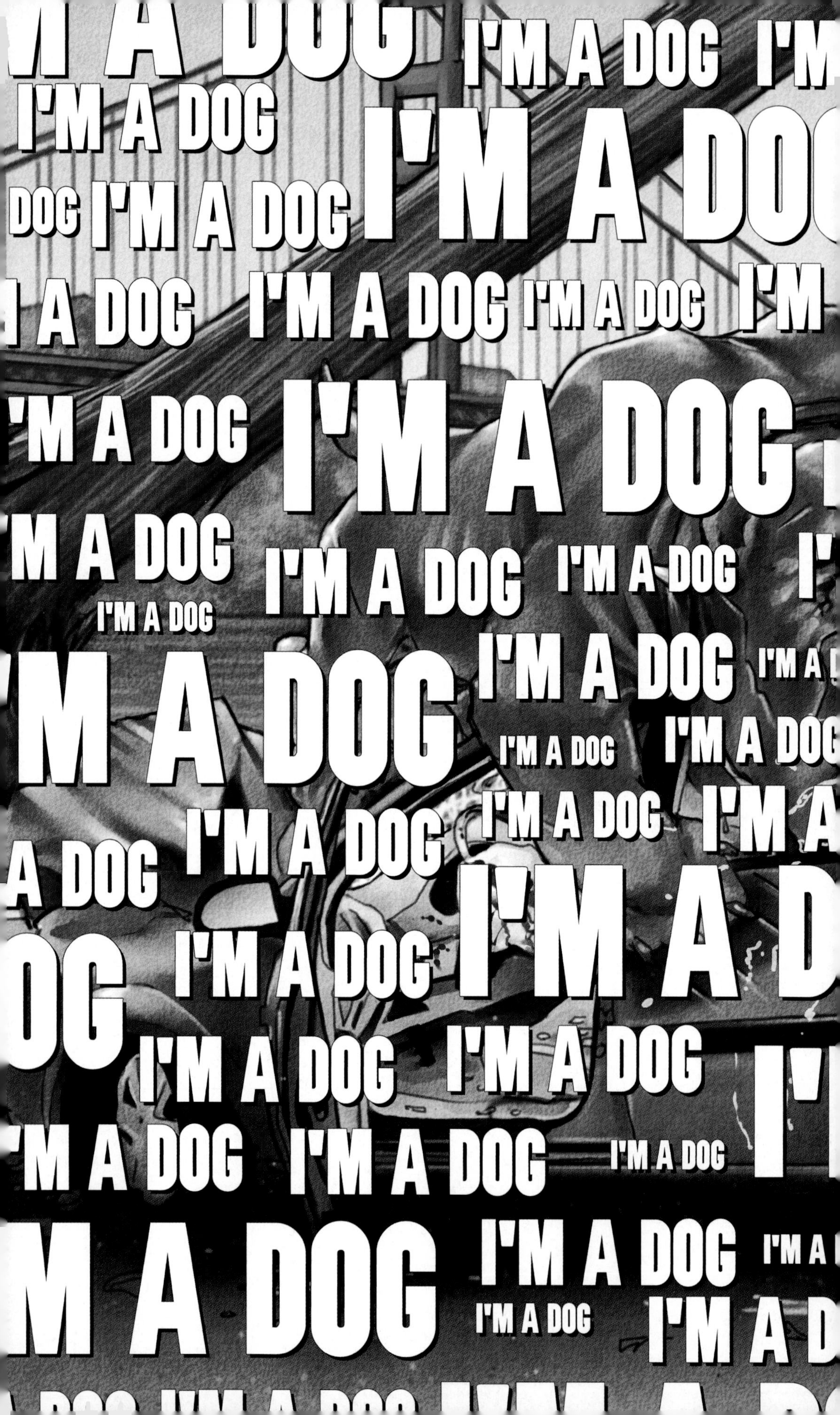

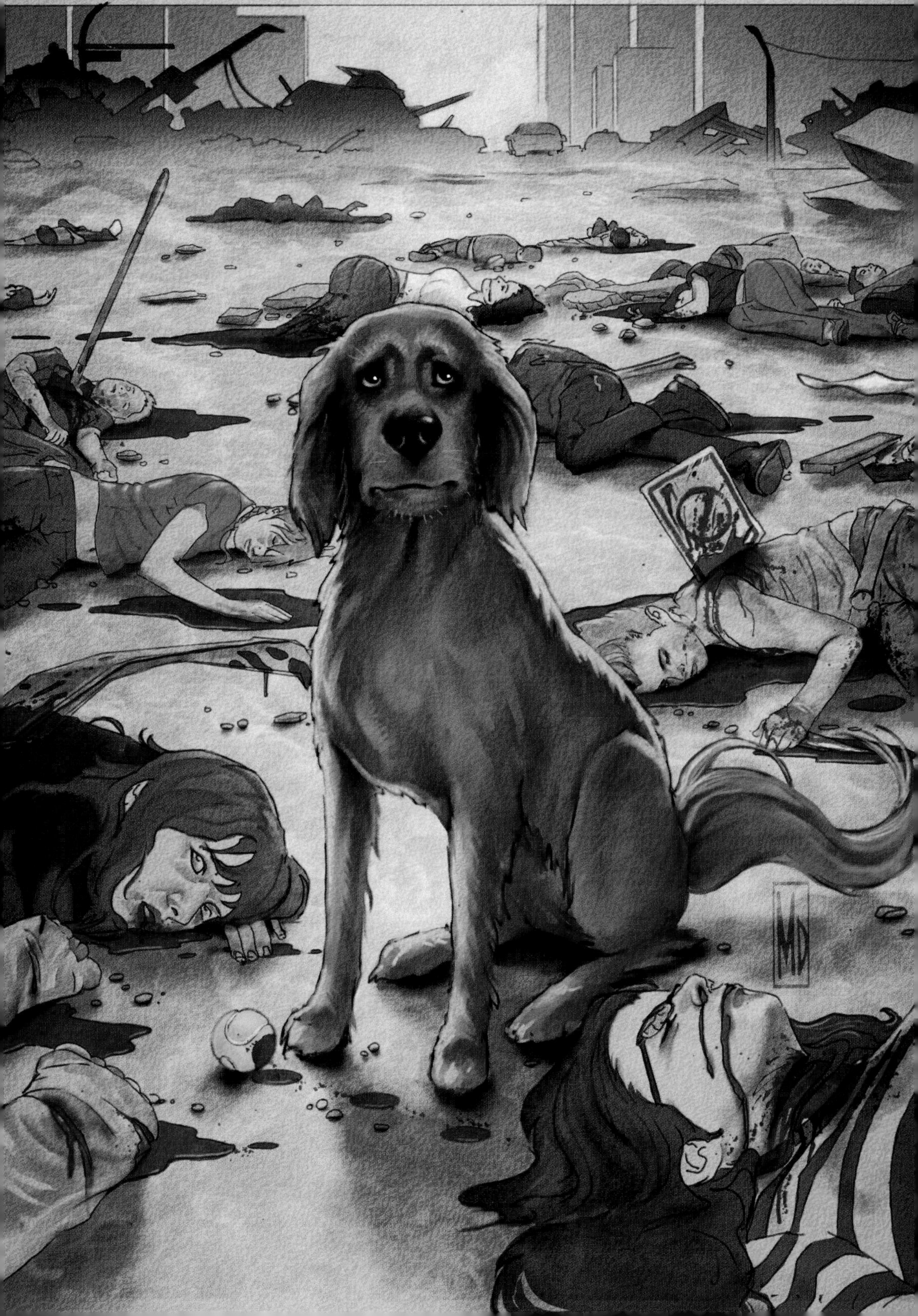

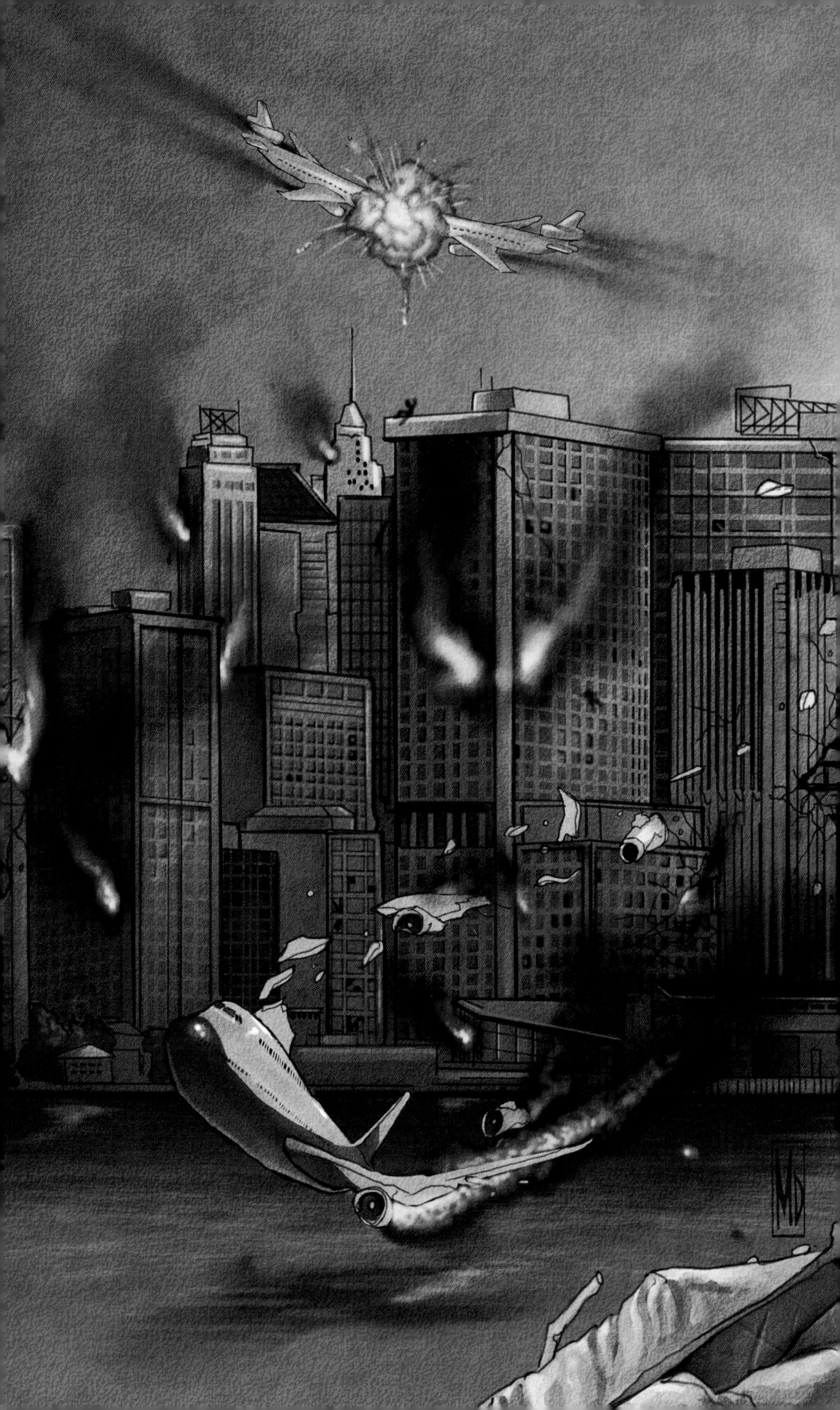

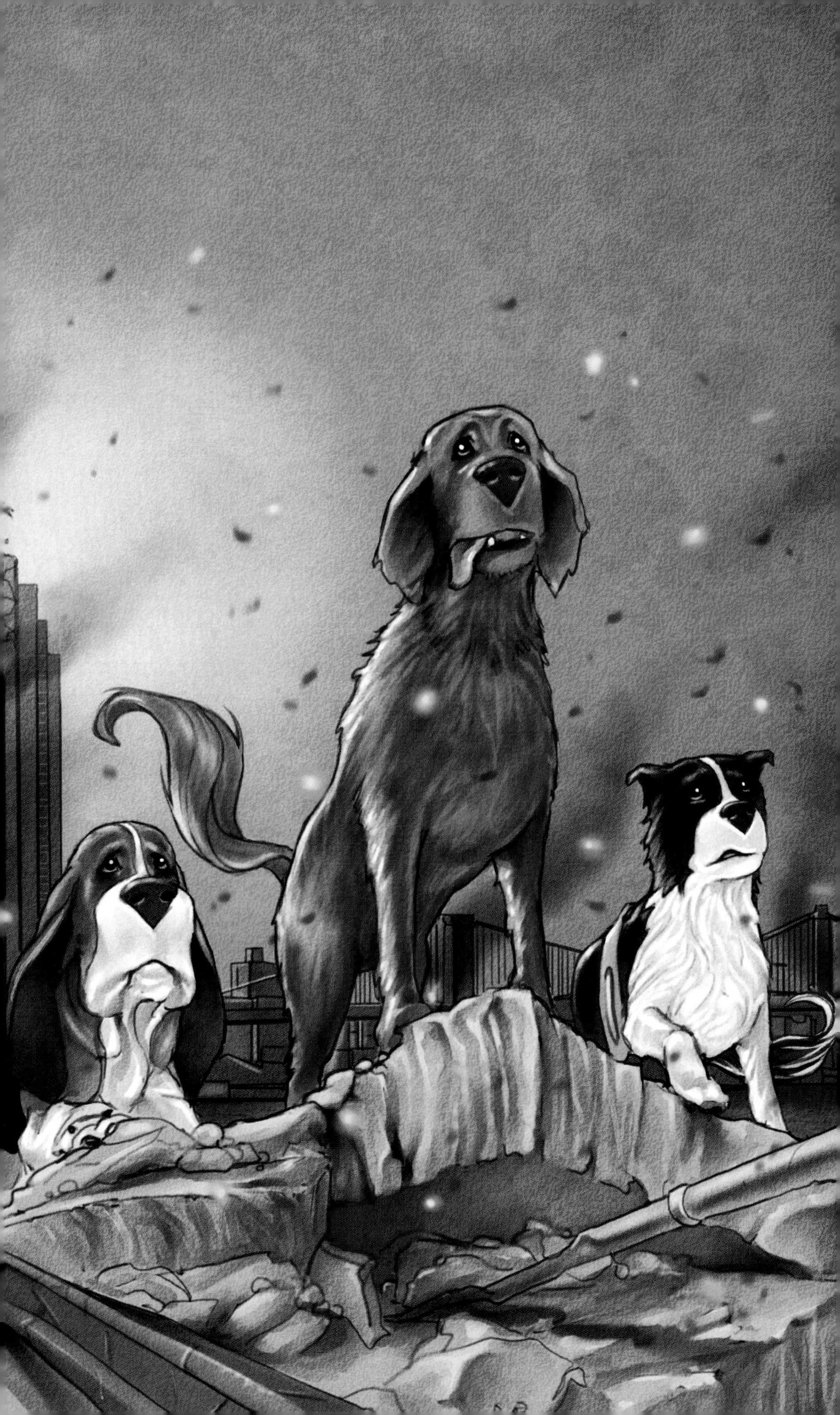

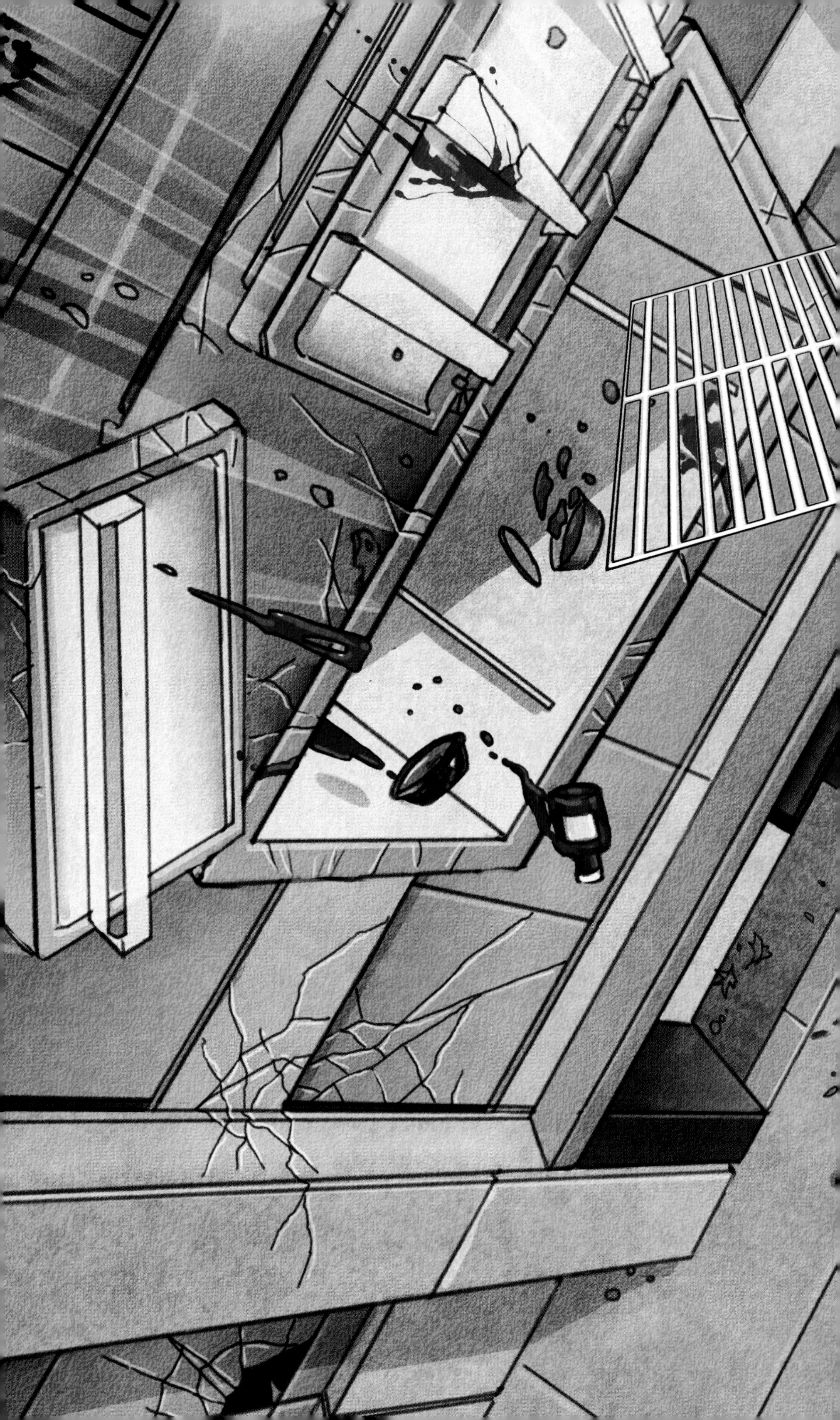

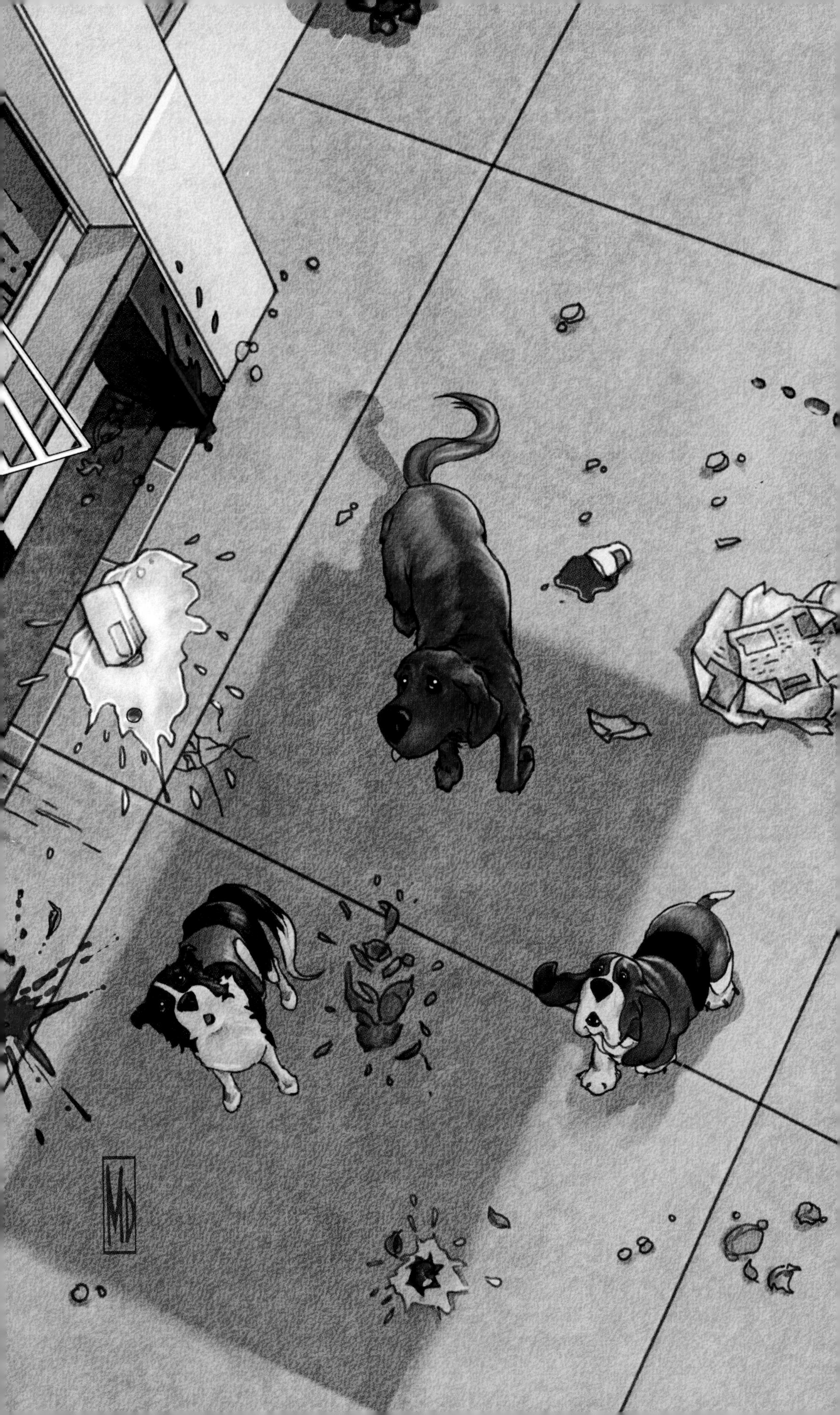

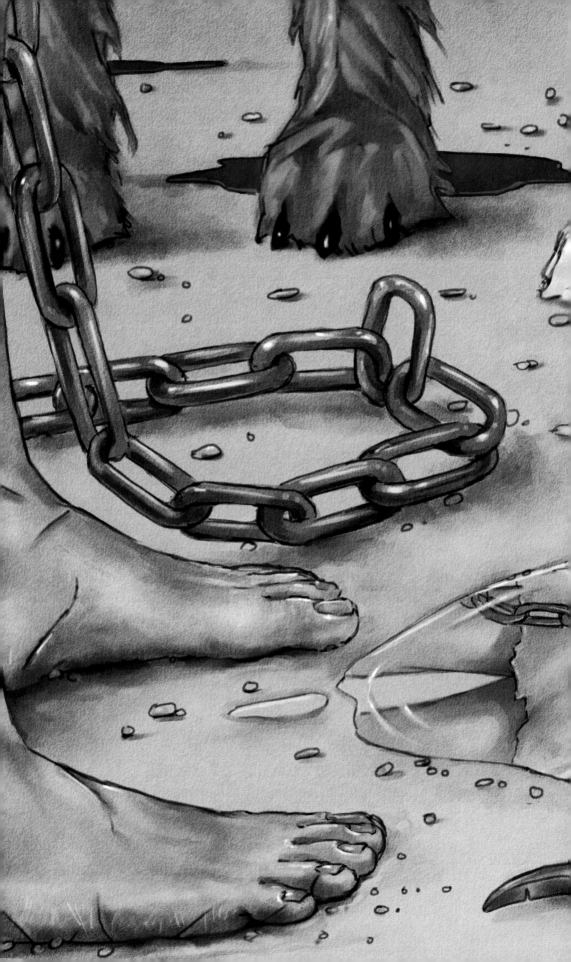

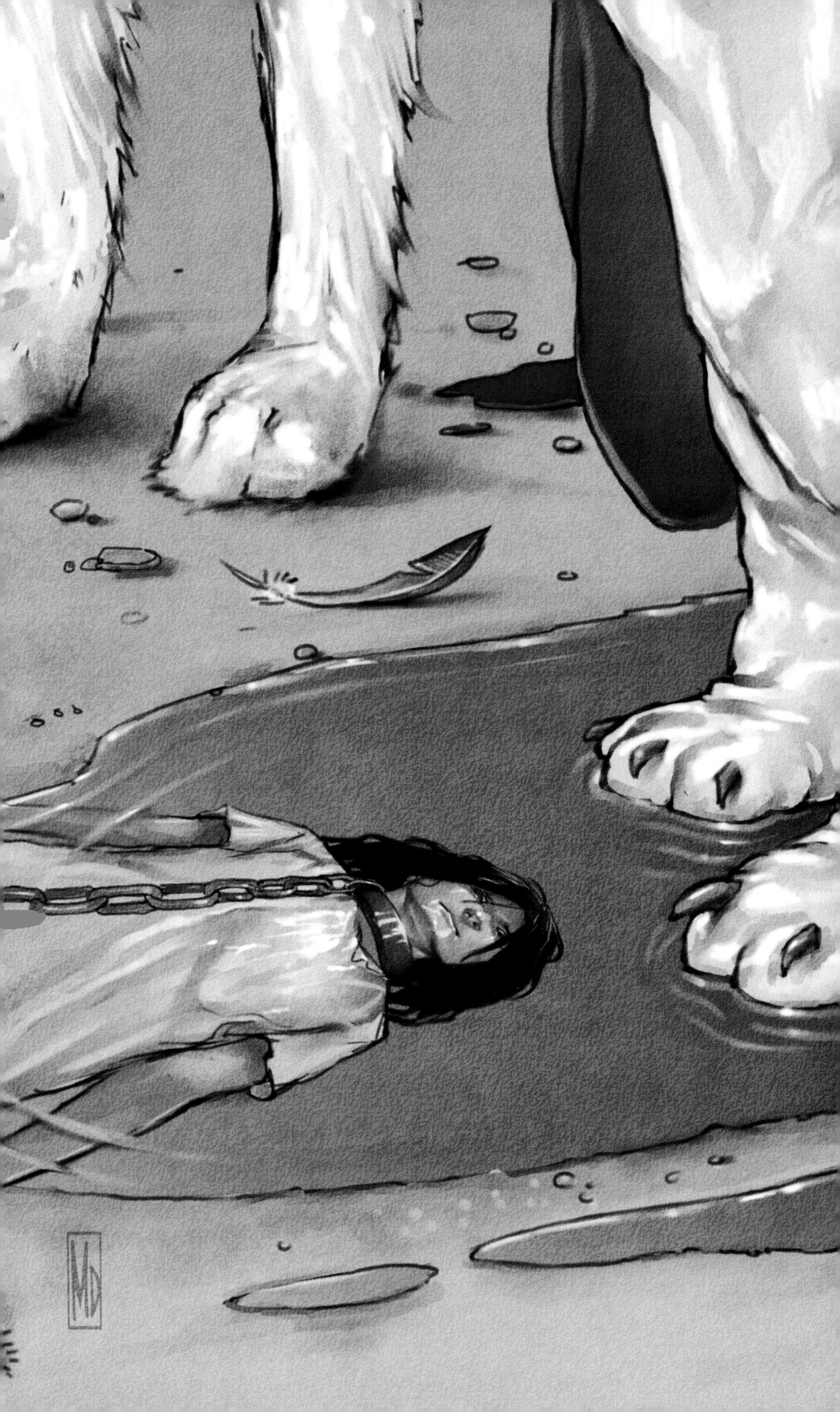

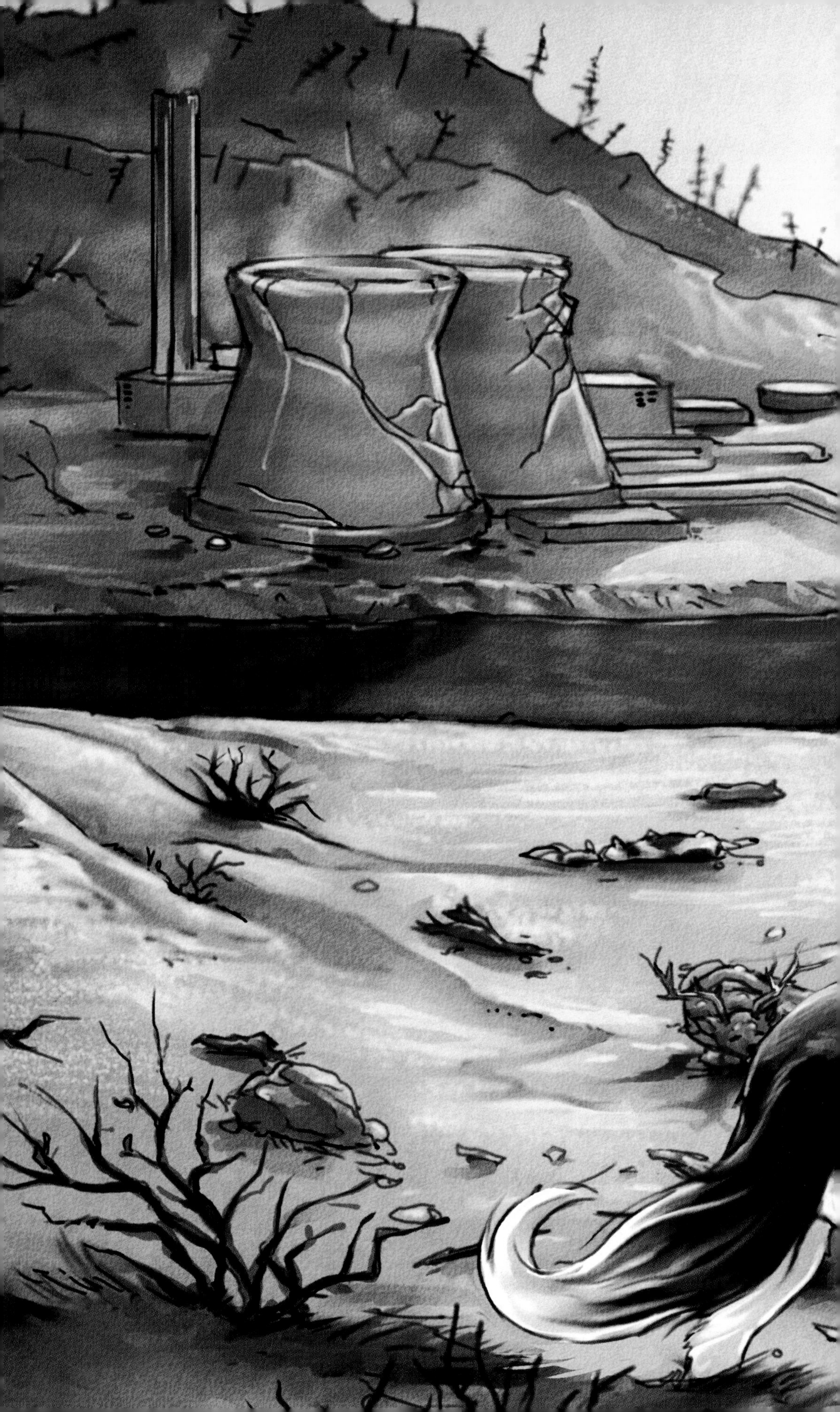

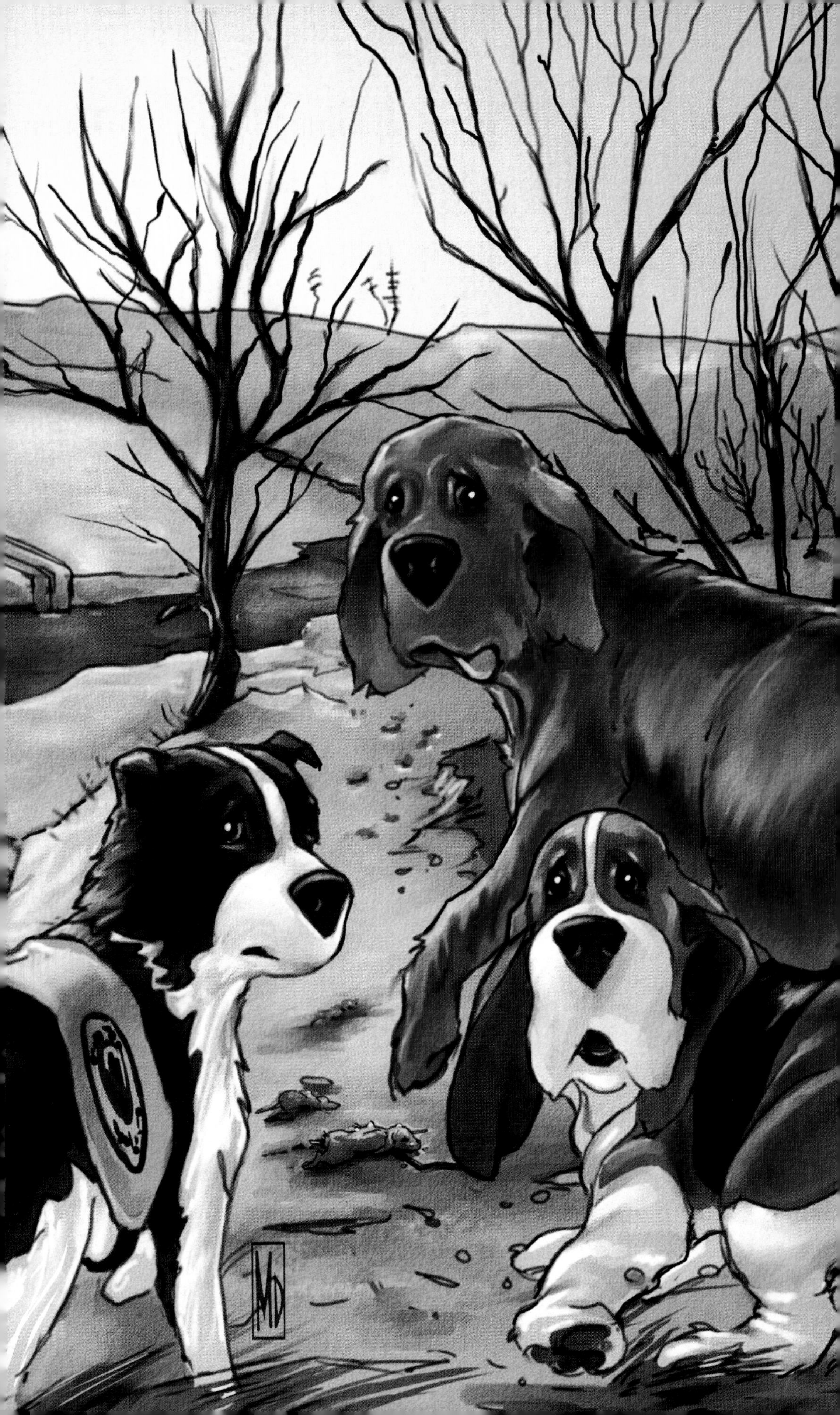

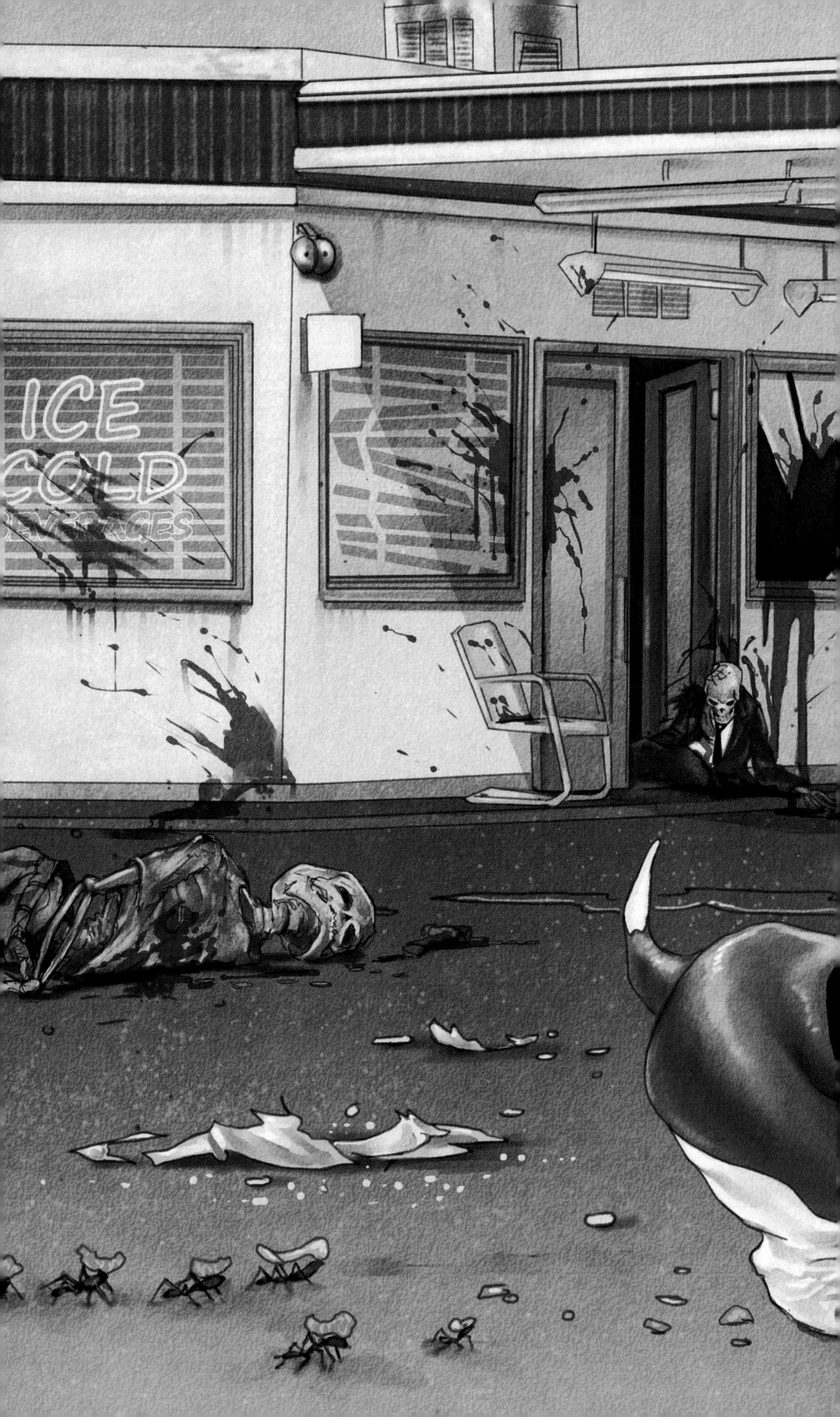
ICE
COLD

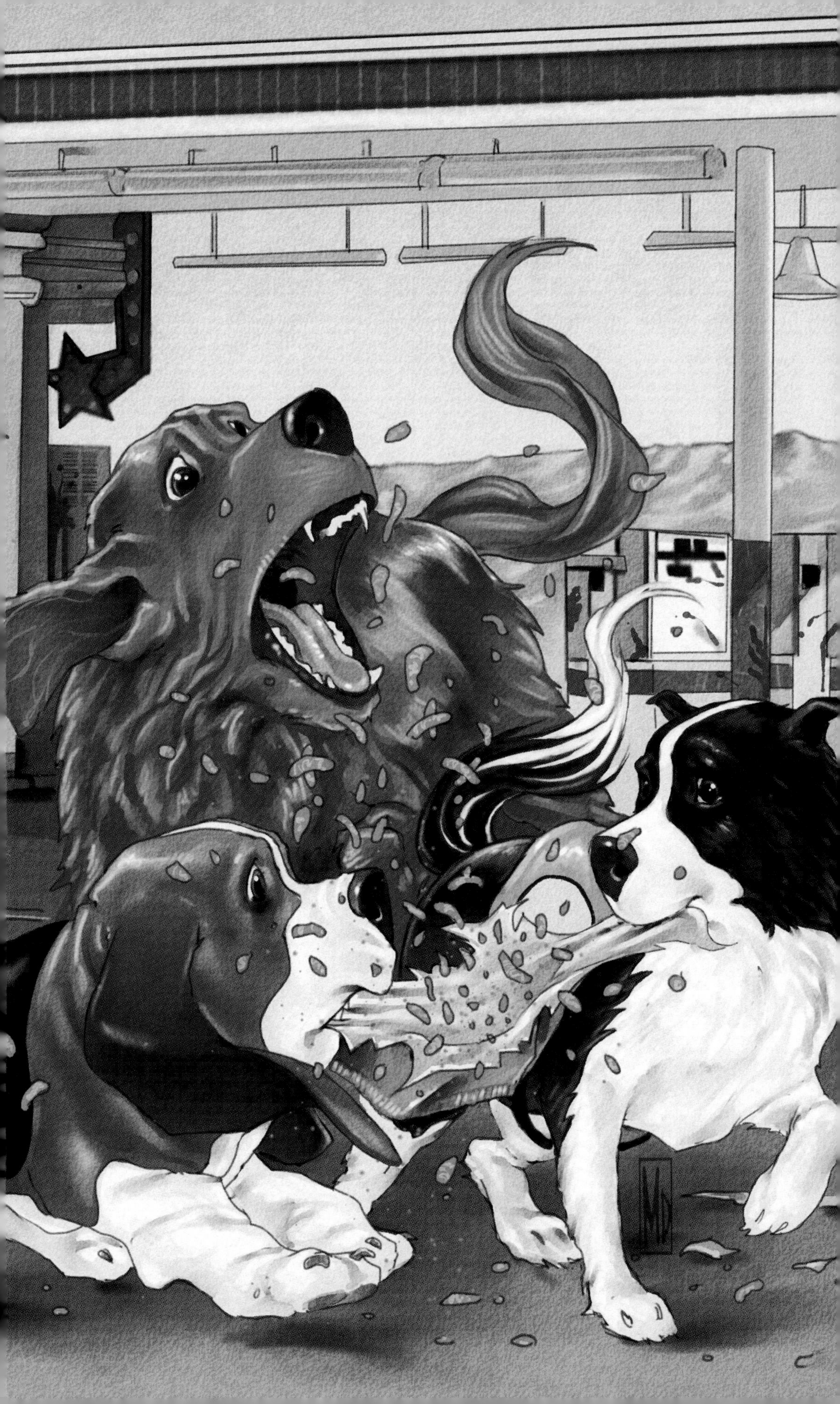

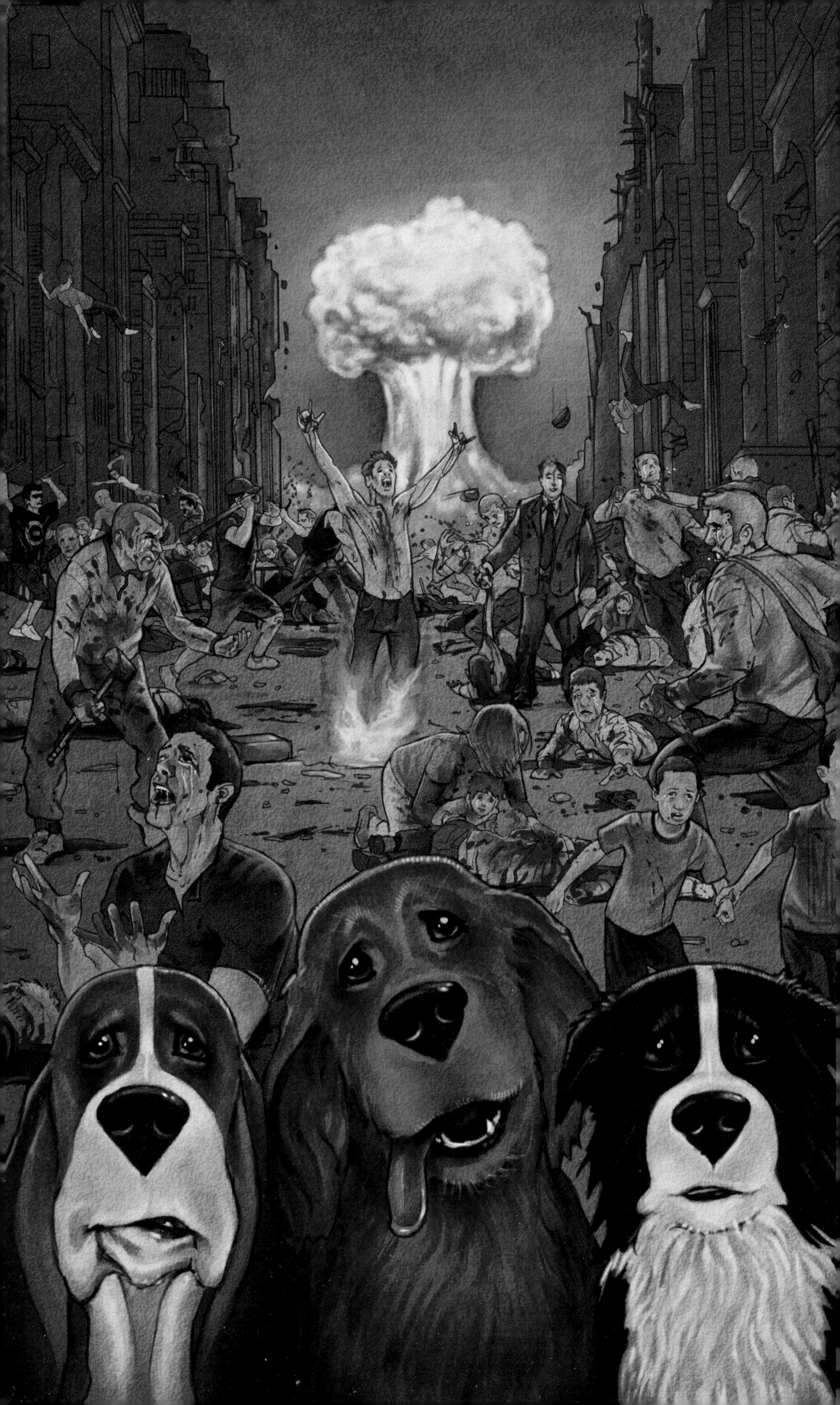